JUDY WEXFORD LEIGH

FLIGHT TO EMBRACE

BALBOA
PRESS

A DIVISION OF HAY HOUSE

Balboa Press books may be ordered through booksellers or by contacting:

Balboa Press
A Division of Hay House
1663 Liberty Drive
Bloomington, IN 47403
www.balboapress.com
1 (877) 407-4847

Print information available on the last page.

ISBN: 978-1-5043-9806-0 (sc)
ISBN: 978-1-5043-9808-4 (hc)
ISBN: 978-1-5043-9807-7 (e)

Library of Congress Control Number: 2018902055

Balboa Press rev. date: 03/26/2018

CONTENTS

PROLOGUE

For six years Victor balked at what he perceived to be God's "call" to become a Christian minister. After meeting Judy and discovering their mutual interests, especially in music performance, his resistance disappeared, but his efforts to find a ministerial job didn't generate results. He was advised to teach at a church-operated school and willingly complied about the same time that Judy began her music teaching career nearby.

Soon engaged, this pair planned a lovely wedding which took place during the schools' Christmas vacation.

Immediately after their wedding, unfortunately, an emotional roller coaster ride began, accelerating with fearsome speed into what Victor perceived as a power struggle, but Judy saw as a difficulty to be quietly worked through. Their courtship had been too short, and red flags had been youthfully ignored. Add to the mix sexual dysfunction, probably stemming partly from Victor's mother's prior sexual abuse with him.

With bulldog determination, Judy refused to walk away. Instead, she calmly and quietly poured into the relationship the same style of boundless analytic concentration and problem-solving measures she had carefully expended on memorizing and perfecting a beloved piano sonata or concerto. Tragically, neither Victor nor Judy knew how to set boundaries or even begin to understand the concept. Consequently problems continued to erupt volcano style, except all "sound effects" were heavily "muted"--so much so that friends and relatives were totally unaware, thinking this couple's relationship was superbly harmonious, even ideal.

When that first school year of teaching was completed, they traveled to a seminary where Judy worked as a secretary while Victor studied theology for more than a year, finally resulting in his becoming a church pastor.

Their marriage, to onlookers, went on happily for nearly forty years. But there were serious rough places and dilemmas that Victor refused to discuss and insisted on "sweeping under the rug," although Judy longed for problem-solving communication. She believed so strongly in the integrity of her marriage vow, that she worked extremely hard to create an ideal relationship in spite of Victor's communication void. She therefore embraced her difficult realities not only without complaining, but with unique creativity for years.

Victor belatedly admits that he had silently longed for, but *never mentioned* divorce. Yet he had absolutely refused all suggestions and requests for marriage counseling. His passive-aggressive tendencies had slowly escalated, resulting in Judy's frustration, hurt, illness, eventual infidelity and abject desperation. Suicide/murder became part of her carefully detailed but miraculously aborted plan.

Finally an ultimatum was advised and delivered, shortly followed by divorce. Judy's emotional chaos expanded, while Victor's relief and elation soared. Then *both* parties became *engaged to others!*

The saga about how this handsome and musically-passionate couple not only got back together, but have since experienced more than two decades of *true romance and teamwork*, is miraculous. As told by Judy, the story demonstrates how family weaknesses, passed down through generations, *can* be OWNED and finally DISCARDED!

Through the manuscript Victor occasionally voices his thoughts, feelings and insights, and together Victor and Judy gratefully thank Karen Giles, Marriage and Family Therapist, for interspersing her astute comments and suggestions. Many names have been changed for privacy.

1

VENTURE

So much to do! Not enough time! Now I was even late to rehearsal for the long-anticipated yearly reunion of the college choral group. It was the first day of May, and next month *was* to have been my graduation from a college in California. As I walked into the auditorium choir loft, I noticed an attractive man sitting behind where I found an empty seat in the soprano section. He noticed *me* and gave a broad smile!

There was something familiar. What was it? Could he be a classmate from previous years? I was intrigued. Surely we must have met in the past somewhere. How can I unobtrusively learn more? I shifted my position to look again as new sheet music was being handed out. Picking one for myself, I passed the remainder on down the row, giving a fleeting backward glance.

There he was! His light blond wavy hair was parted on the side and brushed away from a tan face. It's amazing how much I could observe from less-than-second-long-glances! The varying streaks of blond hair framed an oblong, very masculine countenance. Strong jaw. Regal nose. High forehead above intense blue eyes that spoke even more deeply than his less dramatic mouth. He appeared slim, but strong-muscled. He was sitting in a chair two rows behind me, and a bit to my right, so I couldn't tell how tall he was. But I noticed the length of his bare arms, my eyes following their line to his long, slim fingers.

Aha! He shifted *his* position to where he could see *me* better and even smiled again! Who is he? I'm certain I've seen him before!

When rehearsal was over and all stood to leave, he seemed to unfold his lanky legs and stretch to more than six feet. Could it be six feet three inches? He was wearing smart, well-fitted black-and-white-hound's-tooth slacks and a black silky shirt with the top three buttons open, showing a little bit of bare chest. A smart dresser? Yes indeed!

He suddenly turned and looked the *opposite* direction toward an approaching brunette. He now smiled at *her*, squared his broad shoulders, and accompanied this attractive, slim, dark figure through the nearest exit. They are gone!

"Well, you can't win them all," my brain tried to mollify my ego, as I let out a long and disappointed sigh and headed to another door which was closest to my car. Unlocking my vehicle and flopping onto the seat, I looked straight into the mirror. Disappointment glared back. Determined, I flashed a sly smile at myself, knowing I would see him again *tomorrow* when the choir sang for church. Then again tomorrow *night* he would be at the Reunion Concert performance. I beamed messages of hope into my reflection!

As I drove home it finally dawned on me that I had seen his picture in a friend's dorm room earlier in the year. Then later I remembered he had dated my brother's fiancé's cousin somewhere in the dimly remembered past. Finally the name Victor Leigh slipped into my awareness, and relief relaxed my pondering.

By the end of the encored Reunion Concert the next evening, the lovely brunette had disappeared. Victor was *alone* at the crowded post-concert Reception! I was immediately enchanted as he and I distantly appraised each other over our cups of punch. Moments later I saw my brother-in-law chatting briefly with Victor, so I soon persuaded my sister to ask her husband, who obviously knew him, to introduce the two of us. Happily I spent the remainder of the evening in conversation with this handsome man. When Victor asked for my phone number, I also offered my address, making sure he could contact me. I had moved out of the dorm earlier in the year and was living a half hour away with my parents.

KAREN: IT IS IMPORTANT TO EVALUATE AS YOU PROCEED SLOWLY. IT WOULD HAVE BEEN WISE FOR JUDY TO GIVE ONLY HER PHONE NUMBER. BY OFFERING HER ADDRESS, SHE WAS ACTUALLY BLOCKING THE CHANCE FOR THE "DANCE" OF ROMANTIC PURSUIT. TAKE ONLY

ONE STEP AT A TIME. THIS DOES NOT REMOVE ROMANCE; IT ENHANCES IT BY GIVING EACH PERSON A PLACE IN THE DANCE.

As Victor walked me to my car through a large parking lot, we suddenly both became aware of a car, with its lights off, slowly following us after the reception. Immediately I recognized it was my very-recent-*ex*-fiancé checking up on me, and I told Victor who it was.

Victor: I felt blood rushing to my face, and my hackles were raised for fear this man would attempt to retrieve *my* new interest! So my usually passive tendencies evaporated, and determined caveman instincts rushed through my emotions. I *will not* allow *any* competition to inhibit me from setting up a date with this beauty NOW, *or sooner,* if possible! I detested saying, "Goodnight," to Judy as she turned the key in her car and headed home.

A few days later, the following letter came in the mail:

> May 6
> Dear Judy,
>
> What a tremendous weekend. It was such a thrill to sing with the Chorale again. Music holds a prominent place in my life. I don't have any natural ability along musical lines, but I have had about ten years of piano lessons, five years of saxophone and several months on the organ. Not much of it "took," but I love to play for my own amazement and also derive much pleasure from listening to good music. During high school years I turned to popular music, but after attending college, my tastes gradually changed. My knowledge of classical composers is very meager; however I never miss a chance to attend a symphony concert.
>
> Well that's enough about me. I want to hear about you. Who is your favorite composer? What sports do you like best? Do you like to hike in the mountains or sun yourself at the beach? Are you going to be working this

summer? That's just a starter. I hope you tell me much more than that.

I really surprised myself the night we met, being so aggressive and all. I'm usually just the opposite.

May 7 (sent in the same envelope)

Well, here it is almost summer, and I haven't saved a penny for a vacation. I suppose I should be satisfied with my four days coming up at the Youth Congress in San Francisco.

I just received a notice to appear in person for my veteran's tax exemption on some property my grandmother and I own near college. That means I'll have an excuse to come see you, since I'll be in that area. I would like to come up Friday, attend to the business, take you to the church youth meeting, attend church with you and take you out that night. If you want me to bring my music, I will do so.

This is the best attempt I have ever made at writing a long newsy letter, so I'll be satisfied and quit. Hope you'll not be too swamped with schoolwork to have a date or to write me. I'll be anxiously awaiting your reply.

Sincerely yours,
Victor Leigh

Excitedly I responded, trying not to sound as eager and breathless as I felt:

May 16
Dear Victor,

Thanks for your letter and all you tell me about yourself. I also was surprised at my own unusual aggressiveness in giving you my address, when you asked only for my phone number.

Since I was out of school for a couple months with infectious mononucleosis, I will be going to summer school to make up two classes. I may also be working at a part time job, but I'll need to study a lot to catch up so I can graduate by the end of the summer.

I suppose my favorite composer is Chopin. I play a number of his compositions. I like to go to concerts and swim at the beach, but especially love hiking in the mountains.

I might be interested in having a ride to the Youth Congress. I was hoping to go, but didn't think I'd be able to manage. Since you are a delegate and have to go, maybe I could sneak into a corner of your car.

Call me about the weekend you go on business regarding the property.

Your friend,
Judy

Then another letter came, far different from anything I expected:

June 2
Dear Judy,

I hardly know how to begin. My heart is so full. Yesterday I was down in the depths of discouragement. I may repeat some things I've told you before, but I must tell this story in its entirety. Ever since I was old enough to think seriously of a vocation I have wanted to be many things. I suppose that's natural for a child to want to be like each person he or she idealizes. During my teens my health was so poor, and my grades even poorer, that I took little interest in school or finding out what I wanted to be. My parents wanted me to be a doctor. So rather than disappoint them, I took one science course in high school.

5

Before I started college my mother had me take vocation and IQ tests. The results showed I should be in some mechanical line of medicine. Why shouldn't they? I came from a doctor's family. I had been used to hearing medical terms at the table. As for the mechanical part, what fellow isn't interested in things mechanical? What does that prove? I put little faith in any of this psychology and testing. I will *never* put my child through tests like I had to take!

I began to like medical things less and less. But since I had no other suggestion that met with my parent's approval, I continued toward that goal. Near the end of the semester my grade average was D. I'd been told no students were accepted into medical school with less than a B average. I felt I had failed, so quit studying so hard. I was in despair until I got the army draft notice right after my 18th birthday. I was so thrilled to soon be able to get away from it all, that I failed all my school exams and therefore received no credits for that semester.

When I first went into the army, I had all the high ideals that my Christian background might foster. Five minutes after my introduction to my fellow recruits, I was confronted with a zealous ministerial intern of another faith. He brought arguments I was unable to refute. Study as I did, I couldn't find a flaw in his reasoning. I was stunned, but didn't turn to anyone for help, because I thought I must face this alone. Was I blindly following what someone else had taught me? I couldn't find the answer, yet felt I couldn't give up my faith either. Those principles had become a firm part of me. I knew mother would grieve if she ever found me renouncing my faith. I merely drifted from one worldly pleasure to another.

When I finally got out of the army two years later, I had no desire to go to college; however my parents had other plans, and told me to go back to school, or start paying room and board. I chose the former.

The Christian influences at college changed my outlook and I began to learn answers to my doubts. On my knees in my dorm room one particular evening I poured out my soul in earnest prayer for God to give me a *definite* sign as to what He wanted me to be. Down deep in my heart I felt I *should* be a minister, but I wanted to be sure.

A senior ministerial student was impressed *at that moment* to visit my room. I had just gotten up from my knees when there was a knock at the door. I opened it, and there stood a perfect stranger. Without any preliminaries, he introduced himself and directly asked, "Have you ever thought of becoming a minister?" That was enough for me! I believed it was the "voice of God" speaking directly to me. I told my newly found friend everything, and then we prayed together.

I went to my college counselor the next day and told him everything. He listened attentively but replied, "Fine, but you can't base your life's work on a supposed sign when it may have been only a coincidence. If you are determined to go this direction, why don't you take a religion major rather than theology, so you can go into teaching later if you desire?"

His response deflated my new dream. I felt it had been only an emotional high of the moment. But since I disliked medicine and didn't know which way to turn, I couldn't go very wrong by taking a religion major. When my parents heard of this change, they told me that whatever I wanted to be was OK with them, but I felt their disappointment.

Through the years I had developed the philosophy that the only way to be sure in the choice of one's vocation was to pick one which gave the most benefit to others. I had come to believe this should be a combination of medicine and ministry. Since I did not want to spend so many years in school to become a doctor, I thought I could obtain all the essentials in a nurses' course. Before graduating with my BA in Religion, I took the few necessary pre-nursing requirements and was accepted into nursing school after graduation.

I *thought* I was determined to stick to my course no matter how much I disliked some things. But during the latter part of my first year I became quite morbid from constant contact with the sick. I also felt that what I was learning in class did not challenge my intellect in the least. I received A's and B's without studying half as much as I did in college. After doing little except giving bed baths, I decided I was capable of a much greater contribution to mankind than that. As I look back on it now, perhaps I had the wrong attitude.

Then the shocking news came that my father and two other physicians had been killed in a small airplane crash. I joined one of the search parties, but was fortunate to be in another area when the horrible wreckage was found. Assuming my family would now depend on me for financial help, I bitterly walked away from my nurses' training unannounced. One day I just left the hospital, on the spur of the moment, in the middle of my nursing duties, without telling a soul.

These past few years, since that time when I asked the Lord for a sign, I have been impressed again many times to become a minister, but I would not yield. I passed it off as emotional excitement. The words of some of my teachers would come back to me: "You must have a *constant* burning desire to be a minister!" "If you can be anything else *but* a minister, be it!" "If you feel you *cannot do anything else than be a minister*, you will succeed; you will *know* you are called to the ministry!" My inner voice calling in that direction continued.

Last Monday I started a job that looked most interesting to me. As a county surveyor it offered outdoor exercise, a substantial pay raise, and used some of my college training. Everything went fine the first morning with the survey party, but after lunch my hay fever started to take over. Within an hour my eyes were watering, my nose was running, and my throat burned so badly I thought I couldn't stand it. I wasn't able to adequately do my work.

That night I was completely discouraged and told Mom, "Now that I have failed to make a living with my college education and am not even able to survey for the county, I might as well give up." Before I went to bed I emptied my heart before the Lord in prayer, telling Him I was willing to do *anything*, even be a minister. If I was able to get my old job back, (which seemed impossible at that moment) I would see *that* as a sign that I should become a minister. The next day I called my former employer. Before I could tell him what I wanted, he interrupted me and said, "So you want your old job back?" I fearfully said, "Yes." The reply was, "Well, come on down, and we'll put you to work."

I am so happy that my future is certain, and that the Lord sees in me something left that is worthwhile. Judy, your friendship has meant a great deal to me, spiritually and otherwise. I hope I can be as much help to you. I can't think just what it is about you that gives me inspiration, but one thing that certainly helps is your sincerity. You have increased my faith in humanity. I'll see you next weekend and look forward to meeting your folks and also enjoying some music together.

Your friend,
Victor

VICTOR: Looking back to the time I walked out of the hospital without telling anyone while on duty as a nurse, I remember criticism from my superiors about my slowness, particularly in giving bed baths, as well as everything else. It seemed the *female* nurses were *always* faster and more efficient than I was. This resulted in my being *consumed* with a sense of inadequacy and depression *even before* the

horribly shocking news arrived about my father's death. After that, I remember only a blank numbness, a dark and empty emotional void. There was *no room in my consciousness for recognizing any responsibility to the patients, the hospital, or the nursing school.*

But to me, his letter exemplified twenty-six-year-old Victor's lofty desires, and I longed to encourage him. His revelation also excited me, because I truly had wanted to be a minister's wife for a long time. It didn't take me long to answer:

> June 10
> Dear Victor,
>
> What a story! Thanks for trusting me enough to share your story. I believe in you, and I believe you would make a fine minister. I feel very comfortable being around ministers, since there are so many of them on my mother's side of the family. My minister father, the only child of his doctor father and teacher mother, has had a variety of roles: youth leader, religion teacher at both high school and college levels, a pastor, and is currently a hospital chaplain.
>
> Thank you for the invitation to ride to Youth Congress with you and the others. I want to continue to be an encouragement, and look forward to going. It will be a good vacation for me also. We'll talk more on the phone.
>
> Your friend,
> Judy

Victor arrived on Friday after he tended to the real estate business. The next day we spent more than two hours at a nearby church where I was the summer choir director. Mostly I listened to his playing hymn arrangements on the piano or organ, and I liked his style. From then on, music was our frequent pastime and social activity. I was pleased to discover that we both liked to listen to classical music. We would also often sing together—hymns, pop music, classic and occasionally an operatic aria or duet.

Even though I had performed on the piano since I was a child, after only a few hours together, I noticed that Victor wasn't especially interested in hearing *me* play. But I determined to *not* be disappointed and to *never* let him, or even *myself,* know I felt hurt. In *our* home no one seemed to express negative emotions or admit they existed. It had never crossed my mind this might be a useful or valuable behavior.

A week or so after Victor had visited me, another letter came:

> June 24
> Dear Judy,
>
> I thought for sure I would be sick in bed today. Instead of an allergy, I had a chest cold. I hope you didn't succumb to such an overdose of virulent, airborne, microscopic, protoplasmic, non-filterable virus. I've been getting ten to twelve hours sleep, and my chest has loosened up today, so I ought to be well by the weekend.
>
> My brother and sister have begged mother to go to the Fourth of July holiday circus and fireworks. In case you would like to go, we could get tickets for you.
>
> I would surely like a picture of you to put in my wallet. I'll bet you were looking at the moon last night too. A lot of good it does me! Oh well, just three more days.
>
> Bye for now,
> Victor

When I had contracted infectious mononucleosis earlier in the year, I had moved out of the dorm, back with my parents about a half hour from college, and was bed-bound with an enlarged spleen for more than a month. Slowly recuperating, I remained with them through the remaining school year and summer, commuting to classes until the end of August.

Victor and I saw each other often, even though we had very busy schedules. Most of the time I would go to his home on weekends—about an hour's drive from where I lived. Our time together often included Victor's family—his mother and grandmother, his brother Patrick, eleven years his junior, and his adopted sister, Aimee, twenty years younger than Victor. I thought it was wonderful that Victor treated his family so respectfully. On some occasions he would come to *my* home. Of course my mom and dad were there, and they enjoyed getting acquainted with him. My sister and brother were already married and living elsewhere.

One day Victor and I made a trip to the ocean by ourselves. He insisted we climb up onto a huge rock next to the water. As we were clambering up on the ocean-side of the rock, a huge wave splashed against us, almost knocking us off, but we fortunately made it up safely. When we were ready to return, Victor decided it was best to climb down the side of the rock towards land because the tide was coming in and the waves were gigantic. A surge of panic rushed over me as I peered over the edge where, to me, it looked straight down about ten or fifteen feet. "That's impossible!" I wailed, as I imagined having to stay on top until the tide changed.

Victor gave a confident chuckle. "I'll carry you. You just hang on to me."

I was petrified, but he picked me up and literally carried me down the side of that rock. I still don't know how he did it, but he certainly won my trust that day.

During my childhood I took lessons and became a performing pianist. Often when friends, neighbors or other guests came to our house, I would be asked to play our very old upright piano. Everyone would sit quietly and listen with interest, sometimes asking questions about the composition or my piano study. I believed they enjoyed my music, and loved playing for them. Their applause afterward made my faithful daily practice seem worth every hour of effort.

When I went to Victor's home, however, it was much different. When his mother would ask me to play their lovely seven-foot-four grand piano, as my fingers touched the keys, almost instantly conversation and even laughter intruded on the music. I was confused.

Why was I asked to play? I thought they wanted to hear my music. Did they want only background music? I feel insulted. That must be my problem and not theirs. Victor doesn't seem to be aware of anything unusual, or at least hasn't said anything about it.

Earlier in the school year, before I got infectious mono, I had accepted a music teaching position in Colorado for the following year. In fact, I had received offers for five varying music teaching positions. Then I became engaged to a different suitor still in college in California, so canceled the Colorado job and accepted one in Southern California. When that engagement was broken, I discovered the Colorado job was already taken, and I was glad to keep the already accepted position at a southern California Christian boarding high school about two hours from home.

It had been because of mother's *extreme* dislike of my former fiancé, including her thinking that he was the son of a "nobody," that I very unfortunately had let her persuade me to break up with him! I was still hurting badly. But by the second or third time she ever saw Victor, the son of a *doctor*, she ecstatically exclaimed, "I could love *him* like my own *son!*" Somehow I had "learned" and come to *believe* that parents were wiser than their offspring, and I felt it was my *responsibility* to follow mother's adamant advice. At this point that unfortunately included my affairs of heart, even though I had already passed my twenty-first birthday.

Not long after the above engagement break-up, a delivery man came to our home one day and surprised mother with a gift for *me*—a *gorgeous* floral arrangement from my ex-fiancé. She had immediately placed it on the middle of our dining room table, although she *knew I was bringing Victor home that same evening for the first time* to introduce him to both her and my dad. After Victor and I arrived, and shortly after introductions were over, she explained *dramatically*, to *all of us*, who had sent the flowers to me! Then she quietly lured Victor into the kitchen and told him he better "get on the ball," because my "old boyfriend was trying to get" me back. **KAREN: IT IS A BIG RED FLAG WHEN A PARENT MANIPULATES LIKE THIS. SHE WAS *SHALLOW* IN HER CHARACTER ANALYSIS AND *PERFECTIONISTIC* IN HER REASONS FOR REJECTING THE FORMER BOYFRIEND. SHE WAS ALSO *VERY* MANIPULATIVE IN URGING VICTOR TO PUSH THE ISSUE FURTHER.**

As my father got to know Victor better, he suggested that one way to find a ministerial job would be to start teaching at a denominationally operated school and get to know the Conference officials. These officials, who were elected by church delegates in each Conference area, were in authority over both the church-operated schools as well as the pastors of churches in the same Conference territory. Then he could let them know what he wanted and volunteer to help at a church. Victor liked the idea.

Victor and I made the trip to Youth Congress together. The deeply spiritual meetings we attended, plus the resulting conversations, helped me get to know him better. I admired his character and his desire to become a minister. As a little girl I had listened to stories about my brilliant grandfather who had been a pastor/evangelist/author/college professor. I also had great respect for my minister/chaplain/teacher father. I even had an uncle and two great uncles who were not only ministers, but also Conference Presidents—very talented men with delightful wives.

It was during this time at the Youth Congress that I began to wonder if I was falling in love with Victor. One afternoon we visited a beautiful park where we both were especially intrigued with the Japanese gardens. I thought, "What a delightfully romantic setting for our first kiss." When he *finally* kissed me, I knew my feelings had intensified. My sister, who was riding with us on our return trip, noticed the way I was looking at Victor, and told me to make sure I was sincere! I assured her I was.

When he kissed me again as we arrived home, he told me he loved me.

Now my life is perfect! I have found the man of my dreams—a tall, strikingly good looking minister-to-be! We can be a team, sharing God's work. What could be better and more complete than that?

KAREN: *Judy* had a *superficial layout* without *any clear substance*. She was having a conversation in her own head instead of with Victor. The focus was only on Victor's destiny, and Judy would follow somehow. Judy took it for granted that she and Victor could be a "Team," without having *any conversation* about *future goals* or *Victor's expectations in the marriage*.

There had been occasional times as I talked with Victor or read his letters that *great big questions* had clouded my mind. Occasionally little niggling bits of fear *still* jabbed my subconscious. Is Victor's *life attitude* really *balanced*? Does he *frequently* play the part of the *victim*? Why didn't I discuss these with him?

Our correspondence resumed.

June 30

Dear Judy,

Won't it be wonderful to wake up some morning and not be tired, then work all day and still not be worn out? I hit the sack when I got home from work yesterday, woke up about six-thirty pm, ate supper and went back to bed. I feel lousy this morning, but I'm able to work.

KAREN: ARE VICTOR'S EXPECTATIONS UNREALISTIC? WHAT IS WONDERFUL ABOUT *NOT* BEING TIRED AFTER A HARD DAY OF WORK? BEING WORN OUT AT NIGHT HELPS A PERSON SLEEP BETTER. THIS UNREALISTIC EXPECTATION AND HIS EXHAUSTION ARE SIGNS OF DEPRESSION. FOR MENTAL AND SPIRITUAL GOOD HEALTH, IT IS IMPORTANT WE TELL OURSELVES WHAT IS TRUTH AND WHAT IS REALITY.

I haven't been able to find those pictures that I had ready to send you. This morning when I asked Grandma where they had been put, she said she didn't know, and didn't see why I was in such a hurry to find them. "After all, Judy's coming down on the week-end. Why do you have to send them by mail?" I'll look for them again tonight. No use arguing with Grandma.

Well, enough of my ills and poor business judgment. How wonderful to have someone that makes allowance for one's shortcomings. Of course I doubt that you know many of my shortcomings yet, and oh me, they are so many! I don't know why you should love me, but I never cease to thrill at the thought.

I love you very much. And though I may be too selfish to really know what those words mean, I do know that God and you may help me to understand.

Yours as always,
Victor

July 13
Dear Judy,

I called the Conference office this morning and they said to come over and meet with them this afternoon at 2:00. I was able to get off work, and I didn't have any trouble selling myself. One of the officials knew my parents some years ago, and one was a former teacher during my high school years. Another knew your dad very well.

They gave me the option of five different teaching positions. The first and most interesting to me was at a secondary school in Northern California. I would teach Algebra, Old Testament, World History, English I and II. The other openings are more local. I wonder which one you would want me to accept, but most important I want to go where the Lord wants me. I have to make up my mind this week, so pray for me. I'm going to look over the secondary-level syllabuses tonight.

Oh, by the way, I must take some education classes so will be going to summer school. I'll probably live in the dorm. I'll be able to get over to see you just about any time. Won't that be great?

I must close now and get busy on the Youth Congress report to give in church. I love you, my darling. XXXXXXX (kisses)

Forever yours,
Victor

Victor had accepted the northern California position before we became engaged July 18. Then we didn't want to be separated five hundred miles. So both of us went to the Conference committee meeting and made a special request: Since school hadn't started yet, could Victor be transferred closer to where I would be teaching. They successfully traded him with someone else. He was hired by a church-operated, three-teacher elementary school in Ventura, CA. He was to teach grades five through eight and also be the school Principal.

We were in a park one free afternoon, where we relaxed and talked while lounging on a blanket. When we stood up to leave, Victor put his arms around me tenderly and was holding me when we began kissing. Soon he French-kissed me for the first time. I melted in his arms, feeling absolutely like putty in his hands. Suddenly he stopped, looked at me, and asked in a rather cool and casual voice, "Did you *like* that?"

VICTOR: I now see how foolish that question was. I didn't realize I had *deep* problems I had never dealt with!

KAREN: VICTOR DISTANCED HIMSELF PHYSICALLY AND EMOTIONALLY WITH THAT QUESTION.

I was startled! Couldn't he tell that I liked it? I was certain my body language showed that I was "carried away." I could hardly believe what he was asking. I didn't know how to answer. Instead I turned to him and asked, "Did *you* like it?"

Karen: Good question.

He answered rather offhandedly, without *any* warmth or excitement, "Oh, it doesn't especially do anything for *me*, but I want to do it if *you* like it."

KAREN: Huge red flag! Time to leave Victor!

What a letdown! I should have taken special note of this and talked about it with him at a later date. I knew no more about communication than he did, and I was already so madly in love with him and saw so many wonderful things in him, that I let this go. I never answered his question nor discussed it later.

KAREN: This was *not* an issue of communication. Time to stop! Listen! Think! Wait! *Back up! Victor just told Judy that he was not physically attracted to her at all. It was time to end the relationship. Sadly Judy remained in this fantasy that Victor loved her.*

We had thought to get married in August, but my dad was rushed to the hospital seriously ill with hepatitis. We postponed the wedding and got together on weekends to plan a later December wedding. More letters came from him:

August 23
Darling,

If I could but tell you what is in my heart! My vocabulary is very limited, and when these words are written in cold letters they seem to lose their meaning. I don't know whether I told you before that one of my many failings is moodiness, but I don't like to admit it.

KAREN: Alarm! Red flag. This continues to show depression.

Just before coming to my room, I stopped to look at the moon, and I thought of all the things that I could have said to you today to let you know again that I love you, but I was glum and stoical. I'm sorry. I suppose it's become a habit, a set emotional pattern to just clam up when I feel bad. It takes some real work and time to get bad habits replaced by good ones, but I do want to accomplish it, and I know you will help me. I feel great tonight, and I wish above all that I might have you in my arms and share my feelings with you. So to my dearest one, I give you my heart. It was yours from the first.

Your devoted dreamer,
Victor

August 31
Dearest Judy,

Just a little note to let you know I still love you. I miss you all the time. I've gotten settled in a room I am renting in one of the church member's homes. Several of the parents came to help fix up the school today. We burned a lot of the weeds and finally finished all the outside work at 5:00 in the afternoon.

I forgot to tell you about what the Conference President said. "We already have too many ministerial interns, so don't even *hope* to get a job until next year."

I'm coming down with another sore throat. Pray for me that I may have enough physical strength to keep going. I may have to get this scar tissue in my throat burned out, so I won't have so many sore throats.

Did I ever tell you the story of what happened to me at age nine? Maybe I haven't. There was a polio epidemic in our vicinity, and my doctor dad didn't want me and my three-year-old brother to get it, so he joyfully found a vaccine which he believed would keep us from succumbing to it. He injected my brother and me that very day. Three hours later my brother was *dead*, and I was in a *coma for several days*, confined to bed for *months*, and out of school for a *year*! Unfortunately, the serum had been accidentally contaminated at the plant where it was produced. Several deaths resulted and the company was closed. One of the main contaminants was streptococcus bacterium. I've had many bouts with strep throat since then, as well as kidney problems. When I was a teenager, my father told me, "When you grow old you will probably die of kidney failure." Thank God my kidneys have healed.

I meant to write just one page on one side. That's what I get for marrying such an inspiration. I love you, I love you, I love you—is that mushy enough? Ha Ha! But I do mean it, and to prove it, here is a big smack (penciled picture of lips).

Your lover boy,
Victor

VICTOR: I can't remember much of anything about my little brother except the fun I experienced when pulling him in my little red wagon. After his death, no family member mentioned his name to me or talked about why he was missing. No one explained what had happened to him or told me that he had died—until months later after I had somewhat recuperated. I don't remember shedding a tear, but I do remember my family then giving me a little white kitten to

play with on my bed. It was my dearest friend and playmate as I lay in bed, hurting to even move my arms or legs. But a few months later, before the kitten was fully grown, my Grandmother told me that it strangulated itself trying to eat asparagus stems in the garbage. I remember *that* as a *huge, crushing blow!* Later they brought me a cage of little white mice that my folks kept on a Ping-Pong table in the enclosed porch. But they also soon died! Mother told me she thought it was because my dad pounded a lot on the table when repairing something, and they were either injured, or they died of fright. I only know that one day I looked in the cage and they were all lying *dead on the floor of the cage! That totally broke my heart,* because I was well enough by now to feel joy and enchantment watching them in their play, as well as taking care of them. I experienced *extreme* sadness over *their* loss—much *more* than I was aware of after my brother died!

September 8
Dear Judy,

I am worried about you today, wondering if you will be all right physically, as well as every other way. I hope I didn't keep you up too late last night. What a wonderful time we had together. I love you so much! What would I do if I couldn't see you on weekends?

I was just thinking today, I wonder who those people are that are sometimes heard to say, "Ah, it's wonderful to wake up in the morning and feel that red blood coursing through your veins." It seems to me I can never remember a morning like that, and a lot of people I know can't remember a morning like that either. We are all so sick. I just long for Jesus to come.

I have prayed many times for God to lay me to rest, but then as I think it over, it is selfish of me not to want to do my share in helping others much worse off than I. And now since I have you, Judy, I want to live for you to make your way easier.

The only thing that counts is for you and me to be in God's kingdom together with those whom we have helped, our students, and friends. May God give us strength to work for Him.

Your devoted Principal,
Victor

November 6
Dearest Judy,

I stepped out to get my books that were in the car. As I looked beyond a row of trees, I saw that beautiful harvest moon. How I wished I could be with you tonight.

There is going to be a parent-teacher meeting at the school tomorrow night and I am to speak on "What 'Home and School' meetings should mean to the Parent." All I can think of is some dry philosophizing I've heard in numerous such meetings where parents and teachers alike have nearly gone to sleep. It boils down to only one point, as I see it. Home and School meetings provide a chance for parents to get acquainted with the teacher and the school environment, thus enabling teacher and parent to combine efforts toward a common goal: the best character building and education for the child.

Every day someone asks me, "When is Judy going to sing for us?" Next Friday night will be a program at this church, and I'm supposed to play the organ, so I'll not be able to see you then. For church I play a special and will probably be teaching a Bible class also. The latter frightens me more than anything else.

I can't wait for the weekend to come for more than one reason. One is that my electric razor died. Due to my sensitive skin, it is torture to shave with a safety razor. My face has broken out in a rash and it looks like I'll have to go unshaven all day tomorrow before it goes away.

I can't put down on paper the way I feel tonight, but that bright moon outside sheds a glow much like the glow I feel in my heart when I think of you. Goodnight sweetheart.

Your lonesome man,
Victor

VOW

On December 22 we had a beautiful Christmas wedding. My father was well enough to provide the homily. As we drove to our honeymoon "cottage" [a motel] a couple hours away in Desert Hot Springs, I fell asleep on Victor's shoulder. I was afraid of insulting him if I dozed off, but sleepiness won the battle anyway! When we arrived, I became very much awake as Victor carried me over the threshold, exactly as I had hoped he would.

He set me down and turned to carry in the suitcases. Then he closed the door and suggested I get a shower and get ready for bed. I was expecting a little more affection than this, but followed his suggestion.

Evidently he kindly realizes how badly I need sleep.

I dressed in my carefully chosen wedding-night pink negligee and waited while he took a shower. When Victor then came to bed he was wearing old, faded and wrinkled pajamas.

I was sitting on the edge of the bed, but he went to the *other side* of the bed and sat down *behind* me and announced, "I'd like to start our marriage with having family worship." He got out his Bible, read a scripture and we knelt on opposite sides of the bed for prayer.

My goodness gracious, this isn't like I expected two newlywed lovers to act. I can hardly believe what is happening! Victor could scarcely keep his hands off me before the wedding. We both have struggled to keep our commitment to marry as virgins. *But now he acts almost like a stranger. Who is this man I have married?*

After prayer he climbed into bed on his side about as close to the edge as possible without falling off, and I got in on my side. Silence! Not one move!

Since we left the church after the wedding and reception, he hasn't touched me except when I had my head on his shoulder while sleeping and when he carried me over the threshold. I waited and waited. Still nothing—no hugging, no kissing, no looking into each other's eyes. NO WORDS. No caressing. Nothing romantic.

Wow, this is extremely different than I had hoped! How shall I respond to this? What am I supposed to do? Help me God!

After *several minutes*, and beginning to feel *extremely rejected*, I reached over and gently brushed a finger against Victor's arm.

At my slight touch he blurted out, "Oh, Oh, Oh, I feel so *guilty*! I feel *so-o-o* guilty! Oh, I feel like I *shouldn't be here*!" Then he cried out again with a moan from the depths of his being,

"I *shouldn't be here at all*!"

I turned to look at him. He was staring up at the ceiling with the sheet pulled tight to his neck. The lights were still on.

"I feel so *guilty* being in the *same bed* with you," he exclaimed *repeatedly* with what sounded like agony!

KAREN: Judy *could* have turned over and gone to sleep. They *could* have gone back to their separate homes the next day.

"But Victor, honey, we're married!" I cooed in my gentlest and hopefully seductive voice.

"I know, but I feel so-o-o-o guilty! I feel *terrible*! I don't think I should be in the same bed with you *at all*!"

KAREN: This was the time to at least WAIT! Leave the first thing in the morning. Go back home and ask for professional help.

What's going on with this man? Who have I married? I am not only shocked, I'm mystified, agonizingly disappointed, and left "hanging!"

Not sure what else to do, I slowly slid over next to him, touching him very gently. I spoke to him quietly for an hour, maybe two--or three. I cuddled with him and gradually encouraged some lovemaking. Very awkwardly, very self-consciously, Victor achieved his masculine goal. Spent, we drifted off to sleep.

Oh, this is not at all what I had dreamed of! What happened to the romance and seduction every girl assumes she will experience? Instead, we have only pain—both of us--emotional and physical! Maybe we should have waited until tomorrow. I can't help wondering what this marriage holds for us in the future, but my hope remains undaunted.

KAREN: This wedding night issue was so severe that Judy would have been wise to get an annulment, or at least put the marriage on hold. Judy should have given herself time for personal reflection, investigation and wise counsel.

Back at school, Victor moved into my home, which was one side of the school's duplex for faculty, and we went on with our teaching. I was so proud of Victor. He was *so* handsome. He had *such* a captivating smile. I was *so in love!*

Late Friday afternoon, the *first weekend* after our honeymoon, Victor's mother phoned to announce, "We're coming over tomorrow with dinner." I was unbelievably taken aback! We had *definitely not* invited them, and they didn't *ask* if they could come. It was *our first weekend at home together,* and I had wanted it to be so very special! I'd made an apple pie for my new husband. Well, at least *that* would be special.

Next morning they *all* arrived—Victor's widowed mother, his grandmother, his younger brother Patrick, a very tall and hefty teen of fifteen, and his little six-year-old adopted sister Aimee, who had been our flower girl. They came with a complete meal, grandma *raving* about all the *wonderful* things they brought. "Oh Victor, I brought you pineapple-apple pie! I *know* it's your favorite!"

So Victor ate *her* pie, not mine. Whatever else I had fixed was sort of pushed out of the way. The family stayed all afternoon and evening.

Every weekend they came, *uninvited,* bringing all the food! They knew our finances were tight, and we were working hard, so a *little* part of me appreciated it. But another *much bigger* part longed for a newlywed retreat and privacy!

I wouldn't go to somebody else's house without an invitation! I guess Victor's family does things completely different from my family, and I'll just have to get used to it!

These first months after our wedding *did* bring *many* happy times. Victor was neat and clean, and he picked up after himself. He told me every day he loved me and always kissed me goodbye and hello. He fixed anything about the house that needed repair, kept the yard beautiful and the car washed and waxed.

He had a wonderful voice, and I began to give him singing lessons. I also started writing new arrangements of music for us to perform together. We became well known for our vocal solos and duets as well as our piano and organ duets. Usually we accompanied each other on piano for our vocal solos, and I played for Victor's saxophone solos. He was a careful musician and was willing to practice thoroughly.

I had always wanted to make the best of everything, create "something out of nothing," be practical but unique. My parents had won a kitchen table and four chairs at a furniture store opening and passed them along to us. We didn't yet have a couch for our living room; so right after our wedding we bought a second-hand sofa that dropped down into a bed. I found an orange crate that I covered with some colorful fabric. On it I kept a vase of fresh flowers. The box became our little coffee table. We didn't believe in charge accounts, and if possible bought needed items second-hand. I didn't feel self-conscious about our home. I just *loved* to make beauty with what I could invent or devise at the moment.

It wasn't long after we married that Victor came home one day looking absolutely furious! Wanting to understand and encourage him, I greeted him with, "Hi, Sweetheart! You look upset."

"I'm *very* upset!" He threw his briefcase down onto the kitchen table.

"What about?" I didn't know whether I was intrigued or amazed. This was a side of Victor I had never seen before. I motioned for him to follow me into the living room and sit down with me.

He followed me, but started developing his tirade while standing and gesturing. "The parents of a *very* belligerent, *know-it-all* student came *fuming* to me about the discipline I gave him. They talked *terrible* to me!" he growled.

I'm now not only surprised, but very curious. "What did *you* say?"

"They made me so *mad* I wouldn't even answer! I just turned and walked away!" Then *he* just turned and walked away from *me*, down the hall to the bedroom!

The elementary principal? He just turned and walked away from disgruntled parents? Who have I married? I am shocked! Victor seems to lack the ability to control his anger and act appropriately. I feel fear and can hardly believe what I just saw and heard.

My *teaching* that year seemed more fun than anything I had ever done before. I loved directing the forty-voice advanced choir. We rehearsed four times a week and sang at least one choral number weekly for church, as well as an introit and service responses. I insisted *all* music be performed by *memory*, which included my conducting *without music!*

Every week I taught forty-five half-hour voice lessons and fifteen piano lessons of the same length. I was also in charge of teaching the freshman girls' physical education class that met only once a week. My life as a teacher of high school students seemed an adventure and challenge every day. I was excited to get up each morning and happily exhausted every night.

However, I *didn't* relish directing the "chorus" of about thirty students who had never sung in a group before. Fortunately, we had only two rehearsals each week and not many performances. I didn't have an accompanist for this group, as I did for the advanced choir, and it was difficult to play, direct and also keep order when several students *didn't want to be there*. It was the only "fine arts" class they could find available to fulfill requirements for graduation.

Before the end of January, my principal asked if I would stay on and teach the following year. He said they were *extremely* pleased with my work, and would be willing to *hire* Victor as well, in order to keep me. I replied, "Victor and I will discuss it and pray about it."

KAREN: Judy is compartmentalizing. Her marriage life is in a horrible place, yet she play-acts as if everything is fine. She seems to

lack wisdom or knowledge of what to do in a traumatic situation. She avoids attending to the crisis!

In early February I was admitted to the hospital with the flu. I had over-worked. I also knew I was very confused and stressed about what was happening in my marriage.

KAREN: Neither Victor nor Judy were looking at the truth and reality of their situation. Their thoughts and feelings were not congruent. It was time to look at their feelings and what their intuitions were telling them.

Because of the long distance to the hospital, Victor began to visit me by correspondence.

> February
> Dearest darling,
>
> I received your letter today and it made me so happy. I had been anxiously waiting, hoping you were getting better. My church, in the town where I teach, has asked me to preach this weekend. I have been working many hours on my sermon. I'm not satisfied with it, but I suppose it will have to do.
>
> I talked with your principal about lightening your load, and he spoke up right away and mentioned some girl that you took on as a voice student who didn't *have* to take lessons for credit until next year. What a hedger he is!
>
> I've heard from nearly all the Conferences, and there's nothing in the way of a ministerial job yet. The more I think about it, the less I want to stay here. Of course it isn't what *I* want to do, it's what *the Lord* wants me to do. Pray about it earnestly, for we must let the staff here know soon. Hurry and get well, honey. I miss you.
>
> Bye Bye,
>
> Victor
> P.S. I love you. So there too! XXXX and many more.

In March the choir started touring on weekends and sometimes performed three concerts in one day. When Victor was able, he joined us. On weekends that we didn't tour, Victor and I often walked in the hills together, bringing home wild flowers to arrange in bouquets around the house. He loved both the walking and the bouquets, and told me so. He often complimented me on my cooking.

3

LIGHTNING

Victor loved to rub my back, and I relished his willingness to do it and luxuriated in his attention; but he didn't want me to reciprocate and rub his back *or even caress him*. I felt enormously disappointed, and continued to offer my time and attention. If I started to caress him, he immediately shifted his position and did to me whatever I had started to do for him. That way I couldn't continue what I started. The only touching he would tolerate for himself was strictly sexual.

I *thought* it was a *problem* that I was hungry for sex all the time. We were both terribly naive, and Victor didn't satisfy me. Every time I'd start to move he'd say, "Hold Still! Hold still! Don't move! Don't move! I want to make it last." Then after a few minutes of just lying still, it was over.

One evening when I arrived home, Victor was sitting at the kitchen table studying. I went to him and lightly touched his shoulders, but he pulled away saying, "Don't bother me. I've got to study." So I left him alone, deciding to later give him a surprise at bedtime. I had been so busy teaching, we hardly had seen each other, and I *didn't think I had been a good enough* wife for him.

Tonight I'm really going to fix up. I will be a live "pin-up." He loves perfume and I'll use his favorite. It's about time I quit being a teacher and start being a real lover. After our evening meal I sat in a hot bubble bath for a while, brushed and brushed my hair and put on Chanel No. 5 fragrance. I experimented with some long, colored chiffon scarves, tying them around myself to make a skimpy bikini-like outfit. When I heard him putting away his books, I opened up the bed and sat in what I imagined to be a somewhat reserved but yet provocative pose.

He opened the bedroom door, took just one step, and suddenly stopped as he looked at me. Instantly the most *awful* expression crossed his face, which looked to me like a mixture of anger, rage and hate. For a few seconds there was absolute silence as my mouth dropped open and I held my breath. Then with venom in his loudest voice, he hissed at me, "What *on earth* are you trying to do?"

I couldn't speak! I just looked at him in shock. I felt as if he had shot me! Suddenly he charged on into the room, seized the door with both hands and slammed it closed with all of his might, shaking the whole house. Wordlessly he stomped over to the closet, put on his pajamas, snapped out the light, climbed into his side of the bed and turned his back. That was it! Total silence! No noticeable movement or words the rest of the night.

Silently I cried, not understanding what was going on, because I had not been aware of much irritation earlier in the kitchen. The next day Victor acted as though nothing unusual had happened and treated me basically the same as he had prior to this "thunderstorm"--with some warmth, but no apology or discussion.

Not asking him what was wrong, I supposed he'd bring it up when he was ready. He never did, and I never mentioned it again until years later when problems continued to erupt. What a gigantic mistake! I should *never* have gone to bed with him again until we talked it out, even if I had to refuse sex and force getting counseling!

KAREN: If Judy had understood her *shock* that Victor was *not* who she thought he was, she could have asked herself this question: "If I pretend that everything is okay, what could happen? However, if I face this, what could happen?"

One Saturday night, near the end of the school year, there was a talent show. Rick, who had been a difficult student that I had told Victor about, had performed well, as had my other piano and voice students. When the program was over, I expected Victor to come back stage and hopefully congratulate me, or at least make some sort of comment about the program, and walk home with me. After I thanked all my students and looked around unsuccessfully for him, I went on home alone. Victor was studying in the kitchen, and made no move or comment as I walked in. He acted as though neither of us had ever left the house. After maybe a half hour had passed, Victor got up for a drink, so I asked, "How did you like Rick's singing?"

If Victor thinks Rick's singing is acceptable, that will mean I'm a good teacher. Maybe he'll say he's proud of me.

But instead, Victor turned to me with that same *awful* look on his face again—mean and furious. "I couldn't *stand* his singing! It upset me so much I got up and walked out *in the middle of the song,*" he almost yelled. Then with emphasis he added, "and *didn't* come back for the rest of the program!"

What is with this man? What is going on with him? I am bewildered! I thought a husband would support and encourage his wife. Instead, here is this "tantrum child." I decided it was better to not discuss it more—just drop the subject—for fear of making him more angry.

Before the school year ended, arrangements were made for our choir to make a recording of many of the songs we had learned. We were all thrilled, and it sold well to families and friends. Now I was being *urged* by the principle and also his wife, who was an outstanding musician, to stay at this school and continue teaching the following year. They repeated their offer of a teaching job for Victor, but he finally made his decision to be a minister. He said he needed to go to seminary for further classes. He also emphasized that his "teaching had been only a stepping-stone" to that end.

Our original plans were to move immediately after the school year ended. But right after we had made the recording of our repertoire, the touring choir received an invitation to sing at a denominational World Conference Session in San Francisco a week after school let out.

That was *truly an honor,* and I was thrilled to make the five hundred-mile bus trip with my choir.

We gave a thirty-minute choral concert at the beginning of one evening's meeting, with probably at least a thousand in attendance, our picture appearing on the front page of a leading city newspaper, along with a very complimentary article about the choir performance.

As we traveled in the bus back to the school, I realized my year there had been not only fun, but I felt very rewarded for my hard work, even though our marriage wasn't yet comfortable. When we arrived home from San Francisco, we excitedly prepared for our new venture at the seminary near the east coast.

Ah, what a delightful quest—packing and moving far away. For several days we pulled the small, overloaded and plastic-tarp-covered trailer, sometimes through pouring rain. At our destination we chose a small basement apartment in Maryland, and moved in with our sparse furnishings.

I wanted to keep our home cozy, neat and pretty, but it didn't have to be gorgeous or glamorous. The seminary was selling some used furniture. My college friend, Jacqueline, who had married one of Victor's classmates, invited us to "go shopping" with both of them. They had signed up to take an upholstery class and wanted companionship, as they created new-looking furniture. They even offered to teach us what they learned. Along with their purchases, we bought an old, but sturdy hide-a-bed couch and non-matching armchair for $25 as well as upholstery material at half price. We joined them in our spare moments, Victor and I learning how to use a curved needle to hand sew, and I, using my portable sewing machine, making cushion covers. Now we proudly owned a matching couch and chair and sold the threadbare second-hand sofa we had bought the year before.

When Victor registered for his seminary classes, I found work as a secretary at our denomination's world headquarters in the same area. After a few weeks, Victor began to hate his Greek class, so he dropped it. He often came home frustrated and angry. He talked on and on about how *hard* school was, what a *failure* he was, and how he'd *never* make it!

I tried to reassure him by saying, "You *can* make it. I'm *sure* you can! You are *very* intelligent and capable." I even proposed he find a good counselor who might help him grow more confident.

At that suggestion he looked quite horrified and declared, "I will *never* go to a counselor! Psychologists lead people away from God!"

Surprised, I asked, "Wherever did you hear that?"

Victor sounded exasperated when he replied, "I've heard ministers *and* teachers *and* various other authorities say something to that effect *more than once,* so I *won't* go to any shrink! You can't *make* me!"

Disappointment flooded over me as his words of finality penetrated my depths and desires.

One day, as I was trying to encourage him more, he yelled, "Don't you *ever again* tell me I can do it! I *know* I can't! Don't you *ever* say that *again!*"

I'm beginning to realize this very handsome and superbly gifted man I married has terrible self-esteem. He apparently hates himself! How am I supposed to deal with that? How can I help him? If he doesn't want me to encourage him, what can I do?

I heard that one of the very capable ministers in the office building where I worked was also a fine counselor. I finally dredged up the courage to visit him for support and guidance. At my first of several visits I told him my husband was *adamantly* against counseling, saying, "You're not supposed to tell your problems to *anybody* other than the Lord." This very wise gentleman encouraged me and gave many suggestions, which I worked hard to accomplish. He never charged for the counseling sessions; and I never told Victor that I went to him, because I *knew* he would be angry.

Victor soon volunteered to serve as associate pastor at a church nearby. Since I had always wanted to be a pastor's wife and was impatient for that to happen, I was excited that this was our beginning. Victor had such high *ideals,* and his *motives* for his life direction seemed almost flawless! *Oh how I wish he could be happy with his realities!*

One day Victor confessed to me that he was a horrible, guilty *sinner,* because *long before* we met, he hadn't paid tithe while working for the road department. Now his mother and grandmother were sending us money to pay Victor's tuition. Victor decided we should make up this past lack by paying a *double* tithe for a year, (twenty per cent) *both* on what they sent and also on what I earned as a secretary! So we deducted this before we bought groceries or paid bills during the entire time he went to seminary. How we managed is truly amazing!

I was scrutinizing our bank account one day and noticed we had only about seventy-five dollars to last a half-month. That evening Victor came home and joyously exclaimed, "I bought a speaker!" He was so excited because he'd gotten this "superb piece of electronics" for only $75, and it was to go with our record player. I was absolutely flabbergasted and told him so, but his excitement didn't abate. That meant for the rest of the month I had about three dollars for groceries and not much for gas. Victor had previously asked *me* to be in charge of the money, but hadn't thought to ask whether we could afford the speaker.

How will we eat for the next two weeks? Doesn't he know food costs money?

I bought a large package of beans, another of rice, a huge head of cabbage and a few apples. We already had a large box of rolled oats. We survived and actually ate pretty well-balanced meals. Having been born at the beginning of the Great Depression, I had many memories of how my parents conserved and stretched their meager income; those memories served me well now.

We had only one car, so generally I was dropped off at work and Victor ran any needed errands when he wasn't in class. One evening when I asked if he had mailed the envelopes with checks for bills he spit out, "No I didn't! I forgot!"

"Honey, please try to remember to put them in the mail tomorrow," I gently reminded him.

Again the next day I asked. "Did you get the envelopes mailed today?"

"I forgot!" Victor turned and stomped out of the room!

The following morning, trying hard to keep our lives well organized, I requested he drop off some dry cleaning. Fragments of fear and caution troubled me as he entered the apartment that night. I didn't want to anger him, but couldn't resist checking whether the needed tasks had been accomplished. I waited a while for him to offer the information, which didn't happen, so I gently asked, "Did the letters and cleaning get taken care of?"

He reacted *vehemently* and slammed his hand against the wall. "No! I forgot! Every time I come home you make me feel like I'm standing before the Spanish Inquisition!"

After he calmed down I quietly explained, "I'm just used to checking to be sure everything gets done. I ask myself, did I do this or do that? I'm not doing anything different with you than I do with myself every day. I didn't mean to upset you, and I'm very sorry."

"I don't *like* it! You keep asking me *all the time* if I did this or that. It makes me *mad!* You make me feel like I am going through the inquisition *every day, over and over!*"

I will not ever, ever ask him to do anything again. I will do it myself.

Later I went to the car and discovered the envelopes had fallen on the floor and slid under the seat. They were now a week late. I used extra gas to make a trip especially for these errands.

I wanted so much to be a *perfect,* or at least a *good* wife. I spent time and prayer pondering how to do this, especially after problems arose. One kind of a problem became more frequent. When we would be heading to some new address or destination, suddenly Victor would inquire with an irritated voice, "Well, where am I supposed to turn?"

I'd get out the map and start studying it. "I think the street you just passed *might* have been where we should have turned."

"Well, why didn't you tell me sooner?" he'd ask accusingly.

"I just barely discovered it," I meekly answered.

He'd then swing the car around fast, in anger, and suddenly become a dangerous driver, continuing to ask me what to do. I'd try to tell him gently where to go, as best as I could discover while still studying the map. This began to happen almost every time we drove any place we hadn't been before.

As we were coming in the front door one day after a trip, he ordered me to sit down on the couch and exclaimed, "We are going to *have* to talk this out! I am *sick and tired* of you telling me where to go! I don't want this to *ever* happen again!"

Oh God, please help me! He's the one who asks! Am I to always study the map ahead of time and plan it all out? Or am I to keep my mouth shut and never answer or look at the map when he asks? I haven't the faintest idea what to do! He has never asked me to plan the route and now he says he doesn't want me to tell him what to do. What if he demands I tell him? I'm certainly in a double bind!

I decided when we'd go somewhere again I'd keep quiet and not answer his direction questions. After his demanding several times, I meekly said, "I don't know." Then he *insisted* I look it up on the map. I complied and tried to answer kindly, but often it was too late and he'd have to back-track. Then he was *furious* with me! I didn't know what to change or even how to be! Neither of us had yet learned to talk about our problems.

It didn't take long after we arrived at the seminary to start making friends with other couples. A classmate of Victor and his wife had spent an afternoon at a park with us after sharing our picnic lunches. It had been a delightful and relaxing day, and our new friends were riding with us back home to pick up their car and leave. We were soon to pass a large church where the Brahms Requiem was to be performed in a few minutes. I'd been mentioning to Victor in recent days how much I wanted to go, especially since it was free, and it was close enough for me to walk home afterward. As we approached the church I said, "It's about time for the Requiem to start. Could you just let me off here, and I'll walk home afterward?" He didn't answer me.

I repeated a little louder, "Victor, please let me off here at the church." At that moment he was right in front of it where it was easy to pull over. He still didn't answer. He didn't even slow down, driving home without a word. The other couple said their goodbyes and left as soon as we arrived home. I was *afraid* to be the cause of more anger, so I kept my mouth closed. Victor and I ate supper wordlessly.

After a while Victor said, "Let's go to bed. It's getting late."

I didn't say a thing about how I was feeling, even though I was *achingly* disappointed to miss the Requiem. Silently I followed him to the bedroom, hurt and bitter, but trying my best not to show it. He made no effort to touch me or even say goodnight.

Life can be so very, extremely unfair! This was a time I should have insisted on discussion—taking a stand of some sort. But I didn't know anything about boundaries or communication.

KAREN: Judy had no sense of the *right* to be acknowledged *as a separate person; that she could make personal choices also.*

The next morning I was still very quiet, because I had *greatly anticipated* hearing the Requiem for the first time at a live performance. Missing it hurt deeply!

I don't understand what's happening. I must talk to Victor about this, but will wait until I calm down a little. I mustn't let him see me cry.

Suddenly shouting, harsh words blasted from Victor's mouth, throwing off my emotional equilibrium, "What's *wrong* with you anyhow?"

Startled and frightened, I spoke hesitantly. "Something *is* bothering me, but I'd rather not talk about it now. I'd rather wait until I am more relaxed."

"You tell me *now* what's the matter with you!" Victor shouted. As I stalled, he kept sarcastically pushing me to tell him what was wrong.

I don't want to break down or be a baby. I need to take a little more time to pull myself together and talk about it at a later time.

After his repeated questions and furious demands, tears broke through and I sobbed, "I want to know why you didn't let me go to the Brahms Requiem performance last night. I'm terribly disappointed!"

The bedroom and kitchen of our tiny and crowded apartment were next to each other, and he was standing in the doorway between them. As soon as I blurted out what the problem was, he got this "devil look" on his face again and just screamed at me, "Well, if *that's* all it is, *you shut up!*"

Who have I married? If he's going to do this to me, I'll do it right back! I'm sick of his demands!

Looking Victor straight in the eye and walking towards him, I quietly returned his words, "Well, *you* shut up *yourself!*"

As I was saying it while walking towards him, he backed up so now we both were in the kitchen. Abruptly he stretched out his right arm, swung his whole body around fast, and flat-handed me *hard* on my face, knocking me across the kitchen and into the wall. I suppose he thought he was just slapping me, but it was a heavy, bruising thrust!

Is this coming to a physical fight? This is no way a minister should act! This guy acts berserk! I'm through being nice and loving and kind. I will toughen up right NOW!

I stepped forward to hit *him* in the face, and he grabbed both my arms. He was much stronger than I was. Holding my arms to my sides, he dragged me out of the kitchen, through the bedroom and living room, to the front door. He opened it and gave me a heavy and forceful shove out of the door as he yelled, "You get out of here!"

He slammed the door shut behind me, as I staggered and nearly fell. Turning, I walked out to the street and kept on walking, unaware of time or thirst, hunger or miles. The side of my face swelled up, stinging and aching.

There is something terribly wrong with this man! What has made him act like this? I have never seen any of my relatives, friends or acquaintances act this way in my whole life! Is this my fault? I can't imagine what I've done wrong. I need help! What should I do? Am I going to stay married to Victor? I'm bewildered! I don't believe in divorce. I'm baffled. Does Victor hate me? What have I gotten into? What alternatives do I have? Can't I ever go anywhere on my own without his agreement or permission? This breaks my heart! Am I never to disagree with my husband? Don't I have a right to express myself honestly? This I know: I will never stay married to a man who batters me, so I choose to never do anything that will cause him to want to hit me again! I will always be compliant. I'll do the backing down. I made my choice to marry him. I'll make the best of it!

That was one of the worst decisions of my life!--the part, *"I will always be compliant. I'll do the backing down."* This should not have even been *believed,* let alone acted on. It is *sometimes* good to be compliant. And *sometimes* it is important to back down. But not in this case! Boundaries should have been set. Strong, clear boundaries!

Judy, don't ever destroy your authentic self by denying who you are. Don't always take the blame unless you really are responsible!

As I walked, the idea finally came to me: *Victor is going to be sorry for what he did, and he's going to worry about me. I haven't been home for hours. I will go back. I still love him deeply. He probably is worried because it's dark now, after nine o'clock at night, and I haven't returned home since early this morning.* I turned around, hurrying as fast as I could, walking probably several miles. As I neared the door, I could hear Victor playing the piano and singing. I stood outside and listened as he sang, "Night and day, you are the one. Only you beneath the moon and under the sun. Whether near to me or far, it's no matter, darling, where you are—I think of you night and day."

He's singing love songs! He must really be worried about me, and wants me to hear this.

When I opened the door, he turned and looked at me in a bizarre sort of way, as though asking, "What do *you* want?"

"Victor, I am *so* sorry! *Please* forgive me," I pleaded.

KAREN: Judy was asking forgiveness for *Victor's* sin. It is convoluted teaching and/or thinking that it's all women's fault. *There are also trauma issues with Victor that still confuse him greatly!*

He smilingly came over and put his arms around me, murmuring, "That's all right. I'll forgive you."

He didn't say he was worried—or sorry! He must have believed everything was my fault. He evidently was waiting for my apology! I am really hurting! I can't believe this is real! Will this be the story of the rest of our married life?

In later years, when we talked about this event, he told me his memory of what caused his anger. A few days before, as he complained about his schoolwork and said it was too hard, and I told him he was smart and *could* do it, apparently I had said something else that I had forgotten about. He reminded me that after he demanded I never again say he "was smart and could do it," I had posed the question, "Are you a man, or a mouse?" I *meant* to impress him that he was very *capable of being the leader* of the family, the *man!* But apparently he took it as an insult and thought I was calling him the *mouse!* That phrase made him furious! He must have been brooding over it for several days before he hit me.

KAREN: Yes. Judy didn't know the depth of Victor's self-loathing and how wounded and confused he was. He also had a lack of conscience. There was so much teaching then about *men* being "right!" The *true* Biblical teaching is that a man is to *sacrifice* for his wife *as Christ sacrificed* for the church--gave His *very life* for it!

THUNDER

Victor's widowed mother came to visit us while Victor was still going to the seminary. When she arrived, after our initial greetings, hugs and kisses, we all sat down—I *thought* to visit a bit. But as she sat on the couch beside Victor, she immediately started to kiss and hug him, *ignoring me and not conversing at all*, so I excused myself to prepare dinner. Even before I left the room, she had her arms around him, embracing him, pulling him close against her breast, giving him wet kisses over and over on his mouth, cheeks, forehead and even eyes. Several times I left the kitchen and returned to the living room, because I couldn't believe what I was seeing. She ran her hands through his hair, patting his face, looking into his eyes and pulling him up tight against her. This "lover-type" behavior went on and on and on for probably a half-hour or more while I was preparing the meal. I don't think *any words* passed between them at all, unless possibly there was an "I love you."

Am I dreaming? Is this for real? It seems like she wants me to see her do this! This is weird! I've never seen this happen before between any mother and son. She acts like Victor is a long-absent husband! Even my mother and father don't act like this in front of other family members! There is something very strange in the relationship between my husband and his mother. I guess every family is different, but this is a great mystery to me. I'll just have to learn to adjust to it. To me it is repulsive to see a mother treat her son like a lover. I can't imagine my mother doing that to my brother. Victor is accepting and joining the action as though this is expected behavior and there is nothing to hide! These two are so deeply involved in the kissing, caressing, hugging, patting and looking into each other's eyes that they're not even aware that I have returned to the living room. There is total engrossment! I don't think I have ever experienced with him what she is experiencing! She definitely is the aggressor! But there is no rage or anger from him like there was towards me in our bedroom some months earlier.

It all ended when I called them to eat. There was never a comment about it afterward from either of them, or from me either, unfortunately.

A couple years before I married, I had lived fifteen months in this city in Maryland, working as a secretary at the same Conference institution. At that time I had sung in a very fine choral organization called The Motet Choir. It had performed many concerts in many places, one of them being the National Art Gallery in Washington, D.C. That particular concert had been written up very favorably in the newspaper by the local, renowned music critic. I rejoined this elite choir after our move to the seminary. Now the group was preparing to tour through a couple nearby states, so I asked the director if Victor could come along on the weekend trip. I knew our marriage had big problems, and I wanted Victor to know he was more important to me than the choir. The director refused, so I quit the choir. Now I ask myself, *Was I crazy, or just stupid? Marriage is important, but doing what a person loves, and being who a person is makes a marriage more interesting if both parties accept each other's participation in specific interests, and encourage each other's growth.* Since my marriage *wasn't* working well, I believed it was at least *half*, or *more* my fault, but couldn't have named any reasons if I had been quizzed. I just *believed* I was inadequate because our marriage wasn't very happy. My personal belief system was evidently somewhat screwed.

Victor did not graduate when he finished his class work at the seminary, because he did not pass his orals; however he *did* get a call to minister in New Jersey. Before we moved, we visited both our families in California.

While at his home, he received a letter from the New Jersey Conference president who had just hired him. This man was now having second thoughts about having hired him, because people had told him, "Victor doesn't wear the pants in the family; Judy does." The letter tore me down, making me look like a domineering, hen-pecking woman. I was absolutely shocked, as well as painfully humiliated! Long before I married, I had made the decision to *never* nag my husband, and I knew I *didn't* domineer him. I hated the way my mother often nagged at my father and made *very conscious effort* to be the opposite.

Victor didn't seem to be a bit surprised or upset about the letter putting me down, although I felt absolutely destroyed! I told him, "I don't *want* to wear the pants in the family. I want *you* to be the leader." He just ignored my comments and refused to discuss anything about the letter.

Apparently people must see me in a negative way, and I am genuinely amazed! The president must be trying to encourage Victor to take charge. That's also what I am trying to do, as I back away and invite him to lead. I want a strong husband! For me to come across to other people exactly the opposite from what and who I believe I am, is frustrating and horribly embarrassing! I have made a specific decision to take charge of myself, but I definitely have not been telling Victor what to do or ordering him around. However I am the one who takes action if he doesn't. Victor still doesn't open up and say what he feels. I think inside he believes the letter is true, and I am the obnoxious villain!

I try hard to monitor myself, and pray earnestly for God to live in me and give me humility and wisdom. I am so baffled! Apparently Victor is not willing to do what is needed to change the situation. I will continue trying to change me, allowing the Holy Spirit to do whatever is necessary for me to become more Christ like.

During that respite at Victor's home, in the interim between seminary and ministerial internship, I began to get to know Victor's mother and grandmother better. I felt deep sadness as I listened to the painful description of the death of Victor's little brother from the polio vaccine, as well as Victor's own very serious and lengthy illness. Their dad's resulting depression had been so severe that he had threatened suicide. I hadn't realized how terribly sick Victor had been, and hadn't comprehended the extensiveness of the awful pain and treatment for his year-long, bed-confined recuperation.

There were more stories about the airplane crash that killed Victor's father and the two other doctors, and Victor's quest to help find the downed plane. Victor's mother was still grieving the enormous loss of her husband, although he died a year before I met Victor.

One specific story was repeated more than once with *emphasis* about Grandma's first marriage. Her husband was a minister of God, and apparently believed sexual intercourse was a sin, unless for the express purpose of procreation. He and Victor's Grandmother must have been married for some time without having consummated the marriage—I think sleeping in separate bedrooms. But finally, in a weak moment, Grandma's husband couldn't resist, and the "ultimate" happened. Victor's Grandma was impregnated by that one-time-only incident, and that's how Victor's mother came into being. Then they told the dramatic story of how Grandpa, on his knees by the bedside, loudly implored the Lord to forgive him for this horrible sin he had committed. The narrative was unclear after that. Apparently the marriage didn't last, and the grandfather died prematurely. Grandma remarried but had no more children.

In pondering all these stories, I was just starting to comprehend a bit how Victor had developed problems that affected our marriage, when a new, appalling incident occurred.

It was a hot, muggy afternoon, and Victor's family members generally took naps after church and a large noon dinner. His grandmother went to her little upstairs room, and Victor and I went into the large, main floor bedroom that he had shared so many years *with his grandmother.* There was no air conditioning in that room, so we stripped off *all* our clothes to be comfortable enough to sleep—which we did, soundly, for an hour or so.

We had just awakened, and were both on top of the bedspread, when the door opened *without* a knock, and Victor's mother smilingly walked in. Even though we were totally naked, she didn't hesitate, and came excitedly right over to the side of the bed by Victor. She leaned against the side of the bed, crossed her arms across her breast, hugging herself, and started to twist and sway back and forth. In a tone of voice as if she had just opened a beautiful gift, she exclaimed, "Oh, I just *love* to watch my son love his wife," as she breathed heavy and kept twisting and turning. "Oh, this is *so wonderful* to watch you love Judy," directing her comment to Victor as she leaned over and smiled down on him. But we weren't even touching each other or lying close together!

What in the world is going on? Is she hoping we'll do something physically intimate so she can be a voyeur? Does my mother-in-law want to watch us have sex? Victor hasn't changed his position since she walked in; he is just lying on his back, looking into her face and smiling as though this happens every day!

Victor's mom's behavior escalated until she was almost gasping for breath and making kind of little gurgling sounds as she jiggled back and forth. "I just *love* this! *Love this!* It makes me feel *so* good, oh *so-o-o good* to watch!" she softly squealed in a high-pitched voice.

Victor continued to say and do *nothing* except lie there and smile up at her. He didn't even look or act embarrassed; but I was nearly dying of mortification and was scouring the room with my eyes for something nearby to pull over my suddenly exposed nudity. [My mother always knocked on my bedroom door before she came in, at least by the time I became a teenager. If she accidentally walked in on me partially dressed, she always apologized for intruding on me, then turned and left the room until I could put on some clothing. Privacy was highly respected in our home.] Victor's mother continued to stay by our bed it seemed for five or ten minutes, talking and "oohing" and "ahhing" to Victor while I was unwillingly made a part of this exhibit. I felt horribly intruded upon and mercilessly invaded! Finally she let out a long sigh and suddenly turned and walked out of the room, with no more comment!

After she left, I told Victor how *shocked and violated* I felt. He looked *startled* and *amazed*, and said he didn't see *anything out of place* with what she did! He then nonchalantly got up and dressed and left the room with no more comment. Since I had previously made up my mind to *not* make him angry, I said nothing more and tried, with great difficulty, to bury my feelings. *I'll not press him with questions. I'll just continue treating him respectfully and lovingly.*

KAREN: Victor's Grandmother's husband had a distorted belief about sex being sinful. Victor's mother learned sexuality misconceptions. Now with Victor's problems there are apparently three generations of sexual problems. For Judy to be quiet, keeps them

both in the fantasy that nothing is wrong. It is possible to be respectful and still address the issue of sexual boundaries.

Soon we were traveling to our new destination. Victor became the associate pastor of a several-hundred-member church in central New Jersey, with Pastor Bill Jorgenson as head pastor. We moved into an upstairs apartment not far from the church and found some more second-hand furniture at the Rescue Mission. We bought two dressers for $10 each and later a four-poster bed and desk.

About this time Victor's grandmother flew, *uninvited*, to visit us. We had about five days to get settled before she arrived. On her first day there I started feeling nauseated. She said, "You're probably pregnant. This is *no* time to get pregnant! Your husband doesn't want *any* children, *ever!* Why are you getting pregnant? You ought to be *ashamed!*"

I'm being criticized and blamed before I even know if I'm pregnant! Did Grandma forget it takes two to accomplish that? She scolds and demeans me for having done this horrible thing to Victor, her darling grandson, as though he never had a thing to do with it. I'll just let her talk, and let it roll off of me. But I wonder what she means by saying Victor never wants children? That's news to me! Before we married I asked him about having children. He said then, "Whatever you want will be just fine with me!"

KAREN: Victor made a passive-aggressive statement. It was not a "Yes, I want children" statement and it left Judy open to blame for being pregnant.

Victor was involved in a lot of preaching. Besides assisting at the larger church, he was assigned as pastor of a much smaller church about a half hour away. We alternated weekly between the two places. In the smaller congregation there were about forty wonderfully friendly members. Often, after services there, we were invited to different homes for meals. The parishioners of this smaller church obviously adored Victor. However, there was just one outspoken woman member who didn't think Victor was well organized. She complained to Pastor Jorgenson, who spoke to Victor about this, and then Victor believed himself to be even more inadequate!

Bill Jorgenson was very energetic, precisely organized and did everything fast. He often urged Victor to speed up whatever he was doing. Victor complained, "That is just my speed of doing things. I *can't* go faster!"

One day Bill gave him a painting job and then stood and watched him. Finally Bill demonstrated, "This is how you ought to paint faster."

Victor was and is a wonderful and meticulous painter! I can't imagine somebody scolding him for the way he paints, because he is fast as well as fastidious. Bill definitely was out of line that time.

One morning Victor was in old, junky, torn and paint spattered clothes when he asked me to go to the bank with him to open an account.

I sort of gulped, "You're a new minister here in town, and I'll not go to the bank with you looking like that. I'll be delighted to go with you when you clean up and change clothes."

He just shrugged, turned away and went alone. Later he brought the papers home and I signed them in privacy.

One of Victor's jobs was to do the church bulletins. He typed the stencils and then mimeographed them. The ink could be messy, and it wasn't easy to stay clean, so he went to the church office on bulletin-making days wearing these same old patched and paint-spattered work clothes that looked awful.

Bill confronted him one day. "Why don't you wear slacks and shirt?"

"I'm doing dirty work," Victor replied and didn't change.

After a few weeks Bill gave Victor an ultimatum to dress more like a minister, and he complied. *Ah, what a relief!*

When Victor dressed well, I loved being seen in public with him. I relished hearing him preach. I adored all the things he could do. I was so proud and happy to be married to him.

One beautiful early fall day a gusty breeze was sailing thousands of brightly colored leaves across lawns and down streets and highways. Our phone rang, and it was a new church acquaintance inviting me to make a bus trip with her and her daughter to a Hershey candy factory in Pennsylvania. I accepted the invitation and relished a day of relaxed travel. On our way we rode through Amish country and saw bonneted women and bearded men riding in horse-drawn carriages. After we arrived at the factory we took a tour and were all offered plenty of chocolate samples. Everything was so fascinating but extremely tiring, I realized, as we headed back to the bus. Soon after the bus started home, I started feeling like throwing up and didn't think I'd make it home without causing a nasty mess. But my stomach held on to its contents while I grasped the concept that Victor's Grandma was right—I *was* pregnant! I had been unfailingly faithful using the only kind of female contraceptive available in those days. For three months I now daily fought nausea and also was so sleepy most of the time I could hardly make myself get out of bed.

5

HURRICANE

Pastor Jorgenson was preparing for a series of evangelistic meetings to be held in a large tent. Victor worked with several volunteers from church who helped prepare the area and set up the tent. The podium was built, chairs were arranged, the piano and hymnbooks were put in place. The electricity and P.A. systems were ready to go for the first meeting that was to start the following Sunday night. Friday morning the radio announced a severe storm was on its way. It arrived by noon, and the wind increased in strength. Head pastor Bill and Victor phoned for more volunteers and a dozen or so arrived as the winds built to hurricane force. With sledgehammers they drove the tent stakes deeper and tightened the ropes.

Then came the rain. Tent ropes tighten when wet, so the tighter ropes started pulling out the stakes. Now the men were struggling to *loosen* all the ropes. More volunteers arrived without being summoned as members realized the emergency. After midnight there was a losing battle. Every time a stake was driven in, it just popped back up from the soaked soil with the gale yanking on the tent. Now it was literally one man to each pole, hanging on with total body weight, trying to keep it stable against the ferocious pull.

Upstairs in our apartment I could hear rain pouring as from a faucet. *Never before* had I heard wind as heavy as that night. The blasts felt and sounded as though they would rip the house apart. It was swaying back and forth frighteningly. I prayed earnestly for Victor and the others' safety.

Oh Lord, even though I feel fear, I love rainstorms, wind and all kinds of exciting weather. I sense Your power and control and feel elation living this life You have given me. Bless me and live in me, and please protect us all. Thank you.

Sometime before daybreak Victor came in, soaked to the skin and shivering miserably. He undressed, took a hot shower, put on dry clothes and announced the bad news. Water had puddled in one end of the tent top, and the big ring that goes around the main pole broke. That end of the tent came down on the piano, the chairs and everything that had been set up. As soon as the men saw the piano topple, they hurriedly crawled under the heavy, soaked canvas, and covered the piano with waterproof tarps. The outside of the piano got a little wet from the sopping canvas but not enough to damage the inside.

Victor is a strong and able man. His endurance at physical labor outlasts many others. He quickly ate the hot soup I had prepared and took a sandwich to eat as he drove again into the pelting cloudburst to the downed tent.

Just at dawn, one of the conference men came from retrieving a new ring and "quarter tent" from storage and recruited an extremely strong and brave man to shinny up the pole and put on the ring. Finally the new "quarter tent" was installed with many helping hands. As the ground dried, the stakes were replaced and ropes readjusted.

By the eleven am church service most of the volunteers were in faithful attendance in spite of no sleep. By Sunday night everything was dry enough and rearranged so meetings began as advertised.

At a later time, during this same series of meetings, a storm came up just after the song service started. There was thunder and lightning and all the lights went out in the tent. Fortunately it was a familiar song, so I just kept on playing, and the audience kept on singing. We did several more songs all by ear. The thunder continued so long there never was a sermon.

Besides doing music with the evangelist, Victor and I sang and played a lot of special musical numbers for various churches and other types of meetings. A teenage girl, who was coming regularly to the evangelistic meetings, started talking to me every time she had a chance. She was bright and eager for life and frequently exclaimed, "Oh, you and Pastor Leigh are the most *perfect* couple! I hope I can find a man as wonderful as your husband! I want to be the kind of woman you are! You are the most ideal and perfect couple I have ever known!"

Lord, I deeply sense a responsibility to represent You honestly. Please guide us and live through us. I must never let her know the negative part of our lives.

KAREN: AT THIS POINT JUDY DOES NOT RECOGNIZE THE "DISCONNECT" EVEN IN HER PRAYERS! SHE ASKS GOD TO HELP HER REPRESENT HIM HONESTLY, YET IS UNWILLING TO ALLOW OTHERS TO SEE THE NEGATIVITY IN HER MARRIAGE, WHICH IS DISHONESTY! SHE IS STILL "HIDING" OR "PLAY-ACTING." SHE HAS ABSOLUTELY NO CONCEPT OF HOW TO TAKE ACTION TO *LIVE IN INTEGRITY.*

Summer was fading, and I was expanding. A denominationally operated boarding high school in New Jersey, was frantically looking for a music teacher, and the principal called me. It was almost time for school to start. I explained my baby was coming in March, but they wanted me *now*, desperately enough to pay my train fare twice a week to teach choir, piano and voice lessons. They would find someone else for second semester. Tuesdays and Thursdays Victor drove me to the train station. After a forty-minute ride, a teacher from the school met me at the station to take me the rest of the way.

One of my voice students was in his junior year. Although untrained, he had an unusually marvelous singing voice, as many Afro-Americans do, but no concept of his own exceptional talent and very little self-confidence. I worked hard to build up his faith, emphasizing that God had given him this wonderful gift. God had a plan for him, and using his gift would glorify his Lord. I spent extra time coaching him without charge. Decades later a mutual friend, also a minister's wife, said she had met this man, who was now an ordained minister in the South and superb singer. During their conversation he happened to tell her who had inspired him so many years before. He looked to Judy Leigh as one of the most important people in his early life. He had learned from her that he had worth to God and to the world.

Praise you Lord Jesus for working through me, for transforming this man for your cause.

A heavy storm blew in one night and disintegrated a squirrel's nest in a tree in front of the school. Two students rescued a couple tiny babies from the rain-soaked sidewalk and started feeding them warm milk from doll baby bottles. The cafeteria kitchen cooperated by allowing milk to be warmed, but the student "adopters" were worn out after a couple days of feeding these tiny babies many times throughout both the day and night. Finally one student begged me to adopt hers, which I did, so took it home on the train. The three-inch pink baby was, by now, growing fur, and its eyes were opening. (I understand the other squirrel soon died.) We named our new baby Snookums. He was one of the most delightful pets we ever had, and more playful than a kitten. As he got bigger and could get out of his box, he had the run of the whole apartment—until he climbed up the curtains in our bedroom to the rod and there found a loose piece of wallpaper, which he tugged. Then he jumped from the rod, grabbing the curtains on the way down, clinging there and swinging back and forth. The draperies and curtains were getting little holes and snags, and the wallpaper was disappearing in minuscule spots. Apprehensively I moaned, "We've got to do *something* or the apartment will be ruined!"

The weather was getting colder. Winter had arrived and I was getting bigger and bigger with child. We finally asked the people in the downstairs apartment if we could use the screened-in front porch for the squirrel's home. They said it was okay. On a small table we placed a large, heavy-cardboard box, and inside of this we put a smaller twelve-inch box thickly lined with glued-on strips of warm wool rags. Into it we cut a small entry hole. Snookums hibernated in the small box tucked among the rag strips all winter. That's when I learned that squirrels *do* come out of hibernation sometimes for food or water. The water froze solid, but Snookums licked holes in it.

By now we had discovered that our every-day life-style habits were very similar in many ways. We loved having daily family worship together. Sabbath was such an enjoyable and happy time. The house was freshly cleaned and special dishes were prepared ahead of time. We delighted in playing and singing together at home, especially when we didn't happen to be in evangelistic meetings.

It was a treat to sometimes get to bed earlier than usual. I showered, perfumed and donned my best nightie. It was a wonderful time for making love. However Victor startled me one night with a new demand. "We mustn't have sex any more on the Sabbath." Never before had he expressed such a thing, and I had never heard of, or imagined it. Then he said, "The next time I try to start something on Sabbath, you are to stop me!"

*Is he is trying to make **me** responsible for **his** actions? I want more sex than I am getting, so I'm physically and emotionally frustrated. Yet he demands in no uncertain terms that I am to stop him! I won't obey him! He can stop himself if he feels guilty, which I don't!*

KAREN: THE CONCEPT OF "OBEY" IN BOTH VICTOR AND JUDY'S THINKING DID NOT INCLUDE ANY ROOM FOR THE ABSOLUTELY BIBLICAL CONCEPT OF THE HUSBAND'S PREROGATIVE OF *SACRIFICIAL, UNSELFISH* LOVE FOR HIS WIFE. VICTOR'S SEXUAL BEHAVIOR AND ATTITUDE TOWARD JUDY WAS *NOT* THAT OF AN EMOTIONALLY HEALTHY MAN!

As time progressed, Victor became more depressed. His self-image was so negative that it affected his whole life. He seemed tired *all the time*. He would come home feeling so exhausted that he'd proclaim, "I was *very* worn out at work today because we had sex last night!" He began to tell me more often, even on weekdays, that I was to stop him! "We're having sex *too often*. You've *got* to stop me, because it makes me *too tired*. Sex is very physically debilitating!"

Our personalities were quite different in that if something out of routine happened, it was an interesting experience for me; but Victor fussed and complained, especially if it was an uncomfortable event. For instance, he was given the assignment of taking a blind lady, Bertha, to New York City to participate in a television program. Hopefully she'd be able to "Strike It Rich." Someone in our church had written to the program about her, time had passed, and the possibility had almost been forgotten. Then a letter came saying that she was to come. Victor wrote the story afterward to send home, and it was so interesting I asked to make a copy to save:

Victor wrote:

I took Bertha's elderly mother along to help, because Bertha's blindness hindered her walking. She didn't have a white cane, and she depended on other people to guide her.

An ice storm had struck the night before. In the dim morning light the cobblestone streets in Plainfield looked glassy. Very few cars were moving. I picked up the two women and started to the train station. Cars were pulled over to the side of the road, spinning their wheels. I was about the only one moving with my VW bug and good traction, but I was scared to death I wouldn't make it on those slick streets. Finally we arrived at the train station.

We had been rushing because we didn't want to be late, but found the trains weren't even running yet because of the storm. We waited and waited. Finally the first train came, but we couldn't get on because people were lined up four and five deep along the platform and crowded in front of us. When the next train came, after about thirty minutes, we were fortunate to board.

In New York City we got to the subway station without going outside. But when we disembarked and came up to the street, I was told the taxis had barely started running. They had been out of commission because of icy streets. When I tried to hail one, it seemed they would pick up only executives and business people. They could see we were tourists. I gave up, and we decided to walk the few blocks to the TV studio.

There was a bitterly cold wind. The ice had been melting, and it was sort of misting, which made everything slushy and slick. We were bundled up in our winter clothes and were hurrying along so we wouldn't be late. Just before arriving at our destination, we passed under the awning of a big apartment building. The wind caught the awning full of standing water in its sag, and the icy liquid poured all over blind Bertha. Somehow it missed her mother and me. Bertha's upper body clothing was soaked to her skin.

We brushed her off the best we could and finally got to the studio, only to find it closed!

The only attendant there said, "Well, we may not have a program at all today. The Master of Ceremonies slipped and wrenched his back." We thought maybe we took the trip in vain, but in a few minutes he came hobbling up and opened the door. Other people soon arrived. We were interviewed and given some test questions. It turned out that many of the sample questions they gave us were the ones they actually used on the program.

Bertha couldn't speak very well either, so the studio official tried to get more information from her mother as to her background. They soon cut off the interview and told us we wouldn't be on the first part of the program. We were to go sit in the audience. That really discouraged me, and I felt angry. I thought all our effort was of no use. Toward the close of the program they swung the cameras around, zeroed in on me and announced, "Would Victor Leigh please stand up in the audience. You will be on the program. You are a minister and you brought someone from your church."

They asked me four questions. The last one was, "The Pentagon is on the border of what four states?'" I could remember three: Virginia, Maryland and Washington D.C., but the fourth one I couldn't remember. I looked up and the cameraman was mouthing "West Virginia," so I said, "West Virginia" and got it right. I "struck it rich" for this blind lady. She and her mother held back their hurrahs and elated shouts until we left the building. I was just glad it was over! It was a hair-raising experience for me!"

Whenever he repeated this story to friends, he always emphasized at the end how *foolishly* these ladies spent their "Strike it Rich" money, and how thoroughly *disgusted* he was that he had gone to all that effort "for nothing!"

Victor's "life message" here seems to be "nothing will turn out right!"

For me, life was one big adventure! Challenges excited me and got my adrenalin soaring. I'd have loved to be given the assignment of taking these ladies, but I wasn't in a physical condition to allow it.

Near our smaller congregation was the Mount Holly church. Tim Donahue was the pastor. We became close friends with Tim and Shelley. We often ate at their place, or they ate at ours. The first thing that impressed me when we walked into their small, filled-to-capacity church was the singing. It felt like the walls and ceiling were reverberating from the voices. There was energetic, marvelous, one hundred percent singing, and I loved to go there just to hear it. Thrilling!

The Donahues had two darling little blond girls. One was four and one was two. Suddenly the youngest took sick, and although her mother was a nurse and they rushed her to the hospital, they couldn't save her. She died within twenty-four hours of some sort of "galloping pneumonia." What a cruel turn of events! Their hearts were robbed--stripped of a most precious treasure. Shelley was able to weep freely and verbally pour out floods of pain. But it seemed to us that Tim was more soul-tortured, unable to find mending for his ripped-apart heart. His body language characterized agony for weeks and months afterward. They both clung fiercely to the memories of their daughter's smile, her touch and the music of her childish voice. We spent increasing amounts of time with them, attempting to lessen their load of grief by sharing time and tears with them.

One of the women who wrote scripts for a television program called Faith for Today knew us quite well, and wrote a special play for us. It would be on live TV in New York City. We memorized our parts and made a trip there for rehearsal and another for the live performance. Victor and I portrayed a husband and wife whose young daughter had recently died. Although I was actually five months pregnant with my first child, I didn't obviously "show" yet.

In the play I was "Emily," a music teacher, who owned a lovely grand piano. Emily's devastation over the loss of her child had turned her emotions inward, and she refused to talk about the painful and searing memories, which hearing *any* music now seemed to invoke. Emily silently chose to discard all music activities, because it dredged up excruciating recall. Every memory of her daughter's small fingers learning to skillfully caress the piano keys tore at her crushed heart.

She hadn't hinted any of this to her husband, but he discovered her "piano for sale" ad while reading the newspaper at the breakfast table with her. This generated an intense conversation between them, about how Emily felt, and why she was selling her beloved instrument.

The second act depicted a situation where middle school girls were to sing an important number in a widely advertised church program, but the director became seriously ill just before dress rehearsal. I, as Emily, after first refusing any musical activity, had finally been persuaded to help, *only* because it was an *emergency*, and they knew I could handle the challenge. However, in the process of interaction with the young singers during rehearsal, their loving response to "Emily," and the feedback regarding the remarkable results of her coaching, she, as I played her, was finally able to begin the process of her own healing and recovery from personal loss.

We performed the script with CBS television cameras almost poking in our faces. Victor said it was a "hair-raising experience" too. But I loved it! I longed to do more acting! As a child I had daydreamed of being an actress. When I had then played with other children, I had tried to get them to use the "right" vocal inflections, facial expressions and mannerisms to "be real" when we were playing house or acting out make-believe stories.

Since I was a little girl I had often imagined myself not only being a minister's wife *and* actress, but also an airplane pilot, opera singer, concert pianist and fabulous wife, cook and lover. I imagined being my minister-husband's secretary, taking dictation from him (I learned shorthand in college) and typing his letters. I imagined going to many Bible studies with him and making friends with the people. Although I expected Victor to lead out, I imagined I would contribute to the lessons and conversation.

Victor met a couple at an evangelistic meeting and had made arrangements to study the Bible with them. He asked me to come with him, and I was delighted. I had gone to quite a few Bible studies with my dad when he was teaching how to give Bible studies, but I didn't think to discuss my expected behavior with Victor before we went.

When we arrived, I immediately started asking friendly questions about this couple's life and interests, but Victor really pushed to stop conversation and get the Bible study started. Several times, after he began, there were periods of silence that felt uncomfortable to me, so I spoke up with a comment. After he would read a Bible verse, ask a question or make a statement, he became totally quiet for what seemed a very long, awkward pause. If I had a relevant idea, like maybe putting the Bible verse into my own words, or telling what that passage meant to me, I'd speak up. Or I asked a related question about something in their life.

I began to notice that Victor was getting irritated. I could see it in his body language, but wasn't sure what was causing it. After a bit, Victor would continue calmly, and then have another awkward silence. He had asked me to come along, so I wanted to do my part. I thought we were all included in the study together, so I spoke up again.

Suddenly, as I started to talk, Victor said in a loud, angry voice, "Would you please be quiet so I can get on with this Bible study?"

Surprised and embarrassed I responded, "Yes, of course. I'm sorry!"

Later I spoke again and was quieted instantly with a nasty sounding demand from Victor, "Shut your mouth and don't say *anything* more!"

I'm sure the couple saw the anger in him; they looked shocked! At that point his words hurt, but I was more appalled because I thought, *Now what are they going to think of Victor?*

On the way home I tried to discuss what happened and find out what he thought I did wrong or what he had expected from me, but he refused to talk. He was still too angry! Before we arrived home he blurted out, "I don't want you to go to a Bible study with me again, ever!" Victor didn't have a concept of *practical* application of Scripture and *Holy Spirit led behavior*, so couldn't talk about the *real* issues.

Oh, that hurts so-o-o much! I wanted so much to be a partner in his work.

Before I started college I knew I wanted to learn how to become a secretary, so I chose that as my "minor" while I majored in music. Between my junior and senior years of college I worked as a secretary for fifteen months at our denominational headquarters almost next door to the seminary where Victor later attended. A relative there was influential in my being hired three thousand miles from home. My job entailed my learning processes and duties in a religious magazine's editorial office. Shortly I was asked to compose most of the correspondence myself, and my two bosses just read and signed the letters. I also did editing of articles sent to be published in the <u>Ministry</u> magazine. My editor boss didn't even want to look at them unless they were put into *my* best form. It was thrilling to be trusted, complimented and depended on during that period.

When I married, I expected to handle my husband's secretarial needs. Verbalizing this, I volunteered to do all of his letters and other typing, but he never asked me to do that, apparently wanting to do it himself. When I mentioned it, he acted angry, without answering.

Other times he would be terribly discouraged and pout, "I don't know what I'm going to preach about next week. I can't think of anything. I'm not any good as a preacher." **KAREN: PERFECTIONISM CAN BE A PROBLEM FOR BOTH VICTOR AND JUDY IF IT IS A *SUPERFICIAL VENEER* TO MAKE THEM *LOOK LIKE* GOOD PEOPLE, GOOD CHRISTIANS, GOOD WIFE, GOOD PREACHER. IT CAN EVENTUALLY RESULT IN LOSING JOY, HOPE, AND INTEGRITY. THERE NEEDS TO BE A PLACE FOR THE HOLY SPIRIT TO ENTER IN.**

I didn't then know how to just mirror back what Victor was saying, such as, "You sound like you're really down today." We were both very poor communicators. Instead I'd suggest, "You could start a series on the Beatitudes or a series on the Ten Commandments."

"Oh, that's old!" was his retort. Whatever I brought up, he'd refuse.

I wonder if he thinks I am trying to domineer him. I thought he wanted help from me. We learn too little too late. Whenever he apparently was stymied and didn't know what to do about problems, he would come and tell me about it. I wanted to *fix everything* then. I didn't know how to just listen with a sympathetic ear without giving advice.

At the end of January I quit teaching at the boarding school and occupied my time with painting the furniture Victor had readied for me. He was so handy at making, fixing and remodeling things. He *loved* working creatively with wood, seeming to enjoy doing this far more than any of his "religious" activities. He cut the "feet" off the legs of the old dressers we had bought to make them the same height, and added wood at the back of the top of one to make them look the same depth. He removed the mirrors and frames, which were very different, and filled gouges and cracks with wood putty. After a couple coats of paint we had a matching bedroom set.

DELUGE

Victor insisted I go for my pregnancy needs to a doctor in *general* practice whose office was *only a half block* away. Victor's father had been in general practice and had delivered hundreds of babies successfully, so Victor didn't see any point in paying *extra* for an obstetrician.

The doctor was "knockout gorgeous," and physically I was attracted to him. He seemed to always be in a hurry, though, and would examine me in about three minutes. Then he'd turn to leave the room, and just as he was going through the door he'd ask, "Do you have any questions?" This so overwhelmed me, I couldn't think of any questions to ask. I'd never had a baby, and wasn't around my mother or grandmother to ask, nor did I know people in the church very well.

I just couldn't talk to my doctor! He laughed at the idea of my wanting to have *natural* childbirth, but I studied very carefully and practiced diligently everything I could learn from the only book I could find on the subject.

I asked Victor over and over again to let me *change doctors*. He said, "You're healthy, and you're strong. You don't *need* a specialist. This doctor can deliver our baby as well as anyone else."

KAREN: JUDY MUST *ASK PERMISSION* OF HER HUSBAND?

I was afraid to tell Victor I was attracted to my doctor and scared of him at the same time. I urged Victor to come with me to my appointments, but he told me that his church work was more important.

KAREN: VICTOR'S PRIORITIES WERE NOT THOUGHT OF IN TERMS OF HIS *COMMITMENT TO GOD AND HIS WIFE.* SAD!

I thought if Victor was with me when I went for my doctor's appointment, it would show a strong marriage to the doctor and *convince myself of that* at the same time. Of course I didn't *dare* tell my husband that reason, for fear of more anger, but he didn't want to take the time to leave work for such an *unnecessary* task. So I'd go to my appointment, and then come home to cry in private from frustration and feeling abandoned by both the doctor and by Victor. At that point in my life, since the episode when Victor hit me, I had decided I would not stand up to him. I would obey him, and he would be the ruler of the family. I would do whatever he said. Victor had reminded me more than once that the Bible teaches wives to "submit yourselves unto your own husbands, as unto the Lord." (Ephesians 5:22 KJV)

KAREN: VICTOR LEFT OUT THE HUSBAND'S JOB—THE *GREATER SACRIFICE* OF THE TWO.

I badly wanted a doctor I could feel was a *fatherly* type, or somebody I could talk to who was warm and interested in me *as a person*, but I discovered it wasn't worth asking for any more.

My baby decided to wait five days past the predicted delivery date, and I was getting more excited and impatient. He was tremendously active. It felt like his feet were up under my ribs, and I ached because he kicked me so hard and so frequently.

I *longed* to have Victor watch the birth. The doctor said no, and Victor didn't want to anyway. I wakened when my water broke about 2:00 am. After an hour I got a mild, achy sensation rather like vague menstrual "cramps." Except, when I had my *period* my *menstrual* pain *never* stopped. At *those* times I hurt severely *with no let-up* for sometimes *three or more days.* Now this vague sensation was almost unnoticeable, and it came and went. Finally, when the contractions were about five minutes apart, the doctor said to come to the hospital. The nurse whisked me away in a wheel chair, while Victor went to fill in the paper work, and then *returned home to sleep* without saying even a goodbye to me.

KAREN: VICTOR WALKED AWAY FROM *LIFE!*

At first I was in the labor room all by myself, but after a while an Italian woman came in who was in labor. There was a curtain between us but we talked a little. Then I decided to go to sleep, which I did between every contraction. During the contraction I'd just concentrate on relaxing and breathing, and then I'd go back to sleep again.

Finally a nurse came in and asked, "Don't you want something for pain? Don't you want a shot now?"

"No. I want to be awake when this baby comes," was my determined answer.

"Aren't you in terrible pain?" she asked.

"No, I'm sleeping between every contraction."

"Don't you even want an aspirin?" the nurse almost insisted.

"No. This isn't as bad as my usual menstrual cramps, and I don't take anything for them." I turned my back and returned to giving concentrated attention to my body.

My parents had never suggested giving me aspirin or painkillers for anything, so I was used to doing without. I remember the nurse was just amazed. She said, "Your contractions are getting *really strong* now."

Finally they strapped something to my wrist and said when I hurt too bad I could move my hand to my nose and breath this gas. I breathed it a little but kept falling asleep. Later I was told that the baby was not dropping properly, and they decided to take me to the delivery room anyway. Sometime after we got to that room, a mask of ether was put over my face. When I realized it was anesthetic, I tried to push it away. Later the doctor told me, "You fought us like a tiger, and we had to get several people to hold you down until the ether took effect."

Because of a previous injury, my coccyx bone was malformed and protruded into the birth canal, but *I hadn't been told this before delivery.* They pulled my son out with forceps and *broke* my coccyx bone in the process. The doctor's office was supposed to open at two o'clock in the afternoon and the birth took place at 2:15 pm. I believe they hurried up the process so the doctor could get back to work. I still wonder if I'd had an obstetrician rather than a general practitioner, would he have done a C-section?

Little Steve *could not suck*! The pediatrician showed me how to hold his lips on my nipple with one hand, and with the other hand massage from his chin down the front of his throat, which forced a sucking motion. My milk was coming in heavily, so it did get into his mouth, but he'd sputter and almost choke. It was hard work and tiring for both of us. The nurses wanted me to give up trying to breast-feed him and instead give him a bottle with big holes in the nipple. Since he could hardly suck at all, they also urged my getting a shot to dry up my milk.

"No, I am going to nurse this baby, and *you can't stop me!*" I insisted.

They'd bring him when I asked, but give him a bottle between times. Because he wasn't getting very much milk from me, my breasts became impacted, hard as a rock and very painful.

Victor came to see the baby and me that first evening and stayed maybe fifteen minutes. Later that night it snowed about a foot. Victor phoned me the next afternoon, and I asked him to bring my nursing bras from home when he came to visit, since the hospital said I needed them. But he informed me in *no uncertain tone* that he *wasn't* coming that night, "because there is *too much snow*," even though the roads had been cleared.

I am a new mother and have gone through labor and birth without my husband. I was alone when the doctor *warned me*, after I regained consciousness, "We *hope* your baby is *normal*. His head will look a little different." Steve's head is misshapen—not elongated like many are, but squished from top to chin. He can't suck, cries a lot, and falls asleep from exhaustion after two minutes of trying to nurse! My husband isn't coming to see me. I feel sad, hurt, blue and afraid my baby might have serious problems! It isn't *normal* for a baby not to be able to suck!

I wouldn't admit, even to myself, that I was angry. That would be "sinful."

KAREN: THIS IS A MESSAGE CHILDREN GET FROM MANIPULATIVE PARENTS AND OFTEN CARRY IT INTO ADULTHOOD.

The Italian girl, who had a baby just before I did, was put in the same hospital room with me. She joked that the doctor must have gotten our babies mixed up because, although Victor and I are both blond, Steve had two-inch-long, black hair and her baby was totally bald. Her husband came and stayed a *long time* and saw how badly I felt. I couldn't keep the tears back. I felt bereft and broken. Where was the loyalty and support I needed so deeply? The awful realization had dawned: Victor didn't *want* to come! Snow was just an *excuse!*

It is icier in my own heart and soul than the roads are. I need support. I need love. I feel totally abandoned. My breasts ache badly. I need my husband NOW!!!! Maybe I was getting feverish.

My roommate's husband said, "I'm going to buy some ice cream. Would you like an ice cream cone?"

"I love ice cream!" So he brought me a cone. Yum!

At least some people care about me, even if they are strangers. But it isn't my husband, and I want him to care. I need him to care!

As I finished the ice cream, I started to chill. Soon I just totally "lost it." I started crying and sobbing, and my chills got worse until I was shaking so hard the whole bed shook. The Italian man called the nurse. She piled blankets on me and even brought a heating pad.

Then another nurse started questioning me--had I ever felt this way before? She took my temperature and blood pressure and seemed concerned. I couldn't stop crying. I was completely hysterical. Finally one nurse asked, "What do *you* think is the problem?"

"My husband isn't coming," I moaned. "My husband won't come to see me. My breasts are impacted, and I asked him to bring the nursing bras, but he said he wasn't coming because there's too much snow."

She got downright angry and exclaimed, "I'm going to call him and tell him he *has* to come--*immediately!*"

A little later, when she told me Victor was coming after all, I was able to partially calm down and shakily mumbled, "I want my baby. Please bring me my baby."

She hesitated, and then stated, "We don't know whether you are *able* to take the baby right now."

"I'm *very* able. *Please* bring me my baby," I repeated. "I want to nurse him *right now!*"

They brought him, even though it was against the rules about timing. Victor finally arrived with my nursing bras, and the nurses just turned their backs and left us alone. Normally the hospital wouldn't let visitors come into the room when the baby was there. Victor acted sympathetic and loving, and actually *apologized* for upsetting me. He got to see how hard it was for Steve to suck. With his presence and concerned involvement, my emotions and body finally returned to normal.

My broken coccyx bone was actually "floppy," the doctor reported, which made it difficult and *very painful* to stand or walk. By the end of that week, Steve was able to awkwardly nurse for about three minutes before falling asleep. I still had to hold his lips on my nipple and sometimes do the massage, but he was sucking more and choking and sputtering less.

After seven days in the hospital, Steve and I were released. On arrival at home I fed him, changed him, put him in his bassinet by our bed, lay down and exclaimed, "Now what do I do?" I still had *severe* pain, both from my broken coccyx and also from the stitched up episiotomy area. It felt as though the stitching went directly through a nerve. Even while lying down, just moving my foot an inch hurt intensely where I was stitched. It was all I could do to take care of Steve, and I didn't have any family help since both our mothers were across the United States. I had always been advised against pain medication by my parents, or else they had no idea how badly I hurt! It never dawned on me to talk to the doctor now about medication to relieve my pain, even though it seemed I hurt much more *after* delivery than I did in labor. The pain *didn't diminish at all* for nearly two weeks.

Even though Victor had acted excited when he felt life in my belly during pregnancy, he acted distant and depressed after the birth. I had heard that a lot of fathers get jealous following the birth of their first child, so after Steve was born I wanted to give Victor all the attention I could. One morning I was nursing my baby with one arm and cooking and serving oatmeal to Victor with the other. I was in a cold sweat and shaking from pain, trying to keep Steve from crying so Victor wouldn't get angry.

As I look back on it now, I was acting utterly ridiculous. Victor was able to cook his own cereal. I didn't *have* to wait on him. But the exercise probably didn't hurt me, and it didn't make me any worse physically. I eventually got over the pain, but the trauma of tension and pain may have affected my milk and my son.

Our church members were wonderfully helpful, and I appreciated them immensely. Several ladies brought in dinners for us for a few days. Others ordered and paid for a diaper service for one month. Some even took our washing and returned it clean and neatly folded. When the month was over, I was physically able to use our washing machine in the basement. We didn't have a dryer.

From the very first, Steve cried literally *for hours at a time.* Often his crying would escalate until he was shaking and shuddering. Nothing I did seemed to help. We got a second-hand rocking chair, and I rocked him by the hour. He'd suck a little bit, and then sleep while we rocked. Then he'd wake, suck a bit more for a minute or two, and be exhausted again. Little by little he was learning to suck, but it seemed to take *enormous effort* on his part. Then we'd both sleep. We practically lived in that rocking chair. At night I'd take him into bed with me to try to keep him from crying, but Victor would loudly complain, "I can't *stand* this crying baby! I'm going to sleep on the couch."

Frequently Steve was having projectile vomiting. Because of this and so much crying, we took him to a pediatrician. The doctor gave us medicine to help him calm down. I gave it to him from a dropper as prescribed, and he seemed to be doing better for about two or three days. When I was about to give it again, Victor came into the room, suddenly grabbed the medicine bottle, and yelled, "I don't want my son to be a drug addict," and dumped the medicine down the sink. After that he refused to let me go back to the pediatrician or even phone him. So our baby just continued his crying and Victor continued his complaining. It felt like he believed it was entirely my fault that I had this crying baby, and he wanted to get away as much and as far as possible.

KAREN: VICTOR CREATED A NEGATIVE AND COMFORTLESS SITUATION FOR HIS WIFE AND SON. AGAIN IT WAS PROBABLY A TRAUMA INDUCED TRIGGER-RESPONSE FROM HIS CHILDHOOD.

When Steve wasn't sleeping, I tried bringing his bassinet near the piano, thinking the music would sooth him. But he would scream and cry until I put him back in his quiet little closet-sized room. If he were near any loud noise he'd scream. I could sing to him quietly while rocking him, but I couldn't play the piano if he was near or he'd get hysterical.

It was early spring when the downstairs family moved away, and we moved to ground level. We loved this "new home' and were thrilled when Victor's mom sent us money to buy an old baby grand piano and shipped us the electric organ Victor had grown up with and learned to play. We began performing organ and piano duets often, for fun at home and also for church and other occasions. I soon started taking Steve for walks in the baby buggy. As the weather warmed, Snookums came out of his box and began playing around the screened porch. He was so tame he would allow us to pet him, and he often ate from our hands. I believed God intended for this little squirrel to run wild, and I didn't want him to be confined. So one morning I propped open the screen door so he could explore. He gingerly stepped out, sniffed around and soon came running back "home," so I closed the door. Each day I'd leave the door open a little longer. Eventually the time came when he stayed out overnight. I left the door propped so he could get in and out as he wanted, and I daily put out food and water.

As time passed, he came less frequently and adjusted more to the out-of-doors. I hadn't seen him for maybe a week or two when I went walking, pushing Steve in the baby buggy. This day was still pretty cold, so I wore a heavy, long coat and cap. As I trudged slowly in deep reverie, pushing my sleeping baby along our block, I was startled by a heavy thump on my shoulder. Snookums had jumped from a tree along the sidewalk. He whirled around and around me, clinging to me like I was a Maypole for him to race around in circles. Down to the edge of my coat and back up to my shoulders and down and up several times, round and round. Then suddenly he hopped up into another tree and disappeared. This must have been his goodbye ceremony, as I never saw him again.

One early morning, as I walked, I was thinking and praying about my priorities. I decided my relationship with God was number one, my marriage was number two and my child was third. I wished Victor's priorities were similar, but I never discussed these with him; I was *afraid to*. Before marrying, I had earnestly prayed for God to help me handle any problems that would come, and now I prayed daily for wisdom to be a good wife and a wise and loving mother. I wanted my children to know God, and wanted them to learn to obey, yet I didn't want to be a stern disciplinarian or harsh.

When Steve was about three months old I said to Victor, "I think our baby is old enough to come to family worship." We took time each morning for Victor to read from the Bible and we prayed together. We often sang a song or two unaccompanied. So if Steve was awake, I brought him in my arms, telling him, "We're going to be reading from the Bible about God and singing about Jesus." If he started making even cooing sounds or gurgling noises, I would very gently tap his lips and say, "Shh. It's worship time. We're going to be quiet in worship." I would always smile and be extremely gentle, and in just a little while he seemed to know that worship was a time to be quiet. I would tell him when we were going to pray and then explain what prayer was.

I started taking him to Cradle Roll School at church every week as soon as I was physically able—when Steve was about six weeks old. I brought home "The Little Friend," the pre-school children's weekly paper, and read aloud to him the stories and Bible lessons in it daily, even though he was only weeks old. I did this at a different time than our family worship. While sitting in the rocking chair and holding him, I'd read him his Bible lesson one day, then tell it again in my own words each of the following days of the week. I'd explain things to him as though he questioned and understood. I even repeated his "memory verse" from the lesson each day, as though he was memorizing it. I gave him verbal credit for learning things, even though he was too young to respond.

When he started using his hands and fingers more, we noticed rather severe coordination problems and spasticity. Another thing I observed was that he cried, laughed and made vocal sounds in a very limited range—about four notes—or half an octave. He didn't seem to be able to use his high voice at all.

For seven months I nursed Steve, until my milk dried up. He no longer was getting immune properties from my breast milk, so he started getting sick more and more frequently, with head and chest colds, high fevers and bronchitis. At first he recuperated quickly, but each time he got sick, it would be worse than the time before, and it took longer to get well. The doctor put him on antibiotics and they helped for a while. But after several bouts with bronchitis, then a series of five different antibiotics, trying to find one that worked, Steve got worse instead of better. The doctor wanted him hospitalized.

There he was put into a crib with a net tied over the top, so he wouldn't try to crawl out. He screamed and looked frantic, and I *felt* like chaining *myself* to his bed, but the doctor and nurses ordered me to go home for the night and get some rest. Now *I* felt frantic and wanted to scream! At least *I understood* the situation, sort of, but of course Steve understood only that nothing and no one was recognizable except mommy, and she was leaving! Horrors! I couldn't keep from crying.

When I went to see him the next day he was standing up with his head pushing against the net, screaming and screaming, even though he had a raging fever. They said all he did was scream and try to get out. After two days the doctor told us they had done everything they could, but he was not improving and was in a state of absolute panic and hysteria all the time, so we better take him home. We felt only slight relief, for he was a very sick boy. He clung to me with desperation as we took him to our car.

Through the long, dark hours that night, I sat and rocked him, singing this song:

> "Oh let me walk with Thee my God,
> As Enoch walked in days of old;
> Place Thou my trembling hand in Thine,
> And sweet communion with me hold;
> E'en though the path I may not see,
> Yet, Jesus, let me walk with Thee."

To me it was a precious promise song to sing when I didn't know what else to do.

> "I cannot, dare not, walk alone;
> The tempest rages in the sky.
> A thousand snares beset my feet,
> A thousand foes are lurking nigh.
> Still Thou the raging of the sea,
> O Master! Let me walk with Thee."

Steve's chest was so congested and his head so stopped up that he struggled to breathe, then fell asleep in exhaustion. As he dropped into sleep, he'd stop breathing a few seconds. Shortly he jerked spasmodically and screamed again because he couldn't get enough air. Back and forth— no breathing, jerk, scream, hideous gasp, no breathing, jerk, scream, gasp . . . .

"If I may rest my hand in Thine,
I'll count the joys of earth but loss,
And firmly, bravely journey on;
I'll bear the banner of the cross
Till Zion's glorious gates I see;
Yet, Savior, let me walk with Thee."

[O Let Me Walk With Thee; words,
Mrs. L. D. Stuttle; tune, Edwin Barnes]

Steve's fever rose to 105 degrees. I carried him to our bedroom and woke Victor. "Honey, listen to the terrible sounds our baby is making."

Victor lay prone, but listened a few moments and finally passively intoned, "That's the death rattle. He's dying."

Victor was giving a death message!

Victor just remained stretched out flat and said nothing more and did nothing. He had been trained as a medic during World War II, which ended as he was being sent to Germany. He'd had a year of the nurse's course and grew up around a hospital with a doctor for a dad, so I understood he really believed what he said.

"We've got to call the doctor." I urged.

Still not having made any movement to get out of bed, he resignedly answered, "The doctor said he had done all he could. We were just to take Steve home. There is nothing more we can do!"

This is another death message.

I was angry, but carefully controlling my voice I said, "We can pray. We will *not* just let this child die! Please, get up and help me. We will give him fomentations" (hot steam compresses). We both had grown up receiving hydrotherapy treatments from our parents before there were antibiotics. We both knew how to do this.

Silently Victor got up and came to the kitchen. After we both prayed for Steve's healing, we got everything out and put down the back of Steve's convertible high chair, laying him out flat on it. By now he was unconscious. We put a big kettle of water on the stove right by where we were working and let it boil until the room was very steamy. We wrapped Steve's head in towels wrung from ice water, which we changed frequently. We put his feet into a pan of hot water and kept it hot by adding more from the teakettle, always checking the temperature with our hand. We dipped wool cloths in boiling water, wrung them out thoroughly and wrapped them in other dry wool cloths. We put these "fomentations" on his chest, putting my hand under them frequently to keep checking the temperature so we wouldn't burn him. We alternated the steaming hot packs to both chest and back, with ice water rubs for a few seconds in between hot packs. We did this for hour after hour, silently praying all the while, and finally Steve's breathing began to be easier. There still was loud gurgling and rasping you could hear throughout the whole house, but now at least it didn't sound like the death rattle.

It was nearly dawn when we finally decided he had had enough treatment. His fever had come down a couple degrees. Victor was to preach that same day. I don't know how long it had been since I had slept, and I was so exhausted I could hardly move or think. I also was still angry with Victor for having to beg him to get up and help me with Steve. It seemed like he didn't care if our son died.

I now wrapped Steve in a cold, wet sheet and then in a wool blanket. My aunt, a pediatrician, had once told me to do this for a high fever. I went back to the rocking chair with him in my arms. Again I rocked and rocked, sometimes humming my song. Finally Steve fussed enough so I knew he was at least semi-conscious. Then he dropped into a rather peaceful sleep, even though his breathing still sounded bad.

While I was dozing and rocking, Victor came to tell me goodbye as he was leaving for church. He said he'd ask the church members to have special prayer for Steve. He also had thought of me enough to contact a nurse acquaintance to come and help me.

What an enormous blessing! He really does care!

When she arrived, Steve was still sleeping, and I practically collapsed into bed and didn't waken all day.

At about seven in the evening I heard a different sound that woke me up. A miracle sound! Steve was giggling and laughing. *Am I dreaming? I'm so groggy!* I made myself get up. Steve's temperature was *normal*! He was rocking in his little wooden elephant rocker with all his might, entertaining my lady friend who was caring for him. His nose was only a little stuffed-up, and he was almost well. My enormous anxiety was thoroughly released, and I praised the Lord. We both definitely thanked Him, because we really thought our son was dying that awful night.

He never, *ever* got that sick again. However he *cried truly more than he slept* for the first couple years of his life. During the night I'd walk the floor with him screaming, even though he'd been fed, burped, changed and rocked. The neighbors questioned me, wondering if I was neglecting or torturing him.

Before he started walking, his feet turned out flat to the sides when lying on his back. The doctor said we'd have to get braces for him. He wanted us to get special high-topped shoes that had a metal bar running from one shoe to the other, and gradually turn the bar and shoes to force his feet to point straight ahead. Because we had already seen that Steve's coordination was defective, I wanted his legs free so I could devise routine exercises for muscle development. I refused the shoes and bar and asked for an alternative. The doctor showed us exercises that took about twenty minutes, which we were to do three times a day. They were slightly painful for Steve but necessary if we were to eliminate the shoe-and-bar remedy. We had to carefully twist his legs as we massaged them. Victor genuinely chose to do his share of this, which was a tremendous help! In a few months Steve's legs became normal.

The local "Conference" decided when ministers were to move. It never seemed clear to us whether they just saw a greater need somewhere else, or whether they were dissatisfied with Victor's work. But often we had been in one place only a little more than a year, or at the most, two years. Anyway, it was moving time again!

Is this the way the conference tests their ministers to see if they have the stamina to work for the Lord? Oh how much we need to stay here longer!

We relocated to Plainfield, New Jersey, a much smaller town than Trenton, and Victor again became associate pastor of another two-church "district." We provided a lot of music at both of these new churches and gave numerous programs of music and poetry in the area. Victor loved poetry—loved to read it to himself, but even more, loved to read it aloud to an audience. He did so with beautiful expression and power, sometimes moving people to tears. We also were involved musically in evangelistic meetings. People especially loved our vocal duets, as our voices blended well.

I was exhausted most of the time from lack of sleep and a screaming baby, but Victor didn't help much because he was "supposed to do God's work." When I was pregnant again and started to throw up while changing Steve's messy diaper, Victor *did* come frequently and finish the job so I could run to the toilet.

Because Steve was sick so much, there was a period of at least three months I didn't go out of the house at all, not even into the yard. I longed to be out-of-doors, but if I needed to buy groceries or other things, Victor would say sarcastically, "I am *not* going to stay here with this crying baby!" He insisted on doing the shopping or whatever else needed to be done outside of the house and refused to stay home and let me go.

We didn't even hang our clothes outside to dry much of the year because the air was so sooty in our section of town that it discolored the laundry. Most of the time I hung things on wooden drying racks around the house, and on the backs of our vinyl-upholstered kitchen chairs and Formica tabletop. Even our steam radiators that warmed the house were usually covered with wet things and hangars of damp clothes hung in the doorways.

Finally there was a church outing to New York City. Someone volunteered to baby-sit for us so we could both go. What a Godsend! Among other things, we went to a museum that had many wild animals artfully preserved by taxidermy and placed in gorgeous, realistic settings. The dioramas made everything look alive. I went off by myself and longingly stood looking at the wildlife scenes. It felt like I was "out into the world," finally! I was seeing something different than the toy decorated rooms of our small house. What a refresher! While pensively drinking in the artificial but realistic scenes, tears welled up in my eyes and dribbled down my cheeks. I was looking at what seemed to be God's creation, absorbing the peace and tranquility, storing it away as an inner retreat. It was a healing day, and I felt renewed energy entering my body, brain and emotions.

We were so relaxed when we arrived home to find Steve sound asleep, that as we went to bed we indulged in warm and seductive love-making, followed by some interesting reminiscing afterward. Victor was telling me about his experiences in the army and relating memories when he casually mentioned giving his mom an enema.

Dumbfounded, I said, "You what?"

"Oh, it was nothing. She wasn't feeling well when she came," he explained.

"When she wasn't feeling well, your mom came where?" I just could *not* let this pass without learning more!

"To my Basic Training Graduation. It wasn't anything important," Victor assured me.

I didn't know *any* parents went to army Basic Training Graduation, let alone travel halfway across the United States by train to get there, so that interested me a little. But I had *never* heard of a teenage boy giving his mother an enema, so I came wide awake instantly. I was full of questions and started probing all the details. Victor seemed a little irritated and quite sleepy, so I tried not to *act* upset or shocked, even though what I was hearing seemed as weird as anything I had ever heard before. Apparently Victor's mother had invited him *to visit her at a hotel* after the graduation ceremony. When he first entered her room he found her already naked on the bed with an enema prepared for him to give her. After all my questions about details, I put the story together in my now overwhelmed, flabbergasted mind, and agreed it was time to go to sleep.

Here at Plainfield I started teaching piano and voice students in the living room of our home. Often Steve would stand in his playpen in the dining room, about fifteen feet away, where he could watch us. Once, when I was getting my piano tuned, he started vocally matching very high pitches, as the tuner would strike the keys over and over again to get the pitch tuned correctly. Steve was making clear tones around high C. I had never heard him make *any* high noises before, and he was *exactly* on pitch. He was now about fifteen months old, and I nearly shed tears of joy in front of the tuner. Steve had cried and laughed in such a limited range, and this new behavior amazed me. Even the piano tuner was impressed. Previously I had done a lot of playing with him, making animal sounds—high baby-chick peeps and low lion growls, and such—trying to develop his ability to extend his range. Now that I knew he could achieve higher sounds, I started working with him to sing, and I supposed the worst was over.

But it wasn't long until severe psychotic episodes began. The first time I heard him start to scream like he was being tortured, I ran to where he was standing, white as a sheet, his whole body rigid and shaking violently. He was hysterical and could scarcely remain upright! When I came close to him, he tried to pull away, like he was afraid of *me!* He screamed uncontrollably for more than an hour, and he fought me off as I tried to comfort, soothe and calm him. I didn't know what he was screaming about, and he couldn't tell me. He hadn't started to talk at all yet.

It took me several times, over a period of weeks, to figure out what caused these episodes. One day a car went by on the street in front of our house when the sunlight was just right to reflect off its windows. The car movement threw a moving flash of bright light across our walls and ceiling, which caused Steve to scream and soon to go out of control—out of his mind really—for a *couple* hours this time.

Steve became increasingly more sensitive. He couldn't stand his bath water more than lukewarm. With anything warmer, he screamed as if he was being burned. If he ate an ice cream cone, he'd go into heavy chills after a few licks, even on a hot summer day. It would take a half hour to get him warmed up. In all his senses—touch, temperature, pain, noise, and movement—he was *extremely* more sensitive than the average child.

Every summer we went out of town to the conference campground for camp meeting. Victor would go a week or two ahead of time, with the other ministers, to help set up all the tents. There would also be a few days after camp meeting ended when he'd help break down the camp. I usually stayed at home for most of the set-up and take-down time, but on one particular day I went with him for the day.

One of the ministers lived in a big house at the edge of the campground, and his wife and I were friends. I was outside their home with several children playing near a tilted stack of wooden tent floors near the house. Steve tried to walk up one of these slightly slanted floors and slipped before I could get to him. He fell and got some splinters in his hand. He started crying, and I took him into the house. A nurse friend was there and offered to take out the splinters. I'm sure it was painful, and took a little while to needle them out of his palm. I was trying to comfort him as she did her work when all of a sudden he just passed out on the nurse's lap. After a few seconds he started violent shaking and contortions. He convulsed hard for maybe two or three minutes, then suddenly went limp. We were *shocked*! The nurse asked if he had ever had convulsions before. I shook my head. She said this was a grand-Mal seizure.

After that day, whenever he experienced something painful, he would have a seizure. The doctor ordered an electroencephalogram. I asked him to describe the process to me so I could prepare Steve for it. In play we glued pennies onto his Teddy bear's head, attached strings to them and talked about how we were reading the electrical waves in the Teddy's brain to see how they worked, so we could see how very smart he was. We talked about how Steve was going to help the doctors understand how his body worked.

The EEG was very abnormal, but the doctors (now several were involved) said the problem was *not* epilepsy. They couldn't figure out what was going on! But Victor agreed he "would allow" Steve to take liquid Phenobarbital twice a day to help prevent seizures.

Camp meeting lasted ten days, so the three of us would be living in a tent for at least that long. Each tent had a wooden floor. A double bed and a couple folding chairs were provided. We had a small trailer we pulled behind our car. Victor helped load the trailer with the dismantled crib, a small chest of drawers, a folding table and a large ice chest. The trailer was almost full of stuff--baby clothes, diapers, our clothing, all of our music, Victor's saxophone and Steve's toys. By now it was obvious I was pregnant again.

When we arrived at the campground with our supplies, Victor stopped the car and trailer in front of our tent and explained urgently, "Well, I've got to get busy! They're going to need me out there to help set up tents. You can unload." He was so concerned about *his* image, doing what people expected *him* to do regarding camp set-up that evidently he didn't stop to think about my pregnancy. Actually, I knew I had strong muscles, and my feelings weren't hurt. I was just a bit surprised he didn't help at least with the bigger things.

I started unloading parts of the crib and mattress, bedding and other things from the trailer, planning to put the crib together myself and get everything settled as soon as possible. I was doing double duty trying to keep my eye on Steve and not let him get hurt, when I noticed someone walking up the tent row toward me, but didn't pay attention because I was so busy. Then I heard the words, "Where's Victor?" It was the handsome, eligible bachelor who was a new minister in our conference.

I had previously known James slightly when I was single and working as a secretary in Maryland. He had come to my apartment one night to ask me if I would sing at a special Valentine's program at Washington Missionary College nearby. Thrilled to be asked, I felt disappointed because I was already committed to be out of town that weekend on a choir tour. Sadly turning him down, I got the picture he might have been planning to ask me to be his "date." He never asked me again.

Now I answered him, "He's out helping the men set things up."

"Why would he let you unload this stuff by yourself?" He was obviously shocked, and appeared angry. He stopped and helped me until the trailer was unloaded, the crib put together, and all the furniture arranged. I felt blessed and thankful. It made me think James might have been a better husband than Victor.

Forgive me Lord for even thinking that. I know I'm physically capable of unloading the trailer, but I'm embarrassed that Victor went off and let me do it alone. I'm afraid people will look down on him for it. He is always so concerned about what people think of him regarding "God's work," but not about taking care of his family. I guess he doesn't realize they might be critical of him for not helping me unload a trailer when I'm obviously pregnant.

Eventually James married, was a successful minister, and I lost track of him.

Later in the summer, before our family increased in size, the conference asked Victor to be a camp counselor at Junior Camp. His group of ten and eleven-year-old boys got first prize for best behavior and cleanest tents! They all loved him and almost clung to him to receive his lavish attention.

Victor seems to be very good at leading and challenging these boys, and I am proud of him for the way he directs and relates with those under his care. They all seem to be very attached to him, especially since they won first prize. I certainly hope he will be as good a father to our sons as they get a little older. Right now Victor seems to not want time or activities with Steve, but he apparently relishes all the compliments he's received from camp leadership and these boys' parents.

7

PERIL

God bless my dear mother. She came a long way to help care for Steve when Alan was born. When I came home from the hospital one week later, my firstborn refused to have anything to do with me. He acted as though I were invisible. I had done so much talking and playing with him about the new baby and my being gone, that I thought he was well prepared, but it seemed to have had no effect.

Babies under three years old don't "get it." They can't comprehend their abandonment.

Mother had to leave three days after I got home from the hospital. The day after she left, I started having pain in my genital area, and the next day a large boil appeared. Another one popped up on my bottom the following day, and more the following days. In order to nurse my new son without excruciating pain, I had to lie on the floor sideways with one leg propped up on a chair. Sleep was possible only on my stomach, with my legs spread wide. After antibiotics and several trips to the doctor through a six-week period, to have boils lanced and drained, I was ready to return to church and healthy motherhood.

Then Steve and I resumed our daily walks again. I pushed the buggy, and later the stroller, while holding Steve's hand. Since he had now become afraid of bushes, leaves, flowers, birds that flew nearby or anything strange he hadn't seen before, I started taking a plastic bag with me to collect things to "show daddy," and began explaining everything in detail. I pointed out the veins in leaves and told how nourishment came up the tree trunk into the leaf through them. When the sunlight reached the leaf it would make chlorophyll. I said it was something like our blood circulating through our body. Our walk times were the happiest hours of the day for me.

Alan cried and had colic for about four months, but he didn't have nearly as many problems as Steve. I loved being the mother of two sons. At church, while Victor preached, I sat in the "mother's room" and watched the service through a glass window. As I nursed Alan, I tried to keep Steve entertained and out of mischief. After four months of nursing Alan, I ran out of milk. I still was not getting anywhere near enough sleep, and I lived totally exhausted. I think that's what dried up my milk. **KAREN: YES!**

Steve still cried so much, often constantly for several hours, before he finally slept. After Alan went to sleep, nearly every night I walked the floor carrying Steve, trying to calm and quiet him. My arms ached and my knees wanted to collapse. Steve would soon be two and was a big boy. I often wracked my brain trying to think of someone I could call to help, even for only a few hours, so I could catch a couple hours of sleep. Victor said, "You can stay home and sleep in the daytime, but I have to work all day." So most of the time he just refused to get up at night to help, unless I was ill and couldn't.

Baby food was expensive and we were on a limited budget, so I didn't buy much. Instead I bought a blender and used what we ate, blended, for baby food. Not only was it cheaper, it was probably healthier. Since Steve was having so many problems, I soon was giving both boys whole grain cereal and all kinds of fresh vegetables and fruits. I blended and strained what Alan ate until he got teeth.

Alan was still a baby when one day he broke out with hives all over his body. There were some welts two and three inches across. He couldn't sleep for twenty-four hours. Victor didn't think we needed to call a doctor, so I put a paste made of baking soda and water on them. They went away in a day or so, and came back only two or three times later in his life. We never did figure out what caused them. [As a teenager he acquired psoriasis, which years later turned into psoriatic—arthritis.]

Through all of these problems, I would discuss them with Victor and ask his advice. Generally he just listened, rather than offering any suggestion or comment. Sometimes he'd say, "They're *your* kids, *you* figure it out!"

Victor was a discouraged *child* at that time. *Children* don't *have* answers!

He knew I had always wanted children. Generally he didn't involve himself with them much, but occasionally he helped, and then seemed to enjoy himself.

Now that I stop and think about it, I'm so thankful Victor doesn't usually tell me what I'm doing is wrong, like my friend Helen's husband does.

It was usually after midnight when I got Steve quieted down enough to sleep. But as soon as I touched the sheets, Victor would reach over and want to "make love."

I'd then fight tears while answering, "I'm too tired to feel sexual, and I desperately need sleep."

"Okay, just rub me then," he'd insist.

But that was more tiring than if he had just entered and let me fall asleep. He refused to take care of himself. He believed masturbating was sinful, and didn't want to feel guilty. However he didn't apparently suffer guilt if he wore me out, and deprived me of sleep. While trying to please him, I would often fall asleep. He'd wake me up and insist, "Finish it." This would happen many nights a week. By now he wasn't talking about sex being physically debilitating. He'd say he couldn't sleep without it, and it was *my* responsibility.

One cloudy morning Steve was deliberately disobeying and testing us, as two-year-olds often do. I believed Victor was in a better position to take over and discipline him than I was at the moment, so asked him to. But he did nothing. Gradually I became more and more angry inside, because he didn't seem to *want* to be a father to our boys. Finally I blurted out, "Victor, I don't have any complaints about you as a husband," (of course I did, and that was a lie) "but if you can't start being a father to these boys, you might as well get out."

"Okay," he responded brightly, turning and walking out of the room to get his suitcases down. "I'll be out sometime tomorrow morning."

That was it! He was just going to leave! He looked relieved and happy.

I don't really want him to leave. Our boys need a father. I still love him. I know there are problems, but I think they're more my fault than his. I'm the one that's not in a sexual mood. I'm the one who falls asleep. I don't want to lose him. I'll take responsibility for disciplining the kids. I want him for my husband. I just can't face his leaving!

I was still trying to "back down," so he "wouldn't want to hit me again." If he wanted anything at all, I'd go out of my way to please him, and do anything and everything he asked. I did not stand up to him, or stand up for myself. I believed this was what a good wife was *supposed* to do.

KAREN: YES. THAT TEACHING ABOUT WIVES OBEYING WAS, AND STILL IS, DISTORTED TEACHING IN MANY CHURCHES.

Next morning I went to him in tears and said, "Victor, please. *Please* don't leave. I love you. I *want* you as my husband. Please, let's sit down and talk. I want us to talk about this problem."

We sat on the bed silently for a while. Finally Victor said, "Well, I have tried and *tried* to love these boys, and I just *can't*! I don't have *any* love for either Steve or Alan!" (Alan was six months old and Steve was twenty-five months at the time.)

But there had been *no action, no behavior* that was sacrificial—putting his sons *first!* This probably would have changed his feelings toward them.

In surprise and fear to the point of trembling, I carefully asked, "Before we were married, you said whatever I wanted regarding having children was just fine with you. Was that not true then?"

After a long wait, he finally admitted, "That's right. I was afraid if I told you the *truth*, you wouldn't marry me."

It took me a few moments to digest and accept that confession before I asked, "What did you *really want* in our marriage?"

Victor was obviously *very* uncomfortable with this new question, but commendably he didn't just get up and walk out. After several long-drawn-out deep breaths and some apprehensive sighing, he slowly spoke. "Long before we met, I *knew* that if a husband and wife were deeply in love, when *they had children*, their love would be spoiled, and the marriage relationship would *never* be the same again! So I didn't *want* children, because I've *always* known that having them would *ruin* our love. And it *has!*"

KAREN: DOES VICTOR KNOW WHERE THAT BELIEF CAME FROM?

VICTOR: I certainly didn't know then, but you will discover my growing insight later in the book. I do know my grandma hated men and told me more than once to *not* have children early in a marriage.

"You resent them, then?" I couldn't believe I was even asking this question!

"Yes!" As he gave this one-word answer, his tone of voice warned me not to ask any more questions.

I am again shocked. No wonder he hasn't acted very interested in them. All the couples we know love their kids—the fathers, as well as the mothers. Tim Donahue was terribly broken up when his little girl died. If one of our boys died, would Victor even feel bad, or would he be elated? How can he not be emotionally involved? Something inside tells me there is more to this man's problems than I ever dreamed. I wonder if he believes his being born spoiled the love relationship between his mother and father. That concept is spawning some new ideas.

The Conference asked Victor to move again.

Why do they do this to us? Can't we be in one place long enough to prove ourselves and accomplish some goals? Or are they moving us because they consider us failures? I don't dare ask these questions of anyone, but I want so badly to feel settled for a while.

Victor was assigned to be the pastor of another two-church district, this time in Jersey City and West New York, NJ. He wouldn't have an associate. Tim Donahue had been pastor of both churches just prior to Victor's "call." We even moved into the same house they just vacated in Bayonne.

Soon after we got settled, the Donahues invited us to go camping with them to Lake Sebago, in the state of Maine. I was thrilled, hoping that some of the love and caring for *their* children would "rub off" onto *our* children's father! Victor didn't want to take Alan, and it was important to not make waves. He was only six months old, so even though I *longed* to take him, and *hated* leaving my child with anyone else, I agreed to the idea. We arranged for a babysitter, although Tim and Shelley *did* bring their six-month-old son. Then we hurriedly got our gear together and followed them in our car.

KAREN: JUDY LET GO OF WHAT SHE *KNEW TO BE RIGHT AND LOVING*—TO BRING HER SON WITH HER— ALLOWING VICTOR TO *CAUSE HER SON* ABANDONMENT PAIN AND TRAUMA.

Hours later, when we finally arrived at the lake, the regular campground was full. The park rangers sent us off to a temporary camp, where there was no electricity. Tim and Shelley had loaned us their tent, and they brought their pop-up-tent-trailer for themselves. We were setting things up, making up cots with sheets and blankets, because we didn't have sleeping bags, when I asked Janey, the Donahues' eight-year-old daughter, to "baby-sit" Steve. I thought she was old enough to be responsible. We gave her a flashlight and asked her to play with him for just a few minutes while we finished getting the beds ready.

Before sundown Victor and Tim had looked around a bit and returned to tell us that the lake was two or three hundred yards from where we were camped, and there was a twenty-foot drop-off down to the water. They said we better watch the kids very carefully.

Now it was dark. Janey had been playing happily with Steve by her folks' trailer. I thought only a few moments had passed when I looked around and there was Janey, but no Steve.

"Where is Steve?" I called to Janey anxiously.

"Oh, I forgot," she nonchalantly answered. "I had to go to the restroom and I took him with me. But since it was the girl's restroom and he was a boy I left him outside the door. When I came out he wasn't there."

"So you came back without him?" I gasped.

"Yes. I thought he had come back already." She didn't seem to comprehend she'd neglected her duty.

I'm angry at Janey, but she is only an eight-year-old girl. Now I'm also angry with myself for trusting her to give adequate care for my son.

The temporary camp had no lights, not even at the restroom. Donahue's Coleman lantern gave us enough light to work in our tent area. We had given Janey our only flashlight and she had left my two-year-old alone in the dark, then forgot all about him when she came back out! It's been maybe fifteen or twenty minutes now. It's about eleven o'clock at night in a strange place. My son is *alone in pitch-blackness.* We have heard no crying. Where is he?

I took the flashlight back and ran to the restroom to look for him, calling for him. No luck. Then I ran back and told Victor and the Donahues.

Victor said, "Oh, don't worry. He's around."

He doesn't seem the teeniest bit worried. I can't believe it! I'm panicked and angry to the point of wanting to kick him. But I don't ever let him see my anger. I just pray and ask God to take it away, and usually He does.

There were a lot of other people camped nearby, so I shouted, "Help, Help, Help! My little two-year-old boy is lost. Please help us organize a search party to find him." Victor stood around and acted embarrassed at my antics. He didn't even call out to Steve or start to look for him.

Victor was showing signs that he was not connected to anyone. *He* still felt all alone!

I wonder if he wandered over by the lake and fell the twenty feet into the water and drowned already, and no one will know. I'm panicked! I never should have trusted Janey. I thought she was by the pop-up trailer with her parents. I should have kept checking on her more often.

People soon gathered and asked questions about Steve's size, age, dress, and other details. A few minutes went by as we started organizing how to go about the search and everyone seemed confused. They couldn't seem to decide what to do next and I kept hollering every little bit, "Has anybody seen a little boy?"

Finally I heard someone shout from the far distance, maybe five hundred yards away. They had a bright lantern hanging by their tent. "Oh, here comes a little boy." He evidently saw the light and went toward it.

I hollered, "Here I come," and ran like a crazy woman. Soon I saw this tiny figure stumbling his way towards the light. I grabbed him up in my arms. He didn't cry. He didn't act hysterical. He didn't show any of his usual emotions that any of us could observe. Instead he seemed dazed and confused. He still didn't talk at all. Maybe he felt so abandoned he became overwhelmed. When we got back to the tent, I thanked the other campers for being willing to help, and I thanked God for Steve's safe retrieval. I held him close for a long time and told him how much I loved him.

The remainder of our camping trip included boating, swimming, hiking and exploring. It was rewarding in both activities and relationship with our family-oriented friends. Tim and Shelley were ideal parents and I felt blessed we could watch their loving manner and communication with their children.

Along with Victor's occupation of being the only pastor of our new church, we also were frequently involved musically with various other churches. We had gone to an evangelistic meeting in Newark one night where we were to sing and play. The meeting was in a building several stories tall that had a very large auditorium, shaped in a partial circle with seating from the center going up numerous tiers all around the sides. This building was surrounded outside by high and wide cement stairs leading from several directions up to the main entrance and located in a triangle of main streets lined with sidewalks. This particular night we couldn't get a baby sitter, so we took the boys along. Friends took care of them there and met us in the foyer after the meeting adjourned.

I needed to dress both boys in their snowsuits, as it was winter and very cold. At one end of the long, narrow foyer I got Steve dressed while someone held Alan. My friends had to leave, so I then held Alan as I walked Steve over to where Victor was talking with people, and asked him to watch over him while I dressed Alan.

When Alan was dressed, I went over to Victor to tell him we were ready. "Where's Steve?" I gasped.

"Oh, I thought he was with you," he absentmindedly replied.

"I brought him over here and asked *you* to watch him. Where *is* he?" I felt frantic.

Victor shrugged slightly and threw both hands up. "*I* don't know. I forgot I was supposed to watch him."

His voice doesn't even sound apologetic. Probably he didn't want to watch him, so didn't try to remember. Steve evidently isn't that important to him.

We began looking around. No Steve. Then I remembered all the many cement steps going down from the high auditorium entrance to the sidewalks and streets below. Steve loved steps. I remembered the heavy traffic in the streets surrounding the building. I had visions of him going down steps and across the sidewalk and being crushed by a fast moving car or truck and no one knowing whose child he was or where he'd come from.

I began telling people all around us that we had lost Steve. This time I didn't yell, because I didn't want to antagonize Victor. Many folks started helping us look outside, and others hunted in all the smaller rooms and halls throughout the building, as it was a huge edifice with all kinds of sections. Finally I decided to go ahead and make noise and not worry whether I embarrassed Victor. I called and called and others did the same. In panic now I shouted, "Steve, Steve, Steve, where are you?"

Fifteen or twenty minutes went by, and between shouts I silently prayed, as tears ran down my cheeks. I fought to keep hysteria under control. No one could find him--no sign of him anywhere.

I can't fathom why Victor was not responsible to watch him. Doesn't he care at all? I realize he said he didn't love the boys, but later he tried to take that back and said he was just angry, and didn't mean it.

All of a sudden some of the lights went out. Most of the people were gone, and the caretakers must have wanted to close the building. Then we heard a faraway scream. I knew immediately it was Steve. Victor went running to find the horrendous screaming. The main lights in the auditorium had been turned out. The screaming seemed to come from high up in there. I started yelling over and over, "Turn the lights back on!" until they came on again. Victor climbed the many steps up the progressive balconies inside the auditorium until he arrived at the very top. Steve had climbed all those steps and gone into a little room, evidently housing the public address and projection systems. Victor found him and carried him back to me. *Now my tears are floods of relief.*

Our denomination used to have a yearly event that was very important for fund raising. "Ingathering," as it was called, happened only during the Christmas season in those days. This was a time church members were designated to solicit their neighborhoods for cash donations for disaster relief and missions. Each church was assigned by the local Conference a specific dollar "goal" based on membership numbers. I absolutely detested going door-to-door asking for money, but usually went because it was expected of me. This *particular church* had, for years, done more bar and nightclub solicitation than the door-to-door type, because it brought in more cash in less time.

Alice, a quiet single girl, and I were chosen to do the street and nightclub solicitation duties on Saturday night, "because you are young, so will bring in the most money."

KAREN: WHAT WAS THE BELIEF BEHIND THIS?— EXPOSING YOUNG WOMEN TO DANGER FOR MONEY FOR A CHURCH!

[This *was* giving mixed messages to the world. To my knowledge, this is no longer done anywhere. At that time--around 1960—the New Jersey Conference even suggested to Victor that if he couldn't raise the goal, they possibly might take it out of his salary! He balked and said no! I agreed and was proud of his stance.]

Victor drove the car while we two girls went into various places in the night entertainment section of Jersey City. Sometimes he'd have to drive around the block while waiting, because of no parking spots. We were expected to repeat this routine every Saturday night for about six weeks. We girls both hated it, but were dutifully cooperative at first.

When Victor had been going to the seminary and I had been working as a secretary, I sometimes was asked to pose at the art department of the Review and Herald Publishing Association next door to the General Conference Headquarters where I worked. They needed models to be photographed, sometimes for artists to make paintings that were used in books and magazines. Once I was dressed in attire as the Statue of Liberty on the cover of <u>Liberty</u> magazine. This extra job provided me with added cash to pay our bills and buy food. This particular year one of my pictures was used on the little tin can that all Ingathering solicitors were supposed to carry as they asked for donations. The picture was of *my* holding out an Ingathering can for people to put money in. Now I felt terribly self-conscious to be carrying a can with *my picture* on it *while I was soliciting with it*, so usually remembered to hold it so my gloved fingers covered my face so it wouldn't show. But one night a lecherous-looking man came up to me and tried to grab the money can out of my hand while exclaiming, "That's *your* picture on that can isn't it?"

Embarrassed, I didn't answer at first. Then he started telling some other bystanders, "Hey, this is her *own* picture on this can. Look at it!"

I hung on to my can with both of my strong, piano-developed hands and walked away, fighting tears and wondering what I was doing out on the street so late at night. *I hadn't realized I had let the picture of my face get uncovered. Do these people think I put my own picture on the can and am collecting money for myself?*

Another night, after eleven o'clock, Alice and I apparently misunderstood Victor's directions. We expected to meet at a different place than he understood. Finally he parked, went inside, and after a futile search for us, contacted the manager. He asked, "Where are the two young women who were collecting funds tonight? One was my wife, and I'm not leaving until you find these two women."

That's the kind of aggressiveness I like.

When two bouncers were ready to bodily throw him out, he left; and we finally found each other. Alice and I had waited about forty-five minutes and were nearly frantic, fighting back tears, and trying to evade men who thought we were "street walkers." We had to keep moving fast to various places to avoid being "picked up." Prior to that, while inside the last huge nightclub where the music was deafening, we had experienced our own embarrassing and frightening situations confronting drunk and "fresh" males. Before I managed to get out of the building, I actually had had to physically fight, punching two guys in the stomach with my elbows, to keep from being carried to a back room. Now I insisted, "Never again!"

So on the following New Year's Eve Victor went again, but without me! He took much older and experienced persons to canvass the same area. After I put the boys to bed that night, I stayed up doing various things, waiting for Victor to come home. I was still awake when I heard him drive into the driveway and back to the garage after midnight. I jumped up and unlocked the bolt lock on the inner door, but closed it to keep out the chill. He could walk right in without having to get his key out. Somehow in his hurry and tiredness he didn't realize I had unlocked it, so he closed the door and it latched, but he didn't re-bolt it.

We lived on the first floor, and another family lived on the second-floor. There was a side door off the driveway near the back of our house with a small entry space just inside, and then five steps up to our level. Just inside the inner door at *our* level there was a rectangular entry room about six by eight feet. Both bedrooms, the boys' and ours, opened onto this entry "hall," as well as the kitchen, dining room and bathroom. We never locked the outer door below the five steps, because other stairs went to the basement and to the upstairs family's place. But I insisted that the bolt lock on our inner door *always* be fastened.

We soon retired, and I left a night-light on in the boys' room, as usual. Steve had learned how to climb out of his crib, open his closet and play with his toys, which he sometimes did if he woke up during the night,.

We were finally sound asleep this New Year's Eve when I was awakened by a small noise. I lay there listening, thinking Steve had gotten up and was trying to get toys out of his closet. Then I heard a different, very quiet shuffle sound. I was looking straight through the open bedroom door into the entryway that was slightly lighted by the night-light in the boys' room, trying to decide if I should get up to put Steve back to bed, when I saw the inner door, with the bolt lock Victor had forgotten to check, start to open a tiny bit. I realized what I had been hearing was someone coming in the outside door and climbing the stairs to the inner door. Soundlessly the door opened maybe another inch.

I started poking Victor. He was sleeping on the side of our bed next to the wall. All was quiet. The door opened another inch. I poked harder and frantically whispered, "Wake up, wake up!" No response.

Finally the door opened enough to reveal a head peeking from behind and looking around. Now I hit hard and whispered louder. "Wake up! Someone's coming into our house. Wake up! *Please* wake up! There's a man coming into our house!" I kept hitting Victor's side over and over.

The door continued to slowly open, the head looking this way and that. Finally, while I was still hitting Victor, a man sneakily stepped out from behind the door and just stood there a moment. He was almost as tall as the door--a very big, broad man. Quietly he took small, silent footsteps until his frame filled our bedroom doorway. He was standing about six feet from the corner of our bed. It looked like he had on a leather jacket.

Finally Victor opened his eyes, but didn't sit up or move. He just looked. The intruder slowly took a step forward, moving stealthily toward the foot of our bed. I was petrified. Victor did nothing. I grew gigantically alarmed, but thought only of the boys and not myself. I was afraid he'd hurt *them*. Being robbed or raped or murdered didn't cross my mind.

My children, my children! This man has got to get out of here.

As he took a few more silent, small, slow-motion steps past my feet to beside my knees, I suddenly jerked upright. In my loudest, deepest, mannish voice I passionately roared, "Who are you?"

The intruder mumbled something I couldn't understand. Victor whispered, "He's just drunk and in the wrong house."

All the houses on our street were very similar. Victor must have thought this guy was sneaking so his wife wouldn't wake up. But if he were *really* drunk, I didn't think he would be so stealthy and slow, taking time to look around *before* coming into the bedroom.

Again I defiantly spit out, "Who are you?"

I've never heard my voice sound so loud and vulgar. I'm aware I'm sounding like a big bass. The Lord must be making me sound this way. Maybe he poured me full of testosterone!

I grabbed the edge of the blankets and threw them back at him with all my might and yelled in the same masculine voice, "You get out of here!"

As I swung my feet onto the floor, I lunged at him. My adrenalin was pumping so hard I thought I could crush him, if I could just get my hands on him! But he sprang toward the door fast. I chased him and tried to hit him, but he was gone in a flash. I nearly pushed him as I slammed the door behind his back and locked it. Then he was down the steps and past the outside door in seconds.

KAREN: JUDY TOOK THE MASCULINE ROLE BECAUSE IT WAS VACANT.

It was totally dark in that lower entryway, but the intruder didn't even stumble. Drunk? I don't think so. I was shaking all over, so frightened! I was sure this man had no good in mind. Whether it was robbery, rape or murder I don't know. Immediately I understood that it was God who protected us. Victor never did get out of bed.

KAREN: NUMB?

Am I not valuable enough for Victor to want to protect? Of course he was behind me in bed, and it would have been much more difficult for him to get out. He would have had to crawl over me.

Victor made light of the experience, and said I was "making a mountain out of a molehill" to be so afraid. He jovially restated, "Oh, he was just drunk and in the wrong house."

It took me hours to go back to sleep, amazed and thrilled at God's protection and baffled at Victor's passivity.

The next day I hoped Victor would talk to neighbors about what happened and possibly try to find out who the intruder was, or at least tell the police what happened, but he didn't even mention it the next day. It was as though nothing unusual had happened.

The following summer Victor left again for camp meeting preparation. I hated being home alone.

It was after 10:00 pm. on a foggy, drizzly night. The boys were asleep, and I was sitting at my desk in the dining room writing letters. I was barely aware of the muted sound of water drops plopping from the eaves outside onto the driveway. The dining room sash window was open wide to get as much fresh air as would hopefully crawl from the window and reach my sweaty back across the room. I was scarcely conscious, for a while, of the muffled voices of the rabbi and his wife talking by their window across the narrow driveway.

While concentrating on my work, my cognizance of any noise was vague and fragmented. Everything was humid and drippy outside as I began to notice a different sound.

It is an indistinct whisper. . . . *No, I'm imagining.* . . . There it is again. . . . *No, only silence.* . . . Maybe it is paper rustling across the driveway. . . . *No, it's too wet for that.* . . . The rabbi and his wife must be moving around. . . . There's the whisper again, only louder. . . . *I'm listening to only silence.* . . . There it is again, louder yet. . . . *And silence.* . . . Just dripping. *I must be getting sleepy.* . . . No, I hear it again. It's louder. Something is being repeated.

Joltingly I came out of my "trance." Something *was* being repeated several times, but I couldn't understand. It began to drill into my consciousness that maybe someone was whispering *to me* and was very close! Goosebumps!

I turned around and looked across the room at the window. In the lower right hand corner I saw part of a man's face—one eye and nose and the top of his head. Then the face disappeared below the sill.

The sill was perhaps about seven feet above the driveway. Evidently a man pulled himself up to look in at me, and then lowered himself as his arms got tired. He was doing chin-ups to see me, and he was *saying* something *to me! Am I imagining, because I'm home alone?*

Seconds ticked. The face appeared again, and then the same unintelligible whisper was repeated.

Oh my, this is real! It feels like my hair is rising up to stand on end. Icy chills shoot over my whole body. I'm looking at this face through the screen and now it disappears again. *How I wish Victor was here!*

The face reappeared.

I am face to face with a strange man at my window about ten feet across the room. I'm so glad all the other windows in the house are locked and covered. I feel panic! I will take action!

Jumping up from my chair, and leaping across the room, I flung open the screen, stuck my head out the window and yelled, "You get out of here!" as I heard footsteps retreating down the driveway. I saw a shadow fleetingly move around the corner of the house next door.

If he had still been there at the window, I would have punched him in the face!

I shouted again, "Get out of here. Help! Help! Someone's trying to break into my house! Get him! Help!" I quickly closed and locked the screen and the window and pulled down the shade. Then I called the police.

Apparently there was a policeman right at the corner, because after calling, I went immediately to the front door, looked out, and I could hear the police radio as he drove up. I ran out to him, sobbing hysterically.

As he got out of the car, he asked, "Did the man get in? Did he get into the house?"

"No, he didn't get in." My voice was so shaky and panicked I could hardly describe what had happened.

He asked, "Are you hurt?"

"No I'm not," still blubbering out of control.

"Are you *sure* he didn't get to you?" he repeated.

I was so hysterical, I guess he wondered if I was telling the truth and maybe *had* been raped. I told him my husband was out of town.

This policeman was the kindest officer I'd ever met. He came into the house, searching carefully, looking into closets, under beds, behind doors, everywhere I asked. Then he checked all the windows and doors to be sure they were locked. He said he would be patrolling our street frequently the rest of the night. God bless policemen!

I went back to bed but couldn't sleep, so read my Bible until dawn. Then I quickly packed everything for camp meeting and drove the boys and myself to camp prep. When I arrived, I announced to Victor and the others, "I'm here to stay." I moved into a tent and didn't leave until Victor could come home with me after camp meeting was over.

I wonder if this was the same man who sneaked in New Year's Eve.

8

CHALLENGE

During the years after leaving the seminary, Victor continued his studying. He returned to the seminary twice to take his orals and passed them the second time, receiving his Master's Degree.

Victor and I took a vacation and again visited both sets of parents out west. While there, the doctor decided we should have Steve's tonsils out. So when vacation time ended, Victor drove home alone from California to New Jersey. I flew home later with the boys, after Steve's recuperation.

While we were on vacation, the Conference had made the decision to hire a full-time evangelist, Jacques Andalon. They were also going to hire a former classmate of mine to be Andalon's "singing evangelist," the title given to whatever musician planned the music, led the singing and was soloist for the meetings. This man would also be the evangelist's "sidekick and go-fer," home visitor and Bible study giver.

Prior to this, more than one doctor had told us that because Steve was so super sensitive and prone to seizures, we should think *very carefully*, and *plan a lifestyle* that would give him maximum peace, quietude, regularity and organization, as well as a careful and systematic program of development. The doctor had emphasized we <u>*should make our son our greatest priority*</u> in our daily planning. I carefully and prayerfully discussed this with Victor, but was unable to discern whether it made a difference to him or not. [Many years later we learned that Steve was/is autistic, but at this earlier period most doctors weren't aware of how to diagnose his problems. Fortunately he is now considered very high-functioning autistic.]

Shortly after Victor arrived home, I received this letter from him:

Sept. 20
Dear Judy,

This house is so dreary and lonely without you. To make matters worse, when I arrived, a cold wave had just hit, and the furnace was on the blink. It probably sounds unbelievable, but I had to put on my long underwear and overcoat to keep warm.

Well, there is some good news too (maybe you won't think so). The "Singing Evangelist-to-be"—the man who was going to be the musician working with the newly hired local Conference evangelist, Elder Andalon--was called to an overseas mission field. Since Evangelist Andalon told the Conference he'd rather have me anyway, they're trying to work something out. They would like to relieve me of my pastoring, but cannot yet, so they will send men up frequently to preach for me, and I will be on the team with Evangelist Andalon. We will finish up the evangelistic meetings here; then we will start meetings in two other nearby towns simultaneously, two nights a week for each.

I love you lots. Give the children and both moms and dads and all the family a squeeze for me.

With all my love,
Victor

Now, since I've arrived home, Victor acts enormously thrilled to be changing from being a pastor to "singing evangelist." He has never once mentioned whether this new lifestyle would help or hinder Steve's health and maturing. It's as though I never discussed this with him. I feel worried that this new way of life will be so erratic that the seizures and emotional problems may escalate.

Should I bring this up in conversation with Victor? I'm afraid to, for fear he will think I'm criticizing him for already accepting this new job that he seems so excited to have.

The letter was my only warning that our lives would change dramatically. Victor had settled everything before I arrived home.

As often happens, the Conference changed plans and decided that Evangelist Andalon should start by holding only one evangelistic meeting for the large Newark City Church instead of two smaller ones. He would assist the pastor there for maybe six months. It was finalized. Victor now was Andalon's "singing evangelist."

Finally a replacement pastor for Victor was located, and once more we started plans to move near to where the first extended evangelistic campaign would be held. One morning I was driving home from looking for a house to rent near Newark. Alan was sleeping in his car seat in front and Steve was asleep on the back seat. In those days cars had no seat belts and three-year-olds didn't have to be in a car seat. I was so tired; I lived sleepy all the time.

I was driving on Main street in Bayonne and almost home. Suddenly someone grabbed my shoulder, jerking me awake! I saw I was about to hit a parked car. I turned my wheel as hard and fast as I could. My front and back fenders barely scratched the back bumper of the parked car. I stopped and got out to inspect the damage. A tiny bit of rust was removed from the bumper I scraped, and both my right fenders had a light scratch mark from front to back.

I climbed back into my car with the still-sleeping boys and started on towards home. Suddenly I remembered about someone grabbing my shoulder. No one was there. It must have been my guardian angel. I realized then that I had driven several blocks and gone under an overpass while I was dozing at the wheel! If I hadn't been jerked awake, I would have crashed and badly damaged the car, my children and myself. Wow! God cares!

One evening Victor's newly arrived boss surprised us with a visit to our home. I hadn't yet seen or met him, and neither Victor nor I expected this unannounced visit from him, and we were about to eat supper. We always ate our main meal at noon, so our supper was always very light. This particular night we didn't have much food on hand and didn't have much money to go grocery shopping. I had planned our supper for little boys, not company. I figured our visitor would understand. We ate tomato soup and cottage cheese, with canned fruit for dessert. Evangelist Andalon's frequent comments about our menu, while he ate, were not what I'd call polite, but I figured he was just trying to be funny. My little boys liked to put their cottage cheese into the bowl with their soup and stir it up, but JA, as he requested us to call him, made an ugly face and said, "Eeeouuu! How can they stand that?" Other similar comments shocked me. Was I being forewarned?

We found a place for rent in the town of Elizabeth, picking a second floor apartment we could afford. A family with several children lived on first floor and there was a basement below that. We would move in less than a month.

JA certainly wasn't the easiest person to get along with. He told me—didn't ask me—to be the secretarial assistant for the evangelistic "team." It was "my privilege" to organize the names on "interest lists" and make a card file of persons who were to receive invitations. This was "my responsibility" as Victor's wife, and the only remuneration would be "the honor I got for the job." In reality, I *did* feel rather honored. I also typed some letters for JA, and functioned in several ways to help get ready for the meetings that were to start soon.

As the time approached to be at the Newark City Church, I asked JA whether he wanted me, as part of this team, to play the piano that first day for church.

He said, "I don't know yet. I can't tell you. Don't bother me. I've got too many things on my mind."

Victor said he didn't know either. He didn't know what JA wanted or expected.

I brought it up again a couple times in the next two or three weeks. Would I play for church or would the regular church musicians do it? I figured the regular church musicians would carry on, at least until the ministers entered. But I wasn't sure, because JA had told me he would ask me to play during altar calls and maybe at other times.

Finally our first day at the Newark City Church arrived. I sat down in church near the front with our two little boys dressed up in coats and ties. Alan was a year and a half old and Steve was three. I left them there and returned to the foyer to see if I needed any instructions. The boys were used to being left alone, and generally behaved well when I had to play or sing.

JA was in the foyer with several people around him, pulling together the last minute details. When I previously had asked him about music for church, he just seemed to be very irritated and rudely asked, "Do I have to draw you a picture?" But now I thought I'd check with him one last time. He *must* know by now whether he would need me during an altar call or whatever.

I stepped up, waited for an opening, and then quietly asked if he wanted me to be at the piano at any time. He turned to me, and in a loud, angry voice said, "Judy, you're going to be the *ruin* of this whole thing! If this evangelistic meeting fails, *you'll* be the cause of it!" He shook his finger in my face and almost yelled, "Why can't you plan things ahead of time? Why do you wait until the last minute? You're my secretary. You should *know* what's going on! Don't come up to me with questions like this again, because you're going to make this whole thing blow up in my face, and *you'll* be to blame!"

This happened within the circle of people around him, who saw and heard everything. These were all leaders in this church, whom I hadn't even met yet.

I was stunned! Red-faced and thoroughly ashamed, I went back into the church and sat by my children. Of course I didn't go to the piano; fortunately no one seemed to expect it. I'm a detail person and I wanted to be sure, but I guess JA didn't *know*, and was *afraid* to admit it. I bit my lip hard to keep from crying. All during church, tears kept welling up in my eyes, and I'd have to dab them with my tissue every so often. How embarrassing!

When we came home after church, I told Victor what happened at church. "I'm not going to eat, and please don't bother me." I quietly went into a long, deep closet, behind all the clothes and started sobbing. Victor apparently called our babysitter. She came and took care of the kids. Maybe she didn't even know I was home. I cried all afternoon.

I am a total failure. I am a stupid person. JA humiliated me, and he will hate me the rest of my life. I must be a horrible person, but I don't know what I did wrong! I know I'm not the one to blame if the evangelistic meeting fails. But apparently I don't know how to plan right, and I certainly don't know how to get along with JA. This has thrown me off balance emotionally. How can I cope? I don't know how I'm going to be able to work with JA at all, and yet that is what I am supposed to do?

Shortly before we were to move, I got an infected finger, probably from a tiny piece of steel wool scrub pad. My finger became swollen and *extremely* painful. Three days before the moving date, I went to see a doctor, and he chemically froze my finger as "anesthetic" and lanced it. However he didn't lance it in the right place and nothing drained out. He told me to go home and soak it. I obeyed, and was soaking it in Epsom salts water, alternating hot and cold, but still in *extreme* pain. Not only that, this was my *finger*, and I was the pianist expected to play for all the meetings! The *only partial* relief I had was *when soaking it*, but I was also trying to pack everything for the move. As I was agonizing with my finger and scarcely able to get much else done, I prayed for God to help me.

In just minutes after that prayer, I got a phone call from Lucy Chilson. She had been one of my voice students at Thousand Oaks Academy where I taught the year Victor and I married. She had taken a liking to me then, and told me she had "adopted" me as her second mother. She had emotional problems and had, since then, gotten into smoking, drinking and maybe even drugs. Through the years she had continued writing me from California. She now said on the phone, "This is Lucy. I'm seventy miles from your house. How do I get there? I'm coming to be your live-in babysitter!"

I hadn't invited her nor told her I was going to move, but I *had* mentioned in a letter that I was looking for a good baby sitter since Victor had decided to work with JA. I was totally flabbergasted by the idea that *she* was planning to come *live with us*, let alone arriving *today*! I knew she had *big* problems and never dreamed anyone would consider moving from

California to New Jersey to baby sit! After a few seconds of silence and a couple deep breaths I said, "Okay, you can come live with us, but the first cigarette you smoke or the first drink of alcohol, you're *out of here!*"

She arrived at our house less than two hours after she called, and she was a Godsend! I put her to packing while I soaked my finger, and finally I opened up the infected part of the finger myself, and it started draining. With Lucy's help, we accomplished the move and getting settled. She lived with us for a number of months and was our wonderfully reliable baby sitter! Thank God she stayed straight, and I did not have to send her packing—at least for quite a while.

Steve was still three years old when he wandered away from our house several times while I was gone doing errands and Victor was supposed to be watching him.

KAREN: SHOCKING!

VICTOR: I remember *at least three times* this happened. I was living on "overwhelm" most of the time and felt drained of any competencies—as a minister, husband or father! I felt *any* adequacy was in shreds!

Lucy had gotten a day job, so was available for childcare only in the evening. When I came home and discovered Steve was missing, Victor and I would get in the car to hunt. We always finally found him, often several blocks from the house, just walking along a sidewalk.

The evangelistic meetings had excellent attendance. Our music went very well. I daily prayed for God to help me cope with JA. Every few days he asked me to type, file or organize something for him. He had some sort of appointment which we all knew about, but he had never asked me to remind him of it. He didn't live near our house, so he called me on the phone when he needed me to do something. When he realized he had forgotten this appointment, he called me and poured out his fury over the phone. "You are a *worthless* secretary. Don't you know it's *your* responsibility to see that I keep my appointments? This is all *your* fault!"

I was still hurting from the previous experience with him, so as he talked, the tears started edging over as I tried to defend myself. I didn't know how *not* to be defensive. Then my voice broke, and he could "hear" my tears.

He hissed, "Don't tell me you are crying! What a sniveling baby you are!"

A day or so later Victor told me JA said to him, "Judy sure gets her feelings hurt easily! She really wears her feelings on her shoulder! She's quite a crybaby!" Victor's demeanor, if not his words, seemed to portray his agreement with JA. Then I felt even worse!

I prayed a lot, asking God for wisdom. He answered by adjusting *my* thinking patterns. It finally dawned on me: *None of this is my fault! JA is scared to death he's going to get blamed for something, and he can't live through that! He's afraid he'll fall apart! Wow, this is a new idea! I refuse to be hurt by him again, and there's no way ever, ever again, he'll see or hear me cry.*

KAREN: GREAT! JUDY WAS PRACTICING LISTENING TO THE LORD—A WAY THE HOLY SPIRIT IS ALLOWED INTO A PERSON'S LIFE.

Lucy often *unexpectedly* brought people to our home, usually teenagers, or young people in their early twenties. She was a short, red-haired, freckle faced *extrovert,* friendly, sometimes brash; and she usually wore jeans, western shirt and a white cowgirl hat. She'd pick up strangers on street corners and bring them home for us "to entertain." She wouldn't tell them they were coming to a preacher's home. Then she'd surprise *us* by bringing them in unannounced, and ask us to "give them a concert." Frequently these were kids with *real problems* such as drugs, and at least one had been disowned and lived in the back of a TV repair store. We enjoyed excitement, so almost always obliged by entertaining them with music and food, friendship and love. Some of them came frequently, and we'd listen to their stories, and treat them as though they were our own "adopted" kids.

But one night, about a year after Lucy came to live with us, she came home drunk, and I told her she had to move out immediately. She found her own apartment and a roommate. Soon she set new goals for herself, and we complemented her often on her emotional growth. We still allowed her to baby-sit, and her discouragement binges became fewer and fewer until she quit drinking entirely!

After we finished the Newark meetings, we packed up for three months of travel with the evangelist. We limited ourselves to what we could put in and on our little Renault. We had to figure out how to fit what we needed into this little car, including enough clothing for three months to span two seasons for the four of us. It was summer and hot, but we knew the weather would be changing. Play clothes, casual clothes, dress up clothes, towels, bedding, a huge briefcase of music, Victor's saxophone, portable ironing board, a few cooking utensils, food staples like flour, sugar, oil and salt were laid out, packed and stowed.

Victor knew every inch of empty space, even under the removable seats. We loaded the back seat level with the top of the backs of the front seats. The boys would lie on that blanket- padded pile of travel miscellany and sleep, or they'd take turns coming up front and sitting on my lap. There were no rules about child seats or seat belts in those days. Our suitcases and other boxes were loaded on the top of the car in a pile nearly three feet tall. We drove a "little tower" down the road. People would stop and stare because of the height of the load that was all covered with plastic tarps and tied down, so things wouldn't get wet or blow away.

Sometimes the churches, where we were to have meetings, arranged a place for us to live. But usually we had to find our own place after we arrived. Often we stayed in cheap apartments made over from old motels, or cheap motels with kitchenettes. We were asked to keep expenses down, so no expensive lodgings were allowed. Sometimes people in the church had a room in their home for us to stay. Once, for at least one month, we stayed in a tiny apartment built into the attic (or third floor) of a home. It was the hottest period of the summer and there was no air conditioning! The churches were also supposed to get babysitters for us, but they didn't always do that, and when they did, we weren't always happy with the ones they provided.

Victor bought a toy airplane for Steve's fourth birthday. It had a motorized propeller that seemed to pull the airplane as the child held an attached string and turned in circles to fly it. He excitedly took his son out of doors and showed him how to fly it. But Steve, being very poorly coordinated—even spastic—couldn't seem to do it right. Victor showed him over and over and became increasingly irritated and impatient. I was watching out the window when Victor almost threw the plane to the ground and loudly exclaimed, "I give up. You *can't do it right!*" Then he stomped into the house, leaving Steve still tearfully standing alone outside, bewildered by his new airplane that he couldn't manage to fly.

I felt angry with Victor, *especially* for telling Steve he *couldn't do it right*, but Victor just whizzed past me into the bedroom. So I headed directly outside and put my arms around a very confused little Steve to comfort him. "You are *going to learn* to fly the airplane, because I will help you until you do."

Slowly and carefully I explained how to do it, and practiced the motions with him very slowly at first, without the airplane. Within fifteen minutes he was doing it himself without a problem ever again. I'm sure Victor must have noticed later that Steve thoroughly enjoyed flying his airplane, and he must have known I taught him how to do it, but there never was a comment from him.

Oh how I wish Victor wanted a good relationship with his son, or at least wanted to learn how to encourage, rather than discourage, him.

After traveling and being involved in meetings in various places for three months, we moved back to Trenton, a more central place in the state for our headquarters. We sold our old baby grand piano and bought a new upright one. Now we had a home base, but we continued to travel and be in meetings most of the time, in spite of heavy snow that winter. Then we'd come home in between each series of meetings, sometimes after one or two weeks, and other times after a month or two. We also made what I called just suitcase moves to a number of different towns where we were gone from home for just two or three days.

Eventually we graduated from a Renault to a Nash station wagon. When we were in tent meetings, we would park our station wagon by the side of the large tent near the piano. We'd take the boys to meetings dressed in pajamas and put them to bed in the car when it was their bedtime. They'd be just about twenty feet from where I was sitting at the piano, and I could see into the car.

We devised a streamlined system of unloading and repacking between moves. In three or four days we did all necessary washing, ironing and mending, checked all mail, paid all bills and prepared for the next several weeks. Eventually we got a trailer to pull behind our station wagon. For the next several years this was our life style, which I really loved. It was the most favorite period of my life. Steve didn't seem to be any worse for the experience, at least not at that time.

Since we traveled extensively, our boys had a lot of different doctors. I explained to a new doctor a few of Steve's problems and remarked about his spasticity. Immediately the doctor responded, "Hasn't anyone ever told you he has cerebral palsy? It's quite obvious." I was rather shocked. No one had ever mentioned it before, although I suspected it. Fortunately it wasn't severe. And I *knew* it had come as a result of the forceps delivery and injury to his head at birth.

Sometime later we moved south to Vineland into a parsonage that wasn't being used. It was a small house next door to the church. Victor didn't become the pastor, but he spoke there occasionally. In between our house and the church was a tall tower, much higher than the steepled church. It had three large loud speakers on it, which the church had used for playing music, bells or chimes to the neighborhood at various times.

Once, while we were lodging temporarily in another town, a hurricane blew in. What a surprise to return home and see this whole tower bent in half, with the speakers crumpled and crushed on the ground only a foot from our bedroom window.

Another time, while we were away from home in the middle of winter, the pipes in this house froze and broke. When the weather warmed enough for them to thaw, water came pouring down from the second floor bathroom into the kitchen. Fortunately a neighbor discovered this before we came home, turned off the water and notified us. When we returned, our kitchen floor was covered with water and ice. What a huge clean-up job!

Traveling, seeing new places, living out of suitcases, singing and playing for meetings was one great big adventure for all of us. I loved having so much time to spend with the boys. At each place we lived I planned how I could teach them about life in that particular neighborhood. In the towns we walked a lot, visiting the fire station, post office, library, parks and other places of interest. In the country we walked maybe even more, collecting flowers to press for scrapbooks, looking in books to identify them. We read stories, made up stories and sang songs together.

I felt very sad and frustrated that Victor didn't seem to want to spend much time with us. He was really a workaholic and felt he just *had* to do everything to please JA, even though JA never criticized Victor or put him down like he did me.

As soon as Steve slowly and haltingly started talking--almost four years old--I started teaching the boys the words and melody of songs and writing out harmony parts for Victor and myself. When Steve and Alan learned the words and melody really well, then we'd try singing our parts with them. At first I allowed them to hold their ears, so they could only barely hear us. Gradually they got so they could unstop their ears and still stay on pitch. We did songs "a capella" (unaccompanied) such as "Climbing Jacob's Ladder" or "Heaven Came Down." Shortly we sang together well enough to begin singing for churches or other meetings.

There was one church service I won't forget. The boys were sitting on the front row, as usual, so I could sit with them when not musically involved. They were dressed in suits and ties, occupying themselves quietly with books and puzzles. I was at the organ playing during an altar call, and Victor was sitting on the platform listening to JA. All of a sudden, for whatever reason, Alan and Steve did something very unusual. They almost never fought, but now they started a real fistfight, hitting each other hard and furiously. I couldn't very well leave the organ, so Victor got up, left the platform, came down the steps, calmly took them both by the hand and walked them out the back door near the platform. Soon the door opened unobtrusively, and Victor walked them back in quietly, still with tear-damped faces, but peaceful and quiet. Victor went back to the platform, and I went on playing as the altar call came to a close. Bless Victor! He rose to the occasion.

A marvelous change took place in my life after I did so much praying and thinking about my relationship with JA. Soon I found an opportunity to use my new decision to never allow him to hurt me. Evangelistic meetings started where we had to drive many miles to attend. Sometimes Victor would be asked to preach at a different church in the morning, we might have a singing engagement somewhere else in the afternoon, yet we had to return to the town where the meetings were taking place that evening.

At the night meetings we were supposed to be "in uniform." The men always wore white coats and black pants. I was to wear either black or white or a combination of the two. I had worn a light blue dress that day at two different locations. But this particular evening we were late because of a traffic hold-up, so there wasn't time to change. JA came up to me as I was about to go into the building. "Aha," he said in a sarcastic voice, "What are you wearing *that* dress for? Don't you know you're supposed to be in *uniform*?" He lit into me with many accusations again, so I decided to treat him like he was a spoiled two-year-old, since he was ranting and sputtering similar to one.

I looked at him rather indulgently, like he was cute or funny, just smiled and slowly drawled, "Oh JA, I *like* this dress! If you don't like it, you can just look the other way." He sort of blubbered, turned and walked away really fast.

The next day he *apologized* for the way he had talked to me! That was the most marvelous, interesting and amazing thing I could have imagined! It was the biggest eye-opener I had ever seen. The problem was that *I* had been "carrying an unseen 'Kick Me' sign." *I was allowing* him to put me down. Yes! The more I hurt or cried, the more he would bawl me out. But when I came across as *sure of myself,* he apologized every time! I just pretended to myself that he was being cute, and it didn't faze me--just entertained me! I *refused* to be hurt. There were numerous times like that during the six years we worked together, but gradually those challenging times melted away until they were no more. JA quit trying to hurt me because I refused to be hurt!

One day the pastor of a church where we were holding meetings asked Victor and JA to go with him to visit a couple who "were in a serious crisis." The ministers were rushing around as if in a big hurry and yet acting kind of "hush-hush" about it.

When they returned from the visit, I asked Victor what the crisis was. I thought maybe a child was about to die or somebody maybe was suicidal. Victor replied that a man's wife had committed adultery. As Victor was telling me about it, he commented with irritation, "I don't know why they get so riled up about it!" His voice began to get louder and more exasperated. "I don't know why the man was so mad--why he was so upset! All his wife did was just sleep with another man." He acted disgusted and almost angry that he had been asked to go with the two other men. Why had they needed him?

Maybe it is disturbing him so much that he is in denial about his real feelings. He seems to think it is stupid, foolish or unbelievable that JA, the pastor and the husband are so upset about it. I am shocked. I can't understand. I think it is a terrible thing to have an affair. I know how I'd feel if my husband slept with another woman. I hope it never happens. It couldn't possibly happen to us! I hope to God!

I tried to tell Victor there must be some problem between the husband and wife that needs to be solved. They must need to change something, to talk over difficulties in their relationship. But Victor demanded, "Drop it! I won't discuss it more!"

So Victor doesn't think it wrong for a woman to sleep with some man other than her husband? I've pondered that for a while now and am wondering if he is giving me some sort of hint? I'm about twenty-five pounds heavier than I was before I had children. That better change right now!

I worked hard at getting in shape again, planning carefully what I ate and doing a lot of callisthenic-type exercise. Not ever having been to a gym or talking to a body coach, I designed my own exercises to do twice a day, a half hour each morning and evening. I wanted so much to please Victor with the way I looked, so I slimmed down until I had an almost perfect figure. I tried to imagine what else I could do to make him happy in our marriage. I cooked his favorite foods, altered my clothes, and made some new things on my portable machine. I bought some new accessories, wore perfume and fixed my hair differently. Victor complimented me and seemed very pleased.

We "suitcase moved" to Atlantic City where we were to help with tent meetings. When the meetings were over, Victor was asked to continue some Bible study meetings on nearby Brigantine Island for several weeks. "What an opportunity! After the meetings are over, let's also take our two weeks of vacation while there!" we both exclaimed.

A young couple, Roy and Marcia Pineda, who had been baptized in one of JA's earlier meetings, owned a guest apartment complex on the island; during the summer they rented to vacationers. They had a small, unoccupied apartment in the back where they let us stay without charge, and it was only a block and a half from the beach!

I made a special request to Victor that we do some fun things while on the island. I wanted him to go to the beach with the boys and me; swim, read to Steve and Alan, and play with them, and converse and people watch with me. I wanted to go to the boardwalk on the mainland with him and sight see. It was summertime and we had a free vacation. Whoopee!

Some of the time it was cold weather for summer. Besides that, there were green head flies that drew blood when they bit. Wow they hurt! The boys and I would flap away at them and only occasionally get bitten, but we laughed it off. After only once or twice at the beach, Victor refused to go any more. He was disgusted it was cold. He was angry there were biting flies. So instead, he made offers to people in the church to polish their cars. He would do such a fabulous job that it took all day. He told me how carefully he did it, and prided himself in using cotton swabs to clean the design in the hubcaps. He almost *begged* people to let him polish their car for no charge!

The Pinedas offered to child-sit free if Victor and I wanted to go out and do something on our own. They even offered their two bicycles for our use, but at the first invitation Victor declined.

I was disappointed, but decided to accept the status quo without complaint and make the best of the situation. I wanted to embrace our life together, however it was. The boys and I went to the beach every day after housework and cooking were finished. Sometimes we'd sit and dig in the sand or play tag. Other times we collected shells and explored the beach farther away.

One cold day, soon after the three of us arrived at the beach, we discovered a hard-packed dirt bank over six feet high, which made a wonderful slide. The boys were getting themselves royally filthy, but having fun. Along came a rather plain-looking, dark-haired man with three boys, just slightly older than Steve and Alan, and they joined the sliding party. Soon all were having a great time playing together.

While enjoying the fun of watching, this gentleman started talking with me. He lived in another town an hour away, but frequently brought his family to stay in a vacation house he had built near the beach, and also not far from a motel owned by his brother. His wife had just recently had their fourth child, a little girl, two or three months old. Apparently she was having postpartum depression and wanted the boys out of the house.

It was so obvious that this man, who I later learned was named Tony, *loved spending time* with his sons. I found myself absorbed in noticing how he played with them and joyfully related to them. After meeting him, I urged Victor more frequently to come with the boys and me to the beach, hoping he might learn more "fathering" techniques by observation, but he chose to do other things.

There was a part of me that wanted to tell Victor about Tony, but the greater part of me expected Victor would leave me if he even imagined there was someone who was attracted to me that I might become attracted to. That "second part of me" was more frightening than the "first part." I purposely stayed at "my" section of the beach, or walked the opposite direction from where Tony and his boys came. But eventually they showed up nearly every day wherever we went. Each day I saw him, the more intrigued I was with his style of fathering. He was playing with my boys now also, as though they were his own. Steve and Alan were obviously eating up the masculine attention from him, as well as from his sons, and I was thrilled to see them so happy. I began to look forward to Tony's coming, but I chose to be very conservative and not act flirty or forward. I started praying for wisdom to handle this situation and determined to stay faithful to Victor.

I'm lonely. I need Victor. I want Victor. Why won't he come with me? I've done everything I know to attract him. The only thing I know is to pray and obey.

Nearly every day I asked Victor what he wanted to do, where he wanted to go, but he said he didn't know. I kept cheerful and didn't nag. Every evening I asked him about what he did that day and listened, as he briefly answered with one-liners or a single word. I asked a question or two to encourage more conversation, but he wouldn't elaborate. I told him I really needed him to go to the beach with me. I also suggested going biking or boating.

One day Victor offered to work in Pineda's guest house yard. He was weeding, digging and spreading peat moss. I got the boys all psyched up to go out and "help daddy" spread this peat moss. I thought that was something two and four-year-olds could do as well as they could pick up their toys. After our offer to help, it was only a few minutes until Victor became angry with them because they "weren't doing it the right way." He scolded them, and told them to leave him alone, so I took them back to the beach and figured I probably should never encourage them to try to help him again. Within minutes of arriving at the beach, Tony and his boys appeared. Apparently the attraction was mutual.

Now I'm worried! Extremely worried! I feel like I might fall in love with this man. I'm trying to be very rational about it, and I purposely make no plans for seeing him more. In fact I am making specific plans to not let it go further, and I pray frequently for God to help me.

Finally one morning Victor said he'd go bike riding with me. Hurray! Marcia and Roy took care of the boys. We went early in the morning and had a *wonderful* time! Victor seemed *happy* to be with *me*! What a joyful relief! Maybe he'll want to be with me more.

Another day I persuaded him to rent a small motorboat so we all could go for a ride. The four of us clambered into the boat and Victor steered quite a long way out into the bay. It was loads of fun. On our return trip both Victor and I got a bit disoriented. There was a lot of marshland, and we weren't sure how to find our way to the proper dock. It was getting late in the day, and I think Victor really got scared. But instead of admitting it, he got angrier and started some dramatic complaining. "It's all your fault. You should never have asked me to go." Then again later, "I should never have rented a boat. It was a stupid idea."

I was also feeling some apprehension until we finally found our way to the rental dock. I had been silently praying we would.

As we were getting out of the boat, Victor said, "This has been an *awful* day and a *waste of time! You* should have watched more carefully so we wouldn't get lost. *I* was too busy driving the boat. I'll *never* do this again!"

The last week before we were to return home, the boys and I went with Tony, *in his car*, to the Atlantic City boardwalk. Afterward, I told Victor where we went, but I didn't tell him how we got there, and he didn't ask! Amazing! Unbelievable! I was prepared and *planning* to tell him *everything*, but he acted as if he didn't hear me, wasn't at all concerned, or didn't want to know.

A few more days, and our vacation will be over and we'll head home. Today Tony told me he loves me! I responded by saying I was attracted to the way he treated his sons. I did not hint that I was in love with him.

But I am scared! I'm panicked! What shall I do? We've never even held hands. I've always acted conservative and proper. I don't want to make a mess of my life. Help me Lord! I want to call my father. I know I desperately need someone's help, but that scares me too. I daydream of calling daddy and talking it over with him, but can't bring myself to do it. I'm afraid to. We'll be going home soon and I'll be safe. That will be the end of it.

Meetings were over. Summer vacation was over, and we all left the island and drove the two hours back home. I never expected to see Tony again. A part of me felt very relieved, but another part felt bereft and empty. I hadn't given him our address or phone number, although I may have inadvertently mentioned the town we lived in.

Almost every evening I took the boys out for a walk after our early evening meal. There was a park near our house where we played a little while before returning home. I always invited Victor to come with us, or even suggested he go and take the boys himself, but he didn't ever seem to want to. He always had more important things to do.

One day, as the boys and I were walking to the park, a car stopped beside us. I heard someone say, "Hi Judy." I looked up, and there was Tony in his car right beside us. Unbelievable! I didn't know if I was thrilled or aghast! His work required him to travel all over the state doing troubleshooting. He was staying somewhere in the area overnight and decided to look up our name in the phone directory and come exploring. Of course the boys were excited to see him also. They wanted to know where his boys were. Tony joined us in the park, and we talked a few minutes while Steve and Alan played, then he left.

Every so often he would show up, uninvited. I should have told him never to come again, but it became a bright spot in my day when he did. Now he didn't mention being in love with me, nor did he try to touch me. The conversation was always just friendly with nothing to hide.

Since Steve, by now four years old, had *finally* started talking, but with extremely slow and carefully enunciated speech, I was afraid he might mention Tony to Victor, so I told the boys his name was "Pop-Pop." Another acquaintance in our area was called this, so if they said anything about Pop-Pop then Victor would think it was just this other man.

Oh God, please forgive me for being dishonest. Why do I feel I have to do that?

9

UNDERTOW

Early in September we received a phone call from Marcia and Roy Pineda inviting us to spend a weekend at the island complex one last time before they closed it for the winter, around the beginning of November. Those two friends were always so much fun. They were energetic, creative, humorous, wonderful Christians, and Victor seemed to really enjoy their company. He seemed apparently thrilled with the idea, as were the boys and I. After considerable planning, the time came to go. On the morning of the day we were to leave, Victor had packed his suitcase and had put it into the car trunk. As I was helping put in the last things, Victor said suddenly, "Oh, I've decided not to go. You and the boys go on by yourselves. I have too much to do." He reached into the trunk and took out his suitcase, turning to take it back into the house!

By now I should be used to these last minute lightning bolts. I really should expect them instead of being shocked and hurt. Yet I must *urge* Victor to go!

So I said, "I really *want* you to go. I don't *like* going *alone*!" I felt apprehension and real fear as I spoke.

"You won't be alone when you get there. Marcia and Roy will be with you," he rationalized.

"But you *told* them you'd come! You sounded *thrilled* they invited us." I was feeling desperate.

I saw his fists tighten and his jaw clench before he declared, "I have a *right* to change my mind!"

"What happened? Why did you change your mind?" I still couldn't believe this was happening just minutes before we were to leave.

"I told you, I'm *too busy!*" He now sounded angry.

After more of my gentle pleading, he announced a solid and exaggerated "No," and I knew I must "back off."

As I fought back tears I suggested, "Then *you* call Marcia and Roy and tell them you're not coming."

"Okay," he responded with a sigh, as though it would be a big chore!

He had seemed so *excited* to go, until a few moments ago. What did I do to change that? *Maybe he thinks it will be too cold by the beach. Or maybe he's just mad at me for some reason and doesn't want to spend time with me. Maybe this is his way of showing power over me, deciding the last minute not to go. Maybe he's frustrated with the boys. I don't know why! I am so disappointed! The tears are filling my eyes. I've got to get out of his sight before I cry.*

Tony had found our phone number, as well as our address, before he found us walking to the park, but he had called only once. I had, without thinking then, unwisely mentioned to him that our family would be going to the island this particular weekend, believing Victor would be with us. He said he'd probably be at the motel with his brother, and if I had a chance, to give him a ring. It would be fun to see me again. I told him there was *no chance, period!* I had totally dismissed it from my mind--*until Victor dropped the bombshell!*

I have such enormously mixed feelings! Oh, it is so painful to realize my husband doesn't want to be with the boys and me. A part of me really wants to see Tony, but a bigger part of me knows I shouldn't see him. I'm angry and bewildered at Victor for backing out the last minute, as well as being very embarrassed that he isn't coming. How can I explain this to Marcia and Roy? He hadn't mentioned being too busy until he had already packed and loaded his suitcase. I'm so scared of my feelings. I'm relieved Marcia and Roy will be there, so I won't have a chance to see Tony. It's going to be okay. I don't have to worry. At this point Tony and I haven't done anything wrong! I have no desire to be sexual with him. I just like the way he "fathers."

Steve and Alan both *begged* their dad to go, but he wouldn't budge. After he removed his things from the car and I finished packing ours, we left for the island without Victor. By the time we arrived, it was after sundown. I went to the door, expecting to see Marcia and Roy, but everything was totally dark. I tried both the front door and the back. I pushed hard at some windows but everything was locked up tight. I expected they'd arrive soon, so we waited in the car. I had brought food, so got it out and gave the boys supper. *I'm not hungry. I can't eat with all this crazy stuff going on.*

Since we always lived on a limited budget, I didn't have any more money with me than what I needed for gas and maybe some extra change in case I needed to make a phone call. We didn't use credit cards in those days and I had left the check book with Victor. I had no money to stay in a motel! Even with the windows rolled up, the car got colder and colder. I put warm coats on the boys and they eventually fell asleep. I covered them with the only blanket I had brought. I put on an extra sweater plus a heavy jacket.

It's been over two hours. Maybe I'll have to call Tony. Maybe we can stay at the motel and pay them back later. There's no point in trying to call Marcia because they will already be on their way. Since Victor must have called them to say he wasn't coming, they'll be hurrying. How long will we have to wait here? I'm really cold now! I don't think that blanket is enough for the boys even with their coats on. Now I am truly afraid! I am a total stranger in this town. What if Tony isn't at the motel? I didn't give him any hope of seeing me, and I've never met his brother. I don't even know where the motel is, although I do remember the name of it.

Now the wind is blowing hard! We're going to freeze in the car all night. No point in calling Victor. He's hours away and sound asleep by now. He doesn't care about us anyway. Besides, I probably don't even have enough money for that long a distance phone call. I fought to stay awake driving this far. I know I'd never make it back home safely. I'm furious! How could he have done this to me? I'm exhausted and shivering. What shall I do? Victor has left us, abandoned us, and we are in serious danger! Maybe I can see Tony after all. How exciting! I am so angry!!!

There was a pay phone within sight of the car and it had a directory I could read by the light of a street lamp, so I called the motel and Tony was there! He said, "I'll be right over." He came, and I followed his car to his vacation house. This was the first time I had seen it or known where it was.

Tony got out and came back to my car. "Come on in," he invited. "You can rest here until they come. I'll check back at their house every so often to see if they've arrived, then you can go over there. In the meantime, let's bring the boys into the house and let them sleep where they'll be warm." So he carefully and gently carried each of them, fast asleep, and put them in his kids' beds, and we sat down to talk in the living room. In about twenty minutes Tony checked the guest complex again. All was dark.

Now it was midnight. Tony checked again. No one had come. We were sitting on two different couches in his living room. I kept dozing off. Tony hadn't even tried to touch me. He also was falling asleep. Finally he said, "Come on; let's go back to the bedroom where we can really sleep." We lay down fully clothed on the only full-sized bed in the house. Before morning we made love. I felt both excited and guilty. There was caring, tenderness and gentleness. And wonderful seduction!

When morning came, Tony went back to check the place again. Still closed and locked! He made no more attempt at sex. He just cuddled and hugged and whispered in my ear that he loved me. It so touched me, so moved me at a deep level. I tried, but I couldn't hide my tears.

"Why are you crying? Have I said something or done something to hurt you?" he tenderly asked.

"No. It's just so amazing and wonderful to have someone treat me so special," I whispered, embarrassed.

Now I phoned the Pinedas on Tony's phone and discovered they hadn't left yet. I told them I couldn't get into the guest house and we had to stay at a motel that night. *Again forgive me, Lord, for lying. I hate lying!*

They said they had so many things to do they just couldn't leave when they planned and would get there later today. "We just figured when you and Victor came, you'd know how to get in. Didn't we tell you to go up the stairs in the back and around the balcony to the front? There's one door at the top of the inside stairs that we leave unlocked." I had never been told that before.

I asked them if Victor had called, and they said no. "I came alone with the boys and he said he'd call you to tell you."

"You mean Victor didn't come? You and the boys came alone?" they gasped. "We didn't get a phone call from Victor!"

"I'm so sorry. He said he'd call and tell you he changed his mind yesterday as we were packing the car."

"What happened? Is he sick?" They sounded terribly concerned.

"No. He said he had too much to do. But I don't know what it was. He didn't tell me. I was as shocked as you are. He insisted we go on and have a good time."

"Was there some emergency regarding the meetings or something?" Apparently they couldn't understand his actions any more than I could.

"Not that I know of. He just told me, as we were finishing packing the car. He had even put his packed suitcase into the trunk. Then he suddenly took it out and carried it back into the house! I don't have a good explanation. Are you going to come?" I was worried that I wasn't making sense, still feeling confused!

"Oh yes. We're so sorry you had to take a motel. You are very brave to come without Victor. We're eager to see you and the boys, and we really wish Victor were there also! What a *big disappointment*! We'll sure miss seeing him! Go in and make yourselves at home. We'll arrive sometime in the late afternoon."

I thanked them for instructions on how to get in. "We'll see you soon."

I don't know what I would have done had I not known Tony. I suppose some people would say, "Well, just don't go if your husband doesn't go."

But I'm not going to let him spoil my life. I'm not going to let him spoil our boys' life. **KAREN: GOOD DECISION!** *We have counted on seeing our friends for a whole month! Besides, I think Victor must have wanted to get rid of the three of us for the weekend. This is something we had planned for weeks, together with other people, and Victor seemed genuinely thrilled about it. I don't know what his excuse is for changing his mind. They practically idolize him! I think Victor is not only being selfish, but also rude!*

Tony went with us back to the guest house. He went upstairs as Pinedas explained and found the unlocked door, came down and opened Pineda's apartment for us. I fixed breakfast for the four of us. We played with the boys and then ate lunch together. Finally the boys took their afternoon nap and Tony and I went to a back bedroom where our family had lived that summer. The sun was shining into the room where Victor and I had slept, and we practically fell onto the sun-warmed mattress and immediately slept exhaustedly.

All of a sudden I heard a car door slam and knew Pinedas had arrived earlier than we expected. I nearly panicked, because Tony was still there. We hadn't planned on sleeping so long. I woke Tony and whispered, "Go there," as I pointed to a closet where he immediately and silently hid. I walked out to the front into their apartment where the boys were sleeping. They asked, "Where were you?"

"I was sleeping in the back apartment bedroom where the sun shined in and warmed the room where Victor and I used to sleep."

They were busy bringing things in from the car so I returned to the back room, threw open a window, which didn't have a screen on it, and opened the door of the closet, silently pointing to the open window. Tony quietly jumped out the window, which was about five feet from the ground, ran through the back yard, jumped a low fence and walked back to his house. He had not brought his car. I closed the window and returned to the front apartment as the boys were waking up.

I wonder if the Pinedas suspect anything. If they do, they certainly haven't let on. I feel so guilty! Horrible! What ambivalent feelings! I feel so loved, being treated so kindly. It is such a revelation to me that this is how it could be with Victor. I have not experienced this before, at least not since the boys were born, yet I am guilty. I have committed adultery. I realize I don't want to lose Victor. I really want this kind of a relationship with him, not Tony. I want Victor to love me the way Tony does. I don't like Victor's moodiness and poor-me attitude, but he's the minister I wanted to marry. He's the musician who performs with me so beautifully in our work for God, as well as for personal fulfillment and satisfaction. He's the father of our children. I like all his gifts and talents and his basic personality. I adore his looks. It's just that he somehow doesn't love me. Or doesn't like me. Or feels sorry for himself being around me, and wants to escape. Or something. . . . .

It was fun renewing our acquaintance with friends and catching up on all the news. Marcia and Roy were delighted to play a little while with Steve and Alan after they served us a good evening meal. The next day the boys and I headed home. They slept most of the way, but I was overflowing with dramatic and opposing emotions! How could I live with these? I felt ripped up inside!

Our next-door neighbor, at the parsonage where we currently lived, was a child psychologist whose office was in his home. We had met him and his wife when we first moved in, and had established a casual, neighborly relationship with them. But because he was so handsome and probably near my age, I avoided him as much as possible. I was frequently trying to avoid men. I didn't want them to chase after me. I tried to resist any appearance of being flirty or unfaithful. And I also tried to keep anyone from discovering there were problems in our marriage. I really tried to believe our marriage was normal. But the day after I arrived home from being with Tony, I was desperate to talk to someone. I called next door and made an appointment to talk with the psychologist on the pretext of talking about Steve, because he still had a lot of problems.

When I came to the appointment, I told him what had happened and how guilty I felt. I just *had* to talk to somebody. It felt good to "unload" on someone. What a relief! He listened and sympathized. He suggested I needed to start developing some interests on my own that I liked, so I wouldn't be putting so much pressure on Victor. He, himself, did sculpturing. He said I needed to develop something artistic, something I could get very much involved with, and really loved to do. This would be a way of occupying my time so I wouldn't feel so much neediness for Victor. I felt somewhat better. Then I set an appointment for him to evaluate Steve.

At the next appointment with both my son and me, the psychologist said Steve apparently had an unusually high IQ. He was a four-year-old with an eight-year-old vocabulary, but he would probably never be emotionally normal, for he had some severe problems that possibly had been caused by a brain injury at birth; however he didn't give a diagnosis.

A few days later, still wearing guilt heavily on my heart, I asked Victor, "If you could change even one thing about me, what would it be?"

He replied in his nicest, most genteel voice, "Oh, I love you just like you are!"

There seems to be a hidden phoniness in his tone. Or is it his body language? I sometimes pick this up when he is talking to someone he is trying to impress. He tells me nearly every day that he loves me and gives me a quick kiss. Many women long for that, so I'm lucky to get it. Why do I think he doesn't mean it? Is the problem only mine? He doesn't seem to want to spend time with me. He doesn't want to converse with me, unless it's important business. He doesn't want to talk about any kind of problem. He doesn't want to spend time with our sons. I've just got to quit trying to solve this, accept Victor as he is, and stop worrying. But is he damaging his sons? Many kids don't even have a father! Others have extremely abusive dads. Victor isn't abusive—just uninvolved and sometimes unkind. Can I change that?

Allan Fishkin was pastor of a church in a neighboring town. He and his wife, Ramona, had three boys slightly younger than our two, and we all got together a few times to discuss details and strategies for a series of meetings JA would soon start at their church. Ramona was planning to have all of us come for dinner the first weekend the meetings were to start, and one day she agonized to me, "Oh Judy, please help me plan this meal! I don't know what JA likes. I don't know how to cook for him. I hear he is always running down other people's cooking and telling how he is such a great cook. I'm just scared to death!"

The fact that JA bragged about his own cooking was beginning to become gossip. Sometimes, as a guest in a church member's home, he talked about what he liked to cook--his spaghetti, his eggplant, his black beans and rice, instead of complementing the hostess on her food. If he didn't like something, he was known to exclaim, "I'm not going to eat that!" This sounds like strange behavior for a minister/evangelist. But JA had grown up in the French Quarter of New Orleans, a non-Christian jazz musician. His fairly recent conversion and short-spanned education in a Christian college had speedily propelled him into evangelism. He was a dedicated and dynamic speaker, and extremely adept in bringing people to know and love the Lord. He was just rough around the edges still, but God was obviously using him.

Ramona and I sat down and talked until we decided the menu and plan. I said, "Don't worry about it. I'll help you." The big day arrived. Ramona said she had to be in some sort of short meeting right after church, so would I please go to her house and get things started. She gave me her key, and I went to her home with five boys, their three and our two, and dug right in to the last minute necessities. With food preparation I am fairly organized and fast. Ramona had specifically asked me to "just take over," and tell her what to do when she came in.

"Gluten steaks" were popular vegetarian food at that time. These were made from the protein (gluten) left in flour after the starch was washed out. We dipped them in beaten egg and seasoned breadcrumbs and fried them. An ample variety and supply of other food had also been planned and prepared ahead of time and things in the oven were hot. Earlier, when I was about to add onions to these "steaks," Ramona told me, "No, my husband refuses to eat onions!" Then a few minutes later I remembered that JA thinks nothing tastes right if it isn't loaded with onions and garlic. So I said to Ramona, "I'll quickly cut up some onions while you get out another frying pan, and I'll fry them to serve separately."

I was in the process of peeling an onion when I heard some very interesting conversation in the living room. I wanted to catch the rest of it, so with onion and knife in hand I stepped around the corner of the kitchen a moment to listen. JA saw me peeling the onion and started verbally chastising me again, almost yelling, "I'm hungry! What are you girls doing wasting your time talking out there? Why don't you get this dinner ready? I'm tired of waiting! Are you just now starting to cut onions? I thought you'd be ready to tell us to sit at the table by now."

I just looked him in the eye and laughed as I stepped towards him, holding out the knife and onion. "If you don't like how I'm cutting the onions, you can just come and do it yourself."

I acted as though I thought he was being funny again, and he started to reach out to take them. I repeated, "You may do it." He quickly pulled back and wouldn't take them. Instead, he sort of stuttered or mumbled something under his breath. So I returned to the kitchen. I had learned to turn right around and give it back in a laughing way as hard as he threw words at me. Never again was I as vulnerable to feeling hurt as previously.

At that moment dinner was nearly ready to be served; the table was set and chairs arranged. Ramona brought out other dishes and seated people while I finished frying the onions. We were all gathered at the table less than five minutes later. After Allan Fishkin asked God's blessing on the food, JA's wife, Lillian, started talking to him in French, and a short, intense conversation between them ensued.

Later Ramona told me JA's wife told her what she said in French: "Who does Judy think she is to have the right to come in here and tell my husband what to do and order everybody around? This isn't even her home. Who does she think she is?" Ramona then responded, "I *asked her to take over*, to take charge! She was doing *exactly* as I wanted her to do." I was grateful for that!

After the boys and I returned home from the island, Tony started calling me occasionally. As far as I could tell, Victor just spent a quiet weekend at home while we were on the island. Now the meetings had started at Allan and Ramona Fishkin's church. Business regarding the new series of meetings necessitated my driving back and forth several times to Fishkin's town, and on one trip Tony met me at a market where we talked a few minutes. He gave me a warm kiss, but after my absolute insistence, he agreed we would not touch. One other time I met him at a restaurant. We didn't go inside, but sat in the car about fifteen minutes to talk. He told me how terribly guilty he also had felt, so he had gone to confession. His priest said, "You're forgiven. Just be sure you don't leave your wife." Tony *got* forgiveness!

I still wanted a good relationship with Victor that was fulfilling, and was willing to work for it. I wracked my brain to think up some new way to interest him. I read books on marriage, personal growth and pleasing a husband. I was constantly trying to better myself, to be the woman I believed God wanted me to become. **KAREN: JUDY HAD TO *WORK* FOR MORE *PERFECTION*!**

The Fishkin's introduced Victor and me to a friend who was attending the evangelistic meetings regularly. Mr. Learner had been a Baptist evangelist, but currently owned and managed a piano store. His wife had left him some years previously and married someone else, which devastated him. He felt much shame because of the divorce and decided he shouldn't be an evangelist, so went into the piano business. When he discovered I was a pianist, he wanted me to come and play his pianos and give my own professional evaluation of each one, which I did.

One night Tony came unexpectedly to the meeting, evidently curious to hear me sing and play. He had never said any hint to me that he was even considering coming, and I didn't expect him. After the benediction and postlude I walked towards the back entryway and was absolutely astonished to see him, but scarcely smiled or even acknowledged him. Victor and I had driven separate cars, and as I left the church, I discovered Tony following me. Farther away, and in a public place, I stopped and got out of my car to tell him he must *never* follow me again and we must *never* meet again!

I don't know whether Mr. Learner saw Tony and me glance at each other at the church, if he saw Tony follow me, or saw us when we stopped, but the next day Mr. Learner phoned me. He talked a little bit about Victor and the meetings and how he enjoyed them. Then he said, "Judy, I have been very much impressed that you need to talk with someone. I believe you are having problems that you want help with."

"You're right. I've been praying for God to send me someone to talk to."

"Let's set up a time. I have my two teenage children living with me. Come on over and have supper with us next Monday night, since there's no meeting that night."

The day I was to meet Mr. Learner, I took our boys to Ramona's place. She agreed to baby-sit while I went to supper at Mr. Learner's home. In the afternoon Ramona and I were working in her kitchen when she complimented me about having helped her with the big dinner for JA and the "clan." She thanked me profusely, and then said, "Oh Judy, you are such a wonderful person! You're the dearest friend I have. I just love you so much! I don't think there's anything you could *ever* tell me, or anything you could *ever* do, that would make me not love you. No matter what I ever heard about you, *even* if you had committed adultery, I would still love you!"

"Wow, how sweet you are to say that." I appreciated her comment very much and wanted her to know that. "I had lots of fun helping with the dinner, and *you* are a dear friend."

Her wonderful validation and specific wording about "adultery" prodded me to open up more. In confession I went on, "Since you said that you'd love me in spite of anything I might do, I'm going to tell you something. I'm going to Mr. Learner's tonight because I badly need some counsel." Then I blurted out the story about Tony, how guilty I was feeling, and how I was trying to figure out what to do to repair what felt like my "messed up" life. I hadn't wanted an affair, and I felt so sad, sorry and guilty that it had happened, and I had broken it off. I told her Mr. Learner sensed there was something I needed to talk about, and that was why he had invited me to supper that night. She didn't make much comment, and it was time for me to leave.

Mr. Learner must have been having a hard time financially. He had asked me ahead of time if I liked pizza, and I agreed. When we sat down to eat, I was served an individual small cheese pizza, and the other three each ate a small bowl of corn meal mush. That was all. We drank nothing but water. I felt embarrassed and would have gladly eaten corn meal mush with them, because I grew up eating and loving it.

After supper Mr. Learner suggested a ride, and the two of us rode a bit while he asked a few general questions. Soon Mr. Learner parked on a hill overlooking a valley while I tearfully elaborated my tale, pouring out my whole story: my marriage problems, how I loved Victor and wanted to have a good relationship with him, how I met Tony at the beach, how Victor backed out the last moment for our return to the island, how the Pinedas weren't there and we nearly froze, how we ended up in bed at Tony's vacation home, how terribly guilty I felt, how I now insisted Tony and I never meet again, how I'd miss him terribly, but was afraid he would still try to keep in contact anyway. Then I asked how I could completely and cleanly break everything off?

Mr. Learner was considerably older than I and was barely five feet tall. Since I was five feet ten inches in bare feet, there was absolutely *no* physical attraction so far as I was concerned. We sat on opposite sides of his large car and never were there the slightest questionable things said or done between us. I was feeling *so relieved* to have someone *listen to me--really hear me*!

Finally we went back to his home. He took me into his study where I sat across from him at his desk. He encouraged me to deepen and enrich my daily relationship with God, and he read to me from the Bible and counseled me some more. He asked about my spiritual life and assured me that God really can change us. Then kneeling, he prayed a powerful prayer for me and also for Victor, and I prayed for all of us also. I made up my mind that I would refuse *any* further contact if Tony attempted to contact me. The time went by so fast, I gasped when I looked at my watch. It was way past time for me to return to Fishkin's home. Mr. Learner drove me back and let me out in their driveway. It was two a.m.

I tried the door, but it was locked. No one came when I knocked lightly, so I rang the doorbell. When Ramona opened the door she instantly sneered, "You slut! You're nothing but a whore! You've been out having sex with Mr. Learner. When are you going to do it with my husband?" She called me every name she could think of, over and over. Then she said, "I told my husband everything you told me, and he has already called the conference president. He is going to talk to him tomorrow morning, and your name is going to be filth!"

My mouth dropped open. Earlier in the day she had emphasized there was *nothing* I could say to her that would stop her loving me, "even if you had committed adultery." That's why I was so "brave" (and ridiculous) to tell her. **KAREN: THIS WAS ACTUAL FLATTERY! BEWARE!**

Apparently my "bravery" is naiveté. I'm desperate for help! I want to run away from all this! I want my problems to end. I've broken off with this man more than once and he came and found me! I want Victor to love me! This wouldn't have happened if Victor hadn't backed out the last minute and refused to go to Brigantine Island with the boys and me. I'm the kind of person that doesn't break a promise, period! If I tell my kids we're going to do something, we do it. If I tell Marcia and Roy we are coming, I don't change my mind the last minute. Victor didn't ask me to stay home. He told me to go on without him. I really believe he wanted to be alone for some reason. I think he would have been angry if I had stayed home.

So I said as calmly as I could manage, "Ramona, Mr. Learner was praying with me. He never touched me all evening. I don't think we even shook hands." She didn't believe me. She was positive we'd been having sex. I could not convince her otherwise, so I didn't try any more. I told her I'd leave the first thing in the morning as originally planned.

She has broken my heart. I am far more shattered by her attitude than worried what other people will think. I am more devastated than if Tony had called me names. I trusted Ramona! Can I ever trust again? She told me I am just out for any man I can get. I want only Victor! I couldn't imagine being attracted to her husband.

The tears coursed down my face. I wanted to leave immediately, but the boys were asleep, and I was so tired I would have fallen asleep trying to drive home. In bed I sobbed and shook, and soaked the pillow. I knew now that I must tell Victor before the conference president contacted him. It would be hard, but I saw it as absolutely necessary! As soon as the boys awoke next morning we left.

There was another meeting that night and Victor and I went together in one car and left the boys with a sitter. At the meeting I acted as if nothing had happened, but I didn't go near Allan or Ramona. On the way home, when we were driving on a country road, I said, "Honey, please stop the car and pull over and park. I need to talk with you."

He did, so I poured out my heart to Victor with tears, and in truthfulness told him what had happened. I told him how much I loved him and how much I wanted to stay married to him, how much I needed him to be a concerned and caring father to our sons. I told how I had thought of calling my father for counsel, and how I had insisted Tony never contact me again. I said I didn't want anything like this to ever happen again!

When I finally stopped talking, he coldly asked, "Is that all you have to say?" I nodded. He did not show *any* reaction, by comment, facial expression or body language. It was as though I hadn't spoken and none of it had happened. He drove on home and we went to bed without one word.

The next day Victor stayed around all day and *did* ask a few questions, which I answered honestly. That afternoon when the phone rang and I answered it, Victor came and stood beside me. He whispered, "Is that Tony?" and I nodded.

He said, "Give me the phone." I handed it to him.

"You leave my wife alone! Don't you ever see her again!" He hung up and walked from the room.

That's good! Very good! My husband cares enough to take a stand! What an enormous relief! I'm so glad he did that! He evidently is finally willing to take action, to do something to try to make us close again. I feel sadness, and know I will miss Tony. But my greatest grief is that it happened at all. I'm sad for Tony. He knows I broke off the relationship several times, thinking it was over. He knows nothing of Ramona's anger or what I've told Victor. I'm certain he is filled with pain also. Now I can really work on my marriage. We can start solving our problems.

After this phone call, Victor asked me where Tony's vacation house was on the island, and I told him. A few days later he left the house in the morning as usual, in his suit and tie, saying he was going to go make some visits. I suspected where he was going. That evening, when he returned home, he told me where he had been and what had happened. He drove the two or more hours and arrived at the vacation house I had described. He went up to the door to ring the bell, and from around the back came

Tony. Victor told me he looked horrible. He had about three days' growth of beard and appeared extremely depressed. Victor didn't see how I could ever be attracted to "this unkempt man."

I responded, "It had nothing to do with looks. It had nothing to do with sex. It had nothing to do with my being attracted to him if I had just seen him somewhere. The thing that was important was that this man treated *our* children like his own, and he obviously loved and enjoyed them. He treated me with care and interest and *enjoyed* being *with* me. That's what I long for *with you*!"

Victor reported to me that he made a *big point* of telling Tony he forgave him, and that when we all went to heaven he would be glad to live next door to him. I felt embarrassed about that, because I imagined I heard phoniness again.

That evening Victor started treating me more lovingly. He hugged me and kissed me like he meant it. I felt more love for him than ever and told him so.

In a day or two we went to some gathering where all the Conference officials, including the President, were in attendance. Nobody said anything unusual to us or treated us any different. We didn't know whether Allan had actually called the conference president, or if it was just a threat. Maybe he called Mr. Learner and learned the truth. But that day Victor and I were very much together and we showed it. He put his arm around me and looked at me lovingly, and I was so thrilled and happy!

Oh God, let it be this way forever, PLEASE!

The next morning, while lying in Victor's arms before getting out of bed, I said, "Victor, we need to talk about what happened, so we can plan specifically for it never to happen again. I feel so bad and so sad it happened. I feel so guilty that I was unfaithful. I feel just awful. Let's get some professional help. Let's work out whatever is wrong. I need your help."

As I began my request, he had jumped up and practically thrown on his clothes. As he jerkily dressed he spat out, "I don't *want* to talk about it! You are *never again* to mention *anything* about Tony, the affair, or that it ever happened! We are going to live and act as though it *never happened*!" He walked out the door and slammed it.

What a horrible slap in the face! It felt like a gigantic canon ball landed in my belly and I was all "mush on the floor." What enormous rejection!

That's the worst thing you could have done, Victor! I'm angry! I'm furious! I'm unbelievably hurt! Do you know that is abandonment? You have left me. I'm all alone! You are apparently planning to act to the world like everything is fine, but we can never plan how to keep it from happening again, and that really scares me! **KAREN: VICTOR'S RESPONSES WEREN'T ABOUT JUDY. THEY WERE TO PROTECT HIMSELF.**

I won't fight back. I refuse to beg. I made up my mind after Victor hit me in the face that I will always be submissive. He has ordered me not to say anything about it, so I won't. I will go on as if nothing happened, and I will tell him I love him and treat him the best I possibly can. I will do it in a loving way, in sexual ways, spiritual ways, emotional ways, and psychological ways. Whatever I can do, I determine I will be the best wife possible, and it will never, ever happen again. But I long for Victor to face reality with me!

Perhaps Victor was dealing with his own fears and hurts the best he could. But I was desperate in my own neediness, and I craved his strength, support and loyalty. How could we work together without discussing it? I couldn't even imagine he might be just as scared and desperate as I.

Before the evangelistic series had ended at Allan Fishkin's church, JA had been officially called to Georgia to be a conference evangelist, and he soon moved. Shortly after he arrived, he called our Conference and asked that Victor be released to come join him. If Allan had actually called the Conference President, it obviously was a good time for us to leave. The Conference called and passed the word to us that we were wanted in Georgia, and we immediately started packing.

I remember driving in the middle of the night by the city, Runnymede, where Tony lived, while Victor and the boys were asleep.

Victor has put on the real cool act again. He is not particularly interested in the boys or me now. He is not cuddling me anymore. Although he gives me a peck kiss every day and says he loves me, he still turns his back to me after sex. I miss Tony. I miss the warmth Victor started to show.

The tears are sliding down my cheeks, and I am struggling to keep sobs under control so I won't waken the others.

Oh Lord, bring Tony and his family into your Kingdom. I really would like to live next door to his family in heaven. Heal all of our hearts. I leave all the past in Your hands, and I trust You to work Your plans into everyone's life. I close this chapter of my life with a prayer of submission to You, my God.

While driving, I started having severe pains in my upper left abdomen, and they got worse through the night. Sharp spasms kept increasing every little while. I knew I didn't have fever, and I suspected my body was reacting to the emotional and psychological trauma I had just been through. By the time we arrived at Decatur, GA, and were looking for a place to live, I was having periodic diarrhea and passing long strings of mucous. I chose not to tell Victor, and just gritted my teeth when the pain came. I figured I brought it all on myself, so I wouldn't worry anyone else with it. Sometimes I doubled over and stifled groans, but I was trying to "act like nothing had ever happened." Eventually, after about two months, my pains and other symptoms went away. God healed me emotionally and physically.

I really do love life. I love our boys. I love evangelism. I love to travel. This actually is a rather adventurous and exciting life. I love singing, playing and accompanying Victor. I'm better off than the majority of people in this world. I'll depend on God, and make the best of everything. I will embrace all of life as it comes, choosing to put God in control.

I knew our marriage lacked depth, and from time to time I still asked Victor if we could go for professional counseling, but he absolutely refused. He said he'd be sinning, because he believed we shouldn't talk about our problems with anyone but the Lord. But he couldn't even *pray about them*, at least not *with* me! **KAREN: THEIR MARRIAGE NOT ONLY LACKED DEPTH, BUT ALSO RESPECT, LOVE AND CONNECTEDNESS TO GOD. IT LACKED A REAL FOUNDATION. SUCH PAIN!**

We soon found a nice church fairly near our newly rented home. On weekends when we weren't in meetings we generally attended there. The first week we went, the opening prayer impressed me. This man sounded like he really knew the Lord, and had a close relationship with Him. Another time this same man had another part of the service, and he seemed to be so deeply spiritual, so energetic. I recognized I felt attraction.

No way am I ever going to let anything happen here! Oh God, I'm scared! Help me now! I cry out to you that I'm tempted to get to know him better. Please don't let me do anything stupid. I want my marriage to last. I love Victor. Don't let me sin, even in my heart. I rely on you only! Please protect me! Send your angels and Holy Spirit to surround me, and also Victor. Help this man not to notice me. Save me from temptation. Don't let Satan do his work in my life. I cry to you for help.

I considered telling Victor of my attraction. I longed for him to watch out for me and protect me. But I recognized that he would be angry rather than helpful. So I kept my mouth shut. We started being involved in new evangelistic meetings and were away from home, often several weeks at a time. I began to relax and just trust. We weren't home enough to get acquainted with anyone very well.

Ah, vacation time! We made another trip out west to visit our folks. My mother urged us to have my aunt, a pediatrician in Los Angeles, do a thorough medical exam on Steve. Victor refused to come along; he preferred working in my parents' yard. So I drove Steve to my aunt's hospital domain over an hour away. She ordered a lot of tests, including an electroencephalogram and a cerebral spinal fluid tap. I didn't know what was involved in the latter, nor was I asked for consent for any of the tests and I had no idea what all was involved in the process. Doctors' orders were considered supreme in those days. In order to do the spinal tap, two big medical men were asked to lie across Steve, to hold him down on the table so he couldn't move. I felt enormous fear and emotional pain when I saw that happen and wanted to grab Steve away from them to protect him. But instead I did the only alternative I could think of, squatting down at the end of the table, so Steve could see I wouldn't leave him. He screamed so hard that lots of little capillaries in his face burst, and his face was mottled with red spots for several days. I was nearly frantic and panicked myself, seeing him so frightened. Tears coursed down my own face. I wanted to yell as loud as he did! The whites of his eyes also became blotched with red because of the pressure of his screaming. The EEG was still very abnormal, but the spinal fluid tap was okay, yet there was no diagnosis. We were told again that he did *not* have epilepsy, but he was to keep taking the Phenobarbital for seizures.

One day while we were still on vacation, I left the boys in Victor's care at mother's home while I went shopping. Shortly after I returned, mother took me aside and told me privately that while I was gone, Victor had become very angry with Steve for something. She hadn't been in the room so didn't know what it was, but Victor had apparently shoved Steve over the seat of a wooden chair and was hitting his bottom so hard that she came running when she heard Steve's screams. She saw what Victor was doing and in a very loud voice demanded, "Stop that *right now* or you are going to break that child's back!" He obeyed instantly. She was shocked at his treatment of our son! Actually so was I, and I hoped he hadn't damaged Steve's back where he had so recently had the spinal fluid "tap." I had not observed him being that harsh when I was around.

When I talked to Victor about it later, he just sighed and said he wasn't damaging Steve, and "it was all in her mind." After returning home, we took our son to a neurologist who tested him in several ways. He reported that Steve sensed everything at a much deeper level than most people. Whether it was heat, cold, movement, light, sound, or touch, all of these upset Steve easily. But even *this* doctor didn't give a diagnosis or tell us what to do about it. What frustration!

VAULTING

With summer came the invitation for Victor to be ordained to the gospel ministry. This was a time that Conference officials now publicly recognized that the ministerial "intern" had proved himself capable, and was worthy of a ministerial license to legally perform marriages and baptisms. It also was a very special time to ask for the Holy Spirit to be poured out in the minister's life and work. It was a tremendous thrill for both of us, and I sensed it as a deep call for a closer relationship with Jesus and with Victor. Victor's mother had come earlier for a visit, and decided to stay to see her son ordained. My father also came from California to Tennessee to be there. Since, at this point, our life was going fairly smooth, I didn't discuss any problems with my dad.

The ordination service was held on a Sabbath afternoon at camp meeting in Collegedale, TN, with many hundreds in attendance. After the vows and commitments were made and exhortations given, I was grateful for all Victor's laudable characteristics that were mentioned by others, and thrilled at the commendations he received.

During those ten days of camp meeting I met and became friends with Erica Roderick, wife of the man I was attracted to at our church. She was tall like me, and they had two boys just a little older than ours. Since Victor especially liked the Kirkwood church, we attended as often as possible and became better and better acquainted with Erica and Howard.

Sometimes Victor and I attended Vespers in the evening, often with our children, and occasionally were involved in outreach work like handing out literature or helping at a neighborhood Bible school. The Rodericks were very active in the Kirkwood church also, so we saw them frequently. Howard was the vivacious, outgoing "missionary leader," and he exuded love for the Lord. He and Erica seemed so compatible and fun and I truly admired them. Several times we were invited to water ski with them.

Victor and I had learned to water ski quite well by now, since we were often invited to go with various families or groups. Again we were invited by the Rodericks to come to a lake to ski with their friends. Different people would take turns driving the boat, and it was the driver who made the decision of where and how long to go, and the skier often didn't know what to expect, unless they had specified something earlier. Sometimes, when there weren't too many people waiting for a turn, the boat driver pulled the skier for maybe ten minutes, way across the lake and maybe into some cove before returning. The country was gorgeous and sometimes deer or other wildlife could be observed.

This particular time Howard chose to drive the boat when it was my turn to ski, while everyone else was resting back on land. He kept going and going, a long way from where the others were. Then he turned suddenly when I was going over the wake, and I spilled. Then he stopped, and I tiredly swam to the boat. I was extra worn out because of the long distance he had taken me. It always was awkward and hard to get into his boat, because it had a bum ladder, but worse this time since my muscles were "shot." Just as I got one foot in, I slipped and started to fall. Howard grabbed me with both arms and we ended up standing body to wet body in an embrace. I felt embarrassed and pulled away, laughing. "I don't want any of the church members to see us like this. Let's get back before someone gets worried." I went to the back of the boat to sit as he drove. He kept watching me with an expression that seemed to say, "You are very attractive to me." With resolution I turned away and watched the scenery.

Horrors! Why did this have to happen? Now I know I have to be careful!

Fortunately, about this time the Conference asked the evangelistic team to change plans. A pastor in Knoxville, Tennessee, needed a break from his church responsibilities in order to take care of his wife, who had just experienced a heart attack and needed much home care. It was decided that JA and Victor would pastor the large Knoxville City Church and also hold evangelistic meetings in that city. After exploring the area, we found a furnished apartment for rent on the second floor of a two-family home and returned home to start packing. For a six-month period we would be living in the same Conference but in Tennessee instead of Georgia.

The phone rang one day when we were nearly packed for this move. It was the Pinedas, who owned the guest home on Brigantine Island. They had been vacationing on the island, were on their way back home, and wanted to visit us that weekend. Excitedly we said, "The more the merrier. You can help us move." Both Atlanta and Knoxville were exactly on their homeward route. They helped us load our car and drove with us the couple hours to our temporary new place.

Soon after arriving on a dark Friday night, we discovered the electricity was on, but for whatever reason the gas wasn't. We thought everything had been arranged ahead of time, but now the utility company refused to work on the weekend. Our apartment was heated by gas and the kitchen stove was gas! Now what were the six of us going to do? It was winter! Fortunately I have always enjoyed challenges, and started figuring everything out. We had already picnicked along the way, so weren't hungry. We dressed the boys in their warmest coats, caps and gloves, put two pair of Victor's warm socks over their socks and tucked their pants into the oversize socks. We had two large throw rugs that had just been washed and we used them as blankets for Steve and Alan, putting a sheet over the rugs and tucking it under the mattress to help keep the rugs in place. We gave our company our only full-size electric blanket and a second blanket to cover it. Victor and I used the last two lighter blankets and slept in our heavy coats, caps and gloves.

Next morning the brilliant sun shone warmly through the windows; at least it *looked* warm. We ate a cold breakfast of cereal, milk and apples and dressed for church. Oh, that warm sanctuary felt so good!

After services, lunch was the challenge. Before I left that morning, I had put a can of Linkettes (vegetarian hot dogs) on the windowsill to warm in the sun, along with a package of hot dog buns. When we returned from church, I pulled a rack in the oven part way out, turned my iron upside down on it, propping it up with cans of food from which I had taken the wrappers so they wouldn't catch fire. Victor found an extension cord, and we turned the iron on high. On this makeshift electric stove I heated two large cans of soup in a kettle. When it was piping hot, I removed it and covered it with newspapers to keep warm while I heated the Linkettes. We soon had a good lunch of "hot dog" sandwiches and soup. I welcomed challenges that stimulated my inventiveness.

Oh, I just love this traveling, adventurous life. It is so much fun to stir my creativity and imagination to meet all these situations. I could live like this for years!

One winter day Victor and I went walking shortly after dawn. The sun broke through the clouds on a *very* cold day, and suddenly we were in a fairyland of miniature, rainbow-colored sparkles above and all around us. We looked down and saw the sidewalk starting to collect a fine white powder. It dawned on us, finally, that the very atmosphere was freezing, and the microscopic moisture droplets in the air were falling to the ground as they froze. The bright sun turned these delicate ice crystals into the tiniest, multi-colored jewels dancing all around us, reflecting sunlight like billions of diamonds. I reached down and flipped my fingers through the white coating on the sidewalk, and a little cloud of white flurried away as if it were bath powder. What an amazing sight that neither of us had ever before imagined existed, and it happened in Tennessee, what we considered a *southern* state!

Soon after we arrived in this town, there was an epidemic of Asian flu and Victor succumbed to it, running a fever of 103 degrees. The day he said, "I think I'm feeling like a human being again," I got sick. Some dear people in the church took the boys to their home to escape our germs, and they didn't get sick, but I got worse. A doctor in the church called one night to ask about me. When Victor told him my temperature was 104 he said, "I'm coming to get Judy and take her to the hospital in Little Creek, only a few miles away." He did. After arriving at the hospital, I barely remember being lifted into a tub of water that seemed awfully cold (actually lukewarm to bring my fever down) and then being given daily fomentations (hot steam packs, alternated with ice water rubs) to both chest and back.

After several days I was well enough to notice tiny birds sitting on the windowsill outside my window, begging for me to share the cornbread on my tray. One window had no screen, maybe for this purpose, so I placed a piece outside on the sill for them. Later that day, when my tray had been delivered, but was sitting untouched, the tapping of bird beaks on the windowpane awakened me. I was feeling better--well enough to experiment. I went to the window and stuck my hand out with cornbread on my palm. After a few minutes a bird actually hopped onto my hand and ate. It was so exciting; I think I got well right then. Shortly, doctors, nurses and even other patients, some in wheel chairs, came to watch the birds eat from my hand. Apparently no one else had tried this. In a day or two I went home, exceedingly weak but almost well.

I'm remembering the counsel of our neighbor psychologist next to the parsonage who suggested I find something compellingly interesting in which to involve myself, so I wouldn't feel so needy for Victor. Children and the natural world, in particular birds and animals, are all so fascinating. *They* are my *art*, my challenge, my excitement, and my ongoing hobby.

The folk who lived in the apartment below us moved out, and a new couple moved in. A few nights later we heard yelling, then banging, sobbing and louder racket. Victor and I went down our indoor steps leading to our outside door. Next to it was a locked door in the wall of the couple's living room. We listened a little bit and decided the man was really hitting his wife. Victor suddenly knocked loudly on their door, and in a stern and masterful voice said, "You lay off your wife right now, or I am going to call the police!"

Wow, I had *never* heard him talk like that, and I was *so* proud and impressed. After another fight a few days later, Victor *did* call the police. They took the man to jail to sober up. But the abuse continued so we notified the landlord as well as the police. Finally the landlord moved this couple out and a peaceful family took their place.

After our six-month stint away from home, the pastor's wife recuperated sufficiently that her husband could again take over church responsibilities. We returned home with mixed feelings. We had come to love the people, the terrain, the staying in one place. Now we started frequent traveling again, having short duration meetings in a couple of other states. One short series of meetings was outside our conference, in Panama City, FL.

While there we were invited to go deep-sea fishing. Victor and JA both caught red snapper, but all I could do was "feed the fish" at the rail, even after Dramamine.

While at this location, we went with the church on a beach picnic. As we were finishing up lunch we heard someone ask, "Have you seen the alligators?" Perhaps there was a tourist attraction pond somewhere nearby with alligators, but we never saw it. We didn't realize that Steve, who was playing with other children close by, had overheard the talk about alligators.

Victor was supposed to care for Steve while I helped clean up after our picnic lunch. One of the teenage girls was happily baby-sitting Alan. I looked at Victor every little while to see if he was watching Steve, and then they both got out of sight. I thought they must have gone walking. I decided it was time to check on them and soon found Victor, but he had absentmindedly lost track of Steve, who was now missing again. Victor never *showed* any worry or concern about our son--by word, body language or facial expression.

As usual, I was frightened and inwardly angry, and insisted we go hunting for him. I started silently praying to find him. There were lots and lots of sand dunes and hilly places. We walked a long way through deep sand, heading up to where we had been told the alligators were. We climbed over one extra tall dune and from the top scanned up and down the beach. Away in the distance, close to the water we saw a small child, much too far away to recognize for sure if it was Steve, and much too far away to be heard if we shouted. We rushed in that direction, and when we finally got close enough to recognize Steve, I ran full speed to him and hugged him! He said he was looking for the alligators, but couldn't find them.

Steve has experienced so much panic, hysteria, and emotional problems since he was born, I can't comprehend why Victor doesn't seem to care. I wonder, if it were someone else's child, would he be more caring and watchful?

We returned home and prepared for a new series of evangelistic meetings. When they began, we started announcing that we would have a musical "request night," before the meetings closed. When people turned in the names of favorite songs, we chose some to be vocal solos or duets and others to be performed on saxophone, piano, organ (if there was one available) or a combination. Doing this often involved learning new songs and making new arrangements, and took much enjoyable work to adequately prepare. News traveled, and "Request Night" sometimes swelled attendance to standing room only.

In one "back-woodsy" town in Tennessee we were invited to take part in a funeral. The floor of the tiny country church had almost as much open space between the slats of the platform floor as there was wood. Victor and I were asked to sing with the choir, and we hoped our chairs wouldn't shake so hard with the excited singing, clapping and foot stomping that the chair legs would slip through the cracks. "Railroad to Heaven" was the most energetic song, along with a half dozen others. Someone from the church played excitedly on an old honky-tonk upright piano. We both were worried it actually might fall over as it swayed back and forth on the weak platform. We learned fast and almost relished our fluency in adapting to different cultural lifestyles.

Summer was passing, days were getting shorter, and stores were advertising sales on school supplies. Steve was seven and a half and had never had a day of formal school. Could he manage being in a classroom? What if he should have a seizure when other kids were watching? I had begun teaching him with borrowed materials and whatever I could create at home. He was already reading and understood early math fairly well. But he needed the social stimulus of a classroom. Could he handle it?

We registered him in first grade at a parochial school in a nearby town. Then I started teaching piano and voice lessons at home to people who had been begging me for the last year. Victor was away much of the time with JA, singing at meetings, giving Bible studies and being a general helper and errand runner for him as usual. Someone else was playing piano, since my job had evolved into that of a homebody.

When Steve started school, Alan became so depressed that he just lay on his bed for hours and stared at the ceiling. I tried hard to interest him in games and other play activities, but he wouldn't—or couldn't—get interested. He cried, "I don't have *anyone* my age to play with." The solution to this problem was solved at the dog pound. We brought home a little brown puppy with a pure white tip on his tail. As Tippy and Alan became fast buddies, all depression evaporated.

At the Kirkwood Church where we still attended, there were always snacks and a social time after evening vespers. One night I saw Howard and his boys but not Erica. Upon inquiry, I learned she was home with a headache. Quite a few other friends were standing around talking about going to the county fair. I didn't think I could afford to go, so didn't pay much attention. Then someone asked, "Judy, do you want to go?"

"I'd like to, but don't have any idea where it is or how to get there. And I don't know how much it costs."

Several folks said, "Oh, you've *got* to come. It's not expensive."

Meanwhile Howard's boys were frisking around with mine; and when they heard about the fair, they begged for Steve and Alan to go with them. When I learned the cost, I decided I could afford to spend a little fun money for a change. My sons were tugging for my attention. "I need to follow someone or have someone draw me a map."

Howard spoke up and said I could follow him. "We have to go home and change clothes, but the school is on the way. You could meet us there."

We also went home and changed clothes.

I wish Victor were here. This is the last night of the current meetings he's helping with, and he won't come home until tomorrow. The boys need a chance to be with friends, and I haven't taken them much of anywhere lately. But I'm not sure this is wise—following Howard.

We met at the school where I pulled up behind Howard's car and motioned for him to go on. Instead, he got out of his car and walked back to mine. "My kids are just begging and begging to ride with your kids."

"That's great. Let them come and ride with us." I love kids, so hoped they'd come join us.

"No, they want your kids to come in the car with us," Howard answered.

"Okay, that's fine, I'll just follow along behind." That was the end of it as far as I was concerned.

"It's foolish for you to follow along alone. It's foolish to take two cars. Why waste gas? You might as well leave your car here and ride with us."

He was making a generous offer, but I had some misgivings. "No. I don't want to do anything to upset Erica."

"That won't upset her. You two are friends, and she won't mind. Please come and ride with us."

Howard sounded so innocent and encouraging that I finally was persuaded and got into the back seat of his car. When we arrived at the fair I told him, "I'm going to stay far away from you. Don't think I'm mad. I just don't want there to be any gossip about us."

The boys all stayed together, sometimes with me and sometimes with him. We stayed close enough so we wouldn't lose track of each other, but far enough to avoid suspicion. Finally I allowed my boys to go on a ride with his two boys. Howard and I were both waiting when he sidled over closer to me and said, "I wish I could be on a ride like that with *you*."

"No way! That definitely wouldn't work!" I replied, stressing the finality of my answer.

On the way home we arrived where my car was parked. Howard got out of the car and opened the door on my side. As I was awkwardly getting out of the back seat of this two-door car and feeling almost embarrassingly ungraceful, Howard put an arm around my waist and gave a very quick squeeze. I was startled and instantly quite disturbed, pulling away fast. I hoped none of the boys noticed. But I have to admit I also felt a thrill.

Oh God, please don't let an affair start. Forgive me for even enjoying what he did. Help me! Save me! I promise I will never ride in his car again. This was a drastic mistake.

When Victor got home the next day, one of the first things I told him was that I went to the fair, how I happened to ride in Howard's car, and that I felt awkward and ill at ease. Erica wasn't there, and I realized it was a mistake to have ridden with him, and I'd never do it again. I was worried about upsetting Erica. I felt concern and wanted Victor to know what was going on in my life, for I was determined to not keep secrets, especially of this kind. I *didn't* tell him Howard gave me a quick squeeze as I got out. Victor made no comment or reaction whatsoever and soon walked back outside to do some yard work.

A few minutes later the phone rang. It was Erica Roderick. She was furious! Her voice was caustic, loud and full of scorn. I had never heard anybody except Ramona Fishkin and my mother talk to me the way she did. She yelled, "You are having an affair with my husband." She called me all the names she could think of and screamed, "I want you to know I'm going to call the conference president and tell him you're having an affair with my husband. He's got to get you out of here!" Judy was a five-foot-ten-inch beautiful woman. She could get blamed for much!

When she began to run out of steam I quietly said, "Erica, I'm not having an affair with your husband."

"Well, my son saw him put his arm around you, and he told me as soon as he came home," she blurted out with apparent fury.

"Yes, he *did* give me a little squeeze as I was getting out of the car. It totally surprised and embarrassed me. I pulled away. That's the only thing that's ever happened. I'm sorry I let myself be talked into riding with him. That was wrong, and I'll never do it again. I have never been alone with him, ever. The four kids were with us last night." She continued to rave until she finally slammed the phone down.

I went outside immediately and told Victor we needed to talk. He didn't respond and just kept on working, so I talked while he worked. I told him about Howard's squeeze, their son's seeing it and telling Erica. I told him she was going to call the conference president and tell him to get us moved away. Then I asked, "Please, Victor, come in the house and let's call the Conference President and *both* of us talk to him. I need your support!"

"This isn't *my* problem. You call him if you want!" He kept on hoeing with his back toward me, not even turning his head.

"Please?" I had resorted to almost begging.

"Absolutely not!" He chopped the weeds harder, as though they were his enemy. He wouldn't even look at me or speak another word.

Returning to the house, I called the Conference President myself, right then. When he answered, I identified myself first, and then explained, "I have done a *very* unwise thing." I reported exactly what I'd done, told about Howard's squeeze, his son's seeing it and telling his mother. "She told me she would be calling you and asking you to get us out of the Conference, and I want you to hear it first from me. I have told Victor everything, and will make sure that nothing else happens. It was a *big* mistake, and I take all the responsibility for it. Nothing more will happen, I promise!" He thanked me for the call.

Going back outside, I told Victor about the call, then suggested, "Let's get in the car right now and ride out to Roderick's place. Erica needs to *see* that we are a loving couple and *want* to be with each other. She needs to know there's *no way* I'm going to have an affair with any other man. She needs to see that we have a *firm commitment*, and I also want to apologize in person for having gotten into the car with Howard."

Finally Victor turned and looked at me with what felt like abject disgust and scornful hate in his eyes. He bitterly and slowly enunciated, "If you go, go alone, because I'm *not* going *one step* with you!"

VICTOR: I had formed the habit, long before I was married, of refusing to "look at" my feelings if it made me uncomfortable. My decision was *don't feel* rather than facing reality. I would purposely do anything necessary to block out feelings. So when uncomfortable things came up I figuratively turned to stone, refusing to respond. I just closed off.

Immediately getting into the car, I drove the forty-five minutes to Roderick's home, went to the door, rang the bell, and asked Erica if I could come in to talk. First I apologized for my enormous mistake of riding in the car with her husband, and said it was entirely my fault.

"My husband and I are very committed," I assured her, while wondering if that statement was really true about Victor. "No other man will *ever* take his place!"

She sneered, "I will have *nothing* more to do with you, *ever*! You are nothing but a whore and slut!"

Turning to leave, I politely thanked her for her time and her willingness to listen, then drove the miles home again. Relief flooded over me in spite of Erica's attitude. I had fulfilled my responsibility in acknowledging my fault to both the conference president and Erica, and apologized in person.

On my return, I told Victor what had transpired and my feelings about everything, but he made no response whatsoever, verbally or physically.

The Lord God is my strength! He is encouraging me and buoying me up physically and emotionally. I feel I can hold my head high and not be ashamed. That is a miracle in itself. I constantly reaffirm to myself and to God my commitment to Victor, and daily I renew my determination to love and respect him. God, help me to embrace my marriage in every way possible, even if Victor doesn't!

A few days later Victor left town again for evangelistic meetings in another city. Howard started calling me every day. Sometimes he called twice or three times a day, telling me he was falling in love with me; telling me his wife was not treating him decently. I asked him not to call, but he did anyway. He said he *needed* to talk. He told me about an affair he had in the past and how he had left Erica for almost a year. Finally they had gotten back together. He said he was sorry for what he had done previously, and Erica had good reason for treating both him and me like she did. He said he really did love her. **KAREN: SO JUDY GOT BLAMED FOR HOWARD'S PAST. JUDY WAS WHO ERICA COULD YELL AT AND BE HEARD.**

I told Howard about my call to the conference president, then asking Victor to go with me to visit Erica, and his refusal. Because of the alienation from our spouses, Howard and I were feeling a strong emotional bond. **KAREN: THIS BOND CAME AS A RESULT OF JUDY *LISTENING* TO THE PHONE CALLS. THE *ONLY* THING TO DO IS *IGNORE AND HANG UP!***

One night, when Victor was out of town, Howard called and asked if he could come over. I said no, it wasn't appropriate with Victor out of town. He begged, "I need to talk to you in person for just a few minutes. I won't stay long." After much stalling I finally said, "All right, you may come. That was a weak spot. But if you're expecting something to happen, it won't!" Then I knelt and raised my voice in prayer for God to give me strength.

The boys were sleeping. It wasn't long until the doorbell rang. I let Howard in, and as soon as I closed the door he grabbed me and gave me a big hug and kiss. I pulled away and motioned, "Have a seat here," then I seated myself across the room from him.

Immediately he asked, "What's your bust measurement?"

Repulsion immediately stirred deep within me, with fury hanging on to its tail! **KAREN: THAT WOULD HAVE BEEN GOOD TO VOICE—TELL HIM!** Howard then started to ask another similar question, so I stood, interrupted him and said, "Howard, I am attracted to you; perhaps it could even develop into love. But I'm married, you're married, and I'm *not* going to have an affair with you! At this point in my life I choose to act in such a way that if something someday should happen and we were both free to marry, you would be able to trust me. If I were your wife, I would want to be faithful and true to you. I will *not* do anything with you! Not tonight! Not any night!"

Quickly walking to the door, I spoke while opening it, "Here's the way out." As he left, I closed and locked the door, going to bed a free woman, a thankful woman! However I sobbed with sadness, aching for a close relationship with Victor, and I also cried in sheer relief that God had won the battle for me.

The next morning Howard called, his voice shaking with emotion. "Judy, I want to apologize. I am deeply sorry! I was totally out of line! Because of the way my wife has been treating me, I *was* tempted. *Very* tempted! Yes, I *did* plan to see what we could do last night sexually. But I was totally in the wrong. I ask your forgiveness."

"I gladly forgive you, Howard." Inside I was shaking and weeping. I had *felt* "in love" with him until he asked me what my bust measurement was. But somehow that question suddenly triggered anger, which *exploded* into recognition! I *had* wanted, enormously, gigantically, to be in a love relationship with a man, and this *had* been very tempting. I wanted someone to love ME for *WHO* I AM—not for breast measurement! So Howard's *question* instantly evaporated any temptation, and my need specifically for Victor's love swelled compellingly.

Howard's voice went on resolutely, "Because I have really fallen in love with you, I cannot ever see you again! I want you to know that we can't ever ask you and Victor to come water skiing with us again. I will probably plan for us to attend a different church, especially if we know that you're in town. I mustn't *ever* see you again! I want you to know that I love you, I respect you, and I thank you from the bottom of my heart that you kept me from committing adultery." He hung up. I've never seen or heard from him since.

I wonder if Erica was listening on another line. I hope so.

Now it just so happened that a few days prior to this, friends from another state had visited us. This couple stayed overnight and slept on the hide-a-bed in our living room. The day after I sent Howard away and Victor returned, the toilet in the bathroom this couple had used became plugged, and the water overflowed and flooded the floor. After Victor worked at trying to un-clog it for quite a while, he called a plumber. The plumber had to dig quite a way down in back of the house to get to the sewer pipe and open it. He called Victor out to tell him something. Next thing I knew Victor came back in the house, his face white as a sheet, his jaw set in fierce anger, and viciously growled, "He found the problem!"

"What was it?" I was curious, and couldn't comprehend his fierceness.

143

"It was a condom. I *know* what you've been doing!" His words came with such force that saliva sprayed on my face.

In shock I responded, "Victor, I've not had sex with anyone here."

"Well, how did the condom get in there this weekend while I've been gone?" His rage and condemnation made his voice shake as he spoke.

"I don't know." Then something came to my mind. "Remember, Victor you were here when our friends stayed overnight. They must have flushed it."

Victor continued to glare at me with a hostile, mean and unforgiving expression. "Oh, I know! It *wouldn't* have been that, because it got clogged up just *today*! I *know* what you've been doing!"

Of course the tears poured down my face as I said, "Victor, I want you to *trust* me. I have *been trustworthy!*"

He turned and stormed out, slamming the door behind him.

About this time JA developed some health problems and asked for a change, so the Conference gave him a church to pastor. The Voice of Prophecy radio broadcast organization started evangelistic meetings in Atlanta, GA, and Victor was hired to help with the music, even though the radio quartet provided a lot of it.

When this series of meetings was nearly over, the pastor of the Ellijay, GA church suddenly died. The location was about an hour and a half from where we lived, so the Conference asked Victor to go up every weekend for two or three days at a time to preach and do the pastoral work there. Most of the time he went alone, because I was involved with our sons, our home, and music teaching responsibilities. However, on a couple weekends we got a sitter and I went with Victor.

In this little town lived the Mitzelfelts, who were very active in music. Dr. Mitzelfelt had three doctorates, an M.D., a Ph. D. and a Doctorate in music. He was the main medical doctor in town, but had also organized a fifty-voice community choir, the members ranging in age from eight to eighty years. It was an excellent choir, and among other things performed several choruses from the Messiah Oratorio by Handel.

One weekend Victor and I gave a musical program at this church, which was filled to capacity with town people. Mrs. Mitzelfelt, a very accomplished pianist, played for our duets.

While involving ourselves with these dear people, we were thinking of requesting the Conference to move us here for Victor to become the regular pastor. But then Victor received a call to be associate pastor at the Phoenix Central Church in Arizona with Bill Barstow, and he believed that was God's call to him, although I'd have loved to come to this small musical town.

COMEDY

After packing and driving from Georgia to Arizona, we temporarily stayed in a house trailer belonging to folks who were out of town. It was winter, and that first night there was no heat available in the trailer for some reason! Outside, the rain puddles were frozen solid next morning. Fortunately we had three extra blankets in the car. This trailer was parked on the grounds of a boarding high school, Thunderbird Academy. By the second or third night we moved into one of the tiny apartments on campus where we stayed a few weeks while house hunting and waiting for the moving van to arrive. Bill and Ruth Barstow lived in nearby Scottsdale, and she and I became friends.

While living on campus, Victor got sick with a very bad cold, resulting in his sinuses becoming so stopped up he couldn't breathe well. We went to see a local doctor who sprayed some sort of powerful medicine into Victor's nose to open it up. Now he could breathe well, but soon he had quite a funny reaction to the nose spray. As we started to drive home, I immediately noticed a personality change in him. We stopped at a store to buy a few items. As we were walking down an aisle he started talking, kidding and joking rather loudly. Then he said silly things to nearly everybody we passed. This wasn't his normal behavior at all. He was now actually full of fun and craziness. There was a part of me that liked him that way, and a part of me that was embarrassed. He didn't seem to use very good judgment in what he'd say or to whom he said it.

146

I mentioned to him that he was acting differently, and he said, "Yes, I'm feeling different. I feel really high, like I'm on a drug of some sort."

When we got back to the apartment, he started playing with our sons, talking and laughing, telling jokes and stories. They loved his "new" personality, and didn't want to go to bed because they were having so much fun with their dad. He was really goofing off with them, talking non-stop for hours. I had fun listening to him, but felt concern about the boys being up so late. He kept up this new aura until two or three o'clock in the morning--an absolutely uninhibited high.

Is this what his real nature is? Is he usually sort of rigid and knotted up inside because of psychological problems? Is this who he is when he *feels free*? Or did the drug really change his personality? I can't tell. I like a lot of the change because he seems to be so alive and to really enjoy our boys.

By the next day his high had worn off and Victor was functioning in his usual reserved style. We soon found a house to buy in Phoenix—our first home purchase--and shortly moved in and got settled.

As associate pastor with Bill Barstow, Victor's job was making lots of house calls, visiting church members and giving Bible studies. In this sprawling, sunny desert city his work often entailed traveling many miles. He hated keeping records, so by the end of the month he'd have to "guesstimate," as he called it, the number of calls he had made as well as his mileage for his required monthly report. He'd start to complain, "How am I supposed to know? How do they expect me to remember all these details?"

One day I talked with him about ways of keeping track and suggested he keep a notebook in the car. Then he fussed at *me* because he thought I was trying to tell him what to do. Every month at report time I felt disgusted at his self-pity, but I tried not to show it. He frequently talked to me about his house visits and Bible studies, yet when he wrote the monthly report he didn't put down nearly all he had told me about. Several times I looked at his month-end report when he left it lying open and obvious on the dining table. He was worried he might *over*estimate, so he deliberately *under*estimated the number of visits and also his mileage, so "no one would question his honesty."

Sometimes Victor came home upset because he couldn't find an address, and he seemed disappointed and angry with himself. I wondered what could help him stay calmer and at peace when things weren't going right? If he could just stop and think things through, he could probably plan differently. He certainly is smart enough.

I wish there was something I could do to help him. Maybe there is, but I don't have the faintest idea what it might be. I commend him and thank him often and tell him I love him and am proud of him.

After a few months in our new location, we were invited one evening to our conference president's home in Scottsdale, next door to the Barstow's, for an evening meal. After we ate, president Parish called Victor into a side room. I was in the living room with our boys, and they were playing quietly. The door to this side room was standing slightly open and some of the time I could overhear what was being said.

"Does Judy make you do so much housework that you don't have enough time to go visiting?"

I couldn't hear Victor's response. I'm not sure he answered at all. Perhaps it was a nod or head shake.

"Does your wife tell you what to do all the time or make you do a lot of housework?" He apparently was reprimanding Victor, or at least questioning him about not getting in enough visits.

I have never, ever asked Victor to do any housework! There were probably a few occasions I asked him to change diapers. I do ask for help when we are packing for a move or getting settled in a new place. **KAREN: THE ASSUMPTION IS THAT ALL THIS IS WOMAN'S WORK AND DEMEANING TO A MAN.** *Bless him! He often chooses to do things. Sometimes he mops the floor, scrubs the shower or cleans the bathtub, but he's gone from the house most of the time. I really appreciate all he does, and I thank him for it, but don't expect it.*

After we got home, Victor fumed, "President Parish really put me down! I feel worthless and a failure as a minister." He admitted he *purposely* didn't answer *any* question or accusation, but he didn't say why. It seems that at the slightest criticism he just wilts.

I feel like Victor wants Elder Parish to think the problems are mine and not his. Apparently he made no effort to defend me. Oh how I ached for him to say, "No, my wife never asks me to clean the house. I do occasionally help her, but I don't spend much time with that. Nor do I spend a whole lot of time with our boys. Normally I consider God's work ahead of the family!" How I wish he could have said that, which is true!

I believe Victor is a success as a minister, and I tell him so. He just dislikes the "clerk work" reporting the visits, Bible studies and mileage. I truly hurt that Victor wasn't willing to stick up for me or discuss with me anything he wished I'd do differently.

Fortunately President Parish didn't fire Victor.

The Thunderbird Academy principal asked me to teach piano and voice lessons two days a week. I also accepted several piano and voice students at home and started giving regular piano lessons to both our sons.

When I had taught reading and math to Steve at home, before he started school at age seven and a half, Alan was always listening and learning at the same time. In this new district the conference educational superintendent came to the elementary school and listened to Steve read. She said, "This boy should be in the third grade." He was nearly eight, but his physical coordination was so poor he couldn't cut out things, he could hardly do required pasting, and he couldn't even keep his hand on the page when he tried to write. I shared with her my thoughts: Rather than put him in the third grade with kids his own age and have him feel inept and behind, it would be better to have him totally excel in his mental work while he was trying to catch up physically. She agreed and kept him in first grade. I continued to work with him daily, creating exercises, games and projects for developing coordination in his fingers, hands and arms. I also had the boys help in the kitchen and do chores around the house. They did a good job of washing dishes, house cleaning and working in the yard.

That year both boys got measles and chicken pox. Later Alan became sick again and ran a high fever. Just as he started to get better, his fever returned. His temperature would go up and down, almost normal then up to 104 or 105 degrees, causing him to sometimes become delirious. Finally the doctor diagnosed rheumatic fever.

As he slowly began to recuperate, he started having episodes when he'd complain, "Mommy, I'm *so tired*! I can't stand up any more." Then he'd actually collapse, falling to the floor in exhaustion. Finally the doctor discovered a heart murmur and decided he was not to run or even attend school for the next year! So I also taught him at home, using a big basket of blocks to teach math concepts and borrowed schoolbooks for reading.

In a freak accident Victor badly injured his little toe, stepping into a sprinkler system hole. The pain was so great that surgery was recommended. He finally went to his mom's home in California and there had surgery on his toe. He took Alan with him since I was teaching and Steve was in school.

This is one of the letters he wrote me while he was gone:

Dearest Judy,

I feel like an orphan without you. I'll be so glad when you get here to bring me home. Alan has been a little angel. He's cried only once and that was because he had to go to bed.

The operation was a success. I walked to the bathroom the next day and was surprised my toe didn't throb or pain. I've been walking ever since. I hardly used crutches at all, and on the third day I cleaned and polished my step-dad's car. The stitches won't come out until Thursday, but my foot feels completely well. I bear all my weight on it and would wear a shoe if I could get it on. I've had two swims in mom's pool. The rest of the time I've spent puttering around, playing the organ, listening to hi-fi music and studying. I did get to the city and bought $20.00 worth of used books.

We're all going to sight see today and the others are anxious to leave, so I'll say bye for now. Your picture is looking at me from the top of the piano and I just threw you a kiss. I love you, beautiful. Give Steve a kiss for me.

With all my love,
Victor

When Steve moved on to third grade, Alan started first grade. Both the educational superintendent and teacher decided to keep giving Alan material as fast as he could do it, and he actually finished all first grade material in three months. By the end of the year he had finished all of second grade.

Victor's mother had remarried, which resulted in Victor acquiring a stepbrother, Nate. We had been in touch with Nate and his wife Larell only occasionally, but celebrated with them when they adopted a baby boy. One day, when this baby was four years old, Nate called us from California. Larell had been sick a lot, and he asked if it would be possible for us to keep their son Fred for a while. They offered to pay us well and also cover tuition to put him in a private preschool. We talked it over and decided it might be nice to have three boys, so drove from Phoenix to Riverside, California, to pick up Fred.

He lived with us for over a year, which proved to be one of the greatest challenges of our lives. He had serious problems that taxed our coping ingenuity, but kept our lives from being dull or boring. In spite of everything, he endeared himself to us and set us up for some real adventures a few years later.

I became very good friends with my neighbor, Shelley, who lived across the street from us. There were two children in her family, but because she and her husband loved children so much, they also cared for foster children, sometimes as many as four or more at a time. We had great fun swapping child and animal stories and helping each other when problems arose.

Our sons were given two pet rats, and Shelley's husband built a cage for us. As rats multiplied, he built other cages. We all had fun with them for a while, the boys learning all about mating and the birth of babies. The boys also sold the little babies to a pet store for twenty-five cents each and gave their earnings to a children's fund-raising project at church called "Investment." The pet store then sold them to customers for fifty cents.

Even though Victor's mother lived near Los Angeles and we lived in Phoenix, she loved to sew for me. Now she decided to take a millinery class and made me a very beautiful, wide-brimmed, black straw hat with black chiffon roses attached to the pleated chiffon hat band. This hat looked very classy and expensive, but the only place I felt comfortable wearing it was to church, as hats were quite stylish at that time.

Our church choir had a Bible class before church. I was both choir director and assistant teacher of this class. Visitors often came to it because we developed a reputation for lively discussion.

A woman, who had heard only a little about our church, came to visit one day, and someone suggested she come to our class. I happened to be wearing my new hat, a black sheath dress and high-heeled, ankle-strapped black patent shoes (which made me over six feet tall). Because I was seated in the front row, I hadn't seen her. As usual, I entered into the discussion a lot. This woman noticed me, and after class asked someone, "Who is *that*?" She remarked that she wondered if I was a model or actress. She was informed that I was the associate pastor's wife.

Later she spoke to Victor and asked for some church literature. He said that if she would come by our home the next day, he would have just what she wanted. Victor didn't usually bother to tell me this type of thing, which was typical of his lack of communication.

The next day was rat-cage-cleaning-day, and the boys and I wore old junky clothes. I was in faded and torn pedal pushers, baggy blouse not tucked in, and barefoot. Some weeks earlier I had caught a large king snake near our home, brought it home to tame as a pet, and our neighbor built us another cage. On cleaning day we always took the rats and snake out of their cages. We put the rats on the Ping-Pong table in the patio so we could vacuum the cages and put in fresh wood shavings. A couple of the braver rats sometimes jumped off the table onto the cement floor. Since I was afraid they'd hurt themselves, I had set them, as usual, on my head and shoulder. They were tame and liked this, so rat's toenails were tangling my hair.

This particular morning I had also hung the four-foot king snake around my neck while we were cleaning, so I was decked out with my menagerie when the doorbell rang. Hearing it ring at that early hour was rather unusual, so I presumed it was my neighbor Shelley, wanting to borrow something or tell me the latest funny happening at her house full of kids and animals.

Quickly I went to the door and opened it, as an ear-shattering scream pierced my absentmindedness. It was the lady church visitor who had come to pick up the requested material. She was horrified by the rats and snake attached to my body. She started to apologize, thinking she had come to the wrong house. "Oh, I was looking for the pastor's home," she gasped.

"This is the right house. I'm Mrs. Leigh. Please excuse me just a moment." I removed the snake and rats, and returned to invite her in. Later on we became very good friends and laughed hilariously over the event. She said the contrast made the shock far worse--seeing me in my grungies and fauna the next day after looking like I'd stepped out of Vogue magazine the day before. She discovered that I was a down-to-earth, toes-in-the-mud sort of person in reality, and not a sophisticated touch-me-not.

12

AGHAST

W e desperately needed a second car, so Victor found an old Chevrolet for a hundred dollars. It was horrible looking, but ran pretty well. We paid Shelley's husband to spray-paint it blue for us. We bought new seat-covers for it, but the ceiling and door lining was hanging in shreds, which I just cut off with scissors and left the gaping holes. I was so ashamed of that car; I wanted to hide my face when driving it. But there was no other car available when Victor was using our better one, and driving it was preferable to never going anywhere.

I am embarrassed that my husband can't provide something better than this yucky thing, yet proud that he can find good buys and isn't materialistic. It also helps keep me humble.

Victor also bought a second-hand go-cart for the boys. It wasn't fancy, but its motor ran well. I felt a little self-conscious sitting down close to the ground and driving down the road in this "thing" with the kids beside me, but I didn't feel embarrassed, like I did driving the beat-up car, even after it got painted. At least with the go-cart I was helping our boys and neighborhood kids have fun and teaching them how to drive it.

Suddenly a new medical problem developed. After a doctor's appointment, it was determined Victor had to have hemorrhoid surgery. He was barely recuperated enough two weeks later to go away for camp meeting preparation. I was concerned he might have a relapse and wanted him to know I cared and was thinking of him, so wrote to him.

Hello Darling Victor,

I miss you so this evening. About an hour ago I returned from water skiing. I nearly backed out from going because Alan was sick, so had to pay a baby sitter. Gordon McBride said he needed me to help drive the boat while he helped other skiers learn. The lake was rough—white caps in the first section--but smoother on up the lake. Fortunately the water was comfortably warm. I couldn't help remembering the sheer delight on your face the last time we went together when you sped back and forth across the wake. Today I tried to barely start the feel of jumping—just a teensy bit—but not so as anyone else would see it. I didn't want to make a fool of myself. You are far better than I am at this sport.

Just had to tell you you're missed—especially now at bedtime—last night too. Hope you're managing to get smooth enough food and your "behind" still is improving. Wish I had your "before." Can't get it out of my mind. Glad we were together Saturday night anyway. Sorry I've been probably irritating, frustrating, or finicky-acting the last few occasions. I guess I've just been tired— with being up with the boys, etc. But I'll get over it, never fear. I love you more than ever, and wish I could snuggle up right now so you could give me a potently warm kiss or two or three.

I doubt if I'll come up for camp meeting until Sunday or Monday. Alan is on anti-biotic. His cough is still tight.

Hugs and kisses from your contented
(when you're here) wife,
Judy

Practicing both piano and voice regularly in order to be on faculty recitals and do accompanying and vocal solos kept me busy and mentally focused much of the time. One particularly enjoyable diversion was performing, with another faculty member, the two-piano arrangement of Saint Saen's "Carnival of the Animals." At the performance, Victor read aloud, at the appropriate places, the humorous poem by Ogden Nash which describes the animals portrayed in the composition.

This year I also had a larger load of piano and voice students than previously, both at home and at school. This was deliberately planned so I wouldn't feel the painful lack of warmth and friendship in our marriage. Each time I tried to talk about problems in our relationship or home, Victor still walked wordlessly out of the room, or else said he didn't want to talk more. That hurt deeply, but I wanted to be a good wife so struggled to repress my feelings, which took a toll on my life. Ill health crept up gradually until even the joints in my fingers started to hurt. Was I getting arthritis? I began to feel weak and depressed. I had been on "the pill" for a long time, and since Victor didn't want a vasectomy, I decided to get an IUD (intra-uterine device for contraception).

One Friday the doctor put in the IUD. He told me ahead of time that it would feel like a Mack truck, and it did! But I managed not to yell, and I got up and drove home. The following night, Saturday, we ate pizza and I woke up about midnight with a horrible pain in my middle-- like I was having menstrual cramps, but it wasn't my period. At first I thought it must have been the pizza, but eventually figured it must be the IUD, as it got progressively worse. When daylight arrived Sunday, I called the doctor, telling him I was in horrible pain. It was like I was in very advanced labor, except the pain wouldn't stop for rest like labor pains did. He told me to come to the emergency room, and he immediately removed the IUD.

After I had maybe a half hour of rest, the doctor returned to my cubicle and asked, "Do you feel better now?"

"No, I don't," was my honest answer.

After returning two or three more times over the space of an hour or so, and understanding that I felt no better, the doctor told me to go home, and I soon would. From Sunday until Tuesday I became more and more agonized. The pain was excruciating!

Tuesday evening I was finally admitted to the hospital. It was determined there was a terrible infection, so I was put on antibiotic and confined to bed. Victor asked the church to have special prayer for me on Wednesday night and again on the weekend.

From Tuesday to Saturday I was extremely ill, but felt a *tiny bit* better on Saturday. That afternoon some people from church came to visit me. I didn't know them well and wasn't really ready for visitors, but no one asked me what I wanted. These particular visitors didn't have much finesse, and stayed and stayed and stayed! They may have thought they were helping keep me from boredom. The nurse repeatedly took my temperature and checked on me frequently while they were in the room, but didn't suggest they leave. Finally I told them I didn't feel well and couldn't talk any more. My fever had zipped way up again.

A surgeon was called in to check me that night, and he ordered a stronger antibiotic. Returning next morning, he started examining me again, but suddenly sort of jumped back and let out a loud "Oh!" Instantly he looked remorseful and apologized, "Oh, I am so very sorry!" Although he was obviously embarrassed, he exclaimed, "I'm so sorry to startle you, but there's something in there the size of a *baseball* that wasn't there yesterday."

The infection had localized, and it was decided they should go in vaginally and drain the abscess. Victor was called to come to the hospital and sign papers so the procedure could be done. He came, did what he was asked to do, and *without visiting me, went home to sleep*!

As the surgery progressed, the doctor found the situation much worse than he thought, and decided to open me up abdominally. Victor was hurriedly called *again* to the hospital to sign more papers, then *without checking on me, he returned home again to sleep*! **KAREN: SAME PHRASE AS BEFORE. SLEEP WAS AN ESCAPE!**

A massive pus pocket about eight by three inches was discovered in my abdomen. It had sort of walled itself off from everything else. Little by little they put packing around it until they were able to lift it out unbroken. The operation took over four hours. My belly was poured full of the strongest antibiotic available. After a culture was done, it was declared to be an e-coli infection.

A couple days after surgery, my bed had been adjusted to a half-sitting position when Victor came to visit. He'd been there about five minutes when I suddenly gasped, "I think I'm going to pass out. Would you please put my bed down?" He immediately stood and cranked it down, while commenting it was time for him to leave. After a quick kiss he walked out!

I was in a four-person ward lying flat on my back, when I realized I was still about to pass out. Across from me, where I could see her, was another patient--the young, beautiful woman who had my same first name, Judy. We had gotten quite well acquainted before my surgery, and I had told her about Steve, his occasional seizures, and how I helped him concentrate and *will* his mind to stay conscious, so he wouldn't go into a convulsion. At times it seemed I could keep him from passing out by asking him questions he would try to answer. Judy and I had also discussed cooking and recipes.

Calling softly to this other Judy, I weakly informed her, "I think I'm about to pass out." She jumped out of bed, yelled for a nurse and came to my bedside.

She urged, "Judy, talk to me! Concentrate! I want you to tell me right now how you made that bean dish." It was a struggle, but I forced myself to keep talking—to *will* myself to stay conscious in order to comply. That's the last thing I remember.

Much later, when I began to regain consciousness, I could hear and understand *some* of what people were saying. Apparently they were afraid I was dying. I mentally fought for my life and silently prayed.

Later I heard a woman ask, "Why is she talking so much?"

Another woman responded, "Shut up! She can hear you."

Evidently partially regaining some consciousness, I verbally continued wherever I had left off talking to the other Judy, fighting to stay conscious and alive. Eventually opening my eyes, I saw blurry people all around me. Although hearing their voices, I couldn't respond. *Maybe I'm dying.* That's when I silently told the Lord, *I'm ready to go. It's OK. But I really don't want to die. If it's Your will, please help me to live. But I'm willing to die, and I am ready.*

It was a *beautiful* time that I remember--sensing wonderful peace and love surrounding me, I wasn't afraid to die. Since that profound experience, I've never been afraid of dying. Apparently lapsing into unconsciousness again, I remember nothing more.

On being awakened some time later, I asked why my feet were higher than my head. The nurse explained that the foot of the bed was propped up on wood blocks to keep blood flowing to my brain. I was barely aware a lab tech took blood samples when all went black again.

It was discovered my potassium was extremely low, and an intravenous solution was prescribed. A nurse started poking my arm with a needle, and the pain seemed far worse than before. Over and over she tried to get the needle into my vein.

I will not tense up. I will just let it hurt.

Looking at the nurse's face, I saw huge beads of perspiration appear on her forehead, as her hands started shaking. She looked like she was going to burst into tears as she struggled to do her duty. Suddenly she stood up and ran out of the room. (Later I was told that my veins had collapsed.)

After a few minutes another nurse came, was unsuccessful, and they decided to do a "cut-down" on my foot. Finally they got the IV going there.

During the night I coughed, which jerked me awake. Now something didn't feel right with the IV in my foot. Did my cough yank the needle out of my vein? I pushed the call button and asked the attendant to check the IV because it felt different since I coughed. She looked at it and huffily remarked, "Everything is all right!" as though angry that I was bothering her, and soon gave me a Demerol shot that knocked me out again.

Hours passed. Finally I awakened because--*oh-h-h--my foot feels much worse! It is propped up and uncovered and—Oh No! It is the size of two feet!* The IV liquid had gone into the tissue instead of the vein. Now there really was a problem!

After much consultation and several people coming in to check my foot, someone finally got another IV started in the back of my left hand. A repeat shot of Demerol. More hours pass. I woke up to see someone standing by my bed. A different shift of workers had come, and everybody was checking everything. I said, "My hand hurts. Please—look at it." A nurse took one look, left the room and called others in. Then a doctor arrived and immediately took out the IV.

"I'm really sorry," he apologized, "but somehow air has gotten into your vein." I looked at my hand and saw a space over an inch long that was swollen and hard as a rock which looked like a stick of wood under my skin. The doctor explained that "we all have to be extremely careful," because if air bubbles reached my heart or lungs I could die. My left arm was fastened to a board, which was then tied to the rail on the left side of my bed. A special heating pad containing warm, circulating water was put around that hand, and I was told *not to move my hand for any reason!*

Finally an IV was inserted in my *right* arm, and it was also fastened to a board, which was tied to the right side of my bed.

After another seven days, I was able to leave the hospital, out of danger, but very weak. Some neighbors and friends had taken care of the boys while I was away, but now Victor's mother arrived to help. She was overwhelmed with caring for three boys (our two plus Fred), so called her stepson's home and informed Nate and Larell of my serious illness. Soon Larell, Fred's mother, drove to Arizona and took Fred back to California with her.

My father had decided to take some summer classes at a seminary in Michigan. After hearing of my illness, he and mother invited me to spend the summer with them, which delighted me. They planned their travel route to include Phoenix, and soon picked me up to ride cross-country in the back seat of their car with them. Mother was certain she could nurse me back to health. We drove for a couple of days, finally arriving at Andrews University in Berrien Springs, Michigan. Since the friend's home which they had rented for the summer wouldn't be available for two or three days, we stayed in the dormitory.

We barely were settled in one room when the next day I began to have severe abdominal pain again. My left ovary and tube had been removed during the last surgery, but now I hurt on my right side. I knew it wasn't my appendix, because that was removed at age fourteen. I asked my father to read to me, so I could ignore the pain. But it worsened, and got so bad I couldn't listen any more. I jerked the whole bed each time I felt the intense, stabbing pain. The following day, after a doctor's examination, I was put on another antibiotic for a very large and infected right ovary.

Daddy fixed some sort of a little wall in the back yard of our rented house where I could lie naked, taking a ten or fifteen minute "sunbath" twice every day. They knew I needed vitamin D from sunlight as well as its other beneficial effects. Mother became my nurse, nutritionist and healing supervisor, stuffing me with all kinds of fresh vegetable and fruit juices, wheat germ, vitamins and whatever she could determine might help me get well and build up my health.

Before I had left home, Victor hadn't mentioned anything about plans for a vacation with his sons, but it wasn't long until he decided to take them to a conference-owned, primitive cabin for a few days. I finally found strength to write Victor, and the following was his first belated response letter to me since I had last seen the three of them.

Dear Judy,

I love those syrupy letters. I hope I don't drown. It's 5:45 a.m. and I couldn't sleep because today is the day we go to the mountains, and I keep thinking of all the things to take. It's been 112 degrees here, but I'm sure it will be cool enough for jackets up there, at least in the morning and evening. These two letters I'm sending along are uncensored, and the boys had no help except the dictionary when Alan wanted to spell a word. Steve's letter is already sealed so I'll not open it to read it.

I need to pack so I'll write more later. Kiss the folks for me and tell them thank you for the $100 check. I don't see how they could afford to do that.

Love you heaps and sand dunes,
Victor

Steve's personally hand-typed letter:

Dear Mommy.

I Miss you! I want you to get well soon, so that you can go HORSE BACK RIDING too. We are going to have lots of fun, but most of all I LOVE YOU. Please say hello for me to Grandpa and Grandma.

Good-by.
Steve LEIGH

Alan's personally hand-typed letter:

Dear Mommy.

I miss you. I saw a picture of a Muskrat today. We
went swimming at Saguaro Lake and we had a good time
there too. I hope you will get better soon so you can ride
on the go-cart. I am planning to save up my money so that
I can buy a new motor for it. We are going to the cabin
and it has a little stream going past it.

Love and kisses from
Alan

[I felt greatly rewarded for the effort I had been putting forth daily,
before I became ill, to teach both boys how to type correctly, using a
regular typing class book to help them learn. I decided to do this primarily
for Steve, to help his poor coordination, but Alan wanted to join in on the
fun also. The letters were my reward. The boys were ten and eight years
old. Their joy in knowing how to type with correct fingering long before
their friends had learned was their personal reward.]

Another letter from Victor came in the same batch:

Dear Sweetheart,

I'm sorry my letter was so short this morning. We
arrived at the cabin about 1:30 pm. after taking two
wrong roads. We just finished our supper after playing
in the river all afternoon. The water is so cold it numbs
your feet, and it took all the will power I could muster to
lie down in it for two seconds. So we skipped rocks and
waded and played with a beach ball, letting it float down
stream. The river is very clear and beautiful. Every thirty
or forty feet there's a small cascade or falls.

The pines are quite large, and wild flowers are in full
bloom--some large yellow ones I have never seen, Indian
Paint Brush, and some others, the names of which elude
me. We'll have to sneak off up here sometime, just we
two. The cabin is seventeen miles from the nearest paved

road. That reminds me—how am I going to get this letter mailed? Oh well, you didn't want this letter till next week anyway, did you? The boys just called to tell me the water's boiling, so I'll have to do the dishes.

Later. This cabin is very modern; it has running water (about 15 feet away) but it doesn't run up hill. It's not safe to drink so we have to boil it.

We saw two deer on the way up. One was a big gray doe that looked blue from a distance. The other was a smaller doe and was medium beige. It will soon be sundown and I want to take a walk with the boys. Before I sign off, I'd like to have a little of that syrup I was talking about this morning—a nice smoocheroony on those ruby lips. Stop talking, Judy, and kiss me good night. I love you.

Your hubby,
Victor

Oh how thrilled I was that Victor finally spent some real "fathering time" with Steve and Alan.

About three days after I received these letters, Victor told me by phone that the conference had asked us to move to a new location, Flagstaff, Arizona, where he was to pastor a small mountain church. We agreed he should immediately put our house up for sale.

Dear Sweetheart,

It was so nice to talk with you, but I was sorry to hear that you've been sick again. We came back from the mountains especially for the Father's Day Picnic. It turned out there was such a dust storm that not many came. I'm still blowing dust out of my nose.

No one has come to look at the house in the three weeks we have had the ad in the paper, so it looks like we'll have to put it in the hands of a real estate agent. I'll wait till you get back, but we should do it soon.

I surely do miss you. Hope your trouble is all over by the time you get this letter. Well, it's 8:30 a.m. and the boys are just now waking up, so I'll sign off for now. I love you heaps and heaps.

Your lover,
Victor

Dad's summer school ended, we made the trip back home, and because we had a buyer for our house, Victor was already preparing to move. I was much better, so was able to help with packing.

Rummaging in the garage to organize things, I remembered a box of exotic flower bulbs that I had personally dug from our back yard after we moved in, because Victor didn't like them scattered "here and there" as the previous owner had planted them. There were several kinds of narcissus, tulips, daffodils, hyacinths, crocus, and some rare iris and lilies. He had then wanted to get rid of them, but I begged to keep them if I dug them up. I had wanted to re-plant them at the proper time in a little plot of ground in front of the house that Victor had promised I could use. Now that we were moving, I wanted to be sure we took them to our next place, but they were not to be found.

I asked Victor what happened to them and he retorted, "I threw them out when you were in the hospital. You *knew* I didn't want them!" I calculated the worth, if I were to go out and buy them, to be about $150.00 and secretly cried. My hours of work were trashed. Worst of all, my desires were trashed! **KAREN: IT'S NOT OKAY TO BE DISAPPOINTED, SAD, HURT…**

Then I couldn't find the wheeled, folding grocery cart I had bought with my own carefully saved money. I had started walking to the grocery store to save money on gas. I went again to Victor and asked where the new grocery cart was. He looked angry that I bothered him. "It was in the way. I threw it out while you were gone."

Did he think or hope I was going to die, so he could just get rid of all the things he didn't want? Did he really miss me while I was gone like he told me in a letter, or was that a lie? Do any items I own have value to him? If he doesn't value my personal belongings or my feelings, does he value me at all? Obviously not! Ohhhhh, Ouch!!!

Life is too important to let it be ruined by things that cannot be remedied. I choose to let go of the hurt, forgive, and concentrate on the future. I will now embrace my life joyfully.

Before school started, we managed to get moved to the smaller, high altitude community of Flagstaff, AZ, an hour and a half away. Then I continued making monthly car trips to my doctor in Phoenix for nearly a year before I was released as "well."

In this mountain town we rented a nice home with a double-sided fireplace that gave heat both in the living room and in the kitchen/family room. Steve was ten and a half, and Alan turned nine soon after they enrolled in the little one room parochial school next door to the church. Morton Morris was the outstanding teacher who enriched our boy's lives in so many ways during the next two years.

I became the self-appointed "Community Services" leader in the church and did most of the sorting, washing, mending and organizing of donated clothing, which the church made available to needy people. I considered our own family among "the needy," so was able to get most of the boys' clothes from donated ones and bought very few. I altered clothes to fit Steve and "let them out" as he grew. Then I'd do it all over again with the same clothes for Alan. Any clothing that was still in decent condition after it was outgrown was returned to the church supply to give away.

Our kitchen stove had an extra-large oven where I baked nine loaves of bread at a time, sharing some with others. One day I discovered in a local newspaper some recipes for comparatively large quantities of food types that could be altered in various ways as desired and frozen for storage. Using these recipes, I made my own pie crust mix, cookie mix, and biscuit mix and stored them in tins in our large, second-hand freezer. I kept three big, empty peanut butter jars in the freezer. Into each I put leftovers that would be appropriate for (1) fruit punch, (2) soup, (3) vegetarian "meat" loaf. When full I'd improvise to make a delicious "new" loaf or soup or drink. The leftover juice from canned fruit is delicious in a drink. Pieces of dried bread or leftover beans put through a meat grinder can be added to other ingredients for a loaf. Even the juice from canned olives can be added to soup or home-cooked chili. I saved every crumb or drop of leftovers because I wanted to make-do on the amount of money we had. I made crackers, cinnamon rolls, hot-dog and burger buns "from scratch."

Friends who lived at a lower elevation invited us every year to come and pick grapefruit from their trees. We'd bring back large boxes full, and the boys would squeeze many quarts of juice on our power squeezer and store it in our freezer.

I cut squares of varying sizes of cloth from outgrown and worn out jeans, corduroy pants or other heavy material, and pieced them together in a pleasing design. From this I upholstered a couple chairs and made some throw-cushions and a picnic blanket.

I began teaching a few music students and soon started taking voice lessons from a Northern Arizona University teacher. Inspiration filled me to return to school and work toward getting my teaching credentials. A psychology class was required, but the only one available at the time was for graduate students who had previously studied psychology. When I told the teacher I'd never taken *any* class in psychology, she said she'd help me, so "go for it."

That University summer class met only one day a week in the evening. On the first day of class the thirty of us were assigned several chapters to read. When we returned the following week, our teacher announced, "Divide yourselves into small groups. I want each group to pick a different section of what has been assigned, and then a person from each group will present a discussion on what you have learned."

She then sat down at her desk and said no more! Nobody did anything! Five or more minutes passed as everyone squirmed and felt uncomfortable.

I picked this class because I want to learn, so I spoke up, suggesting how many groups we might have and the number of people in each, and I facilitated this division. When no one else disagreed or contributed suggestions, I described how to divide the material we had studied. I had each group choose who was to be their leader and decide how they wanted to present their part. The class then progressed well as the teacher sat and observed. I felt energized to discover I could just take charge and do it.

One day my teacher and I happened to walk up some stairs together and she said, "Judy, you've *got* to get a doctorate."

Genuinely surprised, I asked, "A doctorate? In what? Psychology?"

166

"Whatever you *want* to study. But you've *got* to get your doctorate!" She sounded like it was very important that I really hear her.

"Why do you say that?" Nobody had ever suggested that to me before.

She suddenly stopped part way up the stairs and pointed directly at my head. "Because you have the ability! You are very capable of getting a doctorate, and you *deserve it.*"

I love that! Should I really believe her? Am I really capable of getting a doctorate? It is exciting to know someone has that much confidence in me. Maybe I can do it.

I treasured that compliment. But by the next day I told myself: *I must never get my doctorate in anything, although the idea is exciting and tempting. Since my husband has only a Master's degree, I shouldn't get a degree beyond what he has. I am sure he would resent it terribly.*

Before the semester ended, there was one special project we were assigned: write about and then verbally report on how we had handled some student, social challenge or class problem, and what we learned or hoped to learn from it. I wrote about Lucy Chilson, who had previously been my voice student at the boarding school where we were the year we married, and who later lived with us for a while as a baby-sitter.

I told about how I had handled all of the frequently dramatic situations that developed with her through the years. Once, soon after I met her at school, she had hidden in the room where I taught private lessons when I had stepped out to go to the restroom. She had actually moved the upright piano which was sitting corner-wise—not flat against the wall— and squeezed into the small space behind it, hiding for some time while I taught another student. Previously she had primed that student to ask me what I thought of her, Lucy, so she could listen to my response. Another time she had sneaked up behind me as I was rehearsing the choir, and suddenly stuck a live snake in my face. Little did she know I liked snakes and had caught many of them myself previously, some to take to school to scare my male classmates! Another tale which I included was about when she came home very drunk, and I physically tried to restrain her from going out to drive her car, which resulted in both of us rolling down a long stairway.

I had been terribly afraid of that psychology class, but I ended up getting the top grade. Yeah!

In this mountain town we heated our house mostly with the double-sided fireplace. Victor had gotten permission from the Forest Service to cut wood before winter. The boys and I had helped him load and unload stacks of it, so we had plenty to burn. We cut our own Christmas tree, and Victor made a stand for it. We didn't own many decorations, and didn't want to spend money on more, so we made our own. I cut paper towel cardboard tubes into half-inch rings. We covered these with aluminum foil or other shiny paper I had saved, and hung them on the tree with red yarn. We took bright colored pieces of old crayons, melted them down in old cans and swabbed waxy designs on shiny gold colored "flats" from used canning jar lids. We punched holes in them with an ice pick and hung them on the tree. We also strung popcorn and made other paper decorations with construction paper or used gift-wrap paper that I had saved. Being snowed in generated creativity and many fun times.

The Big Snowstorm, reportedly the worst in over a hundred years in Flagstaff, blew in about a year after we arrived. Eight feet of snow fell in one week. Three separate storms hit, one right after the other. There was no time for snow to melt between storms, which caused havoc. Several large buildings with flat roofs caved in. The grocery store we frequented had to resort to using twelve-by-twelve-inch wooden pillars to prop up the roof every ten feet or so. Buckets to catch the melted snow under ceiling cracks were everywhere. Even several homes caved in, and strong, willing children were earning good money shoveling snow from roofs.

We decided that because of the continuing snowfall, we'd better shovel the roof of our rented home. We put up a ladder and Victor and I worked for hours. We discovered snow changes acoustics. From our rooftop we could converse with neighbors on their rooftops several houses away without raising our voices. But anyone on the ground close to our house could scarcely get our attention, even with shouting. When our boys called us we couldn't hear, so I went down and checked on them every little while. At lunch time we came down and fixed hot chocolate and sandwiches, then returned to shovel more.

When we first started in the morning, the snow on the roof was armpit deep. When we finally got to the other end of the roof, it was already a foot and a half deep behind us, and it kept on coming. When we finished, we couldn't find the ladder to get down. We had completely buried it, and we literally walked off the roof on snow, and then had to tunnel into our front porch. The next day Victor shoveled the roof a second time.

We tried to clear the driveway, but were no match for that project in one day. We shoveled and stamped a narrow "trail" over the snow to the "street," which was buried. Snow covered the top of our six-foot back fence. The boys had a "whirly-bird" merry-go-round with little seats on it, and before the snow got so deep it completely covered it, each seat was topped by a snow-tower several feet tall.

The roads were all snow-filled so that no cars traveled for at least three days. Only snowmobiles and helicopters could move around. Trains were held up for more than thirty hours. The airport was closed. No mail could be delivered or trash removed. Even after the roads were plowed, mailboxes by the street were long buried. Soon there appeared buckets, wastebaskets or boxes tied to a broom or mop handle stuck in the snow with hand printed signs "Mailbox" and the house number.

During the worst of the road blockage a couple of neighbor men came to our door and asked if we needed anything from the market. Victor joined them, and soon several other men helped solicit the neighborhood for needs, and they all hiked a mile through deep snow to the market, pulling sleds and snow saucers, bringing back badly needed supplies. After the storm, foot-thick icicles appeared from roof to ground. It was impossible to get to church for three weeks.

Steve had almost reached his twelfth birthday. A day or so before the storm I noticed he looked thinner. I had checked his weight a few weeks before, so I asked him to weigh himself again. He was five pounds less than a few weeks before. How surprising, because he was eating more than he ever had. After a meal he'd ask, "Mom, can I finish this up. Can I finish that?" He'd eat every smidgen of food that was left, and want more.

He also started waking up at night complaining of his legs itching terribly. His arms also itched. Then he started complaining of being terribly thirsty. During the storm he woke me up one night after midnight and said, "Mother, I am so, so, *so* thirsty!"

"Go get a drink of water," I sleepily suggested.

"I just finished drinking *three glassfuls!*" he said with exasperation.

Immediately I was wide awake, *shocked*, and wondered if he might have diabetes like Victor's sister Aimee has. Victor's parents had adopted her as a baby, and she became diabetic at age three. I didn't know of any blood relative who had diabetes.

Our heaviest snowfall came the same night I realized Steve was probably diabetic. I knew he *had* to get to a doctor, but no cars could travel! I started letting him eat all he wanted of salad and vegetables but no sugar and limited carbohydrates. I called his doctor immediately, and after three days of waiting for snowplows and all of us working to shovel our driveway, I was barely able to make it to the doctor's office and then to the hospital for tests. Victor stayed home with Alan.

After a five-hour glucose tolerance test, Steve's blood sugar was "off the charts." The doctor was amazed he was so alert instead of unconscious. Steve was asking all kinds of questions about everything in the laboratory where they tested him. "What's this for?" "How does that work?" He was intensely interested in anything he saw that he couldn't understand.

The doctor told me Steve must be hospitalized in order to get regulated on insulin. I asked if he could get a vegetarian diet while in the hospital.

The doctor threw up his hands. "Oh, my no! No one here knows how to do that! He *has* to eat meat!"

"Steve will probably refuse to eat any meat. We are vegetarians." I respectfully explained.

"He *must* eat meat! A diabetic can't *live* without eating meat!" the doctor declared.

I asked Steve if he would be willing to try eating meat.

He nearly yelled back, "Absolutely not!"

Then the doctor asked me if *I* knew where he could go. I answered, "A Seventh-day Adventist Hospital. They'll know how to give him a vegetarian diet."

"Where is the closest one?" he inquired.

I told him, "Loma Linda, California." Then I asked, "Do we have time to try to drive there?" I couldn't imagine having the money for the two of us to fly.

"Steve will probably not live that long, especially with the road conditions. He would die en route!" was the doctor's warning answer.

The trains were not moving yet, and the airport was still closed. The doctor said, "I'll call the airport." With his urging, they agreed to clear the runway for a small, four-passenger plane. They had just acquired new snow blowers and thought by late afternoon the runway would be usable.

We went home, and I packed for Steve, Alan and myself. Very carefully Victor drove us to the airport, with much prayer. We slipped and slid, and more than once nearly landed in a snow bank or off the edge of the road. Part of the road had been cleared specifically for us, but was either icy or slushy. It was terribly precarious.

Finally Steve, Alan and I were ensconced in the small airplane. I had to squelch my panic as it started to hurtle through what appeared to be a narrow tube between snow banks twenty or more feet high. It *seemed* like there was only a foot or two of clearance at the ends of the wings!

Loma Linda Hospital and Medical Center was located in the same town where I grew up, and my parents still lived there. They were to meet us at the tiny Tri-City Airport that was familiar to me. After flying a couple hours it became totally dark, and everyone but the pilot fell asleep.

Suddenly the pilot said, "I should be over the airport about now, but I don't see any runway lights. Do you know this area?"

I looked down, and in a few moments I recognized the main highway lights and oriented myself. "The airport should be right there, almost directly below us, but I don't see the runway lights either. My parents are supposed to meet me right there." I breathed a silent prayer as the pilot started circling lower. Mentally I searched my mind for the location of a different airport, but couldn't think of one I was able to locate. A minute or two passed and, praise God, blue lights along a runway flashed on and stayed on! Another circle and we landed safely, and my folks drove us directly to the hospital.

It took about two weeks for Steve to get his diet regulated and for me to learn how and when to give insulin shots. While we were away Victor wrote:

Dear Sweetheart,

I miss you very much. I should have written more often. I know it must be a nerve strain to keep constant watch on Steve and to learn all the things to do for him. I do hope things are still going fine. When the "Queen bee" is away, this place is like a tomb. Tippy [our dog] misses you too. All he can do is whine, eat and sleep.

Another snowstorm came yesterday, but the temperature is supposed to soar up to 45 degrees today. I hope it doesn't snow anymore till spring.

Since we postponed the revival meetings until February 28, I feel I should definitely stay by a few days in order to organize the visitation and distribution of handbills. I'll start driving Saturday night.

Well, it's time to fix lunch. At least I've had three good meals since you left—two at Morris's house and one at the banquet Sunday night. Do you think it is at all possible for you to play for the meetings when you return, or should I get someone else? Who?

Have been reading your love letters again. What a sweetheart--and beautiful too! Love you, love you, love you.

Your (sterile) lover boy,
Victor

P.S. Squeeze Steve and Alan for me. Now kiss 'em both. I'll see you soon.

I especially noticed the word "sterile" in his letter ending. *Thank you Victor! Now I can get off "the pill" that I started again since I don't dare risk an IUD any more.*

During that half-month while Steve and I experienced medical challenges, the roads finally were cleared sufficiently; Victor could make the long drive to my parents' home, relax for a day, and bring the three of us back to the mountains.

We now bought a used VW mini-bus as our second car and often used it as a school bus. Victor or I took our boys and picked up a number of other students, both going to and coming home from school. Sometimes there would be as many as seventeen in that little VW bus. It's a wonder a policeman didn't stop us. Victor and I traded off as "bus driver" with the teacher. Sometimes Morton and I would be riding alone in the car, because I'd take him to his house before I returned home. He was a very attractive man a little younger than I. His wife worked full time as a nurse but also was an outstanding musician and pianist. I admired her very much.

I agreed to teach classroom music once a week *without pay* at the one-room school, because there was no money in the budget for extras. I wanted our sons, as well as the other students, to get good music training in school.

The kids all loved Mr. Morris, and he took them on frequent field trips. He was also the Pathfinder leader in this town. "Pathfinders" is a worldwide club for youth similar to the Scouts. One month he planned a camp-out for his group of twenty-some youth and invited Victor and me to go with them. He needed a female to supervise the girls. Victor agreed to go with me, apparently happy with the plan. The day came that we were to leave, and I was all packed for the four of us. Suddenly, about an hour before we were to leave, Victor decided he wouldn't go. He just refused, and Victor said I was to tell Mr. Morris, because he was too busy to make the phone call!

When I called Morton to inform him, he was really upset! That left him and me as the only adults. It embarrassed him that just the two of us would be the only adults, and it infuriated him that Victor had let him down. He asked me, "Why won't Victor go?"

Remembering the time Victor decided the last minute not to go with us to Brigantine Island, I also felt not only embarrassment and anger, but also fear. I answered, "I don't have any idea! He won't tell me. He just doesn't want to go. You ask him!"

But Victor had gone to "run some errands" and was not available to speak on the phone when Mr. Morris called. Morton and his wife were *both* angry, and I was livid! Later, privately, Morton asked me, "What is Victor trying to do, set us up for an affair?"

My memories were making me tremble. "I don't know, but it sure seems like it."

"Please don't think I'm angry with you if I hardly speak to you or look at you on this trip," he advised. "If I do, the kids will try to make something out of it. I don't want to start any rumors."

With relief I agreed. So Morton insisted the girls and boys were to be kept somewhat separated the whole camping trip (which was hardly fair to them) to prevent any gossip about the two of us.

Several times after that it seemed Victor was *again* trying to set us up for an affair—so much so that one day Morton told me a *second time* he was suspicious that was true. He also said there was *nothing* that would make him give in to an affair, because he was happily married. However he admitted being attracted to me, as I was to him. He even said that if things had been different, and we had met years before, maybe he might have wanted to marry me. We both solidly agreed, however, there would be no affair! My anxiety was released. **KAREN: SO NO ONE CONFRONTED VICTOR?**

VICTOR: That's right. The idea of setting up Judy for an affair hadn't crossed my mind. If I had been confronted, I would have felt "picked on."

One night Victor and I were to go out with other church members for the yearly "Christmas Ingathering" program, soliciting door-to-door as well as costumed carol singing, but the temperature was only fifteen degrees. This particular night I was getting over a cold, and Victor sounded a bit concerned about whether or not I should go out. He asked, "Are you *sure* you're going to be OK?" He asked two or three different questions that showed he *cared* whether I was well enough. I was so amazed that tears came to my eyes as I *thanked him for asking*. He *does* care after all. He *does care!* That one incident filled me with such joy and happiness that I felt appreciated and blessed for weeks. For a while I felt engulfed in his warmth.

An older couple started coming to our church fairly often. They lived at Grand Canyon, about two hours away. The first week they came, we invited them to our home for dinner after church. Gradually, as we got to know them, we invited them to come Friday afternoon and stay the weekend so they wouldn't have to drive the long distance home at night time.

One Friday I had been rushing around to get the house all cleaned and cooking done before they arrived. I had soaked dried garbanzos overnight and cooked them with a delicious herb-tomato sauce in the pressure cooker. I hadn't yet removed the pressure cap, and because I felt rushed, I absentmindedly forgot to wait for the pressure to return to normal. I tried to take off the lid and it was "stuck." Mindlessly I jerked it extremely hard, and as the lid came loose, the remaining pressure blew the lid off. I had a good hold, so I didn't drop either the lid or the kettle full of garbanzos, but some of the boiling contents splattered on the ceiling, stove and floor. At that moment our friends arrived. Fortunately I wasn't burned, so after welcoming them, I started cleaning up my mess, while trying to stifle my giggling. Mr. Brown exclaimed, "Well, it looks like *you* have your life in control. You're certainly able to handle emergencies!" I smiled and thanked him, glad that some of my father's calm patience had rubbed off on me. The remaining garbanzos were delicious!

There was rain for a little while almost every day throughout the summer in this delightfully refreshing mountain town. Our big garden grew all kinds of wonderful vegetables. The boys helped their dad with the gardening and helped me with the cooking. We picked fresh peas and the boys helped shell them. They loved pulling up brightly colored beets and carrots. We always had more home grown vegetables than we could eat, so we often shared them with neighbors or fellow church members.

One of the families in our church had six children and a small salary. For our frequent church potlucks they always brought one small bowl of beans. I think they were always hungry, because they loaded their plates high and returned for seconds and thirds. I always brought lots of food and was glad they got a good balanced church potluck meal at least two or three times a month.

I was still giving both of our boys piano lessons, and now I added *regular* typing lessons. I knew both would help Steve get more practice in finger and hand coordination. I started them both ironing their shirts and later taught them how to sew on buttons that had come off their clothing. Alan did really well with piano. Steve had a hard time with coordination and had to memorize everything so he could watch his fingers, otherwise he couldn't make them work. I made the acquaintance of a man who was a hairstylist. He offered to cut, color and style my hair in exchange for piano lessons for his daughters. His wife was a talented seamstress and did clothing alterations and made some new things for me, also in exchange for the lessons. It was a good arrangement.

Recently a ski resort called the Snow Bowl had been built near Flagstaff; so some former short ski runs near town had been converted into sled runs. The city park contained one of these delightful areas. Our family took turns going down this rather long, steep hill several times on our sled. One day we happened to have the fastest sled on the hill, thanks to Sears Roebuck. Then someone told us about a snow-covered pile of rocks higher up which other sledders soon packed with more snow. They smoothed it and made it into a short, steep, drop-off from which to start the downhill run. I wanted to try it.

Soon I was hurtling down that hill at such high speed, I realized I would go farther than any of the other sleds had gone. Suddenly some little children ran out in front of me. They didn't see me even though I yelled at them. I was scared I would injure or even kill them, so made a split second decision to tilt the sled and try to turn it off the path. I held tight to the handles, jerked to the left, almost rolling over, but continued plummeting on out of control. I missed the kids, but the sled and I kept plowing at high speed at a slight angle to the run. At the bottom I sailed airborne across a diagonal plowed dirt road and flew into a snow and dirt bank on the opposite side. When my chest painfully hit the top of the bank, I was flipped around and stopped so abruptly it felt like my brain was pounded against my skull. What a headache! I watched my sled cartwheel some distance past me. My light colored car coat was mud-covered and a couple of buttons were ripped off the front.

After catching my breath, I retrieved my sled and said to myself, *I am going to go right back and do it a second time, otherwise I'll always be afraid of trying new things.* So with my bruised chest and torn, muddied coat, that's what I did. Kids ran in front of me again, I jerked and rolled as before, but managed to turn more to the left so I didn't fly across the road. That was enough excitement for one day.

There was a wonderful, huge, gently sloping meadow higher up in the mountains near the Snow Bowl that used to be a ski run. Our family drove up there a number of times, taking inner tubes on which to slide in the snow. Here we purposely planned when to roll off so we wouldn't continue for a mile or so.

On the opposite side of this meadow was a forest of aspen trees that were so intriguing and beautiful at every season. I was curious to explore it when the snow wouldn't hinder our getting there. One fall day I persuaded Victor and our sons to investigate. We walked across the huge meadow to inspect the white-trunked trees arrayed in autumn color. The floor of the forest was several inches deep with golden leaves, branches were still thickly laden with yellow, and the breeze was strong enough so the air around and above us was a fairyland of fluttering and dancing gold, like clouds of butterflies flitting in every direction. It was dreamlike and unforgettable. My heart and mind cried out praise to God for his exceptionally gorgeous creation and our opportunity to be "enveloped" in it for a while that day. I could scarcely stop talking about all the beauty and excitement for days afterward

Many times I took the boys for outings in our little VW bug (not the bus) and explored dirt roads in the mountains. We'd drive until we couldn't go any farther--the road just ended. Sometimes we'd be in "the middle of nowhere" up as high as we could go—driving over rocks and ditches until we could scarcely get turned around. The VW had a "pan" which kept the underneath part of the car from getting damaged. We'd get out and walk or play awhile and then I'd ask, "Which way do we go to get home?" It would be quite a game to see who could lead us back without getting us lost. It taught all three of us to be very observant.

One day Victor, Morton and our landlord, a local dentist, climbed Humphrey's Peak, the highest of the San Francisco Peaks near Flagstaff. Its elevation was twelve thousand six hundred and thirty-three feet. Years later I wished I had gone with them. I didn't then know how much fun mountain climbing is.

Near our church was a high hill with a steep, smooth side that had formerly been a short ski run. Now Sheep's Hill was occasionally used for sledding. The church youth decided they wanted to have a moonlight party. We checked the almanac, and scheduled a night with full moon. A group of us went over in the late afternoon and took lanterns, hot chocolate, cookies, sandwiches, blankets, sleds, and a couple large truck inner tubes. A three-sided, roofed but floorless shelter with a table, some chairs and a fire-pit inside was a cozy and warm respite for snow-soaked, cold bodies.

The hill was too tall to try to take the sleds up even half way. So we put a lighted lantern on the ground to specify the farthest anyone was to go up. This was one of the most exciting evenings I ever spent, and I slid down just as much as any of the younger ones. It was marvelous in the moonlight.

Later, while most of us were inside the shelter serving and eating sandwiches, cookies and drinking hot chocolate, one of the older teenagers decided he wanted a faster, better ride and sneaked up a lot farther than the lantern marker. I happened to look out just in time to see him hurtle past, hit a bump, bounce high into the air and come down on his face into ice and snow. I gasped and yelled, "Help, someone is hurt!" as I took off running ahead of the others.

By the time I arrived at his motionless body, he started groaning, so I knew he was alive. A couple of us who were certified in Red Cross First Aid carefully checked him, discovering his broken glasses and badly bruised and skinned up face. The men gently carried him into the shelter and wrapped him in blankets. This was before cell phones and 911 calls. For a while he wouldn't let us try to carry him to the car, which was quite a long walk through the snow, so we comforted him in his shock, and warmed him to calm his violent chills. Eventually he agreed to let the strong ones carry him to the car, and he was taken to the hospital. Fortunately the injuries weren't life threatening, but took weeks to completely heal.

13

STRETCH

Victor was asked to move again within the same conference. It seems these moves came about every two years. He became Associate Pastor of a church in Phoenix, AZ. When we realized we were going to move, we started looking for a place to buy and came across a repossessed house that we both fell in love with. Immediately I started planning how to fix it up and redecorate. It was a "higher class" house than we had ever had before. There were so many things I was going to do. My spirits just soared because I had new and creative tasks to put my mind on. Then disappointment! We didn't get the house; somebody else got it ahead of us. I shed many tears. But eventually we found another place in Scottsdale we both liked and moved in.

After we got settled at this new location, I started teaching piano and voice lessons again at Thunderbird Academy where I had taught before, although we now lived even closer than we had before. I also taught classroom music for the elementary school on the same campus, as well as some more students at our home. Alan started French horn lessons in fifth grade, and I continued teaching him piano. Steve was in sixth grade and started clarinet lessons. He had such a hard time working his fingers on the piano that I let him quit. Clarinet was much easier for him and he loved playing it. He soon got quite good at playing by ear, besides learning to sight read and transpose well. Both boys seemed to really enjoy practicing, and we loved hearing the music they added to our home life.

This new church was fortunate to have a medical doctor who was also a fine musician. Doctor Lensky asked me to be the piano accompanist for both the adult and junior choir rehearsals he directed. The organist usually accompanied the adult choir in their performances.

A year or more after we arrived, I heard an interesting story about Dr. Lensky from his mother, who was also a member of our church. One day she shyly whispered to me, "When my son first heard you were going to come to this church, he told me he *dreaded* your arrival! He knew you would also want to be involved musically. He felt afraid, because he was *sure* you would try to boss him and tell him what to do. Just yesterday he told me how shocked and relieved he is that you haven't bossed him at all. Instead, he said you are a genuine joy to work with!" That both amused and pleased me.

I get the feeling that not only did my "reputation" precede me at our first church, after Victor finished seminary, but it also preceded my arrival here, and perhaps other places. There must be something about the way I look, stand, act, speak, move—whatever—that scares some people, or causes them to read me wrong. I'm stymied. At least the fear and dread Dr. Lensky had felt finally disappeared, and apparently caring and liking replaced it. Thanks be to God! **KAREN: TALL, STRONG WOMEN GET THESE REPUTATIONS.**

This conference also had yearly camp meeting at Prescott, AZ, in the mountains. Here, instead of tents, were solidly built small cabins where our family of four felt cozily at home. Although I loved homemaking and being a mother, I relished getting away to camp meeting and luxuriated in the social and mental stimulation of varying responsibilities there. One year I was president of the ministers' wives' club. I arranged for all the ladies to meet early each morning during camp meeting for devotions, study and training for the various situations and problems we shared.

As time went on, I became even more baffled by Victor's behavior. He often complained about many aspects of his life. It seemed he was always feeling "poor me." He wouldn't say those words, but that was his attitude. He wasn't satisfied with anything, but he didn't seem to know what he wanted to do differently. When I occasionally asked him what he'd *like to change* about his life, he'd say, "Whatever the conference wants me to do," or "Whatever God leads me to do." But he didn't seem to want, or know how, to look at his *own life* and decide for *himself* what interested him.

One of the pastors who had previously hired Victor as his associate had now become the local Conference President. One day he came to me and said, "Judy, what does Victor *want* from life? He seems so unhappy in his work! What is it he wants to *accomplish?* What do you perceive he *dreams* of doing? I've talked to him, but he doesn't give clear answers."

With a sigh, my answer was, "I wish I could answer that. I don't know. I *wish* I could tell you!"

Then this man also let out an even longer sigh. "I *try* and *try* to find a place for him to be happy. I'm *baffled*, trying to figure out what *Victor wants* to do with his life."

I told him I had tried and tried to find the answer to that question also, but had been unable to.

Before long, I decided to return to school to work more on my teaching credentials. Arizona State University was within driving distance, so I enrolled there. Among the various subjects I took were choral conducting, choral arranging and other elementary and high school music pedagogy classes.

I had never taken a class in any kind of conducting in college, even though I had conducted choral groups and church choirs through the years. My dad had taught me basic conducting patterns when I was barely a teenager. The high school choir I conducted my first year after college had toured, won prizes, made a recording, and several of the singers had, since then, referred to me as the best choral director they ever had. So I started this new class with confidence and joyful anticipation. Near the end of the semester the teacher asked everybody in class to direct a certain composition for the whole class to sing as a choir, and then each student was to write a critique, as specific as possible, with suggestions for each conductor.

After I finished my conducting stint and received about thirty critiques from fellow students, I could hardly wait to read them. Most of them were very complimentary, but one said I had my fingers too far apart; another said I was bouncing up and down from my knees. There were about six slips that had specific criticisms such as these two, and suddenly I was *devastated*! I felt like a total failure as a conductor and didn't ever want to direct again! I went home and cried—sobbed—*very privately* for several days after. However, *I never let anyone know I cried, or even was feeling bad!* I was shocked at my own feelings and reactions! It was days before I could pull myself together and think I could *ever* lead a choir again!

I now realize I'm as bad off as Victor in the self-esteem category. He's not the only one with problems! It's interesting, because he has said he thinks I have all the self-confidence in the world, and he is the one who has poor self-esteem. I sense that he resents my apparent confidence and maybe thinks I have all the talents and gifts. Yet here I am struggling much of the time just as he does. I just refuse to let anyone know I feel inadequate. **KAREN: THERE IS A TIME TO SHARE—WITH YOUR INTIMATE PARTNER AND WITH GOOD FRIENDS WHO CARE.** *Twenty-four good critiques and only six mentioning small specifics I need to work on, and I'm crushed? That's ridiculous!* **KAREN: GOOD PROCESSING OF JUDY'S THOUGHTS AND EMOTIONS.**

In that same class I was asked to be the accompanist for all the choral works we studied. Only when I had to conduct did another student do the accompanying. One day the teacher stood in a different place than usual, and I could see only his back as he directed. He twice remarked—in an irritated voice—that I was missing his cues. So after the second time I smiled and said, "Could you please turn a little more this way or move a little so I can see your arms? I have difficulty reading your shoulder muscles under your coat." He apologized and moved to where I could follow him better.

After class another female student spoke to me with amazement and asked, "How did you *ever* learn to be so *brave* as to dare talk to a male professor like that?" I was nonplussed as to how to answer, because it had seemed so natural, and I hadn't imagined I was being disrespectful, rude or even "brave." **KAREN: THAT IS THE NATURALLY STRONG WOMAN IN JUDY.**

Springtime brought heavy windstorms. When a dust storm suddenly swooped into town, many baby birds were blown out of their nests along

our street. The kids in the neighborhood knew I liked wildlife, and began to bring me baby birds, still alive, which they had found on the ground. Some of the babies were barely hatched, didn't have any feathers and their eyes were still closed. Others were a little older. At one point I had sixteen live baby birds, but in a few hours several of them died.

I mashed up hard-boiled egg and added a little wheat germ, crushed whole-grain toast and milk. Using tweezers, I kept feeding this mixture to the ones that were still alive. Three survived. They gradually feathered out, their eyes opened, and they believed I was their mother. They wanted to be fed every little while, so I took them everywhere with me, even to church in a box. I'd sit where I could leave unobtrusively and feed my babies before returning to hear the rest of the sermon.

When they became full-grown, I let them out of their cage to fly around in the house a bit. Finally I let them outside. By then they were very normal sparrows, except they came when I called them. I held bread in my mouth and they'd fly up and pluck it from my lips. I filled a medicine dropper with water from which they eagerly drank. They'd sit on one of my hands and shake their little wings like baby birds do and beg. Finally they started staying out all night, but begged again next morning.

Camp meeting time arrived, and we were gone two weeks. When we came back, the birds no longer came when I called. My babies grew up and literally "flew the coop."

Tippy, our dog that had been a pal to Alan when Steve started school, was still with us. We kept his dish of food in our screened patio so it would be in the shade and not spoil in the hot sun. He liked the dry chunks to be softened with water. We kept the patio door propped open enough for him to pull it open when he wanted to get in. We began noticing a little bird frequenting the patio. I saw it eating the dog food and didn't think too much about it at first. But one day I looked more closely and noticed it wasn't closing its beak. When it ate, it sort of scooped up the food with its lower bill. I realized this poor little creature was handicapped. I closed the screen door and chased until I grabbed it and cuddled it in my cupped hands.

Looking closely, I saw at the juncture of its upper and lower beak a swollen protrusion like a dried abscess. It was impossible for it to close its mouth, so I decided to "perform surgery." While cradling the bird in my left hand, I gathered peroxide, tweezers and tiny, pointed sewing scissors. I took my patient into the bathroom, closed the door, and laid the bird on a towel on my lap. It was frightened, but I think it sensed I was helping, and lay very still. In only a few moments I succeeded in lifting out the hardened abscess core in which I later found a long cactus sticker. I swabbed the area again with peroxide and put my charge into a little cage with soft food and water. My new pet soon started eating and gradually its bill closed completely, the hole filled in and I set it free. I thanked God for the precious time I had with one of his small creatures and for giving me the privilege of helping it live a better life.

Although I longed for a close relationship, it seemed Victor was growing farther and farther away from me. Maybe about once a year, through passing time, I would say, "I really want to be a good wife for you. If there is *anything* you don't like about me, please tell me."

"Oh, I love you just the way you are!" he always said. Was there a sickening sweetness in his voice?

Again I sometimes asked, "If there was just *one thing* you could change about me, what would you want it to be?"

"Oh, nothing! You're *perfect* the way you are." He spoke with a magnanimous tone of voice as though he believed he was being a "perfect" man to say it.

His answer doesn't have the ring of sincerity. I don't think he really feels that way about me at all. It feels like he is saying just what he thinks he "ought" to say. Or am I dreaming?

Finally, one day I thought I had carefully picked a good time, when he was in a relaxed mood, to talk. I quietly requested, "We need to sit down and discuss some problems that we have." Immediately his muscles tensed and an evil face glared at me. In a *powerfully articulated vocal deluge,* this ultimatum suddenly roared out: "I *know* we have had problems ever since we married! We've been able to survive *without* talking about them! I *demand* that from now on you *never, ever again* come to me to discuss *any* problem about us! I *refuse* to discuss *anything* about our marriage! We have *always* swept problems under the rug, and we will *continue* to do just that, like we *always* have! Don't you *ever* discuss with me *any* problem *ever again!*"

He stormed out of the house, the door shuddering as hard as I was as Victor slammed it closed. He didn't return for several hours. I think he was walking off his rage.

My heart is broken! How can any two people, whether in a business, family or love relationship, live successfully without discussing problems? I always have believed this is part of good living. Life is learning how to solve problems or learning to mutually thrive with them. When two people are living together, whether they're sisters, cousins, college roommates or husband and wife, there are going to be problems that need to be discussed.

I began to get more and more depressed, even though I still tried to fill my life with interesting things such as children, animals, birds, music and school.

It *feels* like I have no husband! We still have sex, but no real lovemaking. Sometimes when Victor leaves the house, he gives me a peck kiss and says, "I love you" in his super-kind, put-on voice. Or he does it sometimes when he arrives home. But that's it! His life focuses strictly around his work. It feels like our sons have no father!

I still love life in many ways, but I am so depressed. I'm wondering, "Is there any man out there who knows how to treat his wife?"

Shortly after this, Victor's mother and stepfather visited us, and we all went to a restaurant, where we sat in a sort of circular booth. I was at an angle across from Victor's mom and step-dad, but I could easily look at the booth next to ours, which was slightly raised a bit higher than ours. There was a rather good-looking man sitting there, and I noticed him watching me. The idea struck me, although I had never done this before, to start a flirtation with him, even though I was in conversation with Victor, his mother and stepfather. They didn't seem to notice at all. I carried on this flirting game very slyly all during the meal. Actually it became a challenge to see how much I could flirt without anyone else noticing. The man was also in conversation with several table mates, but they also didn't seem to notice this game escalating. I felt quite excited because someone was noticing me. I was quite tempted to see what I could pull off, just for fun! As we got up to leave, I said I was going to the restroom, and my mother-in-law said they'd wait at the car for me. This man also got up and followed me. He went into the men's room and I into the ladies' room. When I came out and didn't see him, I decided, *No, I won't do anything about it.*

So I just hurried to the car. I never saw the man again. **KAREN: GOOD DECISION!**

In my discouragement and depression I sat in church week after week near the front and looked at Victor sitting on the platform, even when he wasn't preaching, but he didn't look my direction. Instead of listening to the sermon, I'd just look and wait, hoping he'd look at me.

When Victor was home at mealtime, he'd always be in a hurry and not say anything as he ate. There was no real conversation, although I tried hard to engage his thoughts. When he finished, he'd just get up and leave in a hurry. He didn't ask me out to eat or for any kind of a date. I would look closely at him for rather long periods when we were at home and sitting in the same room. I tried to look him in the eye to smile at him, so maybe I could get him to smile back at me. But he wouldn't *look at me*! *It seems that to him I don't have worth! It's as though I don't exist!*

14

FALTER

The teachers of my music classes assigned us students to attend concerts frequently, which were usually held on campus. I invited Victor to go with me nearly every week or two, but he seldom acted like he even heard my invitation, and silence was his normal answer.

Attending a required concert alone, I saw a good-looking man enter a row ahead of me and sit about three seats to my left. He turned and looked at me, then again, and again. The rows were curved in such a way he didn't have to turn far to catch my eye. He smiled and I smiled at him. I was pleased that he paid attention to me. He had come in with two other people, but when the concert was nearly over, I saw him discreetly tear off a corner of his program and write something on it. I wondered if it might be his phone number and if he were going to give it to me. As we left and were walking out, he smiled again, but didn't hand me anything.

Some weeks later I was at another concert. I walked outside to get some fresh air during the intermission and all of a sudden I heard running footsteps. Here came this same man. Almost out of breath, he said, "Oh, I've been looking all over the place for you. Did you see the paper I dropped for you that other time?"

Surprised, because I had sort of expected it, I answered, "No, I didn't."

"It was my phone number, and I was hoping you'd call me," he informed me excitedly.

His name was Pete; he told me he was a football coach at the university and was recently divorced. This handsome man seemed to have a delightful personality. I was hungry for even a little attention. When he asked me to visit him at his apartment later that week so we could talk and get better acquainted, I agreed. I took some books over and was going to ask him some questions about the university and discover whether we had anything in common. When I rang his doorbell, the door opened almost instantly. Pete was stark naked! He grabbed me and pulled me inside. For some reason I wasn't frightened—actually rather excited, but enormously surprised!

How dumb could I have been to not expect that kind of plan? But I hadn't the slightest idea it would happen like this! Since Victor doesn't seem to enjoy sex with me, something must be wrong with me. I might as well "take myself to school" at this instant and learn all I can about being a good sexual partner right now!

It was nice to be treated warmly, but I soon discovered this was *not* a man I could be serious about. Our values were completely opposite. He was looking for instant sensual pleasure, and I longed for a soul mate. He was materialistic, and I needed someone who valued my character. I also discovered he was an alcoholic, and that is why his wife had left him. I broke off the relationship at our next meeting.

After church a few weeks later, several people were grouped together chatting, including a young man I had seen there only occasionally. As I walked up to join the group, I heard somebody ask this young man where he lived. When he answered, I realized it was the same apartment building where Pete had met me, naked, at the door. The young man then turned to me and said, "Oh, I saw you one time come over to our apartment building. I thought you were coming to visit me!" *I want to drop through the floor and disappear. I am standing in front of the church where my husband is associate pastor, and Victor is standing right next to me. Now this young man says he saw me when I went there? Oh, help Lord! Did he see the naked man pull me inside? How can I give a decent answer? I know I had some schoolbooks in my arm when I rang Pete's doorbell, so I'll say,* "I was doing some school research for one of my classes and needed to ask some questions."

I would not allow my face to show embarrassment. The subject was dropped. Nobody seemed to notice anything awry, and no one ever mentioned anything about it again. Even Victor apparently took no notice.

Thank you, God, that you protected me, even though I certainly didn't deserve it! I know I can't live this kind of a life any more. I hate lying! I hate unfaithfulness!!!!

Victor and I usually went to church now in different cars. He always wanted to go early to tend to "responsibilities." We weren't riding anywhere together most of the time. The boys were getting older, and they began sitting in church with their friends, so often I would be alone. After I saw our boys settled in church, one day I went to my car and drove and drove--nowhere in particular--and cried and cried.

I want a soul mate. I need a friend—someone who cares—anyone who cares! I'm desperate!

I didn't want our sons to know I was depressed, so I acted to them as though I was a fine, happy mother. I also covered my emotions around all the church members, as well as with Victor.

Nearly every week now I started getting up and walking out of church after the opening hymns and driving farther and longer. I even started going past bars and thinking: *Do I dare go in there and maybe pick up somebody? I'm not interested in sex. I just want to find some man who might think that I am "okay." Some man who might talk to me! Some man who might listen to me. Some man who might at least look at me! I want some man to know I exist and to appreciate me!*

I felt *so tempted* to go in one of these places, but I knew if I did, anyone I met would be interested only in sex—and that wasn't what I wanted. I don't think anybody at church even noticed I left. Not our sons. Not my husband. No one ever asked me where I was going, or if I was okay when I walked down the aisle, out to the car and drove away. No one ever mentioned anything about my leaving church and not returning until it was almost over.

I began to experiment with thoughts of suicide.

If I am going to kill myself, how shall I do it? Shall I hang myself? I really don't want to suffer. How do you hang yourself and be sure it's all over in just a moment? Maybe I could get a gun. If I hang myself, I wouldn't want Steve or

Alan to find me. I want to figure out something that will not be too painful and something that will be quick. Something that will be done and over with ease!

I wonder how Victor will feel when he finds out. Will he be glad, or just embarrassed to have the church members know? I think he will be shocked at first, but adjust almost immediately, and with relief start hunting for a new wife. He'll be happy he no longer has to put up with me. He can find someone he truly cares for.

But how will Steve and Alan feel? They will feel horribly abandoned! Victor doesn't seem to love them. Who will love them? If I die, my children will be left without a mother, or even a parent who cares! It will be terrible for them! It will be a horrible thing for them to realize their mother committed suicide! Victor said he had "tried and tried to love them, but couldn't." I can't possibly leave them with him! Maybe I better kill them too.

I came to the point of going to bed at night and lying awake for hours, testing in my mind various ways of killing myself, and studying my emotions and analyzing the determination or resolve I would need in order to accomplish this.

What will my parents feel when they find out? What will Victor's parents feel? How will they cope afterward? It's a compulsion now! It is on my mind almost every waking hour!

I forced myself to go through the motions of being alive and happy, contented and living a normal life. My conversations and facial expressions were almost robotically controlled. FINE! PERFECT! But inside, my planning and mental testing escalated. For at least three months this was almost all I could think of. Simultaneously I was pushing myself to fulfill my responsibilities for being a minister's wife, devoted mother, music teacher, productive student, and "perfect" Christian.

I really missed our previous mountain residence and church. I knew how much the boys loved it when we occasionally returned to Flagstaff for a visit. I decided the three of us would go up there to the mountains for an all day trip on a Sunday and take a big picnic lunch.

I will take the car out on those little dirt roads like we used to do. We will hike and play and have lots of fun. I know the boys always fall asleep in the car after an outing like that. We will go and have a big day of fun and exercise. It will be a glorious time together. Then about dark we'll get into the car, and I'll start driving. Instead of going home, I'll turn to the road that goes down to

Sedona--a steep canyon road I have driven many times before. I know there is a place without a railing or a wall where more than one vehicle has accidentally driven off, fallen a long way, crashing at the bottom, with no survivors. After the picnic, I'll drive long enough to be sure the boys are asleep, then go down this hill as fast as I can until I come to this place, and we'll just whiz off the road. That will be the end of us. What a wonderful solution!

Oh, what marvelous relief! I had a good night of sound sleep. I planned the suicide date. I told Victor we were going to picnic and play in the mountains on that particular Sunday. He said something like, "Well, have fun." I wanted it to be a surprise for the boys so hadn't told them yet. It was exactly two weeks from that day, and I was looking forward to it. The need to end the excruciating pain weighing down my heart had become a tornado of urgency. With the completed plan in place, there was a calming relief and murmur of excitement. This was a new adventure to end it all!

At the university I am being a success in most all I do there. My choral arranging teacher highly commended me for my last arrangement. But I don't feel love from anyone. Victor obviously doesn't love our sons or me. But I can't possibly consider divorce; that is wrong, sinful. My parents would be ashamed of me. This is my only solution! I thought I was a good mother, but now I think I've failed at that too. Something is desperately wrong with me! The world will be so much better off without me! This is a wonderful answer to my dilemma!

As peace flooded over me, I began to take care of the bill paying and getting all the loose ends taken care of, so it would be easy for Victor. My energy and excitement ballooned!

A few weeks before my suicide compulsion had started, I was studying in the music lab at the university and noticed a fellow who was sitting at a piano trying to work out some assignment, playing some, stopping and writing, and playing some more. He was not in any of my classes, but I just happened to notice him, because I heard him struggling with something he was trying to achieve musically. It was *not* conducive to my studying, and was actually keeping me from concentrating, and it annoyed me!

A few days later I was entering a room for class and this same fellow was leaving the room. As we passed he smiled at me and said "Hi." When he smiled, a warm feeling went through me. Somebody noticed me! I didn't think too much about it. But in the next day or two I saw him a couple more times with his warm smile and his "Hi." I wasn't particularly attracted-- just warmed by the attention. To have somebody give me a smile meant so much!

The next school day, after I had finalized my suicide date, I went to my car after class, got in and was starting to turn the key to head home when I saw this same fellow approaching. He walked directly to my car saying, "Hi. I feel impressed that you need someone to talk to today." I was amazed! He then asked, "May I talk with you for a little while?"

Feeling speechless with surprise and amazement, I mumbled, "Sure."

Somehow he gradually began to draw me out, really listening with interest. It was cold that day and I saw him start shivering and pulling his jacket tight around himself, so I finally invited him to sit in the car with me instead of standing outside the window. Eventually I spilled the whole story of my marriage problems. I told him about Victor saying, "I demand you *never again* come to me with a problem. We've always swept them under the rug, and we will continue to do so." I told how he got angry if I even asked how he *felt* about something. Yet, when I asked if he'd like me to change in any way, he'd say, "You're perfect the way you are." Larry just listened and responded in a way that I felt validated. With his consistent feedback and probing questions, I finally told him my suicide plans.

He replied, "Your husband is sitting on a pot of gold, and doesn't even know it!" As he talked, I gradually began to believe that maybe my life was worth living.

That day Larry wouldn't get out of my car until I promised him I wouldn't go ahead with plans to kill myself and my boys. An hour or two later I promised.

As the days passed, Larry began to be friendlier, and we talked frequently. I found out he was married to a social worker and was deeply in love with his wife. Soon I found myself feeling love for Larry, because he showed me my value and saved the boys and my life. I had no desire to take him from his wife or break up their marriage—or even a desire to be sexual with him. He had a good marriage. But he had restored my sanity and self-worth.

One day we each had a break from class. It was a beautiful, warm day, and we went walking out into the hills on some trail we had never been on, when we came to a little gazebo. Without meaning to or previously planning it, we both got carried away and had sex right there in that gazebo. We had never even touched in any manner prior to this. I was shocked, because it had never entered my mind previously, and I thought I had very high standards! It was nearly the end of the school year, and we both knew our lives would take us permanently away from each other. The event put me into a temporary state of "overwhelm." I couldn't believe I had allowed this to happen! I didn't want to be involved with a married man, and he didn't want to be unfaithful to his wife, so we both decided right then that *this would never happen again*! Fortunately, with school ending, we would not be seeing each other again. We said a brief, but *forever* good-bye!

Some years after we moved away, when hope was slowly creeping back that *maybe* our marriage relationship would improve, my story accidentally spilled out to Victor about the suicide and murder plans and my change of mind. But I didn't tell him about Larry, and he never asked. He didn't seem at all concerned about my past desperation. It was like his hearing a fairy tale that did not involve him in any way. But I will always believe it was a miracle of God that saved the three of us—my sons and me. **KAREN: VICTOR WAS ISOLATED FROM GOD, HIMSELF, JUDY AND HIS SONS.**

There was to be a large "camporee" where Pathfinders came from several states to meet at a large site in the Sierra Mountains in California. All the members in our sons' club could hardly wait, but none of the adults wanted to go near where there was snow and cold, even though it was springtime. The leaders asked Victor and me if we would be willing to take them, and we said, "Sure, we'll go." The entire club consisted of about fifteen boys and girls who needed chaperoning. A man in the church agreed to drive the school bus on the trip.

Since the area where we now lived didn't have harsh winters, many families didn't own much warm clothing. In preparation, I got together all the long underwear, sweaters, mittens, caps and warm blankets our family had stashed away. The boys already had sleeping bags and I bought two for Victor and myself, but we later questioned whether ours were warm enough.

We bought a two-burner Coleman stove and a second-hand 12' by 12' tent. Someone in the church loaned us a second tent. We told the club members to bring all the warm clothes they owned and warm blankets if they didn't have a sleeping bag.

It was a several hours' ride in the bus from the Phoenix area, through Arizona to California and then to the Sierras. We hadn't realized the old school bus was unheated, and we belatedly discovered that some of the windows wouldn't close completely. It was dark when we started up the mountains, and the temperature began to drop quickly. After we traveled a few miles, snowflakes started drifting around the bus. I asked the driver to pull over so we could dig out warm clothes to put on, thankful we had brought all the extras that we loaned to others.

The farther we drove, the more flakes came down. At first they just blew off the windshield, but as we got higher, they became larger and wetter. The driver turned on the windshield wipers and discovered *they wouldn't work*! Now we had a real problem! I got an idea and started rummaging for a package of heavy cord which I had tucked in as a last-minute decision before leaving. Then I got out my pocket knife. I cut two long pieces of cord and asked two boys to each tie a piece of cord to the arm of each wiper and bring the ends through barely-cracked-open windows. Then I had them stand inside the front of the bus beside the driver and manually worked the wipers. Success! They traded with others as they got tired.

Finally there was so much snow falling that it was difficult to work the wipers, and the bus started slipping on the pavement. The driver found a wide place on the side of the road, and pulled over for the remainder of the night. Everyone who had a sleeping bag climbed into it. Some of the others brought only one or two light blankets.

It was a small bus, and we were really crowded with all of our camping gear tucked into spare spaces. I suggested that one person lie on one seat and stretch across the aisle, resting legs and feet on the opposite seat next to the person lying on that side. So each seat had a body plus a different set of legs. The floor space under and between the seats was utilized the same. Then stepping over all the leg sets, I wrapped the legs and bodies not already in bags snugly with blankets. Finally everyone was covered and warm. There was barely enough space in the back to sit upright on the floor beside Victor, who was already dozing in a sitting position. Shivering, I finally slept, because of exhaustion. Thankfully, Victor kept his complaints to himself until afterward.

Snow started melting rather quickly when the warm morning sun came sneaking over the trees, and we soon started moving again. Hungry stomachs stopped us for hot chocolate and doughnuts at a small restaurant, after we suggested our young charges use a restroom and freshen up.

On site arrival, we found the designated valley fortunately bare of snow. But the nearby mountains surrounding us were white and gorgeous. We all slept on the floor of the tent with no extra pads under our sleeping bags, because none of us knew any better. The first night I couldn't sleep because of the cold. After going to the restroom where there was a wall heater, I sat on the floor next to it trying to sleep and keep warm, but it wasn't much warmer than the tent. Our *brood* all slept soundly! Victor was in the borrowed tent with the boys, the girls were with me in our "new" tent. Victor actually seemed to enjoy the friendship and camaraderie with his sons and their friends, and didn't complain of the cold!

Cooking was done on our new two-burner small Coleman camp stove. I hadn't counted on the extra time it takes at high altitude, but every stomach finally got filled and no one froze to death. Victor and I, dressed in matching jeans and western shirts, sang some western solos and duets for one evening program.

The camporee was for just one weekend, so Sunday afternoon we packed up and left for a surprisingly uneventful trip back home. This outing with the young folks buoyed up my spirits and excited me. Life is really such an adventure. Even though Victor didn't seem to regard it that way, I felt stimulated and alive again.

My experience with Larry had been so dramatically rewarding emotionally, that with much thought and prayer, I decided to *never, ever* try to commit suicide again. It was miraculous that Larry had suddenly decided to talk to me. He told me he surprised himself, coming to my car unexpectedly, on the spur of the moment. Yes, definitely a miracle.

Realizing now that my life was worth living, maybe I could contribute something to this planet that would make a difference to somebody! I would do what I had to do to survive, finding things that interested me, and keeping my mind off problems as much as possible. But I still often hurt in my relationship with Victor.

We became acquainted with a short and rather chubby red-haired woman, who had an absolutely gorgeous soprano voice. Victor just reveled in her singing. He would exclaim and rave and be in ecstasy as he verbalized what marvelous tone and delivery she had, but he never exclaimed about *my* singing, not even commenting about *anything* regarding my performance or delivery.

I knew my singing was at least better than average, and often was complimented by others. But *my* voice was more dramatic than, and not as lyric as this redhead, whose singing Victor adored. Both he and I frequently performed at various functions and were asked to be the entertainment at a church sponsored banquet. It was a theme program, and we dressed in costume, moving from table to table, singing solos and duets. This time we had an accompanist instead of accompanying each other. The banqueters cheered and encored us, and I loved doing this kind of performance.

Much effort had been spent on arranging music, making costumes, and rehearsing thoroughly with the accompanist. Being Victor's voice coach, I had pushed him pretty hard to get everything ready and wanted him to know it was worth the work. He had, since the beginning of our relationship, accepted my offer to teach and coach him vocally, and always respectfully cooperated and put forth diligent effort to follow my directions.

After the banquet I was hungering for Victor to give me *some sort of feedback*—maybe a compliment—or at least express pleasure in the moment. When we got into the car to go home I said, truly meaning it, "I was so proud of you! You sang beautifully and everything went off very smoothly. You looked wonderful, and I love you so much." I felt enormous love for him that evening, and was so delighted to perform with him. I said, "I think you sang better tonight than I have *ever* heard you before, and it was so much *fun* doing the program with you." He seemed to appreciate my words, and thanked me, acting happy and buoyant.

Quiet then reigned as we continued driving towards home. Finally I softly questioned, "Honey, did I do okay tonight?" There was silence for too long to be at all comfortable. Finally he shrugged or squirmed slightly and belligerently mumbled, "I've heard you do *better*!" My heart was pierced.

The pain of disappointment surged through my whole body. I had worked so hard on the program, and *thought* it a success, but still wasn't able to believe in myself or evaluate myself honestly. The only way I could see myself was through Victor's eyes, so again felt a failure! He was a roaring success and I was a blah-ing *nobody*!

During this period of time there were several church choirs that combined and put on the <u>Messiah</u> oratorio. Dr. Lensky asked the redhead to be the soprano soloist. I was asked to do the alto solos (I had an easy three octave range). Victor was asked to do the bass solos, although he is really a baritone. He had never before sung these solos, and I worked very hard helping him learn them. Victor sang magnificently on his solos, considering it was the first time he had performed them. Because of a cold, my nose was a bit stopped up and I didn't sing as well as usual on the alto solos.

The program was recorded. After it was over, I was hoping Victor would give me some kind of feedback (*why don't I just learn not to expect it?*) and I indulged in a sort of manipulation. He wanted to send a recording to his mom, so I requested, "Don't send the part with my solos. I had a cold and didn't sound very good."

He nonchalantly said, "Okay" and mailed his mom the recorded performance minus my part, raving on the tape he sent about what a wonderful singer the redhead was, but not commenting that I had even done the alto solos. I really asked for that!

Victor liked this soprano's singing so much that he wanted to do whole programs with her! We already were well known for the programs our family put on. Often Victor planned them around a specific theme, and he'd include poetry on the subject. He loved to read poetry, and did it quite dramatically. I also loved poetry, and loved to read it aloud. My parents had paid for me to have "elocution lessons" when I was a teenager. I had taken speech classes in college and even a class in public lecturing. I loved acting and "giving readings," but even though I had suggested it numerous times, Victor *never asked me to read any of the poetry* on a program.

Now Victor asked the redhead to do programs *with him* and got our church organist to accompany them. He would come home from the rehearsal or the performance they gave and say, "Oh, she *read the poems* just beautifully! She sang so marvelously!" I, of course, would be staying home with our sons because Victor said we couldn't afford a sitter. I would like to have heard at least one of the programs they gave, because I enjoyed her singing very much myself. But I never went to one, because Victor insisted I stay home with the boys. I'm sure he was *not* having an affair, nor was he was sexually attracted to her, but somehow he ethereally adored her way of reading poetry, and was "carried away" by her "heavenly" singing. I couldn't compete, and didn't try. I never admitted jealousy to him or to myself, even though I envied her voice and abilities and *did* feel a few pangs of jealousy at times. *Mostly it was abandonment!* There were times I felt so *very alone*—even in a group of people!

As our marriage relationship declined and my self-esteem gradually evaporated, my confidence shattered, and my emotions became off balance. Even though I had won the auditions for soprano soloist in a performance of the Messiah oratorio in Ventura, California, the first year we were married, my voice now began to be affected. My singing was slowly deteriorating. My unusually wide range shrank, and I began to go flat occasionally. **KAREN: AS JUDY'S SPIRIT WENT FLAT! IT MAKES SENSE.**

Although I had determined to never again consider suicide, my self-esteem began to feel like an old rag—faded, smudged and shredded—ready for the trash.

EXTEND

We learned that Fred, Victor's stepbrother's adopted son, who had lived with us previously for over a year, had been rejected by his adoptive parents and returned back to the state. Nate was legally trying to *rescind* Fred's adoption. He was now living at a temporary group home, awaiting re-adoption or foster parents. He now was a ward of the state of California, and Victor requested we take him again as a foster son, and we did.

Then a lady member of our church asked me one day, "Would your boys have any extra clothes they don't need that I could take for a boy about their size who has no legal guardian. I'd like to bring him to church with me, but he has almost no clothes to wear. Steve and Alan had fun going through their clothes and picking things so that they were able to give this lady four complete outfits—shirts to shoes—for this boy named Rudy. He then began coming to the junior Bible classes and church, and also joined the Pathfinder Club. He was just six months younger than Alan, and they were soon good friends; so we began inviting him home with us. At first it was just for an afternoon after church, then it became overnight occasionally, and then whole weekends, when we learned what atrocious circumstances dominated his life.

When Fred, now barely eight years old, came to live with us again, Rudy, who was eleven, sobbed to the lady who brought him to church that he also wanted to live with us. After considerable futile effort to find a family that would take Rudy, Victor asked me if we could take him also, and I agreed. Rudy became a ward of the state of Arizona, and we took him as a foster son. At that time we made a very serious and committed decision to take these two boys as foster children, but treat them *as our very own sons the rest of our lives*, partly because the monetary cost of adoption seemed beyond the realm of possibility for us at that time, and because the boys had a desperate need. Now we were suddenly and dramatically a family of six.

School had barely started. We were adjusting to a bigger family, and the boys were adapting to new classrooms and teachers. I had just finished getting all my lessons scheduled, when Victor received a call *to come to a church in Long Beach, California*, to be associate pastor with Jackson Moreno.

I wondered, *Does Victor always feel obligated to do what the conference offers him? Does he really want to move? This is a terribly inconvenient time! Would the conference insist we move NOW?*

My questions never got answered. It was November, 1969, when we moved, and we found a home to buy at reasonable cost in Lakewood, California, big enough to house our larger family. The boys had to adapt to a new parochial school in Long Beach, and re-adjustment started all over again for all of us. Fred was in second grade, Alan and Rudy were in sixth and Steve was in seventh. Right away I started teaching piano and voice lessons at the elementary school where they were enrolled. Mrs. Mason, a senior citizen and long-time member of this new-to-us church, had been teaching classroom music there for years, and we became good friends.

Soon after we arrived, it became the yearly "Ingathering" solicitation time again. Victor was still adapting to the head pastor, Jackson Moreno, and new responsibilities; he must have felt unsure of himself. Apparently pastor Moreno had asked Victor to do something regarding Ingathering, but it hadn't gotten done. One day when I was at the church and Victor wasn't around close, pastor Moreno came to me and asked, "Judy, why can't Victor just do things on his own? Doesn't he *ever* make his own decisions and follow through on them?"

Answering as honestly as possible, I said, "I don't know *what* he does regarding church business. He doesn't discuss that with me."

Pastor Moreno went on, "It's like he wants me to always draw him a picture for everything I ask him to do."

Later I asked Victor about it and he said, "I wasn't sure how to do it." He hadn't taken the initiative to get it done because the head pastor wasn't around to ask for the details.

Mrs. Mason decided to retire from teaching classroom music at the school, and I was asked to take her place. Mr. Smith, the Educational Secretary of the Conference, suggested I take some course work from Mr. Javier Soldevilla, who taught the Kodaly method of classroom music. I was so fascinated that I ended up taking five semesters from him and got graduate credit for all of it. I started utilizing these things in my teaching and was excited to have first-graders understanding musical concepts, second-graders sight-reading as they sang simple melodies, and third graders singing in three-part harmony.

As we finally got adjusted to our new school, new church and new neighborhood, I finally took the time to meet some of our neighbors. Across the street from us lived a policewoman who jogged every day, which inspired me to start doing the same. Besides trying to build my endurance and increase jogging time, I started taking long walks. There was a lake where we sometimes drove with the boys to feed the ducks. One Sunday, when Victor planned to be home all day, I decided to walk there. It was at least six miles round trip, but I loved going by myself, and having quiet time alone to pray, think and plan as I walked. I continued doing long walks rather frequently after that. Since Victor didn't want to do things together with me, I began creating my own diversions while our boys were in school.

At each new place we had moved we always worked at making it nicer by redecorating and fixing various things. Victor was very handy at this. One day I asked him if he could build some dividers into a drawer in the kitchen for our silverware. He said he could, and didn't make any complaints or act as if he didn't want to do it. A few days later he took the drawer out and put the tableware in a box on top of the counter. Some weeks went by—probably more than a month. Finally one day I said, "Honey, did you get the silverware drawer fixed?" I hadn't mentioned it since the day I made the request.

He took a deep breath and loudly spouted off, "No! I got mad and I pounded it! I got *furious* and *smashed it to smithereens!*"

"Where is it?" I was thinking of the front of the drawer that matched the others in the kitchen, hoping it hadn't been ruined.

After another deep breath and a long sigh, he mumbled, "Out in the garage."

Apparently when he was trying to put in the wood dividers, something didn't go right, and he got angry. I don't know if he was upset at me for asking him to do it, or just furious at himself, or the world. Later I went to the garage and looked. He had smashed the sides, bottom and back of the drawer into little splinters, chunks and powder! The whole drawer, except for the front panel with the handle, was no longer there. Nothing had been cleaned up. I was amazed, and thought he must have pounded on it with a hammer for a *very* long time. I prayed and asked the Lord what to do. I decided to not make any more comment. Actually I felt *guilty* for having asked him to do it, and I prayed about that too. More months went by—probably nearly a year. I didn't mention it or complain about the box on my counter. One day he finally brought in a newly made drawer with dividers in it and put away the silverware that had been sitting in a box all that time.

All I dared say was, "Oh thank you! That's really lovely!"

Victor loved to work in the yard and make it beautiful and well kept. Now, with his "fix-it" talents, both our house and most of our yard looked almost magazine perfect--after we all shared in scrubbing and manicuring them on Fridays. But we had an asphalt driveway that was literally crumbling and breaking apart. Victor decided we should put in a concrete driveway. He built the frames and bought a cheap, used cement mixer. He arranged for sand and cement to be delivered and piled nearby. He then showed the boys how to shovel a certain number of shovels-full of sand and cement into the mixer and add the right amount of water. Victor also showed the boys and me how long to mix it, how to pour it into a wheelbarrow, then into the frames, and how to level it. Just about the time we had barely learned and gotten the first little bit leveled, he said, "Oh, I have to go away."

"You're *going away?*" I questioned with shocked surprise. "Where are you going?"

"I have to go out of town for a few days for a ministers' meeting. You'll have to finish the driveway."

He hadn't mentioned he was going anywhere. No warning of any kind. In about fifteen minutes he got his things together, said goodbye and just left. This was another learning opportunity I hadn't anticipated. And indeed I *did* learn *fast* how to make a new driveway. The four boys and some of the neighbor kids did a lot of the work. We leveled the drive with long two-by-fours we slid along the framing on either side. It was great fun, as well as being somewhat scary that we'd make some drastic mistake and ruin it.

One of the good results of taking foster boys was it kept me so busy I didn't have time to be concerned about my marriage. The three older boys now decided they needed spending money and wanted jobs. We also wondered how we were going to pay tuition for their continuing school. The conference that hired Victor always paid a certain percentage of the tuition for minister's children, but they wouldn't pay any tuition for our *foster boys*. One day Victor heard the school principal mention he was looking for someone to hire to paint the school gymnasium. Since Victor had taught the three older boys to paint things at home, he told the principal they were good painters. They were hired, and they did excellent work on the building.

Since they were becoming more expert with their work, Victor decided to hunt for other painting jobs for summer. He found some home owners who were willing to let teenagers do the painting, since the price was cheaper. Our family was paid a flat rate for each house. When school was out for the summer, Victor took Steve, Alan and Rudy to their house painting job first thing in the morning, got them started and then went on to his own work. Later he'd come back to check on the painting and eat lunch with them. They usually made their own lunches before they left, but sometimes I drove the distance and took a hot lunch for everyone. When our youngest, Fred, and I went, we also helped paint or clean up. Much of the money was put into the boy's school fund, but they were each given an agreed-upon percentage to use as they chose. Three houses were completed that summer.

It was tough keeping the boys in decent clothing, but since I helped out in Community Services, I had the privilege of taking any used clothing I could fix for them. I tried to get pants too long, turn them up to fit, and then let them down as far as they'd go as the boys grew. Then I'd shorten them for the next boy. But one day one of their teachers exclaimed, "Hey, your kids all have high-water pants."

"What do you mean?" I asked curiously.

"That's when you can see the top of their socks below the bottom of their pants."

That day I realized I must stop and think how the boys felt, so decided to go shopping. They each got new pants that truly fit.

I learned to go to swap meets and sell anything we could no longer use, all washed, ironed, mended and folded nicely; then used the money to buy "new" things at the same swap meet. I also sold other things such as two rattlesnake skins I had peeled from snakes I killed while watching the boys practice rock-climbing. I had spread and pinned the skins to dry on Celotex board. I was thrilled they each brought me $10.

The head pastor of our church, Elder Moreno, prepared to have a series of evangelistic meetings. He incorporated a lot of archeology and history into his sermons. He asked me to type them, paying me for my services, so he could give a copy to everyone in attendance. His sermon notes were pretty well written out as a rough draft, and I was to edit them for proper grammar, punctuation, and spelling. He also had me look up every Bible text to be sure it was copied correctly, listing the reference and translation. I also was to research certain historical events in the encyclopedia to be sure dates and information were correct. This took many hours of thoroughly enjoyable work, and enormously helped our budget. I now earned enough to spend a little on myself.

One day Victor's brother, Patrick, phoned us to tell about a voice teacher, Ben Wuest, that his friend was studying with in Glendale. Victor had told him I was looking for a good teacher to help refurbish my own singing. Soon I started taking voice lessons, and later attended a "Voice Teachers' Training Class," taught by my new teacher. In a couple months I became Ben Wuest's accompanist for lessons one day a week. Soon this job expanded to secretarial work for him, then later also becoming his teaching assistant, as well as accompanying for lessons sometimes two days a week.

When Steve graduated from eighth grade, he and Rosemary Orlando were the valedictorians of their class. Rosemary's parents were friends of ours, and their family would eventually become even closer to ours. Shortly after school closed, Steve left for boarding school at Thousand Oaks Academy, where I had taught the year we married, and was a couple of hours away. When he arrived, he worked in the laundry that summer to help earn his tuition for the following year.

Is it fair to send Steve away from home before he's ready for college? He's now fifteen, but I wonder if it is wise for him to go away? He still seems to have social problems. I didn't leave home until I was eighteen. Victor thinks it will be good for him. I will visit him as often as possible.

When I first went away to college, I hadn't experienced all the physical and emotional problems my son had. My parents didn't visit me because my college was too far away and they both worked, but my father soon mailed me a leather-bound, loose-leaf notebook with my name embossed in gold, containing a beautiful character-building poem. Monthly he sent another poem to add to my collection. I felt so proud of that poetry book, and I loved the fact that my father cared that much. It inspired me to collect other poems. Later I added to the notebook things I might want to write in friends' autograph albums, as well as short quips and quotes I might someday want to use. I pictured myself doing public speaking, maybe even preaching, and had taken classes to prepare me for this. This precious gift from my father was now jammed full, and I read out of it frequently.

Before we married, I discovered Victor also loved poetry. He had a notebook about the same size as mine packed with his collections. He used poems in sermons, talks and musical programs, and he was a *master* at reading poetry aloud

Pastor Moreno moved to another assignment, and Victor became head pastor for a six-month period, until another man was chosen. He wasn't used to utilizing a secretary's skills, so Marilyn, his "inherited" secretary, was always looking for jobs to fulfill her contract to work a certain number of hours for a specific salary. Victor got to thinking of his poems and decided it would be easier for him to have them on cards and filed according to subject rather than in a notebook. So he took his poem book to the secretary and asked her to cut them apart and paste them on cards. When that was finished, he decided to do the same with *my* poem book, but never mentioned it or asked my permission. One day I looked for my book, but couldn't find it. Finally I asked Victor if he had seen it, and he nonchalantly answered, "Oh yeah, it's at church."

Only a little perturbed, I questioned, "Why did you take *my* book to church without asking me?"

"I asked Marilyn to cut all the poems out of our two books and put them on cards so they could be filed by subject. She has it all done now," he stated in a matter of fact way.

My mouth dropped open—wide! I was totally and completely stunned! I couldn't believe it! My precious book! My special gift from my father! I treasured it above most all other possessions! Now the contents were all cut up and pasted on cards at church? I was aghast! I let out a yell and could hardly breathe. A part of me died right then! The agony was so great I couldn't even cry at first. I was in absolute emotional torture and unbelief, and couldn't accept what he said as reality.

Groaning, I moaned, "Please bring my book home with all my poems."

"I don't know which ones are yours and which ones are mine now. They've all been put together in one stack. They're not filed by subject yet," he explained with aggravation.

Pleadingly I agonized, "I want them back. I want to put it back together! Please bring them home tomorrow." **KAREN: NO BOUNDARIES!**

"Okay, I'll try to remember to bring them home sometime soon." Victor's voice now sounded increasingly exasperated.

Needing him to know how *important* this was, I *emphasized*, "I spent many, *many* hours when I was in college, using a *borrowed* typewriter, *copying* most of those poems from friends' collections or the library. Then I placed them *by subject* in my own book!"

"Well, you can have them back," he reluctantly sighed.

"There were also a lot of little one-liner things and short quotes in that book. I want those back too. What did you do with those?" I asked, feeling even worse by the minute as I spoke.

"Oh, I have those." Now he sounded bored! "Marilyn just cut them up and put them in a box."

"*They* were organized by subject also!" My agony swelled to the bursting point, as my sobs broke loose.

That stirred more anger in Victor and he uttered in sheer disgust, "I thought when we married, everything belonged to *both of us*!"

"But that was my *personal, private* book, a *gift* from my dad that I have added to through the years!" I flopped onto the nearest chair and started shaking uncontrollably until I remembered his hitting me, and suddenly squelched my hysteria.

Victor, putting his hands on his hips and setting his jaw like iron, gave the order, "Well, when we're married, *everything* belongs to *both* of us!"

Still *internally* shaking with desperation, I begged, "But you aren't to touch my *private* things without my permission!"

Victor's fury now raged! He thought I was totally wrong! He was *certain* he had done *exactly* the right thing, had every *right* to do it, and didn't *have* to ask my permission! He didn't apologize or seem to feel the least bit sorry. I was crushed, betrayed, broken-hearted! My boundaries had been bulldozed! My hurt was ready to explode! But the physical memory of Victor's hand bruising my face forced me to "back down" and say nothing more about it for a while. **KAREN: INCORRECT! NO BOUNDARIES! DOES VICTOR AGREE WITH THIS ANALYSIS? OBSESSIVE-COMPULSIVE PERSONALITY!**

VICTOR: At that time I honestly believed all our possessions were mutually owned. I'm sure I would have realized the opposite if Judy had cut up *my* poetry book. Now my "belief system" has greatly matured.

Time passed. Alan and Rudy graduated from eighth grade. Steve returned home from boarding school and joined them in house painting for the summer. Then Steve returned to boarding school in company with his two brothers. This school was considerably west of Los Angeles. The three were now living a couple hours away, and *they* became a magnet for me to go visit them. Every choir or band concert in which they participated, every birthday or special program begged me to attend. Fred looked forward to the times I'd be gone, because we made arrangements for him to stay with his friend's family. Victor went with me only occasionally.

One day I rose very early and arrived alone at the boarding school worship service in time to hear our boys participate when the choir sang and the band played. By the time we all lunched together and chatted an hour, it was time for me to return home. I drove towards home for about an hour, but became so sleepy I knew I could not continue. An exit sign for Topanga Canyon appeared and was just a half mile ahead, so I knew I could find a place to park and sleep. I began navigating from the fast lane over to the right through several lanes of heavy traffic in order to take the exit.

That's the last thing I remember until I awoke and saw a huge freeway sign that informed me I was in the exit lane for Interstate Freeway 5 going north to Sacramento. Dazed, I somehow *knew* I didn't want to go *there*, but couldn't remember *where* I wanted to go, *where* I had been, or even *who I was*! There was barely time and space enough to get off the exit lane and back onto the freeway, and I just continued to drive on, although nothing looked familiar. It took perhaps ten or more minutes to realize *who* I was, *where* I had been, and where I wanted to *go*. I had missed another turn onto Interstate Freeway101 miles back.

As reality dawned on me, goose bumps erupted all over me, and it felt like my hair was rising on my scalp. Horribly frightening! As I analyzed where I was, from signs, I realized I had been asleep, driving for at least a half hour, and remembered none of it. I started shouting, "Thank you, Lord. Praise you for having my angel drive for me. I soon figured where I had to turn onto Freeway 605 to get back home to Lakewood.

Victor had let the Conference officials know he preferred being an *associate*, rather than a head pastor. Finally a man named Sergio Conti was hired to be the main pastor. He was quite an interesting fellow—a real show-off, an extrovert. His demure and lovable wife became the second-grade teacher in the school where I taught music and we became friends.

Just before this school year ended, Victor received a job offer to be a Convalescent Hospital Chaplain. By now he was sick of church politics, board meetings, and not being invited to preach very often, so he loved the idea. We found a house to buy in Bradbury, which was much closer to the hospital where Victor had accepted the chaplain's job, but the house needed a lot of work. When school was out for the summer, our three boys returned home, and Victor drove them daily, the forty-five minutes, to work on our new home-to-be. They were left off with lunches, tools and instructions, and Victor headed to his new job. He picked them up on the way home. They did excellent work, although Steve wasn't quite seventeen, Alan was fifteen and a half and Rudy was barely fifteen. Some days, when I didn't have lessons to teach, Fred and I would go to the new place with a hot meal for the evening, and we all helped clean up prior to coming home. Before the summer ended, moving day arrived.

Victor, the boys and I had only partially settled in, when we decided we merited a family vacation. Victor had made arrangements at his hiring time to take a week off now, so we all left with backpacks, sleeping bags, closed-cell foam pads, tube tents and food for a mountain trek. Our destination: Lost Meadow, in the Sierras, which our foster son, Rudy, had visited on a school outing and described to us more than a year previously. He had then insisted we *had* to go there some day. Now we were ready. It took most of the entire day to drive to the trail head where we slept that night. After a quick sunrise breakfast, we hiked nine miles to an elevation over 9000 feet. The three boys arrived much sooner than the rest of us and set up their part of camp. Rudy, with his generous heart, returned to Victor and me, and carried my pack the last mile to camp. Then one of the others helped Fred with his.

It was so cold at night that Victor let down one end of our plastic tube tent and put stones on top of it to keep the strong wind from whooshing through the tube, so we could keep warmer. When we awoke in the morning, the mile-long meadow was pristine white with heavy frost. We all had down bags with insulated pads under our sleeping bags so we managed to keep warm enough.

This site had evidently been a hunters' camp. We discovered it had a wood burning cook-stove, built from rocks and cement that was the perfect height for standing while cooking. Close by was a rock-rimmed fire pit. Every night we built a big bonfire and sang camp songs while roasting marshmallows. Hand-cut tree logs had been constructed into a room-sized frame, which I imagined hunters would drape with tarps or plastic sheets for shelter. Within that open space were a rough-hewn table, a few shelves and hooks to hang things.

Nearby, a little spring had been rocked up into a pond about three by five feet with water about a foot deep. Fresh spring water bubbled up constantly from the bottom of this pool, so we drank it. A miniature waterfall about two inches wide and ten inches tall constantly poured out of the pool into a lower trough, which we enlarged to rinse out clothes, using only a few drops of biodegradable liquid soap. The tiny stream from the spring flowed through its self-made, foot-deep trench the entire length of the grass-laden meadow, and contained hundreds or probably thousands of polliwogs.

On one of our day hikes I experimented with a little portable grill someone had given us, but I hadn't used previously. We made a tiny fire pit and soon had an open cooking fire burning. Success! Perfect vegeburgers! (from dehydrated ingredients I concocted at home before the trip.) But once was enough. Using our portable backpack stove was much easier.

Victor decided he wanted to go hiking every day. Sometimes I wanted to just stay in camp and rest or read. One day, when he went alone on a very long hike, he saw a bear in a distant meadow, and came back raving about how beautiful the country was. He persuaded the rest of us to go on the same hike that very afternoon. So we repeated his footsteps--nine miles by the topo map, which made it eighteen for him that day.

The week went by much too fast. We all loved this place so much we went again the next two years. Refreshed from our week long outing, we returned home to finish our unpacking and organize our new home. Now we were only twenty minutes from a parochial school, El Monte Academy, where we registered all four boys. No more boarding school. Steve was a high school junior, Alan and Rudy were sophomores, and Fred was in fifth grade.

At our new house Fred and Steve roomed together and Alan and Rudy roomed together. We got new, unpainted furniture for each room—two bunk beds, two chests of drawers, and four student desks and chairs. We let each boy choose how to paint his furniture. The decision they made together was red, white and blue, but the way the colors were combined was different for each boy, each piece and each room.

After getting new carpet and drapes for our home, we had to tightly limit our spending for a while. Our grocery money had been used and two weeks were left before Victor's next paycheck. We were stocked with basics, but I was about to run out of fresh, canned or frozen fruit or juice. I made it a point of daily prayer to ask God how I could give my family a balanced diet that would include at least a little fruit.

As we got settled, Victor and the boys made more progress with our terribly overgrown large yard. One morning Victor came in with three or four small, green colored but ripe-feeling peaches in his hand. He had discovered a small, old seedling peach tree in the back corner of the yard that none of us had yet noticed. I peeled a little green fruit. The skin slid off almost by itself, and the inside was as pretty, ripe peach meat as I had ever seen. I tasted it and gave some to Victor. Delicious! God is so good!

For the rest of the month we picked enough peaches every morning for each to have a small bowl of fruit. If we picked more peaches than we needed, they'd be spoiled by nightfall, kind of like the Biblical manna in the wilderness. When the paycheck came, the peaches had all been picked and eaten. The tree soon died and in a few months it literally fell over, dead.

One day, after we were more settled, I started to look for my poem book. An occasion was coming up that I thought I might use one of my poems, and I suddenly realized that my precious poem book was no more. In that book had been two poems I had written. One was from my college freshman English class, and the teacher had highly commended me for it. The other was written the first year Victor was in the Seminary. Once, when he was gone all day, I had decided to write a poem, chose the subject, the poetic meter I would use, and finished it in one day. Since then I had reworked it several times. A friend, who had been an English teacher, had shown me one last place I needed to "fix." I hadn't ever followed through with that yet, but always planned to. My only copy of this poem was in this gift book. I didn't have a second copy of either of these two poems. Also in the book was the story poem, "Darius Green and His Flying Machine," by John Townsend Trowbridge. I had grown up listening to my father dramatically recite this to us children, entertaining us sometimes in the car on long trips when we were bored. When I was twelve, I had hand-copied the whole thing and memorized it, so I could say it to *my* kids when *I* grew up, but occasionally I needed to look at it to refresh my memory.

I prayed for wisdom how to bring up the subject of my poem collection with Victor, and gave much thought to how to do it lovingly. Finally I bravely mentioned the "cut up" collection and the poem I recently thought of using. Very irritated, Victor demanded I should just be patient and wait until he was ready. I really tried to put it out of my mind for a while.

I was young, naive and submissive. A dangerous combination. I had never even *thought* of calling the church secretary before we moved, to talk to her about it, or driving to the church myself to retrieve the binder and poem cards. I can handle lots of problems and challenges, but when they involve Victor, I feel intimidated. I don't dare tell anyone about this over at the church, because it would reflect badly on Victor, and that must never happen!

Months passed. "Victor, have you had time to finish unpacking your things you brought from the church? I was hoping you'd come across at least my empty leather notebook that used to hold my poem collection, and find the box of one-liners. I'd also like to sort through all the cards of pasted poems and try to find the ones that were from my collection."

"Oh yes, I think I know where they are." In a few days he finally brought me the whole, un-filed stack of poems pasted on cards. I *did* sort through them and *attempted* to remember which ones were mine, but my torn and bitter emotions kept me from thinking clearly, and tears blinded my eyes as I started to look through the huge stack. I just gave up, feeling like all I could do was just box it all up again and clear my mind and emotions. I *did* look, but couldn't find the two poems I had written myself. Later I asked for the notebook itself, and eventually Victor found it. I was thrilled that "Darius Green" was still in it—the *only one still in the book--* but *not* the two poems I wrote. Maybe another year went by. *Do I dare ask again?* "Did you ever come across the box of one-liners? I was hoping the two poems I wrote might be in that."

"I haven't found that yet, but I'm sure I brought it along when we moved." He sounded confident, but currently seemed suddenly busy.

"Please go through your things and try to find it." *Should I beg or ask permission to look for it myself? I don't want to make him angry.*

The sadness I feel is like I lost my father, plus other loved ones, and the grieving starts again. The book represented dozens (perhaps hundreds) of long hours of work and very precious memories. If Victor had been able to tell me how sorry he was the day I discovered the book missing, it would have been easier. If I could have seen even a speck of sadness in him for his "killing" my precious treasure, maybe it wouldn't affect me so deeply now. But he thought **I** *was the terribly bad person for believing he couldn't do what he pleased with "our" belongings. I have thought about going downstairs to his study sometime when he's gone, to look for these things myself, but I don't want to interfere with* **his** *personal belongings.* **KAREN: THEY WEREN'T ALL HIS, IF JUDY'S THINGS WERE THERE!** *I don't believe that "just because we are married" I have the right to intrude. He has lots of papers and books in* *boxes pushed behind and under things in his study closet. But in a few days I'll ask again—at least one more time.*

"Please, honey. It's important to me for you to find that box of one-liners. Please get to it soon." *Here I was pleading again.*

"Oh, don't worry about it. I'll find it." This time he sounded more like he meant it. So I quit asking.

It was good to have the three boys home with us again, and I still thoroughly enjoyed having conversations and activities with them.

Steve became more and more interested in electronics and found an evening class he could take in El Monte. He hadn't gotten his driver's license yet, so Victor generally drove him to class, and I picked him up afterward, one night a week.

I was still getting acquainted with our new location after moving, and the first night I drove him home on Freeway 605 I saw an exit sign on the freeway I hadn't noticed before. Steve had fallen asleep soon after tiredly getting into the car. While I was thinking about that sign and wondering why I hadn't noticed it before, I guess *I* fell asleep also, and missed my regular exit at the north end of 605. Evidently I took a different exit to freeway 210 going west, and was driving away from home for another ten minutes before I woke up and noticed signs and other things I had never seen before. What a shuddering shock! I felt frantic again for a few minutes until I saw the name of the freeway I was on, and figured how to get off to turn around and get back on going the opposite direction to find my way home.

This is the third time in my life that I have fallen asleep while driving. I must plan carefully for it never to happen again. My guardian angel must be a very good driver, and gets either a lot of laughs or a lot of frustrations with my inopportune naps.

Before the school year was over, Rudy and Fred got into several *very serious* physical fights, which resulted in their caseworkers sending them each to different foster homes. It was with intense sadness that we bid them each a separate farewell, one back to Arizona, but it was not to be a permanent absence.

Steve and Alan continued their schooling more peacefully now, and became deeply involved in music organizations, sports, part time jobs and girls. After another year, Steve graduated from high school and left for college, and Alan did the same the following year. Now the two of us were alone in a 2600 square-foot home. We started to remodel the basement level into an apartment, so Victor needed to move his office to a main floor room. As he was settling things in his new study, one day he volunteered the information that he had looked through *everything*, and couldn't find the box of one-liners. This was the first time he appeared sad, and he said, "I'm *really* sorry. I don't know what happened to it."

I digested that apology with conflicting emotions: warmth and joy that he could comprehend at least a little of the pain he had caused, and exasperation and frustration that he hadn't cared more before this. But I forgave him.

ENDURE

M r. Homer, the boys' former teacher at the Long Beach elementary school where they had attended, decided to form a mountaineering club and invited Victor and me to be members. It sounded fun, so we agreed. Soon he arranged his first trip. It was to be one week long, and entailed considerable driving to get to the particular place in the Sierras range. The final number in the group was five—Mr. Homer, who we now called Chip since he was no longer our sons' teacher, Steve Orlando (Rosemary's dad), Sharry (a girl in her late twenties), Victor and myself.

After a night in sleeping bags by our cars, we hiked five miles with considerable altitude gain to ten thousand feet. We set up camp somewhat below a couple lakes and in sight of a peak called Sawtooth, which Chip told us was 12,000 feet in elevation. After lunching and resting maybe an hour, Chip suddenly said, "Let's go climb it."

I am hoping to find more adventurous things to do at this point in my life, because I don't want to "need" Victor so much. I am seeking to build my own interests and excitement. I purposely choose to not let myself feel abandoned, although there isn't verbal intimacy in our marriage. I am determined to find and enjoy other things in life. So I'll say--

"Sure, I'll go climb it. What do we need to take?"

"Oh, we'll be back in a couple hours." Chip declared.

It didn't look like it was all that far, but I asked, "Do I need to take a jacket?"

"Naw, you don't need a jacket. We'll be back before dark." Chip was already getting up from the rock he was sitting on.

"Do I need to take food?" I am the type who always wants to be prepared for anything.

"No." Chip sounds irritated.

"What about water?" *I'm sure I hike slower than he does since I'm about 20 years older than he is. I think I'll need water before two hours pass.*

"Naw, you *won't* need any!" *Now he sounds like he is scolding me.*

"What about flashlights?" *I wonder if Chip is as good a leader as I first thought.*

Irritated, he emphasized, "*No*, I said we'd be back in a couple hours!"

I wasn't an experienced mountain climber, and didn't know any better than to believe him. No one else commented or questioned anything, so I asked, "Who will join us?"

Wordlessly Sharry and Victor stood up and walked over to where Chip and I were now standing. Steve said he would stay in camp to rest. Chip led the way with Sharry, Victor and me following. I was still dressed only in shorts and tank top, but had on my heavy hiking boots; the others were about the same, because it had been warm all morning. We hiked a couple miles on a steep trail up towards and past the lakes, then "cross-countried" (without a trail) up the side of the mountain at a steep angle. Actually, we just bouldered, using our hands much of the time. It was very hard work, and although I was in fairly good shape, I was breathing almost in gasps! But it was exhilarating! Chip was used to hiking much faster than we could, and kept urging us to hurry. After maybe three hours we got to the top, quite chilled from the elevation and cold wind, and hurriedly turned back.

It took a lot of care going back down where we had bouldered our way up. We picked our way hurriedly, but vigilantly, to get down safely before dark. We kept moving down the "saw tooth" ridge that went the opposite direction from camp. I finally said, "Why can't we cut to the side here to get to the trail?"

Chip reminded us, "Remember how steep the rock was? We'll get down there and then not be able to find a way to the trail. We need to go farther east on the gradual slant of the mountain, which will bring us to the trail at a higher point."

There was a lot of shale, and we "slippy-slid" much of the time. I had put out my idea only once to cut to the south sooner, and offered no more suggestions. But eventually the others said, "OK, let's try cutting to the south now," because it was getting darker and nearly sundown. It also was getting colder, and none of us had jackets or flashlights.

*I should never have listened to Chip. I've hiked enough to know I should **always** have jacket, water, food and flashlight. I'm so thirsty, and a granola bar would help me not feel so tired. I'll not freeze if I keep moving, but I have learned my lesson! I will **never** let this happen to me again!*

We turned right and continued moving carefully down this steep mountainside. Most of the time, now, we could walk upright without hand holds, and slide some on the slippery shale. Finally we could see the trail in the distance that went beside the lakes and on down to where we were camped, but here there was a sheer drop-off! We were above the trail well over a hundred feet. Now what should we do? The sun had just set in a blaze of color, but it was still quite light.

Chip did some investigation and found a steep slab of rock with a crack where he could do a "lay-back," going up fifteen or twenty feet, scoot through a horizontal crack for about seventy-five feet to a "chimney," down which we could probably navigate. I looked up at the steep slab. I had never attempted a "lay back." In fact Chip just now told us the term and showed us how it is done. He said I must literally lean back and pull "up" with my hands grasping the edge of this overlay slab and press "down" with my feet against the lower underlay slab, both of which weren't perpendicular, but were at a steep angle. The pressure exerted on my feet from pulling the upper slab towards my chest will keep my feet from slipping, and I'll walk up the side of the rock mountain—so he says! And so he just did!

He's encouraging me. It will soon be dark and we'll die of the cold. This is my only chance.

I started praying out loud for everyone. "God help us do this. Please save us." Then I said, "I'll go first."

I can't believe what I just did and said!

I grabbed hold of the rock, as Chip just demonstrated, and forced every possible ounce of strength into my arms and legs. I was already exhausted from hunger, thirst, exertion and high altitude. But fear pumped adrenalin into me, and God's strength infused me.

I can't believe I'm doing this. I'm amazed!

In two or three minutes I got up to the horizontal crack. The enormous physical exertion overtook me as I retched hard several times and thought I was going to throw up, but there was nothing in my stomach. After frantic panting and gasping for two or three minutes, I regained my air and composure and eased my way across the horizontal crack, refusing to look the distance down. Finally I was at the top of the "chimney." The others arrived shortly. Chip showed us how to push our backs against the side of the rock opening and our feet against the opposite side, and one by one we worked our way down about fifty feet to solid ground. Not really solid, because everything there was shale and very steep, but we walk-slid down probably another hundred feet.

Just as we arrived at the trail, here came Steve. What a relief to see him with his climbing rope circled around his shoulder and huge flashlight in his hand. Camp was still a couple miles away. Steve told us other campers were also worried about us. As we began our remaining journey down this very steep trail, it became pitch dark, and we were partially feeling our way when Steve's flashlight abruptly went out! It refused to function further. We could see far down in the distance a huge bonfire other campers had built purposely to help us find our way.

Now the trail totally eluded us, and the steep slope was covered with dry brush. We decided to go straight toward the fire, which looked at least a mile away. There was minimum moonlight, and we literally hung on to bushes and saplings as we let ourselves down small drop-offs, stumbled through gullies and navigated over humps and bumps. We pushed through clumps of bushes, moving as fast as we could to keep warm. It was actually almost too cold to *feel* the scratches and gouges tearing our bare arms and legs.

After what seemed a *very* long time, we finally made it to the campfire. It was midnight! Fatigue overwhelmed us! I gulped quantities of water and crunched a dry granola bar as I stretched my shivering body into my down cocoon. Dressing my wounds could wait until tomorrow.

Next day we climbed all morning to get to the top of a pass over 11,000 feet high. It was shale and loose rock, and for every three feet we climbed up, we slipped back two feet. It was exhausting, with my fifty-pound backpack. When we finally reached the top and looked over the exquisite, deep valley and lake below, I rejoiced and exclaimed, "What a gorgeous place to camp for the night!"

Chip sneered, "Camp? We're only going to *lunch* at *that* lake and camp beyond the next twelve-thousand foot pass over there."

I looked where he pointed and gasped, "I can't believe you!"

"Of course we will! We've just barely gotten started today." He was scolding again.

This man is a slave driver! No way do I want to do more mountaineering with him, but I'll really try to cooperate this time. It will be good for me to push myself. I'm glad I have on mountaineering dark glasses, with leather at the sides to shield my eyes. I can't keep tears from trickling down. I'll pretend I have to blow my nose, and I'll secretly wipe my eyes at the same time.

The lake was only halfway down to the trail that crossed what looked like a miniature rivulet far below. Lunch finished, we trekked downhill for a while. After crossing what turned out to be a large, fast-moving stream, we started up the other side after three o'clock.

There's no way I'll complain. I'll just pray for strength. I'm too tired to talk or even smile.

Chip led us into a campsite atop the next pass just after sundown. We barely had strength to set up our tent and heat water for soup. We were too drained to be hungry. Sharry was much younger than we were, probably about Chip's age, but she was totally washed out also. The country was stunning, but hard to enjoy when the body craves rest.

As we were silently drinking our soup, Chip stopped by our tent and sarcastically taunted, "I see you're mad!"

"Too weak to talk," I whispered.

Next morning we were on our way bright and early, and by two o'clock got to our Chip-planned lunch area. As we ate, he pointed to another high range of mountains far in the distance and said, "That's where we'll sleep tonight."

"Maybe *you* will. *I* will sleep right here! Who will stay with me?" I determinedly questioned.

Sharry and Steve happily chimed in, "We will."

I finally had to ask Victor, "What about you?" before he finally said, "Yes, I'd really like to stay here and enjoy the scenery."

We all loafed and slept while Chip climbed another peak by himself the next day. Two nights in the same camp! Luxury!

When Chip returned we explained, or rather *I* explained that a mountaineering trip is for fun and exercise, not for torture. If he was planning these long outings in the future, he needed to find other hikers who were in far better shape than we were or else plan easier trips until we could become more fit. Our trip back was more leisurely, although still very strenuous. When I arrived home, I pulled off my jeans without unbuttoning or unzipping them, I had lost so much weight. But I had a deep tan, a better figure and felt *marvelous*--after my sore muscles recuperated.

When we completed our house remodeling, a woman with a four-year-old son moved into the new "apartment" downstairs. It was fun hearing a young voice and child's play.

Soon after they moved in, the pastor of the church we attended asked if we could possibly rent some other part of our house to a new friend of theirs. This man, Ben, had started coming to the same church we frequented, had studied with the pastor, and had just been baptized. He had been a Harri Krishna and had worn the yellow robe. Prior to that he had lived some other varying, rough-type lifestyles, and now wanted to settle down and live for the Lord.

We rented one of our upstairs bedrooms to him, and he boarded with us. It was interesting getting acquainted with someone who had experienced such diverse ways of living, and he adapted better than we expected. Approximately a year later the downstairs apartment became vacant, so Ben became our downstairs renter. He was a superbly gifted visual artist and interesting conversationalist, and lived in our home over two years. He also did some house painting for us, both at our home and also at our recently acquired mountain cabin.

While conversing with Ben one day, I happened to mention that evidently I came across to some people as bossy, or hard to get along with, or demanding and controlling, or domineering and manipulative—words used by Victor now and then to describe me. I hated appearing that way to folks, and wanted to change whatever it was that gave that impression.

Ben said, "Oh yes, I *thought* that from the first time I saw you singing in church and found out who you were. You just *looked* like that—the way you walked, the way you held your head, the way you were so confident. In *my* mind I didn't know anybody could *be* that way—a self-assured, take-charge kind of person who could accomplish things and organize situations—*without* being bossy and trying to run everybody. **KAREN: SEE! TALL, STRONG WOMEN ARE ASSUMED TO BE LIKE THAT. IT IS A HORRIBLE CURSE FOR PHONY EXPECTATIONS OF CHRISTIAN FOLK, ESPECIALLY.**

When I moved in with you, *I* was afraid we wouldn't get along. But I found you weren't the least bit bossy or domineering. I never saw or heard you manipulate anyone, and you've been kind and patient to the point of utter amazement. I was shocked that someone, who has as strong a personality as you have, is not demanding or overbearing."

"I thank you from my deepest heart," was my relieved response.

This is so encouraging, because Victor still thinks I am domineering and critical. But here is someone who lives right in our house, sees me nearly every day, and doesn't see me that way. Praise the Lord.

My sister was also a minister's wife, living at that time in South Carolina. I had an opportunity to ride with friends who were traveling to that area, and visited her. Being gone from home for over a month prompted more correspondence between Victor and me. Even though Victor was not much of a communicator when we were in the same house, he was a very interesting and entertaining letter writer. I really smiled as I read the following letter from him:

Dear Honey,

I've got you on my wavelength and I could just feel those loving thoughts coming to me from far away. I've sure missed my snuggle-bug. Oh, how I would love to rub your uh—back, and play with your—nose, and run my hand over your—lips, and if I could just twist your--big toe I'd be satisfied. Really, there is so much to love, and I love every inch of you. What a honey-bun.

The reason I'm writing on this small lined paper is that I didn't want to bore you with eight full-sized pages of stark white paper, and besides I need lines to guide my declining penmanship....

Well, it's after 9:15 and I must do some work on finances, etc. so will say goodnight and see if I can find Bomber to rub his back. It's no use, our cat won't do.

Hurry home you melancholy maverick, because I can give you some exciting love, sweetheart, and I don't need a book to do it. Technicolor dreams to you too, dear. I love you.

Your lonesome housekeeper,
Victor

Such sweet and romantic letters! I *love* them. I wish he were more like this when in close proximity. **KAREN: ACTUALLY THIS IS BIG EVIDENCE OF A SPLIT IN THE PERSON!** I wish . . . . . No, I'll not complain, even to myself. I'll accept life the way it is and make the most of it. I'll embrace my life as God has allowed it. Victor is quite a clever writer, isn't he?

A week later a second letter arrived from him. When Victor is with me in person, I almost have to pull words out of him when he tells about events. I have never yet figured out why it is easier for him to write interesting stories like the following, than it is to put them into words when I am with him. Since I was away with my sister, he and our sons, along with his brother, went on their *own* vacation to visit their cousin's family at a farm in central California. He seemed eager to tell me about it in the following letter:

Dear Sweetheart,

Your letter came this afternoon and was it ever welcome. I wasn't sure when you would get there. I'm glad you wrote first and said you arrived safely. It seems like you've been gone such a long time. I want you to go on a backpack trip. We don't have to leave until September 12, or after.

While you were gone I received an invitation to visit our cousins in Central California for a week. I drove Steve, Alan and my brother there and we had a delightful time. The boys slept on the floor at their farmhouse and we were all up and starting breakfast by 7:00 A.M.

Both Victor and his brother Patrick are adept at piano and organ playing and are also fine singers. My husband continued with his tale:

Patrick and I practiced the two duets we were to sing next day for the service, and then I was asked to play the organ almost spur of the moment because the regular organist was sick. I was anxious to get acquainted with the stops, but I had only about five minutes to do that, plus also look up the hymns and responses.

I was very nervous about the order of church service, so went to see the pastor in his study. I found out this was his first day in his new church, and he didn't know the procedures well. He said, "We'll just muddle through together." That wasn't exactly calming news. I got through the introit all right, and then the pedals went dead. I tried every pedal stop. The only one that would work was a blatty horn that I turned off immediately. When I got up to sing with Patrick, I asked the congregation if there was anyone there who could tell me how to get the foot pedals to work. Silence. Patrick whispered to me, "Try the coupler." I did, and it worked, but by this time I had enough palpitations of the heart to last me a month. I don't even remember if our duets were OK. I had to play a meditation just before the sermon, so I picked the shortest piece in my organ book--not the one I had planned to play. Just punched a pre-set button and hoped for the best. Thank God it came out beautifully!

When it came to the postlude, it was a different story. During the prayer I reached over to get a book to choose a postlude and realized that the pastor was at the end of his prayer. So I had to flip open the hymnal to the first song I came to and start playing. I don't remember what it was, but I recall it wasn't appropriate for a postlude. It seemed like I had to play forever, because they dismissed by rows. Of course they were all quite charitable in their remarks afterward, but Cousin Caroline was more realistic. She said, "Well, I'm glad the organ acted up so the members could see how badly we need a new one."

As Victor went on describing his vacation, I felt some real envy regarding all the fun he was having, and I felt some genuine loneliness for him. I also felt elated joy that he was doing all this *with his sons.*

This was a water-skiing vacation. The lake is really an irrigation reservoir about twelve miles from their home. It's about a mile long and a quarter mile wide and has a new boat ramp, restrooms, picnic tables and lawn on one side. So we had a nice place to camp. We arrived at the lake about ten a.m. and on weekdays had the lake to ourselves until five o'clock when folks got off work and brought their boats out. With about fifteen people wanting to ski, our cousin's boat didn't get a rest except to refuel. In four days we used over 155 gallons of gas.

They had an easy slalom ski, so I was able to do fairly well on a single, except when starting in the water. We had a variety of things to do, including the circle board and a large truck inner tube, which was a barrel of fun.

The first day I got so sunburned on my feet and ankles that I couldn't ski the next day. The sunscreen must have washed off, and I didn't keep putting it on after every ski trip. So I had a miserable night. Had to take Tylenol to sleep. I was sore, but skied several days anyway.

Love,
Victor

Victor obviously enjoyed this vacation. He seldom seems to relish any part of his life, and I was relieved he wrote about his fun. When I returned from my sister's place, it felt so good to be home.

I continued teaching voice and piano lessons at El Monte Academy. My time was busy with rehearsals, recitals, arranging music for students, attending seminars and master classes.

Victor started taking courses in CPE (Clinical Pastoral Education), which is chaplain's training, so he could finally become certified. We attended church together, and in public he often held my hand or put his arm around me. Victor is an excellent masseur--a back and foot massager. Now the non-sexual, touching part of our marriage was wonderful, but I missed a more meaningful relationship regarding both sex and communication.

When together at home there was almost no conversation between us unless I *really worked at it*; but if pushed *too* hard, Victor said he didn't feel like talking and would leave the room. If I mentioned anything about wanting to work on our relationship, he would turn and walk out or distance himself in other ways. But it seemed important to Victor to "play the game of marriage" very carefully so the public would believe our marriage was perfect. Perhaps he didn't want or need the interaction I did. Apparently he couldn't handle the idea that *we both* could take the responsibility to improve and grow.

I again started reading self-help books and often asked Victor to let me read to him, or read a page or a chapter for himself. Usually he declined. One of his teachers for Chaplains' training classes, Merv Jenson, began an evening "Communication Class" for the community and invited us to join. Surprisingly Victor agreed, which delighted me. We went for many weeks and discovered it was really almost a therapy group; but just when I thought we were about to make a break-through, Victor decided he'd had enough and quit going.

This class helped me recognize my need to learn a lot more! I had *big* self-esteem issues, suffered from shame that needed to be discarded, was more manipulative than I realized and often monopolized conversations. **KAREN: IT HAPPENS ALWAYS IF ONE PERSON WON'T TALK. THE PERSON NOT TALKING CAN BE AS OR MORE MANIPULATIVE THAN THE ONE SPEAKING. IT IS A POWER ISSUE!** These were only a few of the improvements needed. So for the next *several years* I attended group therapy sessions led by Merv Jenson. These were two and a half hours long, held one evening a week for a ten-week period about twice a year. During the interim months I worked at putting it all into practice.

I was determined to continue group therapy in hopes of doing *my share* of the growing that needed to happen in our marriage. It was rewarding most of the time, but often it was painful. During one period of heavy therapy I just *had* to write. It became an everyday compulsion to spill onto paper my thoughts and feelings that needed an outlet before falling asleep. When I lay my pencil and paper down for the night, tremendous relief tranquilized me. In one period of four months, *ten whole shorthand notebooks were filled* with turmoil, insights, stories and trivia—writing on both sides of every page. It was an emotionally intense odyssey that entailed experiences such as the following, which here is copied from my journaling:

I have spent hours trying to put my thinking and myself together in a new way to change my behavior and response to others. Towels soaked with tears, bushels of prayer, and hours of effort in spiritual refreshment study have poured from my soul for weeks.

Several years ago I made a commitment to God and myself. After a serious neck injury, accidentally done to me while anesthetized in surgery, followed by months of severe neck pain, much of the time being confined in a hospital bed traction apparatus at home, I read several of Merlin Caruthers's books on thankfulness. As a result, I made a decision to *thank God for everything that happens to me the rest of my life!* My current prayer is, "Lord, thank you for showing me how to grow. Thank you for challenging experiences that create a desire for emotional expansion. Thank you for facilitating this process in your own way and with your own timing. Give me insight into problems, wisdom to solve them, will power to follow through with decisions, and joy and happiness."

From last week's group therapy until this week I have been living in what feels like a deep cavity of fear. Of course when with friends or teaching music students—when my attention is drawn to other things, the fear is filtered. But when alone, it grips me. Last night, on the way to group, I tried to put feelings into words. It was like I was in a dark, deep pit, with many people looking over the edge at me, some clamoring and shouting, but some unnervingly silent. It was as though I had just become conscious from either sleep or amnesia and had no idea who or where I was or why those people were about to stone me. THAT'S my feeling all week—isolated, condemned, barred from life—and no way of knowing why!

I have been wanting to run away from them--the people in my therapy group. I'm afraid of coming across to them as cold, because that's what I feel.

Friday evening Victor and I went to a nearby city to attend the Chaplains' Refresher meetings. Most of the week he has been supportive. Yet as we got out of the car in the parking lot, this fear, *fear*, FEAR almost overwhelmed me. The ride had been enjoyable, then it hit again! I felt like running a thousand miles away and crawling into a hole and hiding. I chose not to fight the feeling, but accept it and turn it over to the Lord, deciding to just trust Victor and put myself in his care (and God's), probably acting more passive or quiet than maybe ever before. There was a total lack of desire to manipulate or dominate or use power in any form. I decided that even if I felt BAD, that, in itself, could be a good thing. When we walked in slightly late (my fault), I thought, *"Oh no!"* seeing the place set up for communion [celebration of the Lord's Supper with Scripture quotation, prayer, and eating unleavened bread and drinking grape juice]; then another huge, *"Oh no!"* seeing a foot washing agenda [basins, water and towels ready to commemorate Jesus washing His disciples' feet].

Although speaking quietly and unobtrusively to several people in a friendly way afterward, I *felt* as though out in space looking back at myself. UNREAL! Is this a simple trick of the mind caused by emotions?

Tim Donahue from New Jersey was there. We hadn't seen him for years. His wife, Shelley, was there the next morning, and I felt more comfortable with her. After church they came to dinner with us at my mother's home. Wanting to share what I was learning and feeling, without trying to defend or prove myself or trying to be perfect, I went for a long walk with Shelley in the afternoon. Later that evening Tim volunteered the information that both he and Shelley had been talking earlier in the day about how much more relaxed I seemed now. It was a good sharing time, and my fear was gone!

Maybe much of my fear is of strangers getting close and criticizing me for things I *didn't know were bad*. That must be an "old tape" from my mother—being yelled at for things I didn't know were wrong—or even being punished for something, but not being told for what. That creates shame, then fear. I am choosing to make "new tapes," and during this time of feeling fear, telling myself I'm OK, and trying to act adult. No. I *am* acting from the adult position, not just *trying to*. Perhaps these crazy feelings are part of the growth process.

A few weeks later I became intensely stymied by an assignment for therapy. The following journal entry is from that struggling period:

> Yesterday I wrote out what to say in group last night—about a dozen times—attempting to condense each idea into one sentence. That was difficult—VERY DIFFICULT—not just intellectually, but *emotionally*. I kept feeling the urge to explain, elaborate and give details, finally realizing it was because I wanted to either *defend* or *prove* my position. I wanted to say so much that others wouldn't need to ask *any* questions--wanting to totally bare myself--with the right effects! Each time I'd start crossing out descriptions or embellishments that were unnecessary, I HURT! This was scratching out a part of ME! While writing this sentence now, tears are wetting my cheeks. Time out to get a towel to mop up.
>
> I really *want* to get rid of a part of me—but it's still SAD. Hopefully that is part of the grief process over some of my "death"—that part of me that was eliminated in all the re-writing and planning what *not* to say. The cutting, chopping, and rewording—all of it was SO HARD! Organizing thought is fairly easy, and it's one of my assets and joys. But I shed tears off and on for about three hours

while doing the assignment because it *felt* like I was re-writing—recreating ME instead of just an assignment. That was *so* difficult! Maybe that's why there was so much fear all week.

The following is the result of my struggle to write, while shedding many tears:

These are three things I'd like to accomplish tonight in group:

A. Share five one-sentence statements of things I learned last week.
B. Have one question answered.
C. Work on overcoming my fear of expressing my feelings, especially anger, to Victor.

A. Five things I learned this week as a result of my work last week:

1. Both last week and the week before, when you, Merv, asked me the same question again, I assumed you were insinuating my bad behavior. So I tried to project an OK image of myself, accommodating you by answering each time with a lie, which resulted in my being angry at both you and me.
2. Because of my contract with you and the group to give up manipulating, I realize the processing of my behavior takes priority over everything else, including reporting on assignments.
3. I haven't expressed my true feelings to *anyone*, especially my husband. When a child, contrasting my father's behavior with my mother's, I made a decision to be like my father, who never in my lifetime of observation showed any impatience, anger, loss of temper, or other "immature" behaviors, but was strong and Christ like.
4. I manipulate by talking too much, apparently for two reasons: either defending myself or else trying to prove myself, usually coming from a not OK position.
5. I *can* take the time, put forth the effort, and have the ability to discern and clarify my main point first, state it simply, then choose whether or not to elaborate or embellish it, according to the appropriateness of the situation.

B. My question is: What was the significance of my going to Mindy first last week when directed to tell three people I would be straight about expressing my anger. Yvonne mentioned it was *very significant,* and apparently others agreed.

C. You suggested working this week on my fear of what might happen when expressing my anger to Victor. I'd like to do that tonight.

Merv and the group gave excellent feedback when I read the above assignment aloud to the group, but at the time, I couldn't "hear" him because of my overwhelming guilt for what I perceived as bad behavior in group. My journaling continued:

> When my "work" in group was finished, there was no elation like I hoped. There was a little relief, but still a desire to avoid everyone. No happiness or joy. Just scared feelings and wanting to withdraw. But I *chose* to act differently and conversed with several people during intermission. When Merv Jenson told me after group was over that my work was excellent, I felt only a *little* better. But *during* group I was so dense—the feeling of barely becoming conscious and not quite relating to reality— that his "stroke" [compliment] fell on deaf ears, thinking it was criticism! And when I obeyed and checked it with three people, as Merv required, even then a blanked-out daze overwhelmed me—totally unreal! *When their repeated responses finally entered my brain, it dawned on me they were all compliments, which at first I didn't even want to accept!* But eventually I did! Maybe this is a little like Victor feels sometimes.
>
> This process of growing is threatening and scary, but it is also enormously important. In group last night a part of me—the part that manipulates, wields power, dominates—that little part died. Today I am feeling— not fear—but fatigue, laziness, disorganization—my day is just totally washed out, my body only half alive. Numb is a good word. Fortunately, I will have a short day teaching lessons at school, and there's only one student

to teach at home tonight. **KAREN:" YES. THIS IS A NORMAL RESPONSE TO THE HARD WORK OF THERAPY.**

Later my journal entry portrayed growth and change in my feelings:

> I don't feel as much fear today as yesterday—only about certain aspects of myself that are hard to trust or predict. Wanting to just "sit out" or "wait out" the numbness, so I can get on with living, yet doing things while waiting—like writing in my journal, mending and cooking--is my solution. I love Victor. Hopefully he loves me. For sure there are some others who love and appreciate me.
>
> <u>Often, however, a huge NEED for *reassurance* overtakes me—validation that others love me because of my *"loveableness"*—the inner me—the way I AM—and not just because of physical attractiveness.</u>

The latter is fun to know, but not nearly as necessary as the knowledge *I'm OK right where I am*—even if not "growing" at the moment. Is this what Victor needs too? I *hope* I am lovable!

ᴇXPAND

It seems like I journaled incessantly—often waking in the middle of the night to pour my very soul onto paper before I could return to sleep. Sometimes I skipped meals to write events and feelings and record episodes and victories such as this interchange on love with Victor:

Last night, during and after dinner, we had a "fight," or "peaceful negotiation," or whatever it might be called. The whole thing left me relieved, happy, stimulated, challenged, elated—and a little sad and subdued. I now know a teensy bit more about the REAL Victor, how he sees me, and how he thinks and feels about our relationship—previously and currently.

Yesterday morning, as Victor was leaving for church, I was feeling disappointed to miss his sermon because of an injury to my leg, temporarily requiring no walking, so asked what was the subject of his sermon he would be preaching.

"Knowledge," he replied. He had been doing a series on what he calls "Peter's Ladder" (2 Peter 1:2-10: "…. add to your faith virtue; and to virtue knowledge; and to knowledge temperance; and to temperance patience; and to patience godliness; and to godliness brotherly kindness, and to brotherly kindness charity…."KJV)

"Please tell me more about it at dinner time. Too bad I'll miss it." I genuinely was interested.

Hoping, as usual, that Victor would initiate conversation first when dinnertime arrived, we sat in complete silence, Victor looking only at his food, while we ate for maybe ten minutes. I finally mentioned, "Tell me about the sermon you preached today."

"Well, first I gave a review of the last two sermons." He talked about faith and virtue and briefly described them. Then he started talking about love as being the foundation of these attributes —how a person cannot have faith, virtue or knowledge without first having love. He went on: "For instance, in the relationship between husband and wife, a man learns to know his wife through loving her. He cannot know her unless he first loves her."

My mind shifted into "Fast Forward:" *How's that again? Is he saying he cannot know me unless he loves me? It seems to me knowledge stimulates love into existence, not the other way around. If Victor chooses to love me simply because of his own internal attraction and not because of any knowledge of me, it seems to be a turned-inward kind of love. It is as though he loves only whatever he <u>imagines</u> me to be. Which leaves the real me out! Is that the problem in our relationship? Maybe that's why sometimes I feel unloved— unknown, unheard, un-listened-to, and unobserved.*

I want to be loved primarily for my choices and reactions to life: for my adventuresome spirit, my optimism, joyfulness, imagination, my ability to appreciate varieties and types of people, for my love of life, my ability to concentrate and search a problem to its roots, creating a way to solve it. I want to be loved for engulfing myself in feeling for the sheer pleasure of it, yet throwing myself urgently into action for the dynamic exhilaration of it; for being able to instantly drop into a state of deep thought for the quietness and self-fulfillment of it, and for the ability to shed tears as easily over another person's pain as my own.

Please notice me for how I evaluate, discern, discriminate, create, enjoy, observe, question, resist, fight, expound, inquire and listen. Be intrigued with me before loving me, and choose to search me out and test me, explore me and gradually learn to appreciate me because of what is found. Since I am forever growing, expanding and enriching myself, I hope Victor's love will continually be stretching to new horizons also. And I'd like this to be reciprocal—each loving the other <u>because</u> of their growing knowledge. Victor has hid so much of himself from me that it is difficult to find him.

These thoughts burst almost instantly into my consciousness as he said, "A person must *love* someone in order to *know* them."

There was a l-o-n-g silence before my reply. "I don't understand that. It seems to me you must *know* someone first before you *can* love them."

Victor brushed back his graying hair, as though to clear his mind, then tossed out the comment, "Well, think of God."

Feeling totally blank as to what he meant, I asked, "What are you referring to?"

With a sigh, Victor carefully elucidated, "You can't *know* God without first *loving* Him."

I was enjoying this discussion and didn't *dream* it was upsetting Victor. So I said what I felt: "But *I can't* love God without first knowing Him!"

"Well, you have to have faith," Victor emphasized with growing volume, "in order to accept there *is* a God, in order to search Him out."

Naively, and more subdued, I responded, "Weren't we talking about love, not faith?"

His body language shifted instantly! He was about ready to leave the table in anger or disgust. That's when fear, and the memory of the heavy thud on my face, joggled my mind. Whew! Now *my* gears shifted. "I really *want* to understand what you are telling me, and really *appreciate* your willingness to be patient. Questioning you isn't because of disrespecting your view. The fact that you see something different *intrigues* me! I admire your sticking up for something *beyond* my comprehension. By my expressing *honest* misunderstanding, I was *hoping* you'd have *more* to say about your convictions. If you tell me enough about them, perhaps you'll persuade me to agree with you. I *like* the kind of discussion we were getting into, and enjoy mind-bending thinking where there is struggle to grasp an idea, then support it or revise it for myself. I've *wanted* and *needed* more of this kind of conversation."

Instead of his being relieved, he looked all the more irritated, lost and even dejected, mumbling, "I don't think it's *worth* discussing! I have no desire to *prove* anything, and we both are right, depending on how you look at it. I *won't* discuss it anymore!"

Tears were forming in his eyes! This was new behavior! His words rang true, honest and open. The phone rang, and he left the room to answer it.

When he came back I commented, "You were feeling bad before you left the table, weren't you?"

Without even sitting down again at the table, Victor raised his voice, "You *never* let me say what I want to and hear *my* side. You *always* want to argue! I don't want to tell you *any more at all* about my sermon!"

Subdued to almost a whisper, my words trembled out, "I don't like the 'never' or 'always,' but I accept what I think you meant—you felt blocked. Is that right?"

"Yes, you wanted to take the *opposite side!* I've been reading lately—maybe I shouldn't even tell you--that people who *always* take the opposite side have emotional insecurity and are *very* unsure of *themselves!*" he forcefully emphasized!

"Do you feel I *often* take the opposite side from you?" barely beginning to comprehend how I had contributed to *his* emotional upset.

Still standing, Victor answered with a belligerent, "Yes, I do!"

"Thank you for telling me the *truth* of how you feel," purposely speaking as meekly as possible. "I thought in most matters dealing with everyday life such as eating, sleeping, money, planning, kids, and so forth, we were usually in agreement. I didn't *know* you felt opposed, except in very rare 'intellectual' discussions."

"Well, you don't do it as much now, but you *used* to take the opposite side in almost *everything!*" he blatantly blurted.

"I certainly was never aware of that, and am *truly* sorry! You need to tell me, inform me, when you want to finish without interruption. *Please* tell me when you feel blocked. There's no way to know how you feel if you don't *tell* me. Please *help me* be aware! I *can't* learn it all alone! These times in the past, I had *no idea* you were hurt or thwarted. I cannot change something I'm not even *aware* of doing!"

Silence stretched long and thin. "If you believe different from me on *any* issue, Victor, *tell me!* I respect your differences. Don't deny them! Would you be willing to state when you disagree with me, rather than 'go along' with me?"

He sighed, and spoke condescendingly, "I'll try to do that."

After a moment or two he seemed to relax, then he smiled and put his arm around me as he said, "Now, I *don't* feel like telling you more of my sermon."

"I accept that," I responded. "If you want, at a later time, to tell me the rest, please remind me not to interrupt you."

"Okay," he answered rather dejectedly.

"I know you much better now than before dinner, and feel very happy about that." I wanted him to realize my delight in his telling me honestly what he *felt*. "Your willingness to share how you *feel* thrills me! I love you even more because of my added knowledge about you."

He wordlessly kissed me and left the room.

Part of that new knowledge is the fact that he feels *I am the one who has blocked* his sharing of himself. If he *feels* that, then it is his *reality!* I couldn't have known without his telling me. But it took bravery, persistence and hard searching on my part to excavate it from where he had been hiding it.

Relief and elation are both awakening within me as a result of Victor's showing vulnerability and freedom to speak the truth. There is also disappointment in the conversation ending just when it was beginning to be stimulating. In the future I must restrain my questioning.

Now it suddenly dawns on me that he probably wants me to love him for *himself* and not for my *view of him*. That's why I'm always struggling to learn more about him and feeling sometimes frustrated in the attempt. I also want to be loved just because I AM. Maybe my struggling to get to know him will lessen if I love him just because HE IS. Maybe our whole problem lies around our differing life views of what comes first—love or knowledge. Wow! What a concept!

Enough of my journal for now! I did *long to do things* with Victor, but even more I longed to have *conversations* with him. Usually at home he occupied himself with work in the yard, garage or in his study. For many years we had often given musical programs, frequently with our sons joining us, and often had to turn down invitations because of full schedules. Now I discovered that recently he had deliberately been turning down requests for us to do programs, but hadn't told me about them. He no longer seemed to *want* to sing with me or *work on any music together*. Although frequently reassuring myself that our marriage was at least average, my body, heart and brain still felt lonely.

Do I cause this lack of conversation? Do I block Victor? Why haven't I discovered this before? I loved conversations with my father because we explored all sides of a subject or an idea. What am I looking for? What is a real husband? Is my imagination unrealistic? An affair is definitely not the answer.

Sometimes men slowed down, looking at me as I was driving. Sometimes a smile was returned. On more than one occasion I stopped and met the driver, chatted a bit, then said a firm goodbye. But a few times there was more development, lunching together or chatting in a park with males who had interesting lives and were mentally stimulating. Twice I allowed things to go too far before stopping everything. But having good *conversation* and *honest feedback* from several of them moved me so deeply that I began to think through carefully what I'd really *like* in my relationship with Victor, or with good friends of either sex. The following is what eventually evolved in my journal:

> You have reached out and touched ME.
> What was it that caused you to break the common barrier that so often separates people from relationships?
> Was it courage or spontaneity?
> Assertiveness or adventure?
> Motive is sometimes evasive, so let it pass. What matters is
> I HAVE BEEN TOUCHED.
> I have been warmed,
> > stimulated,
> > excited,
> > and unalterably changed.
> I HAVE GROWN.

This experience has created a new dimension in me that I will never allow to die. Perhaps it was only one chance out of a million that our paths would converge closely enough to afford the possibility of meeting. Yet they did, and you noticed, and followed whatever inner impulse directed you at the spur of the moment. Thank you for giving me the gift of yourself. Sometimes relationships sour. Let's keep ours delicious, however often or seldom we taste. One possible means is to avoid building expectations of which the other is not aware. So I will state what I'd like:

> Love
> Acceptance
> A listening ear
> Freedom to be myself
> Appreciation
> A share in your awareness of and focus on life
> Intellectual stimulation and challenge

Guidance and information about your kind of world about which I know so little.

I have no expectations. I only want to discover you. I want to get under your skin and feel something of what you feel, view things with your perspective, savor things with your relish. I want to know what is important to you and why.

I want you to attempt to discover who I am. A difficult project, for I am still struggling at it myself, and continually changing.

I want more of what we have already experienced, and am adaptable to varying time and space needs, remembering this is a reaching out from our present state and not meant to change it.

I'd like to help create an atmosphere where we both are free to talk about anything we choose, including irritations, dislikes and anger, knowing our purposes are not to change values, make demands or manipulate. I believe humans scarcely can discover *themselves* except in relationship with others. We BECOME by taking down the walls of defense and opening ourselves to others' BECOMING.

I want your suggestions, your observations, your creative ideas about how I can grow.

And what do I offer?

> A share of myself –
> Zest for adventure
> Love of the beautiful
> Imagination and fantasy
> A capacity for deep and creative thinking
> Open-mindedness
> Sexuality and sensuality
> Happiness in your presence.

And I give to you
Freedom to be yourself
A listening ear
Acceptance
Appreciation
Love

I want to be a part of your life for an indefinite period, with no hooks or strings attached. I want us both to be honest and verbal should we have need to change the relationship, and have no recriminations, because our lives are richer than had we never met.

I have become more human and real for having written the above. Although my decision was to end each of these passing relationships, they were valuable in helping me think through what I want and need to contribute in the future to facilitate deeper and more flourishing friendship relationships. My painful realization is: this is what I want with Victor, but can't figure out how to achieve it.

I took myself to a highly respected counselor who recommended we both go to a well-known sex therapist couple. Victor refused, so I went alone. After my first visit, Victor decided to join me after all. It was expensive, but profitable. These two therapists, a husband/wife team, were genuinely caring and interested in helping real people with valid problems.

We were given a number of sexual assignments to do at home over a period of several visits. Once, when we were doing an assignment, I asked Victor to do something slightly different than he was doing. He became angry and refused to do anything more that day. When we went back and reported, the female therapist said to Victor, "I see you are an emotional hemophiliac."

"What do you mean?" he questioned.

"When you barely get pricked, you hemorrhage," she explained.

After several weeks of doing assignments, we came away with a better understanding of how to show love and caring to each other in intimate ways.

One day there was an advertisement and article in the newspaper about a seminar called "Self-Esteem and Transformation." A psychologist and author, Nathaniel Brandon, would be the coach for two consecutive weekends. It was expensive, but since I had a lot of students and could pay for it myself, I determined to go. Registering, but not mentioning my plans to Victor until ready to leave Friday afternoon, I expected some kind of negative response. While going out the door, I told him only when and how long I would be gone—both this weekend and next weekend—but didn't even hint where or why I was going. Victor only shrugged slightly and nonchalantly replied, "Okay."

Does he care about me at all? Are other husbands this passive?

It took over an hour to drive to the seminar, and I prayed most of the way. It was very scary to go alone where I had never gone in the city, hunting to find the right place, parking and finding my way to the right building and room.

But far more frightening to me was the possibility of disappointing God, or deliberately doing something that might damage my sense of peace and comfort that I joyfully expect during my Sabbath hours.

I am committed to Jesus Christ and believe with all my heart that He is my Creator and Redeemer, and that the seventh day Sabbath is a holy memorial of His creation of our universe. I want to make sure that this will be a day of re-creation and expansion. I don't want anything to block my experience of spiritual refreshment and emotional renewal this holy time gives me. Believing God is leading me to these seminars, I earnestly pray that He will keep my mind on Him and give me wisdom and discernment of truth and error in all I hear.

The seminar was exciting, as well as inspiring and challenging, helping me understand myself better and discovering how others experience me. Although somewhat overwhelmed, doing exercises with people whose various cultures and life views encompassed a wider spectrum than I had ever experienced before, this obviously benefited my social and personal growth. I knew God had led me to the right place at the right time.

We were given numerous assignments. For one, after the teacher verbalized a phrase, we were to write as fast as possible anything that came to mind. After a moment of writing, the leader repeated the phrase, and we were to write anything more we thought of. This is what came tumbling out from my subconscious into surprising awareness:

The teacher's phrase: "If I were willing to accept my childhood, I . . ." was repeated many times, and this is what my hand produced after each repetition:

> Would have to forgive my parents.
> Would love myself more.
> Might remember more.
> Might feel lots more pain.
> Might grow up.
> Might be able to leave my childhood behind.
> Would remember lots of fun times.
> Would remember really scary times.
> Would hate myself for not responding differently.
> Maybe would learn not to hate myself

The teacher gave another phrase: "If I could accept my childhood, my mother . . ."

> Would be relieved.
> Would be surprised.
> Would feel less guilty.
> Would feel like she lost control.
> Would feel ashamed.
> Would be shocked.
> Might yell in hysteria.
> Probably would say it wasn't true.
> Might try to force me not talk about it.
> Might be able to accept her childhood.

"If I could accept my childhood, my father . . ."

> Might approve.
> Might not like some parts of me.
> Would be thankful.
> Would be happy.

Would feel validated.
Would feel rewarded for his efforts.
Would think I had always accepted my childhood.
Would feel uncomfortable.
Would still be very straight laced.
Would keep encouraging me.

"If I were willing to see what I see and know what I know, I . . ."

Would quit humiliating myself.
Would tell my mother to peddle her embarrassment elsewhere.
Would listen to my instinct.
Wouldn't worry if everything didn't turn out like expected.
Wouldn't allow anyone to convince me I'm dumb or stupid.
Would believe in myself.
Am learning to do just that.
Would feel very embarrassed right now.
Would feel like a fool right now.
Would say, "So what!"
Would ask, "Where do I go from here?"
Can trust my instinct.

Another interesting thing this psychologist had us do—after much teaching preparation—was write our "life history." He gave us a half hour.

Life History (half hour version)

Born energetic on Friday the thirteenth, in the United States. My father said they should have called me "Dyna," so my nickname could be "Dynamite." Even at three, life was exciting, such as doing crazy, wild things, like balancing my tricycle over the swing seat, then sitting on it while my brother pushed me—until the swing chain broke and I went sailing, but made a three-point landing—enjoying every second of it.

Then along came my mother, feeling ashamed and embarrassed about what other people would think of me—or really her—for not training me better. The painfulness of being physically punished and verbally and psychologically humiliated for doing what I thought was fun and exciting and acceptable impacted me early. Mother could humiliate me, in the presence of the people who meant the most to me, so severely that she convinced me I was a shameful person, which resulted in my cutting off relationship(s) because of severe embarrassment, unable to face them any longer, feeling totally unworthy.

Yet there was a spark, determination and fire that burned within, and I soon bounced back, discovering new ways of creating adventure, joy, life and friendship. When my life was put back together sufficiently to be satisfied, happy and creatively fulfilled, she chopped me to bits again for several days at a time over maybe one tiny thing. Trying to protect or defend myself, I was psychologically pulverized into abject devastation until no longer able to fight or react in any way. Instead I became a chameleon complier—a "goody-goody"—even to the point of kids in school shouting that name to me across the playground. It was more important to try to please my parents and other adults and authority figures than to please my peers.

Became a B student, college graduate, excellent pianist, popular. Married, had kids, became an "ideal" cook, housekeeper, entertainer, mother and wife. But was a farce and didn't know it until, after years of unhappy marriage trying to please my husband and never showing my feelings or revealing my needs, I discovered in one traumatic half-hour, during an in-law confrontation, that all my husband's family detested me (although I loved them dearly) to the point they could hardly stand being around me. They saw my husband's incessant unhappiness, blamed me for *all of it* and pitied him. They also thought me responsible for all our sons' problems. Realizing then that all of my life had been spent forcing myself with gigantic effort to be perfect—as I thought "they" wanted— and discovering instead that I was unforgivably terrible—like my worst imagination—a total ogre—I decided, "To hell with trying to please people, especially relatives and husband."

After weeks and months of devastated depression and crawling into my hibernating hole until healing could begin, I began to search for my true identity. Gradually looking inside myself for answers to feelings, needs and wants, I told my husband, "From now on I'm taking care of me, not us. You can do the 'concerning' about us for the next 25 years." He is also growing.

My mother was informed of my capability of making my own decisions, doing my own thing, and from now on I would! Beginning to grow, and discarding some of my former behavior, I was pleased to realize that much of my previous way of relating really *was* me. I could be that way because of wanting to, and not to impress or please someone else. Reaching out for old interests and new adventures, I'm now working on a Master's degree in piano pedagogy and am being urged by the piano faculty at the university to switch to a straight performance major because they insist, "people will want to hear you."

Most of my fears about being alone have been discarded, and I now hike quite often, with only my dog, in the mountains--through snow, rain, fog, hail or heat. Last year I did my first rappelling, currently am taking Sierra Club's Basic Mountaineering Training Course, and have plans to make it to the top of Mt. Shasta next month. I have faced my sons with the growing knowledge of myself, and shared with them the parts of me that were a hindrance, and my progress in changing that. I encourage them to do the same, assuring them of my love and acceptance. No matter what direction they grow, they don't need to worry about my approval or lack of it. I will merely be cheering them on in whatever they do or don't do.

Establishing new relationships and regaining my sexuality, I *like* me, and am taking care of myself by walking, jogging, and hiking regularly, intending to live to be 150. My many desires include wanting to hike in the Himalayas, becoming an airplane pilot and maybe even sky diving—or at least learning to parachute. I will continue exploring as much as time allows, and expect to die in the mountains, while enjoying the great out of doors, by something like lightning striking me, a boulder crushing me during an earthquake, or drowning from a flash flood. I will live every moment to the fullest and experience every emotion, even the painful ones, to the fullest, until that moment I can no longer experience life.

After we wrote for thirty minutes, the teacher gave more insight and instruction. What? Write my history again? In five minutes?!!

Life History (five minute version)

I was born with aliveness and vitality, losing it at an early age—but not completely. It was squelched out of recognition much of the time by my mother. She didn't do it purposely, and I couldn't have changed that as a child, since I didn't even know how to as an adult. But there was enough inner sense of aliveness to keep searching. For the last five years I'm finding new ways, though still regretting my earlier inability. That's reality. Now growing by leaps and bounds, experiencing pain and pleasure, joy and sadness, fear and courage with intensity, I'm alive, aware, and quite a bit more at peace with myself, not fearing death, but only intense physical suffering. I'll not dwell on that fear.

Generally liking what I do, and finding more interesting challenges daily, my plans are to live to 150. No one will believe I'm past 70. Perhaps I'll have earned three advanced degrees in various areas of music and psychology.

I will remain a sexual and beautiful person up to the last moment, but my beauty will not be just physical. It is, and will continue to be, an inner radiance that comes from accepting myself and learning that I am neither greater than nor less than any other human, in terms of worth or value, recognizing my superiority in some tiny little personal gifts, and realizing my inferiority in many other areas. Being comfortable with that, I will die in some sort of exciting activity such as rock climbing, rappelling, water skiing, sky diving or falling off a cliff while scaling a mountain. My death will not be from deterioration. It will be somehow just circumstances of natural events, and it will be sudden and swift—instantaneous.

Yes, at 150, I'll still be good, close friends with lovers and ex-lovers, husbands or ex- husbands, kids, neighbors--any who are still alive--and also with the rest of the folks that now detest me. I hope they enjoy it.

Triple surprise!!! Next we were asked to tell the whole story of our life—in one minute? Oh help!

Life History (one minute version)

Born alive. Will die alive until I'm dead, not wanting to erase anything I've survived, and choosing to enjoy all I've experienced--damn it--the pain and the pleasure! Some of the pain I created. Much was created for me. I choose to create pleasure, and relish all of life with exultation. EXPERIENCING (in contrast to DENYING) is pleasure. I will die while living life to its fullest, whether in a cast in bed wracked with pain or having a heart attack while falling off a cliff.

Condensing my life story into five minutes, and again into one minute, really aided my understanding of what my priorities are. Life's desires and purposes suddenly became more focused than ever before.

This seminar was repeated annually, and former alumni were given a very special cost break, which allowed me to repeat it. The value of this seminar experience was so great that I participated several consecutive years, finally becoming an "assistant"—one who handed out tissues for tears and sat with people who needed extra comforting or special explanations. There were many new and different exercises each seminar repetition, and each time the assignments had a slightly different "twist." Some of my responses were:

"One of the things I wish people understood about me is . . ."
I'm learning late in life about how to relate, and still make lots of mistakes.
It's okay to have best friends a lot younger than I am.
Even though intelligent, I can be very down-to-earth, comfortable and fun.
The most important thing in my life, now, is learning to be close to people.
I don't want to intimidate people.

"When I was young it would have meant a lot to me if . . ."
I knew an alternate way of life than having to please people.
My mother would have allowed and encouraged me to talk about my feelings.
I had recognized it was OK to be me.
My mother wasn't ashamed of me.
I had realized my value.

"One of the needs I sometimes try to deny is . . ."
My need to cry.
My need for sex.
My need to be respected.

My need for intimacy with a man I love.

My need to find a man I love who wants to be emotionally and physically intimate.

My need to "hoop it up" and holler in exuberance.

My need to express anger.

"If I were more honest with myself about my needs and wants . . ."

People close to me would probably be angry and frustrated.

Discouragement would set me back.

I'd discover it was totally impossible to meet all my needs and wants.

People important to me would feel threatened.

If only half of these needs could be met, I'd be marvelously happy.

"As I allow myself to understand what I am saying . . ."

I'm really seeing my wants and needs and making progress in filling them.

More people are attracted to me.

I feel afraid.

Fear will not stop my growth!

Experience will teach me what is appropriate.

At the last seminar I attended, the teacher again had us do the life history writing in the three time limits. Some of my concepts had grown.

Drama of My Life (one minute)

Girl becomes woman. Searches for love by other people's standards. Finds hate, irritation, enemies in greater number than friends and fun. Gives up on pleasing others some years after becoming adult. Decides to please self. Searches for self. Finds real life. Truly finds God. Discovers love from many of the people who hated, rejected, or belittled her, when her excitement was more than they knew how to deal with. Found security in not having security. Finds excitement as much in aloneness as togetherness. Loves self as much as others and vice versa because she lives in cooperation with God. Feels and looks younger, has more adventures planned, imagines scads of ideas for the future to choose from.

APPREHEND

New Woman Magazine was one of my favorites. One day, probably early in the year 1990, I discovered in it an advertisement for a contest: write my concept of "What Makes a New Man." Inspired, I began to write what to me was admirable in a man. There had been no "affair" for a long time, and I retained hope for my marriage to improve. Victor was still the most handsome man in the world to me. We just didn't have a real relationship. I told him about the contest and worked very hard on my entry. Thinking it was quite good, I showed the finished product to him with a sense of pride. We were sitting at the table when he read it, then angrily threw it back across the table with, "That's impossible!" pushed his chair back, and wordlessly stalked out of the room. Such disappointment!

It was mailed to the magazine, but no acknowledgment was received.

Some terrible nightmares had been disturbing my sleep. One day I persuaded Victor to let me tell him about one of them. After my last word, he said disgustedly, "You evidently must have just had an upset stomach!" then turned and walked out of the room again. Frustrated and hurt by his constant unfeeling attitude toward me, my hopes and goals got dislodged so badly that I told myself out loud, "Well, if I can't beat him, I'll join him! I will totally turn off *my* feelings! I will learn to live without feeling! I will cut myself off from all emotions! It seems to work for him. I'll just *make* it work for me!"

It was approximately a year later when I discovered a lump in my breast. It was cancer. I had a lumpectomy and thirty-seven radiation treatments over several months and was on Tamoxifen pills for the next five years. When the realization of cancer hit me, I firmly self-talked again: *"I did this to myself! I made a decision to cut off my emotions. God never intended for me to do that. Having once almost committed suicide, unconsciously I've done it again. Now I speak in a loud voice inviting all my emotions back! I choose to feel them all! God gave them to me for a purpose! I will not squelch them! To cut them off is just another way of killing myself! I will never do that again! Forgive me, Lord. I'm yours, and I choose to live for you."*

Through the years, as I racked my brain trying to discover creative means to better my marriage and myself, I had started a poem. From time to time I added to--or changed--my self-talk, so likewise revised or added to my poem. I wanted it to express my determination to never run away from problems, but to embrace them instead. I chose to face the risks of immersing myself in whatever it would take to move ahead. I chose to grow in character until my beautiful (though often painful) experience of life would overflow to others with blessing, encouragement and challenge. Eventually the following poem emerged:

Embrace Life
A many-hued arch spanned sky's canopy...
Pastels, transparent as light, luminescent pinks and purples,
With black jags piercing their softness;
Glaring scarlet, partly blinded by swirling clouds of depressed gray,
Lightning-spiked vibrant orange, lush green, royal blue,
But smoky haze dulling patches of ecstatically glowing rainbow.
Question.

Aghast with wonder, uncertainty, elation, dread...
Desiring to grasp, instead retreating,
Wanting to block the view above:
Awesome! Awful! Amazing! Audacious!
Fearful! Dreadful! Paralyzing, Intriguing, Challenging.
Paradox.

249

Higher Voice within whispered,
"I love you. Embrace life with Me!"
Angrily retorting, "It hurts! I hate it! I'm afraid!"
Pianissimo words crescendoed to electric, cymbaled shout:
"Embrace Life WITH ME!"
Silence

Thunder Voice rolled on and on, pulsating echoing message:
"Live life joyfully! Endure it peacefully!
Love it energetically with abandon!
Let ME create excitement, adventure, patience, beauty, love."
God articulated,
"EMBRACE!"

Deepest soul core trembled in trepidation and happiness...
In apprehension, then resignation, joy.
Spirit swelled, enlarged, expanded,
Rose at last to the challenge.
Stand.

Stretching, tripping, tumbling, painfully grief-filled...
Until swirling gray clouds massaged brokenness.
Exhausted, sleeping uneasily, healing slowly commencing,
Morning stealthily slipped over horizon.
Awaken.

Groggily groping to grasp faint flare of light...
Extending every slight sinew and tenuous tendon...
Until prickled, awakening excruciating agony.
Struggling forward, faltering, groaning, in anguish praying...
Prone.

Resolve returned. Stance recovered. In exultation vaulting, soaring...
Until color reflects from face and heart...
Until hands immerse in prism's light...
Until fingers caress different tints and shades...

Until body, mind and emotions absorb refracted rays…
Love.

Until precious pearls and emeralds of lasting relationships
Pour into empty hollowness,
Inundating with floods of multi-dimensional love and caring…
While following the curve to horizon.
Glory.

The pot at rainbow's end
Is not attained by those who reach for gold,
But by those who fly to embrace each variegated strand,
Finding jewels of greater value overflowing,
Starting new rainbows reflecting from other faces and hearts.
Peace.

Reflecting on my life and marriage, doing what felt like deep, intuitive self-analysis, the whole problem often seemed to be all *mine*. *I* was the one who had affairs; Victor hadn't, to my knowledge. Intensely desiring companionship, friendship, communication, loyalty, adventure and humor in relationship *with* Victor, I hoped, lost courage, then regained it periodically. Finally, I decided to make another attempt to show Victor my dilemma in such a way that he could truly comprehend, and carefully wrote out my perception of our current relationship. As a last resort, I dictated it on tape and asked him to listen to it *with me*!

Dictated letter written December 7, 1991:
Dear Victor,

I must tell you my thoughts and feelings regarding our marriage. Apparently our current status is two separate individuals existing under the same roof, with a non-negotiated, non-verbalized truce as the primary bond. Your actions and silence seem to show that your concept of marriage is two people play-acting the husband-wife game for the convenience of living. It must never include *real* communication, baring of soul, or deep sharing of ideas, goals, needs or feelings. If no confrontation or uncomfortable event takes place, then it is apparently a good marriage. Is this really what you want?

For the sake of reputation, finances, convenience, and to avoid worse loneliness, I currently choose to stay married. I haven't the remotest idea how to change my dead emotions. The idea of this tape was precipitated when my counselor, Lena Talbot, informed me that you, only one week ago, told your Ministers' Support Group that she leads, "Judy and I have a *wonderful* marriage, the best it's ever been!"

It was only a few months ago I had almost given up hope for a marriage like I believe God wants for us. It was so hard to tell you that, but I did! And I *meant* what was said! It took tremendous courage! How can you say our marriage is the best it has ever been?

When I asked for intimacy, you walked away. When I inquired whom you considered your closest friends (because I wanted so much to be your friend), you responded that you didn't feel any need for friends. When I mentioned we seldom did anything together, you said we couldn't afford to. When I said we didn't have a real marriage, you retorted there wasn't a man in this world that could please me. But I don't want or need to be "pleased." I want you to tell me what you don't like about me and help me grow. I want to scratch off your film of pretense, break through your walls of make- believe, and find the squelched Victor Leigh.

Fifteen years ago you made a promise to your sister that you would come to her graduation. You didn't come or even apologize! I told you how awful it was to disappoint her, especially since she sent you an invitation, which you tossed and forgot about, so she sent you a second one. She called three or four different times during the month to remind you, and tell you how important it was to her that you come. But you didn't. Oh how I sympathized with her and told you so. Then you said angrily that *I knew,* before I married you, that God's work would *always* come before family. But *that* day was the *first time* you ever told me! I didn't *know* before I married you. I probably wouldn't have said, "I do," because that premise seems to me Biblically wrong. That wasn't putting God's work first. That was disdain! The *first priority* in living out our relationship with God is *living His love in our families!* Following this we are to live out God's love in our church and our profession. God has sent us into the world to serve Him as His witnesses *by serving others!*

Each time I felt a desire to leave you, instead I made renewed effort to reach out to you, to build our friendship. The night after my last graduate recital I stood in the kitchen, with tears streaming down my face, and pleaded, "I am your wife. I NEED you to be a husband to me." You slammed some cupboard doors and walked out of the room.

Later that evening I asked you some question regarding our relationship, to which you sarcastically retorted, "I don't *have to* respond to that!" The hurt was so intense and the need to talk to someone so immediate that I left home a half-hour later without telling you. My talking and crying were done at Faye's house. My return home was more than twenty-four hours later. By that time I was sure you'd be frantic about me and ready to talk. When I pressed you--days later--to talk about it, you countered that my leaving was just a manipulation.

When we finally went away for a weekend—the first together in many years--I took along a magazine article about ways to achieve intimacy in marriage. It had multiple-choice questions regarding various aspects of sex and suggested husband and wife discuss their similarities and differences. After we answered and discussed three questions, and you discovered my tastes were not a carbon copy of yours, you angrily threw the magazine into the corner of the room and said that was no way to spend a romantic weekend. We watched your choice of TV after that.

When we went for sex therapy it was suggested and agreed upon that we set aside time to spend together to develop our *friendship*. We mutually chose Monday mornings and Wednesday evenings. That lasted maybe a month until you suddenly started doing your own thing at those times, such as playing tennis with other women, with no explanation and no substitution of a different time schedule.

It was more than ten years ago that I started having a number of terrible nightmares about us. I am going to tell you just two of them:

Dream Number One: I was struggling to climb a rickety scaffolding about thirty feet high to get into our kitchen. My toddler baby and I were naked, and the rough wood boards scratched and hurt as they swayed and almost buckled under us. I could see you, Victor, in your suit and tie sitting at the kitchen desk, looking down as you talked on the phone. You appeared happy, contented and very involved in conversation regarding your work. My baby and I were crying. I called to you loudly and repeatedly, "Victor, please help us! Please, please help us! I'm afraid we're going to fall!" But you wouldn't respond.

I changed my request and started pleading, "Please look! Look at me!" You looked up, but looked right past me as though I didn't exist, never acknowledging my presence, and returned to talking animatedly on the phone.

Suddenly I found myself in the kitchen. You were gone. The baby was gone. A living cloud, a sort of "monster" cloud of evil gloom, was about to enter the kitchen door. It was trying to get me. The door was open, but piled furniture and boxes filled the space between the door and me. I knew I must get it closed before the cloud got in, or be doomed. It was a life-and-death struggle to climb over the things, but using my last resources of strength and ingenuity I managed to barely reach the door with the tip of one finger and push it far enough to latch just as the cloud was pressing against it. Then because of my emotional tension and anxiety and the sudden relief, I turned around and started screaming hysterically, "Help, Help, Help!"

You woke me up and asked what's wrong, and I told you it was a nightmare. Going back to sleep, the dream-scene changed. I was in a basement that had rough cement floors and large, unfinished rooms with half-windows near the top. The floor had many telephone wires lying on it and extending to other rooms. There was the sound of your dialing the phone in the distance--dialing and dialing. If I could just find the right cable and follow the sound, you might be there. I was trying to untangle the lines to follow one, but it was so dark and confusing.

Finally I realized a window had been open, and the monster cloud had entered! It surrounded me with total darkness, pushed me over, and pressed me face down against the cold, filthy cement floor. Harder and stronger it bore down, squeezing out my very life and breath. But I prayed for God to help me, even though I couldn't speak. Suddenly I received a message in my mind: "You are going to survive. You will be all right."

Dream Number Two: You were a carved soldier in the center of a white marble "bas relief" decorating the side wall of the room. This artwork was life-size and covered the entire wall. You were a very strikingly handsome Christian soldier in Biblical-time garb, appearing to head full-speed to lead your followers into "Christian warfare." You had your helmet, your sword and your shield. In the carving many others were marching into battle with you. All looked animated, determined, happy and courageous. But in reality everything was unmoving, silent, beautiful, gleaming, polished, carved white marble.

In contrast, I was very much alive, human, and vulnerable. You were still my husband, and I wanted to honor and obey you. You were wordlessly telling me to eat the contents of a large white canvas bag that was on the floor beside me. There was a ragged hole in it, and I was trying hard to follow your instructions. Quite a bit was eaten all ready, judging by the hole in the solid mass. I again painfully scraped a bit of frozen, crystallized substance into my hand. My fingers ached from the cold. The icy crystals had pricked them in many places and spots of blood showed at the broken skin. Still I got small amounts and fingered it into my mouth. It didn't taste bad, sort of like frozen root beer.

After eating for a little while, I suddenly felt the side of my face go numb. Frightened, I reached up and touched it. Hard and cold, it felt like polished marble. In a panic I realized that what you were trying to make me eat would turn me into a marble "statue" like you. The numbness spread to my neck and shoulder, but I wanted to continue to be alive, moving, acting and feeling, not a gleaming white marble decoration on the wall. Horrified that I might have eaten so much it was too late, I knew now to *never* touch the contents of that bag again. I prayed, "Please God, rescue me! **End of dreams.**

After telling you my plans to leave you, you finally agreed to go with me for counseling to Dr. Roland. My plans had finalized for a trip to Canada to investigate a job possibility there, but we had a few more sessions before that date. The last counseling session before I left, you said you realized you had some problems and decided you would work on them for your own sake. I was so thrilled!

While away, and after some indecision, I finally decided to stay with you, since you gave your word to get help. But the very first counseling session after I returned, you told Dr. Roland a different decision: that day was your last session—you couldn't afford more!

Since I had already told you my decision to not leave you, my conscience persuaded me to keep my promise, even if you didn't keep yours. Although feeling no romantic love or sexual attraction, I chose to treat you lovingly, and I have. Lonelier at home than anywhere else, I have built life apart from you, arranging activities and finding some degree of intimacy with hiking friends, students, relatives and others.

We cope fairly well with life in the same house. But our sex life compares to a marathon runner thirstily gulping down a cup of water at a wayside station, except it's more like plodding, and I am the empty cup tossed in the trash.

You are valued by me as a human being and as the father of our children. I highly respect you as a minister and chaplain. You give tremendous service at the hospital and fill so many needs in the lives of others. You are enormously valuable and loved by so many. I see you as a most handsome man, as kind and caring "out there," as hard working and reliable in everyday tasks, as helpful and giving to many people, as dynamic, warm and interesting to the "world." But you have not been there for me when I needed you, except on rare occasions, for all these years. Is this all we have to look forward to for the rest of our lives?

Sincerely,
Judy

Victor listened silently to the end of the taped message, got up and walked out wordlessly. The next day I courageously asked him to play this tape for his Ministers' Support Group meeting which was being facilitated by my counselor, Lena Talbot. I didn't think he would, but surprisingly he did. The following day he returned the tape to me with only these words:

"I played the tape at the Support Group." He made no other comment and left the room.

My dreams are becoming an ongoing source of great comfort. I have learned from reading and counseling that each of us has an emotional or psychological "parent, adult, and child" within us. The baby climbing the scaffold with me I understand to be my inner child that was squelched most of my life and uncared for during my marriage. Our nakedness symbolizes my vulnerability and willingness to expose myself to learning, change and maturity. I am currently getting counseling and searching for a better relationship with Victor. I am learning to nurture my inner child. The message that I will be all right stays with me constantly, day to day.

Victor's intentions are so good and right in much of his effort to do God's work and fight spiritual battles. But because he is so emotionally blocked, he seems as impenetrable as marble. I am learning from the second dream to never again believe I must, for Victor's sake, squelch my feelings and needs for the sake of peace. God didn't intend that kind of obedience. From now on I will spend more time alone in nature where God recreates me with health of mind, body, spirit and emotions.

ULTIMATUM

Nearly a year after this December 7 letter was written and read to the Ministers' Support Group, the Convalescent Hospital was dedicating a new acreage of land for a gorgeous and intimate garden for the use of the patients. There was a special Celebration the evening of October 18, 1992. I came for the festivities, and while greeting many acquaintances and meeting new ones, at least three different women at three separate times voiced to me their individual opinions. The context of their comments went something like this: "You are *so* fortunate to be married to Victor. He is the *kindest* man I have ever known! You are so *blessed* to have him for a husband!"

Graciously I thanked each of them, and realized he probably *was* the kindest man they ever knew, because that is the way he relates to *others*. I also feel a huge stab of pain, longing for that kindness for myself, but have not told anyone.

One of the board members present that night was a man I had dated a few times when I was in high school and he in college. After the celebration was over and Victor was tending to his finalities before leaving for home, I saw Gene, now a retired minister, sitting in the lounge and went over to speak to him. He had recently lost his wife, and I wanted to give him my condolences. We talked a little longer than I had expected and did a bit of reminiscing while waiting for Victor. To my surprise, Gene interjected a statement that really took me unaware: "Judy, I have always loved you."

"Thank you. That's sweet of you to say that." I warmly basked in that comment for a while. It felt good to know someone noticed and cared.

That night I couldn't sleep, thinking of what Gene had said. Here is someone who obviously likes me and is not deeply connected to anyone close to me. I desperately need to talk to *someone* about my dead-end marriage relationship with Victor and think it would be safe with him. Next morning I called him, telling my need to talk, and we agreed to meet later in the day.

After somewhat explaining my marriage situation and my long-term efforts to improve it, he said, "Judy, this has gone on long enough. You *must* write an ultimatum and *force* Victor to some sort of decision regarding your relationship!" After he made several key suggestions along with more discussion, I agreed to do that. He prayed with me that God would guide. The next day this is what I wrote:

> October 20, 1992
> Dear Victor,
>
> You tell me you love me, but you refuse to discuss any problems we have. I *want* you for my husband, but you aren't there when you are needed. We live under the same roof, apparently playing the husband and wife game acceptably to the general public, but I want us to be *soul mates* and *best friends*--have lots of fun and laugh together, be able to sympathize and cry together. I've tried everything imaginable and get no decipherable response from you.
>
> This is my request: Before the end of the year, please find a counselor and get into therapy.
>
> Look at the following concepts or behaviors: assertiveness, awareness, integrity, aliveness, personal happiness and joy, describing feelings, expressing wants and needs, saying no to what you don't want, saying yes to what you do want, choosing to make plans for yourself or for us.

Look at these and discuss them with your counselor. If you choose to work on any *one* (or more), please tell me, and I'll wait *as long as necessary* for you to work it through. But if you choose to work on *nothing*, I will file for a divorce after three more months—that would be the end of next March.

I am praying for both of us to learn how to love each other the way I believe God intended. Please let me know what you decide.

Judy

I called Gene and read it to him. He said that was *exactly* what I should say; he'd be praying for me. I knew if I just handed it to Victor to read, there would be no response. So I read it out loud to him that night, Thursday Oct. 22, 1992. When I finished, he suddenly rose from his chair and left the room hurriedly as he almost inaudibly mumbled his only comment, "You go find an attorney!"

I wasn't sure I even understood him correctly, so figured I'd wait and ask him later. The next day, as he came in from work and passed me in the kitchen, he monotoned, "I told my boss and quite a few others that we are getting divorced—you're divorcing me."

Astonished, I gasped, "But I *didn't* say I was divorcing you! I want to know if you're willing to *work* on anything! Are you?"

Totally devoid of expression, these words tumbled out of Victor's mouth, "I can't do all that you demand! That's impossible! I give up! You get the attorney! I'm not even going to bother. I told everybody you had an affair!" In absolute silence he slumped past me into his study and even closed the door without a click.

Shock! Disbelief! Utter amazement! Humiliation! Pain! Anger! Hurt! Agony! I'm frozen in place! I gape at this man, this apparition—or the space he momentarily occupied before escaping. He's an emotionless animal, an unfeeling chunk of white marble! He's only a skeleton of a human being. He's a cold machine!

This is the same man who has heard me ask, numerous times through all these years, if there is *anything* he would like to change about me, and

261

who has *always* answered, "I love you just the way you are!" and he often still gives me a "peck kiss" on the cheek as he leaves for work, saying, "Love you." But he *refuses to discuss problems!* In fact he says, "We have *always* swept problems under the rug, and I *demand we continue to do that!*"

For a few moments I hardly even realize that he's left the room. This is unreal! Judy, get a hold of yourself RIGHT NOW! MOVE! DO SOMETHING! DON'T JUST STAND THERE!

The rest of the evening is a blur. The remainder of the week is drenched in fog. But sometime, as blank days slowly slid into oblivion, as hurt hours flooded past in a blur, as crying nights slumped into a wet pillow or a sopping towel, my determination began to grow. Fury chomped its tail and raged.

Finally, during defiant and morosely desperate night hours when comfort and sleep had eloped, I lunged out of bed, yanked a notebook from a haphazard stack on my desk and grabbed a pen. Angrily my rear thumped hard onto the sturdy oak chair behind me. After a couple noisy deep breaths, I slammed the pen down against the wood desk top with a resounding whack, but that released only a miniscule mite of the tension and emotional pain wracking my body. I picked up the pen again and started to write as fast as possible. My imagination was aflame, and my heart on fire. My brain, silently roaring, was conjuring up ideas which overflowed with more speed than they could be flung as words onto paper. It was *now December*, two months after our divorce was filed. The words in my head lurched on, trying to win the race with my fingers and writing utensil:

Agony! The searing, pulsating, jabbing constancy of the rejection is overwhelming. The abandonment, the being discarded, deluges and floods my being. The finality has dawned. There is no hope! There never should have been. I still hear Victor's words as he was packing, getting ready to move out—the loud, forceful, angry words:

"I don't *like* intimacy! I don't *want* intimacy! I *never* have, and I *never* will! When you ask me how I feel, it gives me the *paralysis of analysis!* I don't want *anyone* to *ever* ask me how I feel, because I don't *know* how I feel, and *I don't want to know!*"

On and on I wrote until my soul emptied itself on paper. I wrote what I *imagined* Victor's unspoken marriage contract was, or at least what I now perceive he must have *wanted* it to be! I felt like a galloping wild stallion, picking up speed as I wrote. The signs were there from the beginning—in actions, words, letters. How could I have interpreted them in such a convoluted way as to seem like a good thing? How I wish I had been willing to see the red flags before we married.

Back then it seemed to be a storybook romance. This was the man born to be mine! The musician who could, with me, make magnificent melody. So long ago I thought every facet fit, every detail developed as desired, every handsome hope happened, every exciting event endured. My emotional night must be over; the morning of reality was dawning. That's what I thought—*then*! Back then! WAY BACK THEN! **FAR BACK IN THE DARK AGES!!!!! KAREN: WOMEN OFTEN SADLY IGNORE THEIR INTUITION. SOME HAVE BEEN TAUGHT TO BYPASS SUBTLE SIGNS, EVEN BLATANT ONES—SIGNS THEIR MOTHERS, SISTERS AND FRIENDS HAVE ADVISED THEM TO IGNORE.**

VICTOR: In retrospect, as this book is being completed, I realize now that what I was *feeling* then, when we first married, was this: I, Victor Leigh, the *spiritual* leader of our family, must *require* certain Biblical principles to be *unquestionably* upheld and *faithfully* carried out. I believed that because the Biblical Abraham *commanded* his "household after him, that they shall keep the way of the Lord" (see Genesis 18:18, 19 KJV), I thought I must also *command* my wife to obey God. It was *my* total responsibility to do this. I *believed* this was what the world *expected* of me, if I was to be a *proper* husband! But I also felt *totally inadequate!*

I continued deluging my paper with pain, imagining what Victor might say to me *right now*, if he was capable of expressing his thoughts regarding our divorce. Going on, I fantasized on paper that the following were Victor's bitter and condemning words to me *right now*:

You made waves in my life.

You rocked my boat too many times.
You didn't unconditionally accept my unspoken contract.
You have refused to submit to me.

My imagination regarding Victor's *thinking* was based on my experience as his wife. It wasn't necessarily what was *really* in his mind. But I drained my imagination until there were no more words to write and I could face a different world.

After many agonizing hours, and who knows—a day, a week, a month or so—or more—I was able to begin to face my reality: Apparently Victor has wanted to *rid himself of me all along* and just didn't have the guts to do it. Now he seems happy and relieved, more relaxed than he's been for months. He wants to leave right now! Maybe this "animal" isn't as emotionless as I thought! This cold machine is at least *starting* to warm up, but maybe for a drag race—the opposite direction!

My wonderful and terrible rocky-road-roller-coaster marriage is starting to make sense to me. Life is about growing, not stagnating! Living is a process of gaining insight from problems and moving in new directions. Who wants a boring life? I've always loved challenges. Now, I see there is a real story to tell! Who knows all the paradoxes and conundrums that will yet develop? What ecstasies and tragedies will transpire? What sort of a climax will evolve? I know now I want to TELL MY STORY—no matter what waits at every turn and detour—no matter how it resolves. I will buy a mini-tape-recorder.

I asked Victor to stay through the Christmas holidays for our sons' sake, since they were planning to spend that time with us. He complied, but started sorting his things and packing. On New Year's Day, 1993, he moved out. Our divorce was finalized eight months later.

PRISM

Thinking—recording; reading—recording; writing—recording; crying—recording! It's March 21, about two and a half months since Victor moved out. Life is still never boring, although sometimes sad and lonely, and often very colorful.

Last night I finished reading a book by Barbara de Angeles called, <u>How to Make Love All the Time</u>. It has made a profound impression on me. One of the things she teaches is how to write what she calls "love letters" to *yourself!* The six things this kind of love letter is to include are:

1. Anger and blame.
2. Hurt and sadness.
3. Fear and insecurity.
4. Remorse and responsibility.
5. Intention and wishes.
6. Love, forgiveness, understanding and appreciation.

Now I will write a letter to myself, read it aloud while recording it, then listen to it carefully, as frequently as I need to hear it, until my emotions get transformed—I hope! Working to change the relationship between Victor and me, I want to heal and get back to the state of love, even if we don't ever remarry, choosing to *release* Victor and *empty myself of negative emotions. God please help me. I'm counting on You!*

Dear Judy,

I am angry with you for being afraid of Victor, and disgusted you weren't brave enough to confront the problems, which started before you were married—like when he first French-kissed you. I'm furious you even slept in the same bed with him the night he angrily refused your loving seduction. You took it so calmly when Victor walked out of the talent show and said he couldn't stand your student's singing and wouldn't stay to hear the others. Your passivity galls me. And it absolutely appalls me that you didn't tell his mom to get out when she walked in on you without knocking when you were both naked on the bed.

I'm dumbstruck you accepted the blame for Victor hitting you, and aghast that you decided to stay with him. It is terrible to think you always must submit in order to keep him from repeating that dastardly act.

This letter writing to myself is certainly a challenge! The above takes care of point No. 1—Anger and Blame. Point No. 2 is to include Hurt and Sadness. There certainly has been an enormous amount of that.

I wonder why you weren't absolutely inflamed when Victor's mom came to visit, and she and Victor looked into each others eyes, kissing and hugging like lovers for at least a half hour, while you fixed dinner that time during your first year of marriage.

It displeases me that you didn't write Victor an ultimatum years ago. I'm infuriated you let him wield his passive power over you, tear you down and nearly destroy you. You should have refused to stay in a relationship where you and your boys were treated as non-persons. You undoubtedly didn't *know how* to un-numb him or persuade him to face his reality, and he didn't know how to express his rage, guilt and low self-esteem, so that he could overcome them, and I am grieved by that fact.

It's OK to hurt. It will not last! You've learned to tolerate a lot and can hold your head up and move on. You are not going to break or die, and you enjoy independence and aloneness already.

Now I'll attempt writing point No. 3: Fear and Insecurity. These emotions are still raging in me.

Sometimes worry fills me that Victor will grow a lot and really change, and you won't recognize his growth and will miss the chance of having a great husband. Someone else will get him, and you'll be alone—an Old Maid, despised and rejected because you couldn't see gold and diamonds lying in front of you. Yet I'm almost panicked you might think you see something valuable where there is only fool's gold. Don't go there!

Do you fear you'll fall apart if Victor marries again? Are you afraid you'll always see yourself as a super failure if he makes another marriage stick? Will Victor always blame you for being an awful wife? Actually, I'm almost terrified he will, with his charm, persuade the whole world that that *is true* about you, and you'll be hated forever! But inside, you *know* that is *not* true!

One thing I've learned in counseling and group therapy: I *do* have remorse, lots of it; but I'll not let it drown me. And I certainly *am* responsible for my own decisions and actions, which is point No. 4, Remorse and responsibility.

You allowed yourself to be his victim. Your passivity was as bad as his. You are as responsible as he is for allowing things to go on this long. It also astounds me that you actually believed for a while that suicide was better than divorce. You were so weak, naive and self- blaming. It's pathetic you didn't know how to break through the mask and iron walls surrounding the frozen man under all those layers. It's tragic you doubted your own sexuality and believed for so long you were abnormal. You should have *forced* the conversation to sexual issues that first day before they deteriorated so much. I *despise* your being unfaithful! I *loathe* infidelity!

Now I need to set goals and make strong decisions about my own behavior and set boundaries for myself. Here are my intentions and wishes for my future, which is point No. 5. And following that, I will continue— always—to move into love, forgiveness, understanding and appreciation, as designated in point No. 6.

I'm *positive* you can let Victor go and find a rewarding life for yourself. What are you hanging on to? Don't you love him enough to release him? I can see you are petrified of the guilt probably more than the pain. Can you dump guilt? Don't you dare return because of that! Give yourself time to heal and flourish. This can be a time so filled with your generous love, that you will reach out with tenderness, compassion and caring to many, many people—any gender, any age.

You are a sleek, female cat—tiger or panther—moving through her world quietly, yet with power, strength and grace. You are somewhat tamed, but you know how to protect yourself, hunt and find what you need.

Don't look for alley cats or plain old tomcats. Don't look for kittens. Don't latch on to any crude, mean lions. Out there somewhere are partially tamed, big male cats—smooth, fun and intelligent, who want to mate for life and true love. They want to share excitement, joy and tenderness with a feminine feline who knows how to strut her stuff at the right time, but is calmly waiting without a flip of the tail. She knows how to capture whatever is life-sustaining. She also knows how to have a good romp in the hay or jungle. You are that cat! You have your life in control. I admire you! I commend you! I love and cherish you! You are courageous, resourceful and enormously loyal! You are a wonder!"

When I had finished reading Barbara de Angelis' book and made the decision to write and record a letter to myself, my spirits felt so extremely low—depressed—worthless— aimless—that I expected to need to listen to this tape while going to sleep every night for the next few months, or weeks at least. But after writing, recording and listening to it three nights, there was no more need. It wasn't listened to or looked at again until the writing of this book. The tape itself was thrown out two or three weeks later. I KNEW WHO I WAS!

Light had finally shown through the cracks of my broken emotions, and the healing rays had become prismed into a multitude of exquisite colors.

21

EXHAUST

My sister was chapter president for a Singles Club in a nearby city and was contacted by a man who had lost his wife to cancer a year earlier. Jim was interested in finding some single women his age that might like to get acquainted. She gave him my name and specs and immediately called to inform me. This was in July of 1992, shortly before our divorce was final. Jim soon called and we started communicating. Shortly we were able to meet and spend time together getting acquainted. He was an excellent conversationalist and definitely not passive. He planned interesting things and soon started talking about a wedding--our wedding!

We would move to his farm half of the year and travel in his motor home the other half. I would always come with him to the tennis courts when he played, but since I wasn't as good a player as he was, I would find my own partner. Since he made the living, I would not teach any music students. His spinet piano was just fine, and I didn't need my seven-and-a-half-foot grand. He would handle all the money, including what little I had. I went along with all of this, for a short time, because it was such a welcome change. **KAREN: THIS WAS ACTIVE CONTROL, INSTEAD OF VICTOR'S PASSIVE-AGGRESSIVE CONTROL.**

But soon there were misgivings, and I felt an urgency to pray even more than I had been previously about my situation. If it was not God's will to marry Jim, if it would turn out worse than my first marriage, I wanted God to make something happen to cause us to break up. I already had enough emotional traumas, and felt I couldn't bear more. And I *did* want God's approval on my next marriage, if there was to be one.

After we traveled to meet Jim's son, daughter and mother and visited his farm, each in a different state, Jim moved his motor home into my back yard. But I soon sensed his dissatisfaction, and was rather expecting him to tell me things weren't right for us.

We were conversing in his motor home one day when there was a knock on the door. When Jim opened it, there stood Victor, a smile stretching wider than I could have imagined. Jim invited him in, and before sitting down, Victor joyfully proclaimed, "I want you to know I'm the *happiest* I have *ever* been in my *entire* life! I'm engaged to a *wonderful* woman, and we are getting married next June."

Instantly I broke down and started to cry, *shocking both of them as well as myself*! No one said anything for a little while. Finally I sobbed, "That hurts so much to hear you say you are happier than *we ever were*, even in our courting days or any time since then." Appalled at my own blubbering, I excused myself and left to go back into my home. Jim suggested he and Victor go play tennis.

Embarrassed and dazed, I isolated myself until bedtime, trying to sort everything out. After an almost sleepless night, I rose at 5:00 a.m. the next day to write:

Dear Victor,

Can't you realize how much it hurt for you to bring me the "good news" that you felt happier than you have ever felt in your life? There is a part of me that hates you for that! I never hated you before. Can't you understand that what I felt for you all those years was deep, profound love when I asked for counseling and was dissatisfied?

My "losing my love" for you was a result of your rejection of me, which started within days after we married. A part of you hated my guts, and it hurt so badly! I wanted so much to be what you wanted me to be--to change and grow to become your partner and companion. I wanted to inspire you, support you, excite you, be your secretary, go on Bible studies with you. You wouldn't let me! I'm human and made a great many mistakes. My mannerisms turned you off. I interrupted you in conversations and bored you with details. But I want you to know I didn't *ever* choose or *try* to "run" you, intimidate you, overpower you or "wear the pants in the family." I wanted *you* to be my *leader*, my helper, and my supporter.

The excruciating pain of the letter from the Conference President who first hired you, after you finished seminary, is still with me. I longed to figure out how *not to be* what he described—the one who "'wore the pants" in the family. I wanted to encourage you in *your* leadership, but you didn't let me. My heart is in a million pieces when I realize there was *nothing* I could have done all of those years to make you happy except keep out of your way and keep my mouth shut.

Alan hadn't started school when a different Conference President asked you whether your "helping with housework" kept you from making enough "calls." You told me recently that *his questioning* escalated your anger towards me and *sealed your decision* to "pull away" even more. But you didn't let me know! Victor, I loved you from the very core of my being, likely much more than you now love Clarice.

Please remember: Immediately after returning from the trip in the motor home with Jim, I requested our sitting down to talk. I *didn't* smilingly say, "I have good news to share with you." Instead I told you there was "something heavy" we needed to talk about, not wanting to hurt you. But even then I ached while telling you, "Jim is willing to back out now and leave, because he recognizes I really belong to you."

At first you didn't even answer, but eventually said coldly, "Thank you for telling me." That response hurt enormously. When I questioned you, you admitted you were *relieved* I found another man.

Perhaps I shouldn't have told you about my affairs. That must be what made you decide you could never love me again. I don't blame you. I did wrong. I had been in horrible agony with a husband who pretended there was nothing wrong and said he loved me, when in actuality you were bitter, resentful and had no desire to work at closeness.

Right now I feel devastated, having spent thousands of dollars on counseling, used concentrated energy reading dozens of self-help books, and prayed untold hours struggling to be the woman you wanted. That is all gone! Down the tubes! Garbage now! You say you are happier than you've ever been before. I believe you! You seem elated, look younger and more handsome, radiant and in love.

Jim has backed off. He moved too fast in the beginning and now questions whether we are even compatible. But he does *not* see me as intimidating, overpowering, overbearing, and critical as you see me. Instead, the problems he verbalizes are that I can't fit in with his goals of tennis, ping-pong, shuffleboard, horseshoes and snow skiing. I was excited about learning these fun things. Jim thinks I'll resent giving up my friends and piano teaching. **KAREN: YES, JUDY WOULD DEFINITELY RESENT JIM FOR HAVING TO SACRIFICE HER PIANO, TEACHING CAREER AND HER FRIENDS!** But *right now* I don't *want* to play or sing again, or teach music. Right now I *hate* listening to music! *It tears me up!* Jim says he now wants me to get as many students as possible and progress as if we were never to marry.

You are fortunate to find someone you are compatible with—someone to love you. During all those years when you were so depressed and *felt* unloved by me, if we could have just *admitted* our problems and *talked* about them, maybe we could have resolved them and rekindled our love, or else decided to separate.

Victor, I still love you! There are many things about you that I miss. My only reason for moving out of the bedroom was self-respect. Each time you asked me when I was coming back to join you in the bedroom, I *wanted the situation to change*, but couldn't continue any longer without *acceptance, love* and *effort* on *your* part towards intimacy.

God can work miracles in our emotions. And though my feelings have been kicked down so many times that they currently haven't strength or bravery to rise into awareness, I truly believe they *could* be reborn. That could have happened with determination to learn *how* to love.

Because I still care for you, you are wished the best in your new love. Today I threw away the large cardboard heart valentine I created for you with love on our anniversary. I haven't the vaguest imagination what the future holds. Not consciously choosing to die, I'm not sure if I want to live. You are not to blame. You are free to love another and still be respected by me. May God bless and strengthen you and give you wisdom and ability to love Clarice as I wish you *could* have loved me. Please learn how to communicate and be intimate with her. Don't live in denial!

Jim said you told him it didn't take long for you to get over any pain of divorce because you could see it coming for a long time. Why didn't you tell me you wanted it years ago? I know "why" questions are useless, and don't expect an answer. But why did you force *me* into going to an attorney and acting on the very thing I had been trying to avoid, but which *you wanted*?

Your love meant more to me than music, hiking, reading or life itself. I'm sorry you couldn't love me passionately, and I couldn't return love for pretense. Right now I can't imagine how to endure the next days, weeks and months, facing the reality that you are far happier than you ever were with me, even in our courtship days. But I will survive! God bless us both.

Judy

The following weekend Jim took his motor home away and that was the last I ever saw of him.

Victor soon responded to my letter with the following:

Dear Judy,

I somehow thought that since you said your love for me was dead, and because you said you loved Jim, I thought that would soften the blow you were "afraid" was coming. I don't blame you for hating me. Unconsciously I suppose it was to "get even" for your loving Jim and the rest of them.

Judy, I too have love for you, but it's more like pity and sorrow for the pain I've caused you. That's not a strong basis for remarriage or even attempts at counseling. I guess my faith is not strong enough to overcome thoughts that may never be obliterated: "I wonder if I'm doing 'it' as well as Tony or the others that made love to you." And what about the thoughts that you might have: "I wonder if he loves me as much as Clarice, or was it just guilt or pity that brought him back." It tears me apart and hurts me to say this, but I don't think it will work for us to try to get back together, even for counseling.

Judy, I think you are a fine woman. I have forgiven you for the affairs. I have done mean things to hurt you, and you say you have forgiven me. But it doesn't wipe out the past. It's too late, Judy. Please don't do anything drastic. You are still a good person. If things don't work out with Jim, I'm sure there is a male friend of a relative or a man somewhere who would be delighted to have you as a devoted companion.

You certainly did everything you knew how to do to make the marriage work. I thank you for that. I should have been honest with you years ago when it would have been easier to start life over with a new partner. If you don't want me coming over to the house when you're there, just say so and I won't come over.

Victor

Finality seemed certain. My friend Susan suggested I start a prayer journal of thankfulness. She said I needed to start a habit of thinking positive thoughts, being thankful for all the blessings I have. Thanking her for the excellent idea, I decided to jot down things I'm thankful for on arising, no matter what my "mood" is. Remembering it first thing in the morning was the hardest part. Over and over I didn't remember until halfway through the day, but then I put it down on paper.

Soon after that I was driving down the freeway when the memory jolted me again. Being thankful for anything seemed totally preposterous at the time. But I had made a decision and determined to keep it. Searching my brain to think of something, I spoke out loud, "Lord, thank you for the variety of colors of cars. It would be so boring if they were all the same color, even if that was red." In a few minutes I saw a huge, spreading tree totally bare of leaves and noticed a beautifully intricate design created by the branches and twigs, and imagined trying to sketch them. Then I thanked God for the splendor He creates in the natural things of this world.

The following are a few entries from my prayer journal of thankfulness:

"Thank you, God, for Susan. She seems to make more sense to me than anyone else since Jim broke up with me. She has helped me understand that neither Victor nor I are ready for another relationship, because we haven't finished the business between us. **KAREN: YES!** She helped me see the importance of finding out who I am, learning to *be without* a man, learning to become involved with projects of my own so that I won't spend time needing a man."

"I am truly grateful for health and strength, for hearing and eyesight and the sense of taste, touch and smell. Thank you for food and clothing, warmth and shelter, a good bed and my dog, Buster. I appreciate a car that runs well and my income from students. Thank you for a functioning brain and the power to make choices." **KAREN: AMEN!**

"I highly value the calls from my sister and mother today. They were such a tremendous comfort to me. Thank you for the gorgeous, sunny, clear morning as I walked up the hill. I'm relieved that my house mates are being more cooperative with each other. I'm blessed that today was the best day I've had for two or three weeks. I didn't feel shaky three-fourths of the day. I was able to concentrate on my teaching."

"Thanks for a good sleep at night with warm blankets and not gaining any weight this week. I was elated that my cholesterol was down from 297 to 233. I felt blessed that gas prices came down. Thanks for red and the compliments I get wearing it. Thank you that I could study and cook today from the nutrition book Jim gave me before we broke up, and also look at his picture without falling apart."

"I appreciate the opportunity you have given me to make a difference in the universe. I really value Victor's effort to be more open with me. Thank you that I can learn from my dreams. I'm thankful for getting a lot done today—closets, washing, sorting, check writing, ironing. I'm thankful my brother is teaching me about investing."

"Thank you that the policeman is trying to get the car license of whoever smashed the side of my car while it was parked by the music building where I was teaching yesterday. I'm grateful I wasn't in it. Because of your grace I can leave my problems in your hands, whether we find the hit- and-run driver or not. Thank you for my calmness in teaching today."

Merv Jenson, the teacher of some of Victor's classes in chaplain's training, a good friend and fine therapist, wanted both Victor and me to get counseling *specifically* for the purpose of "finishing our business" regarding our relationship. Neither Victor nor I were ready for another relationship, and that was so obvious to Merv. I saw it then, but apparently Victor didn't. Merv Jenson didn't plan this to patch up our relationship.

Merv persuaded Victor to come *with me* for counseling, but wasn't expecting this to change anything except help us empty our emotional garbage bags and give us wisdom to keep from filling them again. God help us both!

Shortly Victor and I both attended a session with Merv Jenson. He gave the assignment to Victor of writing me a "love letter." Then he set up another appointment for later in the same day. Victor wrote the following:

Dear Judy,

I'm sorry for all the grief I've caused you. You have a beautiful voice. You've had your vocal problems like most singers. One time, when you asked me to tell you what I didn't like about your singing, I felt at a loss to come up with the technical terminology to address the problem. You are a good voice teacher and I have always felt inadequate to suggest anything in the way of improvement of voice production. Through the years of many voice teachers, books read and suggestions given, you came up with a good philosophy or method of teaching to develop in the singer all of the different qualities of the voice and not making a hobby horse of just one quality and in the process trying different techniques to suit the person and his or her unique situation or personality.

The night we sang the duet, "La Mano," I thought you sang well. I don't know why I dwelt on the negative. <u>Perhaps it was the idea of being competitive rather than encouraging one another. The latter is where I want to be now</u>. **KAREN: MY UNDERLINING. WOW!**

VICTOR: Before we were divorced I felt inadequate as a musician, father, preacher, husband and person. It had seemed that whatever I suggested, *SHE* took as "wrong," even though Judy didn't say so. She believes she was only wanting to broaden my perspective with a *VARIETY* of ideas and often just kept elaborating

on creative alternatives more than validating mine. I mistakenly took every suggestion as criticism, resulting in *my* feeling worthless because *my ideas* seemed worthless to her. The only way I could conceive of having worth was to be *better* than her. That way I could "win."

Karen: Victor and Judy were both competitive, but underneath that was Judy's motivation to help Victor shine as much as he could. And Victor's self-loathing made him hear everything as Judy's condemnation. If Victor could have said that he "felt condemned", and Judy could have expressed her love for him, they could have moved into a deeper understanding of each other.

As to the red headed singer—I can't even remember her name—I was very enamored by her *voice*. But in comparison to yours—well, yours and her voice are just different. You both have unique qualities. I like the warmth of your tone, the feeling you put into your singing, the close attention to pronunciation of words, the vibrancy in your voice, your body language, and the pleasant expression on your face as you sing songs from the heart.

When we spent that first weekend together in your hometown, we sang and played for hours. How thrilled I was with your voice, and with you and your piano playing. I didn't have the security and the self-worth at that time to give the compliments, the encouragement and the love that you needed. I'm sorry for that. Please forgive me.

Lovingly,
Victor

At our second counseling session that same day, the above letter was discussed. Victor was assigned to write another "Love Letter."

Dear Judy,

You mentioned this morning how disappointed you were in my love letter to you because it didn't have much emotion in it. Now hear this:

I didn't marry you because of your voice. I married you because I loved you. You were and are a beautiful person inside and out. Your lovely voice and expert and expressive piano playing were a bonus I hadn't expected to find in anyone.

I remember our rapturous courting days when I tried to keep you occupied with me every weekend so Reese wouldn't have a chance to get you back, and Joe wouldn't have a chance to take you out again. No suitor was going to steal my queen away.

Talk about passion—remember how sometimes I couldn't keep my hands off you? Where has that passion gone? I don't know. However just the fact that I can write about it lets me know that it's there, buried under garbage. It's there waiting to be resurrected.

Lovingly,
Victor

Victor had told our counselor at the first session that day that *he wanted* to try to get back together with me! A mixture of fright and hope stirred within me. Am I going to be so stupid that I'll remarry a man who is still frozen, non-communicating, and often unfeeling? Or will I be so stubborn and blind that I'll not recognize Victor's growth, maturity and rekindled love? For more than a month we continued weekly counseling sessions.

One day I visited Victor at his apartment, thrilled with his new, respectful, attentive and loving attitude. Then the following day, it not only disappeared, but anger, resentment and bitterness replaced it. I just had to express my feelings to Victor regarding this dilemma:

Dear Victor,

How I ache tonight. Hurt and panic chase each other. Our two sessions in one day thrilled me. Although neither

Merv nor I had planned for—*or even imagined it*—you said you *wanted* to get back with me! Your *insisting* that's what you wanted prompted me to start believing perhaps you were serious about *really* wanting that. You even related you *told that to some people at your work*! But I've needed to talk to you and question you, because you say you still have hostility towards me.

Last night I felt really lonesome for you, so after phoning and talking awhile, courage stirred me enough to ask if I could come over. You acted happy to see me, and we enjoyed watching the news together. The way you decorated your apartment impressed me, and your lighting the candles and offering to rub my back thrilled me. Feeling almost romantic, I also felt scared to let my emotions go free. For years you pretended to not be angry with me, but I felt it at a deep level anyway. How can I trust that you mean what you say without our being in real communication? Since you didn't offer much information, I felt a strong need to question you. **KAREN: GOOD PERCEPTION!**

I worried that you were just "pretending" when you said you wanted to play tennis regularly with me. When you asked me that same evening to go to the upcoming Alumni Homecoming with you, saying you were "*ready for the public to see us as a couple again*," my hopes started to soar. I began to think maybe I could enjoy going to a movie, a concert, out to dinner or to the cabin for a weekend with you.

I asked a lot of questions last night and was both surprised and pleased that you seemed delighted to answer them openly and honestly; but worried inwardly whether there was too much questioning on my part. That's why I humorously asked, "Could you handle one hundred more hours of talking like this before we decide to get back together?"

You responded pleasantly that if we remember to use the code word like Merv suggested—to stop conversation when it gets out of hand—you thought we could manage well. We agreed on "elephant." I had no idea then that all this turmoil was in you. Couldn't you have been honest and said "elephant" that night? I would have shut up immediately.

Coming home the next afternoon and seeing your car in my driveway pleased me. I was about to suggest we go out to eat when you said you had to be home by seven. Not trying to pry; the question just popped out, "Whatcha' doin' tonight?"

You answered that Mr. Peterson [Clarice's ex] was going to return your call at seven. You wanted to ask him about Clarice.

Then I asked you, "If he gives you a good recommendation for his ex-wife, are you going to want to get back with Clarice?"

You sounded hotheaded and smart-alecky when you answered, "I'm not going to promise!" and then told me you didn't like my "inquisition" last night. Yet you hadn't said the code word or asked me to stop. *I can't read your mind!* **KAREN: PASSIVE-AGGRESSIVE CONTROL AGAIN!**

Then I asked you, "Didn't you commit yourself to trying to get back with me—not pressing me for time?" Instead of answering that, you told me it was while you were writing the second "love letter" to me you realized you didn't know if you were really committed, and that you are emotionally unstable. I believe you, but it hurts to have allowed my emotions a step toward loving you and the very next day get rebuffed with your anger and hostility.

Neither Merv nor I expected these counseling sessions to reunite us. Neither of us hinted for that. Merv just wanted for us to learn to bury our garbage and not create more. It was all *your* idea to work towards our getting back together, and you amazed both of us with *that idea of yours!*

If Clarice finds out that you called her ex to ask about her "hang-ups," she may feel angry with you and have second thoughts about wanting *you!* Nine years is a long time after her divorce, and much could change. The ex could decide to give you a glowing report about her *falsely* for any number of reasons—his own hang-ups included. Or he could, in bitterness and anger, give bad reports that are not true. I'm not going to put hope in a man who will have me only if his girlfriend's ex-husband gives a bad recommendation. I'm worth more than that!

Judy

Not long after this Victor was assigned to write another letter for his therapy:

Dear Judy,

You asked me about the vestige of hostility left in me. Well, some of that hostility stems from the realization that several men had sex with you, some of whom you hardly knew. You say you wouldn't have me in the bedroom because you didn't know me—(lack of intimacy). You knew some of these men for a few hours and you gave yourself to them—one flesh.

You said I was sexually using you. What were these other men doing? Did they really love you? Or were they using you? I'm sure my performance wasn't the best, but I did try. After we went for sex therapy, I thought we were doing well together. The reason I went back to playing tennis on Monday mornings was because I thought your interest was waning!

It would have helped, had I known about my hang-ups with mom. How could I get sexual with my mother? That was a no-no. How could I make love to one who had to be in control of everything, like my grandmother? How could I be sexually passionate to my grandmother who hated men and controlled me more than mother or dad or anyone else?

I also felt *inferior* to you in every way. How could I, *an inferior slave*, make love to the Queen?

I've done many things to hurt you, some in an infantile spirit of revenge. I don't wish to dwell further on "histrionics," but I needed to get this anger out of my system! I'm sorry if this letter further hurts you. We both hurt each other. I'm sorry for that.

The reason I wrote this letter is that I previously denied and tried to cover up the hurt and the anger. Now it is released. You don't have to respond to this if you don't wish to.

Sincerely,
Victor

In the above letter, Victor wrote about his grandmother being such a controlling person. I am now remembering about some years earlier, when our boys and I stayed with Victor's mom and grandmother for an extra week or two after Victor flew back to his pastoral duties. Mom and Grandma were preparing to move to a different home and needed help packing. Victor's brother Patrick, who still lived at home, was away for the weekend. I was to sleep in his much younger sister Aimee's room at the back of the house, because she was away at college.

After preparing for bed, I had locked the back door of the house which was right next to "my" room. Grandma came a minute or two later, unlocked it and sarcastically enunciated, "Don't you lock this door! Patrick is coming about midnight and will want to get in."

"I don't feel safe sleeping with the outside door unlocked. I'll hear him come and open it before he gets to the door," I explained.

Raising her voice even more, she shouted, "No! Don't you *dare* lock it!"

In compliance I stated, "Okay, I won't right now. But after you go to bed I'll lock it."

I could see the fury rise in her. Now she stomped her feet as she yelled, "I *demand* you leave this door unlocked!"

Smiling calmly I said, "Okay, grandma, it's all right. I won't lock it now, but I will before I go to sleep." Her temper tantrum was beginning to amuse me.

She started screaming and grabbing her long hair, which she had let down for the night. She was in her flannel nightie and bare feet, stomping like a two-year-old, yanking hard on clumps of her white hair, flailing her furious words at me. "You do what I say! Don't you *dare* lock this door! It is to stay unlocked *all night!*"

I had never forgotten the night a man sneaked into our unlocked home and the fear that engulfed me then, and knew I couldn't sleep now with the door unlocked. Indulgently I repeated, "Its okay to leave it unlocked now. I'll lock it later and open it when I hear Patrick drive in the driveway."

KAREN: Great way to respond to a temper tantrum!

Grandma's tirade went on for probably five minutes before she stomped off, still yelling, to bed. Never before had I seen an adult acting out so totally in a childish tantrum. I *did* lock the door, went to sleep, heard Patrick's car come in, unlocked the door before he got to it, re-locked it before going back to sleep and unlocked it before grandma was up the next morning.

Victor had to share a bedroom with this grandma from the time he was about ten until we married, except when he was in the college dorm and the army. Any time he came home during that sixteen-year period, he slept in that same room, which was always called and considered "grandma's room." No wonder he has expected me to be like his grandma, or has "put her face on me," as Merv calls it. But that controlling, angry behavior is so foreign to me.

My father was my "emotional model." He *never* appeared to lose control! My personal challenge was to emulate him *as well as possible!* I determined to *first* think through and silently name what I was feeling in response to events. My *second* responsibility was to make a decision about how I would respond before allowing any words or actions to have their reign.

As I mentally separated my future hopes and plans from my real and currently present life realities, my emotions became much calmer. However, it wasn't long before Victor's roller-coaster emotions and reactions rocked me again. In an attempt to state the problems clearly to him, I wrote again:

November 11, 1993
Dear Victor,

> I'm still struggling in bafflement regarding your anger at my questions that night at your apartment. You say you felt like I subjected you to an "inquisition" that romantic Wednesday night.
>
> When I came to your place that night, you again said you wanted to "get back together with me." You even invited me to go to the upcoming college Alumni Homecoming with you, saying you were "willing for the world to see us again as a couple." Yet you haven't even mentioned it since, or said you changed your mind. What's going on? You need to know why so many questions were asked. You are confusing me!

Here you are, a man whom I've loved deeply for decades in spite of:

1. Sexually rejecting me in rage in the first three months of marriage. No reason ever given.
2. Professionally rejecting me in anger the night you walked out of the talent show and said you couldn't stand my student's solo, so refused to listen to all my other students—first six months of marriage.
3. Hitting me hard in the face and telling me to get out, and never a spoken word of apology—first year of marriage
4. Telling me before four years of marriage had passed that you had *no love for our two sons*, and you *knew* before we married that you never wanted children; but you *didn't tell me the truth* back then

because you were afraid I wouldn't marry you. You are correct. I would *not* have married you then, had I known.

5. Telling me recently that when I asked you to leave some years ago (because of No. 4 above), that if I hadn't changed my mind and begged you to stay, you would have left and *"never given a backward glance."* **KAREN: Hurt! How Sad!**

6. Your *deciding*, after the Conference President questioned you whether I demanded your help with housework, to *never be close to me again*—but not hinting that decision to me.

7. *Demanding*, fifteen years after marriage, that I *never*, under any condition, ever again discuss problems with you. We had always "swept them under the rug" in the past and "we would continue to do so from now on!" Plus - -

8. Many more times you made me promises and broke them, <u>putting "God's work" as your priority, more important than family, in your belief system.</u> **KAREN: Do Victor and Judy even know what that means? VICTOR: I didn't realize then that the Bible teaches that my Family is my first responsibility. Only after *their* primary needs are met should I tend to church work. Judy agrees.**

That romantic Wednesday night this man, YOU, whom I've loved in spite of all this, tells me he's *"ready for the world to see us as a couple."* Yet you had already planned to call Clarice's ex-husband the very next night to ask him for a recommendation for his ex-wife! And now you tell me you had already decided, (before that romantic Wednesday night) that if Mr. Peterson gave a good recommendation, you'd marry her instead. **KAREN: Would Victor trust what the ex said because he was a man? VICTOR: Gender didn't matter. I just needed a second input besides Clarice.** Can you, Victor, begin to understand my need for questioning you? Sometimes even *I* can't tell when you're pretending!

That one night you were loving and kind, but the next evening you were a totally different person—short tempered, irritable, impatient, unkind and really cruel. Rip, rip, tear, tear, crush, crush, stab, stab, cut, cut went my hopes, my desires, my *respect* for the man who had told both me and our counselor he wanted to get back with me! The pain was searing, burning, and torturing me all weekend! But I foolishly still hung on to a thread of hope until you came Monday evening and told me your decision was final to marry Clarice.

Shivering and shaking in bed that night, I felt nauseated and tried to get to the bathroom, but was too weak and fell to the floor. Crawling to the phone, I called Alan to come help me. He piled blankets on me and brought the heating pad and a basin to use. I vomited a half dozen times that night, retching so much it woke up my house mates. I discovered I had a fever of over 102 degrees.

What were you *trying* to accomplish during the weeks of counseling after you said you wanted to come back to me? What you *did* accomplish was rolling over me with a steamroller and flushing my remains down a toilet—pouring gas over my emotions and igniting them with napalm.

I have been addicted to a liar, a deceiver, a blackmailer, a betrayer, a dishonest, cruel, pretender ---

Or else—an unstable, emotionally sick, bewildered, confused-thinking human being ---

Or possibly—a damaged, crushed, seared, burned, knifed, stabbed little boy who hasn't been able to grow up yet and feels lost in the night.

Whatever the case, I have allowed myself to be sucked into your whirlpool and have nearly drowned. By the grace of God I've grabbed hold of a limb and am struggling to gasp for breath.

I told you yesterday never to try to come back to me again. The trigger was your saying, with your *kindly* *"pretense voice,"* that you wanted to spend Thanksgiving with the boys and me. Can you imagine the gigantic will power it would take me now to keep from crying in front of our sons with you in the house on Thanksgiving? Can you imagine my wanting to do the work necessary to have a big dinner for "company" who has just told me a *second time* that he wants to marry someone else?

All these years, I've *needed* you to nurture and protect *me* as much as you have needed me to nurture you. I've needed someone to *value* me instead of belittle me. I've needed someone to *say* what they didn't like and help me work to overcome that.

You have never known the real me! I am not an ogre! You are still so filled with the rotten stuff of your childhood. I'm not blaming you, and would give anything I own to assist you in working this through! You have been searching the world for rhinestones when you've had a diamond mine in your own back yard. You have refused to mine the diamonds. I will continue polishing them myself. My intention is to find and *make* happiness and reach out in love and kindness to people in whatever way God leads me.

If you don't marry Clarice, or someone else, but down the years discover how to ditch your skeletons, smash your ogres, *grow up*, become honest, and decide you want to come back, I still could reconsider. I know that underneath your almost impenetrable armor is a loving man of God; yet I also know it would take far more than a year to break through your walls of steel.

Judy.

P.S. I have written another page—more potent but different. However you'll get it later only if you request it!

November 22 Victor requested it, so I gave him the following:

P.S. I've been thinking about what you told me just before we divorced—that *supposedly I knew*, before we married, that you believed God's work came before family. It seems to me that all other people, especially females who needed a man's help, were more important than your wife or children or even your sister. You *do* remember, don't you, promising to be at her graduation (after repeated reminders from her) and yet doing something for someone else that day instead? And you seemed to be angry that she felt hurt and gigantically disappointed.

Now, since you have discarded me, I fit the category of the "widow" in the Bible who needs help. Perhaps, now that you've decided you want Clarice to be *your family*, you will be so kind and gentlemanly, magnanimous and thoughtful to consider *my* needs and our sons' needs as "God's work." If so, that would mean that now *our* needs should take precedence over Clarice's needs. You might also tell her that *before* you marry her. You recently told me that I *knew* that's what you believed before you married me, but you didn't actually *tell me* until you divorced me. I'd like you to give her this letter to read so that won't happen a second time.

Seriously, I hope you find happiness and peace. I *will* find it! You MUST find integrity, real love, commitment, reliability, and stability if you want *any* marriage to succeed.

Judy

Soon I was informed that Victor had started attending one of Merv Jenson's therapy groups. I was relieved and enormously pleased that he had decided to at least *try* it—for Clarice's sake, if not for mine. I would continue going on a regular basis to Lena Talbot for counseling.

22

NEGOTIATE

If Victor marries Clarice June 13 as planned (my birthday), she may pressure him to sell our house to get his money, even though he has verbally promised me he would *never* force me to sell! I definitely don't want to sell now! Victor hasn't asked for any money yet, but maybe I could get a loan to give him $20,000 cash now. Later, when I choose to sell the house, he could be paid $40,000. That wouldn't be anywhere near what his share is, <u>but it might sound good to him</u>. **KAREN: The words I underlined are manipulative.** He is about out of money, and I'm trying to plan ahead. In his need for cash *now*, he might even quitclaim the house over to me.

Victor hasn't spoken to me since the day he told me he was going to marry Clarice. I asked my attorney to do the negotiations with him. This is the letter the attorney wrote:

> December 10, 1993
> Dear Mr. Leigh:
>
> This letter shall serve as a written offer on behalf of Judy Leigh to purchase your interest in the residence. Under the terms herein proposed by Judy, this purchase would provide you with immediate cash of $20,000 and an additional $40,000 upon the sale of the residence at a date to be determined by Judy. . . .

Seven specifics were listed and a request was made for Victor to call the attorney regarding them. Later, the attorney called me and said Victor received the letter and left a phone message that he would accept $20,000 now and $40,000 when I sold the place. That thrilled me.

Three days later Victor left a message on my phone saying that the above arrangement was unacceptable to Clarice, and she said I would have to pay the $40,000 off in fifteen years at $222.22 a month without interest. My income currently won't allow that.

Dear Victor,

The offer I made through my attorney was not meant to take advantage of you. I want to negotiate in a way that will be a win/win situation—so we both will be happy.

You gave me a verbal promise to *not* make me sell this house as long as I want/need to live here. I thank you for that and trust you will *keep your word*. Please realize there is a good chance I might not want to sell for many years. That leaves you no money to move into your new marriage with a firm financial footing. Refinancing and giving you $20,000 cash right now might help you. Perhaps you haven't stopped to consider these factors:

1. A few months ago you told me you couldn't get a Visa card because your credit rating was too poor. If that is still the case, my bank adviser says it would be impossible for *you* to get a loan, or even *the two of us together* to take out a loan for you, if your name is still on the title. However, *my* credit rating is excellent, so I qualify for a loan without your name. My care of our finances through the years must be worth *something* to you—the fact that I could get the loan to give you, but not with your name. The divorce agreement does not require me to give you *anything* until I sell the house, which I'm not ready to do; and you didn't *ask* for anything until after I made you the offer. I want you to succeed in your marriage; that's why I made the offer.

2. If I give you $20,000, I will have to pay interest on it as long as I keep the house, but *you* could invest it wisely and be earning interest or make a down payment on a house.

3. If you sign the house over to me, then the following part of the divorce settlement would be nullified: As long as I live in this house I "shall maintain the family residence in good repair and shall be solely responsible for all normal expenses associated with maintaining the home and yard. In the event that major repairs or improvements become necessary, *defined as any repair or improvement in excess of $100,* Petitioner [myself] shall obtain the written consent of Respondent [you] before making any such repairs or improvements, except in case of emergency, and the cost of such major repairs or improvements shall be shared equally by the parties."

Do you really want me to keep in touch with you for the next several decades to ask, first of all, for your written permission to make any repairs and improvements over $100, and then require *you* to pay *half of everything*? I would like to leave you and Clarice free to build a good life together without my having to contact you. It seems like nullifying this part of the divorce settlement might be quite valuable to you.

4. If you sign a quit claim deed, then I would be responsible at the time of sale for all costs of real estate agents, points, closing costs, appraisals, etc. and you would not have to pay any of this. This alone could run into thousands.

5. I've done some checking with authorities and professionals before making this offer and have been told that it is fair.

My attorney is currently out of town but will be back in his office this Thursday morning. Alan tells me you leave Friday to visit Clarice. Please reconsider the offer with the above information in mind. Thanks.

Sincerely,
Judy

Before Victor left, he called and sounded almost as if he was crying. He came across as though he was "begging mommy" to help him financially. He was "so totally broke" and needed money because they "don't have any money at all and your offer is totally unacceptable." He said he was leaving tomorrow. I told him he'd have to wait for any decision until after Christmas.

23

RETORT

M ost of the following chapter was written in my journal between Thanksgiving and Christmas, continuing almost daily, through several weeks. Although it was originally written only for personal benefit, I later developed a growing compulsion to copy it and give it to Victor. Finally, unable to hold back any longer, it *was* copied and delivered to him on January 3, 1994, along with the following one-paragraph note:

> Victor,
>
> I started writing out my feelings and thoughts on Saturday night following Thanksgiving before you returned from visiting Clarice. A week later I wrote more, basically for my own therapy. Without realizing it at the time, my writing gradually changed into letters to you. I've let these Journal entries rest awhile, thought it through, and am finally inviting you to read them. You have both my permission and encouragement to read *all* of what follows to Clarice and to your therapy group.
>
> Judy.

COPIED FROM MY JOURNAL:

I wonder what it's like to feel alone but happy--to not need anyone to nurture me or to keep me company. Can I learn that? If I don't accept a date with a man for the next year, will I be able to stay home on a Saturday night and feel comfortable? Just now I've spent two hours watching TV and am still alive and not crying. I'm lonely and a bit scared, but thankful for the love of our sons and many others. I'm healthy, intelligent and creative. I'm strong, gentle, loving and independent. My future is in God's hands.

Today I ache. I cry. I'm so very sad, feeling gigantically rejected. Yet somehow my mind tells me I'm fine! Free! Released from the bondage of struggling to please my husband! It seems there was nothing I could do right, being damned from day one. Victor has been insensitive and callous. I should have left him the first year we were married. Looking back now at what has happened during the last couple weeks, anger at Victor's cruelty fills me! If he had just stayed with his first decision to marry Clarice, my adjustment would have been nearly settled by now. Instead he has emotionally pummeled me over and over by being sweet one day and hateful, with changed plans the next day. And I was ridiculously passive, buying into it all, thinking he honestly wanted to get back with me--imagining he meant it when he said he really loved me and wanted us to be remarried. To do that on one day, and then verbally stab me with change of plans and attitude the very next day, over and over, back and forth, is vicious!

Victor followed my request and read the long letter I wrote on November 11 to his therapy group at their "marathon,"—a day-long session. This, in itself, is miraculous! He called me afterward and was crying, saying he loved me and realized the things he had done to me were terrible. He asked my forgiveness, which I gave him, and said the folks in group thought I must have super-human love to still consider going back to him. God gets the credit.

The next day he asked to come over to talk. He hugged and held me a long time and said he was "falling more and more in love" with me each day and was surer than ever that we'd get back together. He emphasized that he had decided to read Clarice the same November 11 letter and would probably lose her, and he hoped to get together with me. He also said he promised to go back to therapy in January and work on himself. However he "just had to go up to see Clarice" and would leave Wednesday.

Exactly one week later, after returning from Clarice's, he called and asked to come over again. He explained that he had decided to pray for a sign. If she still accepted him, after reading my November 11 letter, Clarice's acceptance would be God's sign he should marry her.

I don't believe God works that way, and the whole thing sounds terribly immature.

After she read it, she said she wasn't ready to make a decision and tossed it back into Victor's "ball park." But he insisted it was all up to her. **KAREN: Yes. Again making a woman and the Lord responsible for his life.**

In doing this, Victor's sensitivity is comparable to a hunk of shattered granite.

When he had to catch the return flight, she still hadn't made her decision. That night, after he arrived home, she finally called to say she'd accept him in spite of everything. They would marry June 13 (which happens to be my birthday). When he stopped telling me his story, he bowed his head silently and finally whispered, "I'm so sorry."

You're starting with Clarice before you marry, just like you started with me before *we* married. When we were courting, I asked how you felt about having children and you answered, "Whatever *you* want is all right with me." But after we had Steve and I became pregnant again, you tried to *force* me into aborting. **KAREN: Choosing death over life.** You really are sometimes a self-centered monster. Just look at these wonderful sons of ours. Steve is the first-born that you "knew you never wanted, even before you met me." Alan is the one I was carrying when you finagled getting an Indian secret and made a quantity of the two kinds of tea. When you insisted, I *did* drink a quart or so until I started having severe cramps and realized what I was doing and dumped the rest out, praying earnestly that God would forgive me and let me keep my baby. **KAREN: Severe**

manipulation. Whew! Close call! He answered my prayer and I'm proud of both our sons.

It was when Alan was six months old and Steve was two, that you said you didn't love either of them, even though you had "tried and tried to." I always had wanted six children until you told me that. I wasn't going to leave them with a man who couldn't love them. That's why I was going to take them with me in the car and plunge off the steep road to kill the three of us. **KAREN: You can have compassion now for those that do!** In my crazy insanity I thought *that* was the most loving thing I could do. Can you imagine yourself thanking the "stranger" who finally persuaded me not to do it, even though this gentleman's kindness and deep caring toward me resulted later in our making love? You have Steve and Alan now to love you and care for you when you get old *because* there was someone who cared enough to pull me out of a suicide/murder mode into sanity when you, my husband, didn't even notice my absence during the many weeks I skipped church—even though you were on the platform and could see me when I stood up, always near the front, and walked out in plain sight of everyone there. No one ever asked me why!

<u>We are equal sinners</u>. You tried to murder Alan *before* he was born and I planned to murder both him and Steve *after* he was born. <u>He'd be dead if I hadn't disobeyed you.</u> Now isn't that <u>just lovely behavior for a minister and his wife</u>? **KAREN: My underlining. A big yes!** And guess what? During those "affairs" I didn't use birth control. I figured if I got pregnant, I'd have an abortion! Fortunately, I didn't! I learned that from *you*, sweetheart! Isn't that just gorgeously beautiful? Do you understand now that maybe once or twice in your life you *were* a "stuffed shirt"-- <u>meaning that underneath your mask you were different than what you tried to make yourself look like on the surface</u>? **KAREN: My underlining. Perfectionism; unwilling to let anyone see the real you!** Of course you surely must remember how you have pitied yourself and complained how terrible it was that I called you a "stuffed shirt" a few times!

297

I hurt. I am angry. I loved you and still do. But your behavior sucks the life out of the lady who supported you, nurtured you, complimented you, worked hard to build your self-esteem, mended, washed and ironed your clothes, cooked for you, bore your children (which you didn't want but enjoyed producing}, scarcely ever complained about finances or poor living quarters or even being treated as a nothing.

Right now I want to beat you to shreds, kick in your teeth, stab you until you bleed to death! Yet a part of me wants to hold you and kiss you passionately until you are so carried away you forget Clarice. There is a part of me that wants to be friends with you, possibly even with her, but for now the pain of it all is excruciating. I have to close all doors and say a firm goodbye in order to survive.

Leave me alone, you miserable man. Get out of my life, you respectless fool, you pretender, you liar, you wimpy, washed-out mama's boy. Yet I believe down inside the hidden, screaming core of your being, Victor, you have pure motives, great gifts, and wonderful talents. Your looks and personality I love from my deepest heart, because I see you subconsciously *wanting* to be loving and caring. YOU WERE SO DAMAGED! You still don't understand that, and don't know how to overcome it. So you have floundered in self-pity, pain, rage and hatred all these years. I wish I could hold and comfort you, encourage you and tell you I recognize you tried so hard! I know you did! But I tried *also*, and I need *you* to recognize that! I wanted you to love and accept me the way I loved and accepted you.

Do you remember the collage you made up years ago at some seminar you went to? You were assigned to make one on a paper plate that described your history. Quite a while ago, when you were organizing your desk things, you threw it away. I pulled it out of the trash that same day and kept it hidden all these years. Only a short while ago I threw it away--after your first goodbye letter to me, which I received before Jim broke up with me.

That collage was the most honest thing I've ever seen you do, so far as your emotions and subconscious are concerned. The first picture pasted on the plate was the cartoon bust of a man with a flowered kerchief covering his head and face. Your verbal description to me was, "At first I was blinding myself to reality." You did not interpret more about that picture, but to me it was so symbolic. The kerchief was covered with brightly colored flowers, rather symbolic of "all a bed of roses" while refusing to look beyond yourself to see the real world--people with genuine emotions and authentic needs. You also were refusing to see the real *you*--the good, amazing parts, as well as the ugly and mean.

The next picture was a cartoon drawing of two roads crossing each other. There was a signpost at the junction that had direction arrows and road names: "Eeny, Meany, Miney, Mo." Your interpretation: "Then I came to crossroads and had to make a decision." The symbolism: "Eeny, Meany, Miney, Mo" is *infantile* choosing, not *adult* maturity.

You put next on the collage a cartoon of a rat (obvious symbolism) wearing a silk derby (extremely interested in appearance), but leaning over with his head on a table fast asleep--or at least with eyes closed and chin resting on both "hands." Symbolism: still refusing to become a part of the life around you, and being totally helpless to do anything because the chin was keeping the hands from being free. Your verbal description: "I was still asleep."

After that you drew a tiny cross, less than an inch tall. Your interpretation: "Then I came face to face with the cross, and now I'm a preacher."

The picture you chose to illustrate the "preacher" was a rabbit (a symbol of sexual virility and procreation). But it wasn't a *real* rabbit. It was a *stuffed cloth* rabbit. There was only stitching marking the "fingers" on rather rounded, ball-shaped hands (symbolism: helplessness to really "take hold" and do anything). The ears, instead of being straight up and keenly listening like most rabbits, were both drooped way down (better to keep from listening to what people say that way). Eyes: no pupils, but just expressionless black blobs (still refusing to see reality). The mouth, which was hanging open dumbly as if the only thing it could say was a dull "blah," declared to me your refusal to communicate. One of the rabbit's "hands" was raised like a policeman when he orders someone to stop (refusal to be close or intimate) and its other "hand" was held behind his back like he was refusing to shake hands (refusal to problem-solve). Its attitude: arrogant, swayback posture, with fat stomach sticking out in front (which reminded me of the Biblical message to the Laodicean church in the book of Revelation, "I am rich and increased with goods." (Revelation 3:17 KJV)

But the attire impressed me the most. It was fancy, formal, striped tuxedo pants, ruffled tuxedo shirt, elegant long black coat with tails and a gaudy, huge watch on the side with a long chain hanging down in a decorative loop. You apparently have an enormous vested interest in "looking good" to everyone—including me.

When I asked why you chose the picture of the rabbit, you replied, "I couldn't find a picture of a man dressed like a preacher."

Subconsciously you must have *wanted* me to have an affair, so you could blame me and pity yourself. Apparently you needed an excuse to get out of the marriage when you were ready—or at least have people feel sorry for you staying in it. [**KAREN: Does Victor agree this was true?**] [**VICTOR: I can recall only one occasion when I really wanted this.**]

Do you remember when our sons were still in elementary school in Flagstaff, you asked me to go with you to Phoenix? After we got there you told me I could stay at Pastor Cook's place while you did your business, rather than take me with you. I was shocked and said I felt terribly uncomfortable about doing that because you hadn't asked them ahead of time if it would be okay. And besides, I thought Mrs. Cook was probably away at work.

You drove to their house, she was gone, and yet you asked Pastor Cook if I could stay there while you did your business. He agreed, but shortly after you left he said to me, "I've got to see a man about a dog and will return after your husband comes back." He *refused* to stay alone in his own home with me there, even though I was practicing the piano in a different room from him. He didn't want his reputation ruined. I was *terribly* embarrassed that you purposely put me into that situation, and you made fun of me for feeling uncomfortable. I wouldn't be surprised if *he* thought you were trying to set us up for an affair. **VICTOR: I trusted**

300

Pastor Cook and I trusted Judy. I couldn't imagine that anyone would frown on my doing this. I wonder if I possibly have a mild Aspergers Syndrome problem, and that's where Steve's autism came from.

I was amazed a few weeks ago that you brought up Tony, and surprised you even recalled his name. Please remember that you chose to divorce me *before* you knew about any affairs, except for Tony. There were *no others before that*! You said recently that I was "so in love with Tony on the island." That is not true! You *drove me to that one*!

Victor darling. Sweet, tender Victor. Please remember, shortly before we stayed on the island, I went on a *rigid* diet and lost weight. It was for YOU. I exercised a half hour every morning and evening and got back my good figure because I loved YOU. YOU were the man I was in love with and wanted to be with. YOU were the man I wanted to be beautiful for. YOU were the man I wanted to go biking, boating and walking on the beach with. YOU were the man I wanted to play with our sons and me. YOU were the man with whom I wanted to make passionate love. Your distancing frightened me. I couldn't figure out why you didn't want to spend time together as a family, even though we were on a family vacation.

Tony was there on the beach every day. He was only a *chance substitute* for the one I *really wanted*—YOU! He played with our boys. I wanted YOU to play with them. He treated our two sons as loving and fatherly as he treated his own three boys. He was there. YOU weren't, even though I invited you, actually *almost begged* you to come with us every day! But I still loved YOU and wanted YOU. Although I felt scared—enormously frightened—of the way my emotions responded to this "stranger on the beach," we *did nothing wrong* that whole summer!

Tony was the only person I knew to call. Fighting back tears and panic because I wanted YOU, there seemed to be no alternative. We needed help immediately! Tony provided his vacation home. He carefully carried in *your* sleeping sons and put them to bed lovingly. Certainly what happened was not premeditated.

After telling you what happened, I asked for us to get counseling. You refused! You *demanded* that I was to act as though it never happened and *never speak of it again*! Oh what denial! Oh what hurt!

Did you know that your refusal to acknowledge reality and work through the problem was cruelty? It seemed even sadistic to me!

Just think! You carried your bitterness, jealousy and rage with you *all these years* rather than being willing to face it and get help. Refusing to discuss it, which would have facilitated leaving it in the past, shows me your ignorance and stubbornness.

To be hated is more comfortable than to be ignored! To act like someone doesn't exist is the *ultimate insult!* Many times you have acted like I wasn't there—refusing to even acknowledge my presence in the room or respond in any way to my speaking to you, often walking out mid-sentence.

Even Morton Morris, long ago in the mountain town, said in real anger, "What's Victor trying to do? Set us up to have an affair?" He sensed you were *trying* to, but we didn't!

Before I had *any* affairs, I came to you each and every time I was tempted, told you I loved you and needed you to be my husband. I wanted YOU sexually and romantically. I *didn't want other men!* I wanted YOU. I could tell you were disgusted with me often, but I couldn't read your mind to know what you *didn't like*, and you *refused to tell me*. But when I approached you with these needs and requests, you pushed me farther away and withdrew more. I thought I was *abnormal*, and *maybe* I could learn from other men and come back "educated" in how to love, and you'd accept me then. Ridiculously stupid, wasn't it?

I don't blame you for not being able to love me sexually now, since I told you I had several affairs. However I'm remembering the night after we married. You weren't able *even then* to feel comfortable making love, nor many times since. That was *long before* I had ever been with another man. I don't accept responsibility for that! I was a virgin when I married you.

Nobody can read another mind. How could I know what you needed and wanted without your telling me? How could you know what I needed and wanted without my telling you—which I did, but you closed your mind to it and said I was being critical.

Do you remember the many times you *were* told how *thankful* I was to have married YOU and not Reese or the other five guys who proposed to me? It was YOU I wanted. It was YOU I cherished. It was *your* love, respect and care that excited me! My love *can't* last forever while being pushed away.

I know I have many faults, especially talking too much, interrupting you, cracking my knuckles, wanting all the details, and I guess sometimes unknowingly being bossy. But I so much wanted to overcome my weaknesses!

I never *dreamed* you wanted a divorce. It was brought up only because I wanted you to be aware that the problems were *very* serious and *important*. Shocked beyond belief the next day after giving you the ultimatum, I couldn't believe what you said—telling your work friends that I was divorcing you! It blew my mind! How long have you hated me? I wanted us to be bonded with cement so strong nothing would break us apart!

I hate your guts for lying to me many times that everything in our marriage was *perfect* and *nothing needed to change!* You *hogged up* all my time and effort to selfishly keep up your front to the church and world without stopping to consider you were *robbing me of my life!* Wouldn't it have been far more honest, loving, and even *Christlike* to have sent me out of your life *before* you hit me, so I could find someone who truly valued me?

Burt Dennison, [a pastor who lived near us who had recently finished his theoretical work in Marriage and Family Counseling and also was a member of the Minister's Support Group Victor attended] said the other day, "I think Victor's problem may be developmental."

I asked, "What do you mean?"

"Something probably happened early in his life that caused him to stop maturing emotionally, and he has never gotten past that point."

"At age thirteen or fourteen?"

He responded, "Earlier."

I questioned if it was when your brother died, when you were eight or nine.

Again he said, "Earlier."

I was surprised.

Then he asked me, "Haven't you seen a little two-year-old boy become so angry with his mother that he runs away from her, but soon stops and looks over his shoulder to see if she's still watching him?"

My response was only, "Wow!" Burt likes you. In fact he *loves you* and highly respects so much about you. He did not say this to criticize you, but to help *me* understand and accept your erratic behavior.

Nancy, your niece by marriage, was visiting Alan that day you told him about your new love. She asked if you had told Rudy yet. Later she told me that you responded to her question, with obvious fury on your face. "No, I've *never* done much communicating with our foster son! I've known all along he's wanted Judy sexually!" What's that all about? Do you think I ever had anything but motherly love towards him, let alone inappropriate actions with him? I never contemplated or daydreamed of it. I have always treated him exactly the same as Steve and Alan. Just because your mother *messed you up* doesn't mean your ex-wife is like *her*, treating any son like she treated you! You really *have* put your mother's face on me, haven't you?

I told Rudy and Rosemary about this; they need to face the truth too. I want them to love and support you, but they need to know how mixed up your thinking is just now. They're neither angry nor bitter--only shocked at what you said! You have *never even hinted to me* that you felt that way about Rudy!

Nancy also told me that when you first announced to Alan your engagement to Clarice, you told him you were happier than you'd ever been before. That doesn't seem very fair to Alan to insinuate you weren't ever happy with his mother. Do you suppose he felt hurt when you told him that? Maybe he felt *intense pain*. Did you ever consider that?

My anger towards you doesn't stem from the fact that you are going to marry Clarice. You need to know that. You have a perfect right, <u>with Bible grounds</u>, and no doubt she is a very lovely person. **Karen: I don't think Victor is without sin in his treatment of Judy. So it's not just Judy that sinned here.**

My anger stems almost entirely from your *crass insensitivity* and inability to know when you are insulting and *vicious!* You have shown *enormous disrespect* for me during most of our marriage. You have toyed with me like an animal playing with what it plans to kill, seeming to thrive on the pain and agony you cause. You have been a brute! A jerk! Telling me you were falling in love with me more and more every day, only two weeks ago, is a good example!

Why am I going on and on? I WANT you to hurt! I WANT you to feel guilty! I *don't* want another woman to suffer horrible pain from your treatment as I have! My heart is filled with *pity* for Clarice unless you grow enormously! It is abject insanity for the two of you to get engaged after being together so little. As I understand it, you've been with Clarice only parts of three weekends in your life! The rest of your courtship has been by telephone. This is absurdity!

You're putting responsibility for your decisions on her! Are you going to later resent *her* for "wearing the pants in the family" like you did me, even though it's *you* who *forces* her to do that? Please, I beg of you, *get yourself into therapy*—intensively!

I have had several talks with Pastor Tom and Ruby Hanks. Last Friday Ruby said, "Judy, for years you have been there to take Victor back no matter how he treated you. <u>He hasn't had *incentive* to grow up. The time has come that you must sever all ties—totally cut him off—never allow him to do that to you again. That is the *most loving thing* you can do for him.</u>" **KAREN: Yes!**

Merv *didn't* suggest therapy for the purpose of getting us back together! YOU said that's what YOU wanted! Please remember, we agreed *only* to study how we caused our problems and discover how to stop that kind of behavior so our future relationships could thrive.

A few weeks ago Alan said, demonstrating quite astute wisdom for being only about half your age, "Mother, you've got to face the reality that daddy doesn't *know what commitment is!* When *you* make a commitment, it's like you put on blinders and never turn to the left or right, but plow on through until you've completed your commitment. I don't think daddy is *capable* of making an emotional commitment." He has read this letter, so knows I'm telling you this. But actually I believe you didn't know what or whom you wanted to commit to, because you hadn't learned to know *yourself* well and love *yourself* as God loves you. **KAREN: Victor apparently wasn't able to trust God to commit to Him. I believe that he was very isolated as a child due to his illness and the loss of his brother. And there was no one to help him grieve.**

Why did I stay with you? My belief system said you weren't *consciously* trying to be a pretender; your heart *wanted* to be in the right place. I even believed you didn't *purposely* hurt me when you acted as if I didn't exist. I actually believed you *wanted* to be honest and truthful. That's why I begged for counseling. That's my reason for choosing to stay with you and treating you as lovingly as possible, even though you had drowned my romantic and sexual spark with your evil ways, *which have gotten worse over the years.*

I *want* to totally forgive you, but the struggle feels super-human, especially as this evil seems to creep out even more as you strive increasingly to grow. Maybe there is so much trauma buried deep inside you, that when you open a tiny crack, the inside pressure forces steamed garbage to spew. Since I've been closest to you, I'm the one who gets third degree burns. It still hurts badly, and I can't seem to find any anesthetic ointment or bandages that take away the awful pain.

Each time I've healed a bit, you scald me all over again, pouring out your love farce--asking me to go to the alumni homecoming and telling me you are ready for the world to see us as a couple, then the next day treating me with verbal brutality and never informing me you changed your mind about the homecoming. **KAREN: And you believed him each time? Even though Victor never repented for his behaviors?**

You must be intensely angry with both your mother and grandmother and think I'm like them. You've put their faces on me. You *don't have a clue* as to who is really underneath the face you occasionally look at—who *I* really am!

Through the years you have told me that all I could do was criticize and criticize you. Well, seldom were there even critical thoughts about you. I was so proud of you! But now you are reaping the rewards of *calling* it criticizing, because I *now* am consciously, purposely and forcefully criticizing you with all my might! Wake up, you sleeping fool, to the reality you have denied for decades. You are *far worse* than a stuffed shirt!

Tears are flowing. I'm actually sobbing now. Oh Victor, it is so *hard* to say goodbye! There are so many *wonderful* things about you, so many delightful times we had together in spite of the horrible, heart-rending bad times. How can I say goodbye?

Why couldn't you have believed me when I said we needed counseling? I wanted YOU for my husband--my tall, handsome, talented, smart, creative, hard-working Victors Leigh—the singer, the preacher, the teacher, the superb musician, the helper, the fixer of anything that broke or wouldn't work. I wanted YOU! YOU! YOU! I was crying out for YOU all these years! Will I ever stop grieving for what might have been?

Several years ago Lena Talbot told me, "Judy, you must start building a close network of friends around you. Start telling them what is going on between you and Victor, so they'll understand. I believe the situation is going to deteriorate, and you need to prepare yourself for the worst." I have her permission to say this. She also has read this letter before sending it to you, and so has Burt Dennison.

I hope you can recognize that reading Barbara De Angelis' book, <u>How to Make Love All the Time</u>, was one of the things that stimulated this writing. Do you remember the part about "Love Letters" that *you read out loud* to Steve and Lauren when we visited them? Well, this is my "love letter" to you. I couldn't possibly want to spend the time doing this if I didn't care for you deeply, love you enormously, want you in the worst and best way. The *very existence* of these pages is *proof* that you are *immensely* important to me and *always have been!*

For years I have felt that you weren't really *capable* of loving me sexually *or* romantically either! I believe your mother is partly responsible for that. It has seemed your love was more of the caliber of a child for a gold charm bracelet, a silly woman for a diamond necklace or a teenager for a Rolls Royce. I don't think you have known love at a deeper level than that. So sad!

What am I trying to accomplish with this writing? Hopefully heal. Be honest and speak my true feelings. Share what is real and painful. Help you overcome denial while craving for you to recognize your deep, heavy guilt. Acknowledge my own guilt. Let you know you are forgiven and still loved. Make closure. Say goodbye. Empty myself so I can be at peace. Try to get some sleep. Challenge you to grow more. Inspire the *real Victor* to open up—to be willing to learn *intimacy* and *communication*—with *someone else* if you can't with me!

December 22, our Anniversary.

Wanting to stand openly and honestly before God, I even told mother about my affairs. God has forgiven me for them. I hope I stand forgiven in your sight, but that might not be humanly possible. I believe your forgetfulness and mismanaging of money and situations that Lena Talbot, her husband and others as well as I, thought might be Alzheimer's, was just steam escaping from the volcano of rage you suppressed for so long.

Mother told me she has wept almost all night many times since I told her what was going on between us. She was angry I even *considered* going back to you. But I told her I love and care for you and truly believe you *want* to be truthful, honest and loving.

I believe in marriage and was one hundred percent willing to work on it--at least up until the last two weeks. I've been a *fool* to trust you, to keep on loving and wanting you when you didn't want me. I am going to break that pattern.

Please do not contact me in any way except through my attorney or Alan. And please, under no condition, ever contact my mother again. Her emotional and physical health has deteriorated rapidly the last three months, and she can't handle any more traumas regarding you. Please know that you have seen her for the last time. Don't even say goodbye.

Thanks.
Judy

HAPPY FREE THIRTY-NINTH ANNIVERSARY

24

RELEASE

Emotions are crazy sometimes. In order to try to calm mine, I decided to try a tender letter approach:

January 6
My dearest darling precious Victor,

In sorting out and putting away Christmas decorations, today I came across this bear ornament, [a stuffed-cloth-Christmas-tree-ornament in the shape of a brown bear with "Victor" painted on it in gold—a gift to him from a nurse at the hospital sometime in the past] which I'm hugging to my face with tenderness and love, with sorrow and heartsickness. I am longing for you. Aching for you. Wanting you. Three nights ago the journaled letter written periodically through November and December was sent to you. I kept a copy and have read it many times. Somehow there is comfort in reading it, especially the parts about my love for you. My *current* love. Yes, I've been *extremely* angry with you for the rejection and pain, but still can't seem to dump hope.

It is a struggle to face the reality that this is the end. If it is the end, then I must hold to the no seeing, no speaking, and no contact—to keep my sanity. But even now I'd give it another try if you were willing. We would have to learn how to *not* push each others "buttons." I'd have to learn how to limit questions and be less analytical. That may be as difficult for me as intimacy and expressing feelings are for you.

Two or three times before we separated you asked, "When are you going to join me in the bedroom?"

My reply was always, "I can't, unless we can learn some intimacy and communication." Each time, practically holding my breath, I waited for you to make the first move. It hurt every time you walked away. All those months I missed sleeping with you. But I could not—and still will not-- take *all the initiative* to problem solve.

The day you said: "I was reading in the Bible that the gospel is the good news of reconciliation, and I'm praying for us to have a reconciliation," you gave me excitement and hope. I waited for you to say, "I'm ready for us to get counseling." But you said no more and walked away.

Somebody recently told me that when you were at the singles retreat, you looked terribly sad —like you could cry at the drop of a hat. They said you admitted to feeling awful that I was engaged to be married to Jim. Did they read you correctly? I thought you were relieved! It was foolish— really childish—to let him sweep me off my feet. But getting back with you seemed impossible, with all your hostility. If you really *did* feel bad, I'd have given a lot to hear that *from you*! You seemed to blossom, grow, thrive, excel, and radiate, after you left me.

It's about seven months until you say you'll marry Clarice. A lot could happen in that period. If you don't marry, remember I'm still here—willing to work—but not if you are emotionally attached to someone else.

Cherae Morrison called today to get your brother's new address. She said she saw you in the market six or eight weeks ago and you were radiant—more so than she'd ever seen you before—and you told her you were in counseling with me and were planning for us to get together again. Did you really mean that?

However, please don't respond to this unless you have ended your relationship with Clarice and have given yourself time to grow and heal. God bless you in your future, wherever it is.

Judy

Before Thanksgiving Victor had loaned me a book he had recently read: Barbara Johnson's <u>Splashes of Joy in the Cesspools of Life</u>. It so impressed me that I had made notes with my feedback as I read, and tucked them between the pages. Now I am returning the book with the above letter—leaving the notepaper sticking out so, hopefully, he'll be curious as to what these papers are. These are some of the notes:

Thank you; thank you for sharing this book with me. I believe God led you to discover it. He has blessed us both in the reading. I have always wanted to know you better. Some of that desire is fulfilled in reading a book you chose to buy and read, and then sharing it with me.

I had no idea this was something more than a spiritual fun book, or that it dealt in depth with grief. [The author lost her father and her two sons and her husband sustained an injury that handicapped him for life.] Thank God I have it to read now.

Why couldn't you be reached? Somehow that very state of longing for intimacy seemed to be a turn off to you. Perhaps it was my desire to love you *intensely* that drove you away. My isolation, my being discarded and abandoned, was eroding my health, my self-esteem, my strength and my sanity. That's why I allowed you to persuade me to proceed with the divorce. You came once and said you decided we hadn't prayed enough together. I agreed and wanted to pray more with you, but you never made that offer. I could not value myself and continue being the *sole initiator* of any transactions between us.

I'm glad you read this book. Perhaps you are learning to feel. Perhaps you are learning to express what you feel. It would be a privilege to observe that and to support and nurture you in the process. But it is not to be— your choice, not mine.

In my mind I am "gift wrapping," you, as suggested in the book on page 59: "Next, picture a long flight of stairs. At the top is the throne of God, with Jesus sitting on it. Imagine yourself climbing up these stairs, carrying your beautifully wrapped package. When you get to the top, put it at Jesus' feet and wait until He bends down to pick up the package and place it on His lap. Picture Jesus opening your package and taking your loved one in His arms to hold him...close."

Now I am carrying the box containing *you*, along with all my hopes, dreams, desires and heartbreak. I'm struggling up the "steps" to give this gift of you to Jesus. This gift of *you!* Precious, precious Victor! But the grief weighs me down so much that I am falling down on the steps and haven't been able to pass the box on yet. Oh, how the struggle hurts. But I *will* leave you in God's tender care. I have to in order to survive. How long will it take me to make it up the steps the rest of the way? I still can't face turning my back and walking away—back down the steps and on with my life. So help me God!

Forgive me for hi-lighting your book without your permission. But a great part of me just longs to talk with you. I still want so much to express myself to you and have you really hear me. So this is my showing you what is important to me.

How I wish you had used a hi-lighter when *you* read this book. The two or three books I've read *after* you read and *marked* them gave me a double sense of pleasure—the pleasure of the book *and* the pleasure of learning more about what you valued—what was important to you.

Because you have shared so little of your deep self with me during our marriage, I scarcely know you, yet long to understand you, comprehend you, and see deeply into your heart. Learning about you through books has been exciting. But how much more thrilling it would have been for you to share yourself spontaneously from the beginning! This is what I was asking for when you interpreted it as criticizing.

The time we hiked to Cottonwood Meadows to "acclimate" the day before our last backpack together, we sat under the trees by the lake and you told of the meetings you had recently attended about the Holy Spirit. I loved your sharing! You not only opened up intellectually, but also divulged a bit of how you felt! At that time I thought, "Wow, Victor is really a deep thinking and marvelous man." I wish you hadn't kept closing off after that.

This last note was tucked in at the end of the book:

> You are now completely gift-wrapped.
> I have finally climbed the stairs.
> At long last I have handed you totally to God.
> He has unwrapped you and is holding you warmly and affectionately in His arms.
> He is smiling and laughing with you in your joy.
> I have accepted His promise to care for you and help you grow.
> You are totally released as I turn around and start back down the steps.

Just now I pause and look back. You are radiant. You are
happy. You are content.
God bless you.

Love,
Judy

One day, while my emotional pain was flourishingly potent, this
thought flashed across my mind: *Eventually* I'll feel better. A part of me
wants to put into words what I am feeling *right now*. Maybe someday I'll
want to remember. On the spur of the moment, as I was ready to leave for
church, I grabbed my mini-cassette-recorder. As I started out the driveway,
I began recording—with no plan as to what I would say.

On this eighth day of the New Year I'm on my way to church. My
heart is so full. I want so much to stop hurting, and yet I realize it is
through our pain that we grow.

*Judy, pay attention to what you are doing. You almost nicked that parked
car as you pulled into the street.*

I've made many mistakes, but did the best that I could. I love Victor. I
always have, and always will. But the pain is so great, the hurt so extreme,
the disappointment so excruciating, that I sometimes wonder how to get
from one day to the next. This week I've cried louder and longer, perhaps,
than in my entire life. I've been glad there was no one at home, and have
beaten my hands and arms on the bed and floor until they bruised. I have
screamed in anguish while driving alone in the car, hating myself for
hurting so much—for being weak.

*Now I'm detesting myself for letting tears flow and blocking my view. Judy,
blot your eyes with tissue before you miss the next red light.*

I will eventually find the route my Higher Power has chosen for me,
and trust He knows what's best. My emotions are being ripped apart right
now, but I could no longer live with Victor under the circumstances.

Evidently he could no longer live with me either. God has put someone in his life—or at least allowed it—that may help him heal also. I don't know whether or when God will put someone in my life to help me heal. Recently thinking it would be Jim, I've accepted the death of that wish. Coping with his rejection, I'm still alive and healthy.

This morning I was reading a verse written on a card. "I have seen his ways and will heal him. I will lead him also, and restore comforts unto him and to his mourners." (Isaiah 57:18 KJV). Personalizing it becomes: "I am the God who created you, Judy. I see the pain you're in. I understand it because I've been through pain. I've made you a promise and I'll keep it. Judy, I have seen your ways, and I will heal you. I will also lead you and restore comforts to you and to your mourners."

Struggling to believe in myself, I am determined to claim this promise. Thank you God for already starting to heal me. Thank you that my mourners will be healed. But I wonder, who are my mourners? In Bible times people were paid to mourn. Others mourned because they were close to the deceased. In my case I believe the mourners are my marvelous friends who have heard my poured-out heart. Dearest Faye, my closest friend, has listened to me for hours at a time. How can she do that? She is patient, loving, understanding, loyal and sometimes the one who lays it on the line and says, "Judy, stop setting up expectations!" It's a wonder she doesn't run the other way when she sees me coming. Precious Faye.

Oh, my! It's hard to hang on to this recorder while I drive. I finally was able to retrieve it off the floor at a long stoplight. Let's see, I was telling about "my mourners."

Susan has also been a tremendous encouragement to me. She listened to a lot of my bellyaching years ago when I was teaching her voice lessons before our divorce. At that time she listened with love because she had been through a divorce from her minister-husband. She has grown so much. Now she is a real inspiration to me. I must be careful not to fill her with too much of my pain.

Others that are fresh in my mind are Burt and Darleen Dennison. Previously Victor and I have joined them occasionally for social activities. Last year, when I was teaching Darleen voice lessons, I poured out my heart to her regarding our marriage problems. When calling her the other night, it was Burt who answered. I told him my desire to invite Darleen to go walking with me again and also wanted to take her to lunch. Emphatically he stated, "Please do not mention Victor or the divorce, because it is too depressing for her!" I haven't called her since. I'm not ready to squelch my pain yet. But I have hurt her. How many others are there?

This probably isn't a very good idea to try to think and record my thoughts while I am going somewhere in the car. I'm glad no one else is here, because I know my driving is erratic.

The other day I asked Burt to let me read him a letter I had just written to Victor, but hadn't yet sent. [The letter quoted in the chapter, "Retort."] I needed his feedback. When finished, he warned me not to ever be alone with Victor, not to answer the door if he knocked. He thinks Victor could be dangerous. Lena Talbot, my counselor, alluded to that some time ago. She said he has buried so much that it could finally just explode. Yet usually I see him as outwardly kind and gentle, loving and tender to people other than myself, and previously, even to me.

I wish he could just put his arm around me and say, "Judy, I am committed to you one hundred percent. I am willing to work out everything that is a problem." Apparently he must have things buried from his childhood and needs inner healing. I hope he will allow God to reveal to him his own realities and face them.

For a long time I've known that God could change both Victor and me. I'm willing to be changed, but he needs to be willing also. If he cannot see what he needs, it is because he is damaged. I forgive him. I forgive myself. Now I realize at this point I have to give up! It's totally out of my hands. God, I give you my life. I give you my love. I give you my emptiness and loneliness.

Sometimes I can scarcely think. Sometimes I don't have the energy to work. Somehow this gaping hole that's in the middle of my soul and body feels like everything has just been blown out. It helps to remember the verse that ends, 'Underneath are the everlasting arms.' (Deuteronomy 33:27 KJV). I haven't the strength for anything, Lord, except to rest in your arms. Thank you for my life. Thank you for my health.

Thank you for the healing that you will continue to do. You will allow me to experience only the pain that draws me nearer to you and creates in me Christ-likeness. So by the power of the Holy Spirit, live your life through me every moment of every day. Teach me to love. May this experience make me more willing to love others and accept them where they are. I choose to honor you in my thoughts and actions, my loving and speaking. I praise you for putting peace in my heart and taking away the pain in the future. I recognize some of this has to do with *my* growing, *my* will power, *my* need to change *my* thinking patterns. Help me to focus. Teach me how to dwell on things that are pure, lovely, good and true.

Here's my street to turn left. I'm nearly to the church so I'll have to wind up this recording soon.

I realize my responses to Victor were faulty. Some were in dismay, some in hurt and anger, some in great fear; some were in love, but some were just blatant rebellion.

Is there a reason for me to record this? I feel like I'm being called to write a book. If good can be done, then help me speak onto this cassette what needs to be said.

Now I have arrived at church. God, I leave my life today in your hands, in Jesus name.

I decided right then to save the tape, but didn't listen to it for a long time. By the time I parked the car, I really couldn't remember what was recorded. But soon I started recording nearly every day and sometimes several times a day. Much of the rest of this book has been transcribed and edited from tapes.

25

MEDIATE

After Christmas, and receiving a bill from the attorney for phone calls, letters, and the time spent making them, I decided to go another route. This was too expensive! It became clear to me that I must treat Victor with respect as a friend, and deal directly with him. There just wasn't enough extra in the budget to pay an attorney for calls and letters I was capable of making.

Our realtor friend, who had been a personal friend of Victor's mother and had originally found the house we bought for our present home, might be a good adviser. I called her, told her what was going on, and requested that she come and meet with Victor and me. The tentative appointment was set for the evening of January 30, 1994.

> Dear Victor,
>
> It was my idea to have the attorney be our liaison, but after receiving a bill from him for phone calls and letters, I've decided it's too expensive to negotiate through him and will communicate directly with you.
>
> You have offered me a very fair deal: $20,000 now and $40,000 later without interest. I hope that offer is firm with you and not like ropes of sand, such as your promise in October that you'd never try to make me sell the house. I want to cooperate. But since reviewing my budget, the

possibility of my paying $222.22 per month, as Clarice apparently wants to require, is questionable. There are some other ideas I'd like to discuss in person with you.

Evelyn Monroe has agreed to come and answer questions, give advice and notarize anything we decide to put in writing. Our sons are invited to be here also. I'm waiting for answers from them about time availability, tentatively planning for January 30, late afternoon or evening. Would you be willing to come and discuss this in person with us at that time, or would another time be better?

My anger is pretty well spent, but I don't yet know how to get rid of the hurt. It has been there so deep for so long. Loving challenges, I was determined to do whatever it took to bring us together—even if the process was rocky and painful. The gradual increase through the years of my confronting you was the result of my *love* for you! Seeing your great unhappiness and pain resulted in my pushing you to deal with your childhood regarding your mother and grandmother. Even though you perceived it as *not* unconditionally accepting you, it was *because* of my unconditional love that you were confronted.

I first read Scott Peck's book, The Road Less Traveled, quite a while ago. One of the reasons you were asked to read it was because of his definition of love. This is how I remember it: "Love is the willingness to *extend* yourself for the purpose of your own or another person's growth." Believe me, when I confronted you, it was not on a whim or in anger. It was something *carefully thought through* and *prayed about a lot* for an extended period of time. *Because I loved you*, I did only what I felt impelled to do to help each of us grow, *regardless of the consequences*. It always was *very scary*! It took all the courage I could muster to tell you things that bothered me sexually, emotionally or otherwise. I was *always* trembling inside! It especially took *extreme nerve* to tell you about my affairs. Maybe that wasn't wise, but I wanted to be as honest and open as I hoped you'd be.

You've grown enormously in so many ways, and I am proud of you—of your determination. It is a remarkable thing to see someone as willing to change as you are. I give God the glory for guiding *me* and giving me the *strength to confront* you again and again through the years. Merv Jenson sings your praises about your willingness to be vulnerable in making breakthroughs in group.

Some weeks before your last therapy marathon Merv said to me, "Judy, you have done more therapy for Victor than I have." That greatly surprised me. He said he was referring to all the things I've said and *written* to you, but particularly the things *since* the first divorce discussion started. He and I worked very closely together during your therapy—*not* him telling me what happened in group. That would be unethical. But *I told him* about *all the conversations between you and me* and your reactions and responses.

The extremely difficult thing for me now, as I see your personality blossoming and your assertiveness expanding, is to accept that another woman is receiving the benefits of your efforts. It was always *you* I wanted. But I wanted *all of you*, including the buried, deeply hidden parts that were there, but which you were too afraid to ever let me see, or even to look at yourself.

Can you imagine the way God could have used us if, after all our problems, we *together* could have made a breakthrough? If we were willing to acknowledge our mistakes and weaknesses, we could share what we learned with others, either one-to-one in counseling them, in public seminars, or even in a book.

Now you've made your decision to marry Clarice. It may work, and it may not. All the people I know who are aware of your situation question whether it will work. Many think you'll end up not getting married. I say to them, "Victor has grown tremendously and learned much about relationships and openness. I believe he will marry her, and it just *may* work well, because she has a totally different personality than I have. Victor has never felt comfortable with my personality."

It's difficult enough to have a marriage with someone you know intimately for a long time, but much more difficult if you don't know the other person well. Somewhere recently I was reading that fifty percent of first marriages break up, sixty-five percent of second marriages fail, and seventy- five percent of third marriages don't make it.

You love Clarice, and I have accepted you will marry her. It will be painful to see you and talk to you, yet because of my love for you, I still choose that. Time will help me handle seeing you with her, and it will also eventually take away the pain, but the now is so difficult.

Judy

On January 30 Alan came to the meeting regarding the sale of the house. Steve and his wife, Lauren, lived in New Mexico, too far away to make the trip. Rudy, our older foster son, and his wife Rosemary (Orlando), a schoolmate from elementary days, also came. They are still as emotionally close to us as our own sons. Before Victor arrived, I said, "I want each one of you to know I didn't ask for or want this divorce. It was Victor's choice. I still love him and am ready to work at problem-solving."

Victor brought his landlady with him. He is currently renting a room from Valerie Pierce and her husband. They are good friends from church, and Valerie is a beautiful blond, strong-willed lady. Victor's brother evidently suggested he bring someone to be "on his side" for emotional backing and support. Maybe Patrick thought I was going to tear into Victor.

When Evelyn Monroe arrived, she told us she had just finished a class in mediation! She requested we meet at the dining room table—Victor on one side of her and I on the other--with everybody else around the table.

Evelyn explained how much the house would be worth now, and that Victor's half would be approximately $100,000. She reported that Victor had told my attorney he would accept $60,000—the $20,000 now and the $40,000 paid off in fifteen years.

Rudy asked, "Why would you accept $60,000 if $100,000 is your half."

"Well, I wanted to be fair to Judy," Victor responded.

Rudy wouldn't drop the subject. "Why do you want *to be fair* to Mom?"

Silence reigned for a squirmingly long moment.

So Rudy asked Victor again, "Do you want to be fair to Mom because you *love* her?"

After a long pause, Victor answered, "Yes, I do. I really do."

Then, turning to look straight into Victor's eyes, I said, "I love you too."

Another question came from Rudy: "Why are we sitting here talking about how to divide the property? Maybe we should be talking instead about how you two can get back together."

Victor replied, "Too much has gone under the bridge. It's too late."

Now Victor proceeded to tell all of us that this $40,000, to be paid off in fifteen years, was totally unacceptable to Clarice, and he refused to sign, even though he had already told the attorney he would.

That statement brought our negotiations to an end. But we discussed the idea of meeting later.

Rudy went to Victor and gave him a hug, so I decided to hug him also. We might as well be friends. So I went up to him, (he was now standing) and gave him an embrace.

Victor said, "Thank you for being so *fair*!" It was almost as if he was shocked at my fairness.

This was new insight for me, so I replied, "I have always loved you, Victor, and I always will! I *want* to be fair!"

Surprisingly, his response was, "Well, don't give up hope!"

We were standing there in each others arms. The other folk had passed us and gone on out the front door.

I took a step back. "What do you mean by that?"

"I still don't know," Victor took in a big breath, "what is going to happen after I move away—what's going to happen between Clarice and me."

After the others left, I told Evelyn about Victor saying, "Don't give up hope."

When Evelyn called Victor the next day, she commented, "I saw you and Judy in an embrace. Is there any hope for reconciliation?"

"I told her not to give up hope just to make her feel good. I should never have said it, because there is *no* hope."

Evelyn relayed that information to me and commented that there was strong finality in Victor's voice.

The next day Victor told me he was going to move to Clarice's area on Friday, February 11, 1994. He had a chaplain's job waiting for him near there.

26

EXULT?

I've got to talk about Nancy. She became one of Victor's "shoestring relatives" by the marriage of Victor's brother, Patrick. Apparently she must be on some kind of search for truth in her life. When going through a divorce in the past, she became atheistic, but has been gradually coming back to a belief in God. She talks with me about some of her concepts, and we discuss some of our differences, but I endorse her freedom of choice.

Before December I shared with her a lot of things regarding Victor and me, partly just because she kept asking, and partly because I wanted her to know my dilemma. Will I never learn to keep my big mouth shut? She came across as having gained a lot of wisdom from her own marriage and divorce. At that point it seemed she was encouraging me to let Victor go. She apparently believed then that he was emotionally sick and had severe problems.

On Monday, January 31, Nancy called me again. She was markedly more upset about Victor's and my divorce. She told me she had "been praying earnestly for God to lead" and she felt impressed to talk to Victor and try to set an appointment to see him before he moved. She felt she had to try to see if she could stop him from going. She said she realized it was her "own selfish interest," partly because she didn't want the family to be split up. She said she had some special things in mind that she wanted to say and do with Victor the last Saturday before he was to move.

She had decided to go on a fast, and she asked me if I would join her tomorrow in a week long fast, with concentrated prayer that Victor would not marry Clarice, but would decide to stay and get back together with me.

This is really something unusual! I have been a church member all my life and *never* have I had even *one* person in the church or in my family ask me to fast and pray with them. I know that many religions consider fasting and prayer a spiritual discipline that helps one to focus on character growth and stabilize one's thinking and emotions on problematic issues. If Nancy, who seems to be spiritually unsure of herself, wants me to join her in fasting and praying for *my* ex-husband, that God would somehow alter or mend our relationship in a good way, I am humbled!

I prayed, *"Lord, help me to listen to this girl! Help me to have discernment and not do or say anything that might devalue her, but support her in this project. Please center our thinking and praying, in spite of some disagreement. And Holy Spirit, please stabilize the thinking and emotions in both Victor and me, so that we make no spiteful or frivolous decisions about our future."*

The next day my answer to her invitation was to join her, going on a juice and broth fast, since I have not been able to deal well with a total fast. My legs cramp terribly and I get nauseated from the tamoxifen pills I must take for breast cancer. But I could go on this type of a spiritual fast.

That evening, after giving her my answer, I felt tremendously impressed to write another letter to Victor.

Tuesday, February 1

Victor, these are things I thank you for. These things I'll remember forever with love:

Back rubs.

All over body massages.

Foot and leg massages.

All the many repair jobs of washers, dryers, garbage disposals, broken furniture, broken toys.

Furniture refinishing.

Your neatness and organization of your closet.

Willingness to eat most anything I cooked.

The touch of your face to my face.

Your carefulness and taste in dressing.

The brickwork in front of our house.

Your gardening and bringing me the produce.

Picking apricots and other fruit.

Your singing.

Your singing "All the Things You Are."

EVERY SECOND WE SPENT AT THE CABIN AND HIKING TO AND FROM THERE.

ALL our backpack trips.

Your willingness to let me hike alone and go on trips alone, to seminars alone.

All the FREEDOM you gave me.

Shampooing carpets.

Painting rooms.

Choosing and planning WITH ME how to remodel the kitchen.

Planning WITH ME how to fix up the cabin.

Scratching my feet and legs for hours after my hysterectomy surgery when I itched so badly from the Morphine.

Putting up Christmas tree lights and other lights outside the house.

Cuddling me when it was cold at night.

The smell of your after shave.

The way—the style—how you play 40's, 50's and 60's music. You have a real flair.

Allowing me to teach you voice so you developed such wonderful singing ability.

The way you looked in your red nightshirt.

How you keep on working and working hour after hour in the yard or cabin and never seem to "run down." Amazing!

For ALL the RARE times you shared your opinions, needs, feelings, ideas.

Sometimes being willing to listen when I talked interminably.

The time, after you moved out, you came over for something and really looked at me. You commented on how good I looked and asked if my red high heels were new.

Your planting flowers one of the last times you worked in the yard—putting impatiens in front of the porch and geraniums in the flower box. In spite of my anger, your loving gesture of the flowers moved me to tears. I just didn't let you see them.

Your love of candles and fires in the fireplace.

Your brushing my hair.

Your regular polishing my car and getting it serviced.

Your love.

Your desire to please.

Your safe driving.

The years we were in evangelism TOGETHER.

The traveling, the planning, the practicing, the performing TOGETHER musically.

The being TOGETHER with Steve and Alan during those years.

Playing games and painting together.

Laughing at the filth and cockroaches and inconveniences that we lived with TOGETHER when we traveled from city to city in evangelism with JA, the evangelist.

Musical programs we've given all through the years TOGETHER. My heart broke when I found out that recently we've been asked to give more programs and you declined.

I wanted to work in the yard with you TOGETHER— not me in the front and you in the back.

I love the cabin. We were TOGETHER there. I have always loved our togetherness.

The backpack/camping trip on Catalina Island that YOU initiated and did most of the trip planning. I loved it. Remember the buffalo just outside our tent at night?

The stinky toilets? The fourteen-mile walk to and from Emerald Bay? The mother wild pig and her babies along the way?

The glorious sights we saw underwater while snorkeling TOGETHER? Do you remember our holding hands while we glided along with our fins moving slowly? Remember the eel and the shark?

Climbing Mt. Shasta TOGETHER with cold, fear, violent gales blowing snow and sand in our eyes and the gigantic effort we experienced TOGETHER.

Oh Victor, I wanted us TOGETHER. In recent years we've hardly even eaten meals together, hardly ridden in the same car together—even to church. Only after the new pastor came to the last church we attended did we even sit in church together. Seldom did we read together, play together, walk together, plan together and work together. In some of the years we *did* cuddle together at night. Thank you, thank you for that!

The cabin, to me, symbolizes TOGETHERNESS. I felt so bereft, so bewildered, so hurt when you told me you would limit our time there to once a month. All those previous years were dedicated to arranging my plans to fit your ministry. I had hoped that in our "empty nest" years you'd come at least twice a month to the cabin with me for at least part of the year. But you said your responsibility as an elder in the church and a music committee member was more important!

Oh Victor, I did everything for the purpose of our bonding, wanting you to "find yourself" in therapy so you'd have more *self* to experience with me.

Judy

The letter was finished after midnight. I could hardly wait until the next day to deliver it to Victor's car at the hospital. Currently I'm still fasting and doing lots of extra praying. Randomly I'm opening the Bible, not believing it's a wise way to study, but just looking for ways for God to speak to my heart.

Again I feel impelled to write Victor another letter.

> Wednesday, February 2
> Dear Victor,
>
> Did you subconsciously mean it when you said, "Don't give up hope" after the meeting this last Sunday, even though you now regret it? I believe you said it because a part of you—a deep, strong, stable, enduring part--doesn't *want* to give up. I believe that's why at the cabin recently, even though you had "made up" with Clarice, you embraced me tenderly and said, "Maybe someday we'll get back together." I still believe you meant it and want it.
>
> Remember the pastor we knew who married Barbara? He left his wife and moved halfway across the United States to live with her. That's farther than you'll be from me when you move. He stayed married for about a year. Then he came back, told his ex-wife he'd made a drastic mistake and wanted her back. She refused to marry him right away, saying he'd have to court her. They also got lots of counseling and both learned how to make many changes. She told him, "No sex until we are married." And finally, after quite some time, they remarried. A friend asked him why he came back to his wife, and he replied that it dawned on him he had given up all of what he had worked for. He had given up everything. "A horrible mistake."
>
> Merv Jenson called Monday night to ask about you. I told him about our meeting with Evelyn and your statement, "Don't give up hope."
>
> I also told him that in October you promised me you'd never make me sell the house. Later you called my attorney and told him you'd accept $20,000 cash now

and $40,000 when I sell. You called again a few days later and said you changed your mind and you'd only accept the $20,000 now plus $40,000 paid off monthly without interest in fifteen years. Now you say that is unacceptable to Clarice.

Merv about exploded, "She has no business telling Victor how to handle the finances and settlement. No "other" woman has that right!" He emphasized *that* should be between just the two of us.

Merv further commented, "If she is going to do this to Victor *now, before* they are married, I pity what will happen *after* they marry!"

Since she has twenty more years of time than you do, she can keep working. She's that much younger than you. I don't know how many years are left for me. If I were her, and planning to marry you, it would be against my integrity to even *think* of pushing you to settle with your ex-wife in any particular way, because it ought to be between you, her and God.

You said you were marrying her because she was ninety-five percent submissive. That comes across as *anything but* submissive—persuading you to break your promises to me. I have really hoped to learn to like her, but my respect for her has taken a nosedive. Please don't let her take away your ability to stand on your own two feet.

Love,
Judy

After the writing was finished, I was sitting by my window reviewing Bible verse cards and praying, when suddenly there was the sound of a car engine. Looking out to discover the source, and seeing Victor *backing out of my driveway*, I dashed out the front door to catch him. When he saw me, he stopped.

Surprised and breathless I called, "Here's your mail and another letter from me."

"Oh, thank you for the letter you gave me yesterday." His tone of voice sounded genuine.

"You're welcome." Then I asked, "What were you here for today?"

"I got the amplifier for my keyboard," he answered. "I am going to play for a program later in the day."

I tried not to show how eager I was to impress him. "There's something on your amplifier for you to read. It's not a letter. It's just something I wrote for myself, not intending to give it to you. But after reading it to the Divorce Recovery Group I attend, they suggested you read it, so it's with your amplifier."

He turned off the motor, got out and went to the back of the truck to look inside the camper shell. He hadn't noticed the envelope before, but he saw it and took it into the cab.

I then asked, "Did you get your hat?"

"No. Where is it?"

I asked him to wait a minute. Going to the garage to get the bag that contained both the hat and the stuffed-bear Christmas tree ornament, I brought it to him. He'd left his hat at my house the night he told me of his final decision to marry Clarice, when I asked him to leave after he whispered, "I'm so sorry." He now took it, thanked me, and drove away.

Since the January 30 meeting, and after some studying of my resources, I had discovered my income from teaching music was leaner this last year than the previous year. By phone I then notified Victor he wouldn't be able to hear whether I would even *qualify* for the $20,000 loan until after he arrived at Clarice's place, because my income tax appointment wouldn't take place until the day he left for up north—Friday, February 11.

Now it was Friday evening, February 4—one week before he would drive away in his truck—and I was sitting by the fireplace, reading my Bible verse cards, thinking, praying and watching the fire. The solitude welcomed me and yet felt almost overwhelming at the same time. My emotions were conflicted, and I stayed away from the kitchen and any thought of food that might tempt me to break my fast.

The next day I went to church. Afterward, Susan invited me to her home for dinner, but I declined because of fasting. The afternoon and evening were spent by the fireplace again, knowing that Nancy was with Victor that day, but not knowing what was transpiring.

My journal note written Sunday, February 6 said:

> Tomorrow will be the last day of my "fasting" (juice, broth and a few whole grain crackers to keep me going) and prayer. Nancy asked me to pray particularly for her confronting Victor to face his own truth. She was meeting with him yesterday. I haven't heard how it went. It is scary to think of trying to get back with him and heartbreaking to think it is over. My prayer is that God will bring about whatever helps each of us to grow the most and be the most effective in our lives. "Thy will be done. Give me courage to stand for integrity and truth, fortitude to never give up growth, ability to heal as soon as possible, and courage to change anything you lead me to recognize needs changing. I pray for increasing wisdom, alertness, discretion, openness, patience, self-control, maturity, spirituality and love."

That night, in a phone call from Nancy, she told me she had had a strong impression this past Friday that Victor was going to cancel meeting with her the next day. She wasn't surprised when she found a phone message Friday night that he was sick. Immediately she wondered if it was just an excuse, so she called back to ask if she could at least go to church with him.

He agreed, so the next day they met at the church where Victor's and her families had attended for years. Because of bad weather, they didn't picnic after church as originally planned, but went to a restaurant. She decided to say nothing about Victor coming back to me, and just listen to him. One thing he mentioned about me was "the sweet letters, but they still had barbs in them."

Nancy then told me on the phone, "Victor is going to Clarice because she is someone who loves him and accepts him. He doesn't feel you do." Then she emphasized, "*You* are not nearly as loving a person as Victor, and I don't think you even know *how* to love!"

I'm rather startled at Nancy's quick-change attitudes towards me. But because I value her as a person, I'll listen carefully in spite of her put down.

She said, "I am going to bow out and not contact you for a while, because I realize my *own* hopes and desires of how this will turn out probably won't happen. I am going to end the conversation and leave it in God's hands."

Before she could hang up, I quickly asked, "Do you think Victor might stay here if I asked him to?"

"Yes! I know *exactly* what you should do! Put on your white pantsuit, smear mud on your hands and knees, go to his house and say, 'I crawled on my hands and knees the whole way to get here, and I'm going to tell you I'm wrong. If you will take me back today, you don't *ever* have to go to counseling again, and I'll take you into my own bed tonight. I accept you just as you are.'" Abruptly she added, "Our conversation has been long enough, and I'm hanging up!"

Click. Her drama was worthy of a stage!

I knew the smearing mud and lying wasn't right, but some of what she said made sense.

Feeling desperate, and knowing if anything was to be done, it had to be *now*, I prayed, *"Lord, I've got to do it my own way, but I'll take a chance."* It felt like I prayed the Biblical Queen Esther's prayer that ended with, "If I perish, I perish." (Esther 4:16 KJV)

If he doesn't accept, I'll be no worse than I am right now.

Next morning, February 7, my finger shakily dialed Victor's phone number. "I need to talk to you. Would it be best if I came to your place or you come to mine?"

"I need to talk to you too. I'll come there." His voice sounded as urgent as I felt.

"I have homemade soup, so you can lunch here," I dared to cut my fast short a partial day.

Victor arrived in a little while, put his arms around me and held me for what seemed a long time. It felt so good to be hugged. I invited him into the living room "so we can talk before we eat."

I allowed part of what Nancy had said to be my words, but was so distraught I was not totally honest. Desperation distorted my thinking, but knowing both Nancy and I had been fasting and praying, I fervently clung to my faith.

334

"Victor, I've been wrong. I have criticized and blamed you. I want you to know a new woman—the *new* Judy. I don't want to hurt you anymore, and I ask your forgiveness. If you should decide to stay here and not go to Clarice, I will take you back into my bed tonight, and you don't *ever* have to go to counseling again."

He looked at me, bewildered! Stunned! Shocked! Speechless for moments! Then he put his arms around me and said, "I have been praying for a sign, because I haven't known what to do. Last night I think I got it."

"What was that?" My extreme nervous tension just *would not* let up.

"Clarice told me on the phone last night: 'Until you have the *cash in hand* for your share of the equity in the house--$100,000—so you can buy *me* a house, all wedding plans are off.'"

As he paused, I tried to absorb this new piece of information.

Then he continued. "I'll break up with her tonight."

Now *I* was astonished! The date was Monday, February 7, 1994. We talked a little while longer and soon he said, "We're not married; I better not stay here tonight."

It was with relief that I agreed, because at this point Victor's indecision had squelched *any* current sexual urges.

He suggested we get married in March, but I told him about my promise to God, Lena Talbot, Merv Jenson and myself to give myself *a year* to heal. I was ready "to try again, but not to make wedding plans yet."

Then I asked him to *please* "keep all of this a *secret* for a while!" I emphasized to *not* tell *anyone* yet. I didn't want to tell our sons or my house mates, because I hardly believed he'd really break off with Clarice.

Victor said he would call Clarice at nine that night to tell her he had decided not to move after all, and he'd call me back right afterward. Amazing! He requested we have prayer to praise God that he was going to get us back together again. We did, and then we ate lunch and he left with light steps and apparent joy in his heart.

Now it was after 9:30 pm. that same evening, and he still hadn't called. I figured he must have spoken to Clarice, and she talked him into moving after all; however, *after 10:30* he *did* call and casually said, "Hi, how are you?"

335

As soon as I answered "Hi, I'm okay," he related that he had gone by the hospital after leaving me and told some of the folk there that he "wasn't going to move after all."

Anger swept through me, because I had requested he *not tell anyone yet*! My impatience escalated, and finally I blurted out, "Did you talk to Clarice?"

The result of his phone call to Clarice, which I had been expecting ever since *nine* o'clock, *finally* came out but ended only a little of my suspense. "No, she wasn't there. I just left a message."

"What was the message?" My frustrations were growing.

"I just said I wasn't going to move after all, and I was going back to you."

"That's all?" I couldn't believe what I was hearing.

"Yes," was his only response.

I was nearly horrified by his crude and clipped announcement! Would he break up with the girl he was engaged to with just a brief sentence on the phone? *Victor is being unfair and cruel! He hasn't grown nearly as much as I thought;* but verbally I exclaimed, "I've been sitting by the phone waiting *over an hour* for you to call!"

"I'm sorry. I should have called sooner." I had to listen carefully to catch his almost whispered words. "Actually I just got to watching TV and *forgot.*"

He's still the same old Victor, and apparently he doesn't think about Clarice's or my feelings! I could explode this very minute, but it wouldn't accomplish anything!

With a very controlled and quiet voice I stated, "I'm really upset and disappointed in you!" *But I wanted to cry and scream, and maybe even slap and kick!*

He asked when we could get together again, so I explained we couldn't the next night, Tuesday, because it was my student piano recital.

As soon as it was said, I thought, *Oh no, he may show up and I don't want him to come!* Unfortunately I didn't mention my feelings. Victor ended the phone conversation by saying it was too late to talk more.

The next evening, after the last student had finished playing at the recital, I got up to announce about folding up the chairs and putting them away. As I looked into the audience, there was Victor sitting in the back row with a great big smile on his face.

This man has invaded my boundaries! These people all believe he's marrying another woman. He suddenly shows up here, and I'll have to explain what I don't even understand yet myself. I'm absolutely livid, but must control myself. I'm aghast and feel riled up. Why can't we keep the troubles between us private? For the last few months nothing has stayed settled, so right now I'm in a walloping quandary! My fury is seething!

Announcing to the students and parents that "I'll meet you soon at the refreshment table," I turned my back, pondering, *Here's a good time to close up the piano, cover it and push it back. I must stall for time to pull myself together and decide my next move.*

Then Victor came bounding up onto the platform with a huge grin, as though I was going to be thrilled to see him. I wanted to run far away, not wanting to even *speak* to him, but forced myself to be honest. "I'm embarrassed! I feel awkward! I don't want to talk to you right now! Please don't talk to me!" Turning away, I walked back to the refreshment table.

Shortly I noticed that instead of leaving the place and going home, which I wanted and hopefully expected, Victor looked bewildered and was sitting by himself at the back of the room. Thankfully he at least didn't enter in socially with anyone.

Such a rush of emotion! I want him, but not here, not now! Let us get things settled in private!

After everybody left, we drove to a park to talk a few minutes. He informed me that he told *all the staff* he saw today at the hospital that he was breaking up with Clarice and coming back to me!

Rage surged through me again, over and over! But I only listened. I had *specifically* asked him *not* to tell *anyone* yet, and wanted to know if he could hold to his word and value my requests. Then he explained he also told the staff he wanted his old job back, but the administrator wasn't sure whether or not she would oblige. His "retiring party" was already planned for Thursday, two days from now, which is the day prior to his planned move. His truck, plus the trailer he planned to haul, was all loaded and ready to go.

"Have you heard from Clarice since you left the message?" *I can't help asking.*

"No, and I don't think I ever will." He sounded really sad. Evidently he has no intention of calling her again. Still feeling flabbergasted and perturbed at him, I didn't dare say *one word* about it. My long-existing habit! However I *did* emphasize, "*I, myself,* am going to *have* to go back for *more counseling*! I don't know how to handle some things you do, such as your coming to the recital uninvited!"

There was no response regarding that statement. We sat in silence until he changed the subject to tennis and gave an invitation to play.

We agreed to play tennis the next night, and parted with friendly words.

Clarice called *me* the next morning "to affirm your going back to Victor."

I told her we weren't going to marry until Victor and I could work out some problems, which would be *at least* a year.

She counseled me: "There are plenty of women who want a man like him; he's the world's most precious treasure. You should buy a new dress, fix yourself up, send him flowers, and *pay for his way to the singles retreat* he told me you plan to attend." I inwardly smiled at her "counsel." So she is *passive*, is she? I thanked her for calling and hung up.

All day my emotions felt stormy and chaotic. Still feeling panic about talking more to Victor about my *frustration and anger*, I realized *there's no possible way to go back to this man unless I can confront him, unless there is freedom to tell what I feel! He has so invaded my boundaries! If I perish, I perish!* [Again alluding to the Biblical Queen Esther.] That evening I bravely divulged how intensely irked and ill-tempered I felt regarding his coming to the recital.

He listened! He didn't get up and walk away! He didn't slam any doors! Instead he admitted he didn't understand.

I told him I regretted that, and hoped we could talk more about it. I *didn't* tell him how furious I was about his blurbing it all to the staff at the hospital! I *didn't* tell him how agonized I was about his not calling me when he promised, but forgot and was watching TV instead! I *didn't* tell him I thought his phone message to Clarice was awful! I was too afraid he'd totally close off to me if I did.

I choose to deal with just one thing at a time. I'm not sure if that is good or bad—"stockpiling" all these emotions; but I've got to give myself time to think clearly and evaluate Victor's emotional state before dumping too much garbage on him.

The tennis courts were loaded the next evening, so we decided to go to the yogurt station instead. Purposely looking in before we entered to see if anyone we knew was there, we still missed seeing Burt Dennison, who had his hair styled differently that day, was wearing a pink sweater and was with a group of youth from the church he pastors.

Going to the counter to order, and hearing my name called, I turned around and recognized him. Stepping closer I hastily whispered, "Victor broke up with Clarice. He wants to get back with me." Victor was still placing the order, so I sat at a table away from Burt. Then Victor went to him and told him he was coming back to me.

As we ate, I again reminded Victor of my promise to God and myself that it would be a *year* before making a decision about marriage.

He said he didn't know how he could wait that long.

Putting on a brave front, and speaking firmly to him, my words revealed, "I have plans for this Friday night with Susan and her sister. The remainder of the weekend I'll go to the cabin with a male friend who is going to help with a project there. The following weekend is the singles retreat I'll attend." So we said a friendly goodnight without making any plans for meeting again.

Nearly every day I continued talking on my mini-cassette-recorder, telling about that day's events and re-verbalizing conversations. Sometimes I did it several times a day, such as the following:

> This is the Friday Victor was to have moved away, but instead is moving back into his apartment. He has been staying with his friends, the Pierces, who temporarily rented him a room in their house. I decided to invite him to go on a Valentine's early lunch date with me next week. There also were more things I needed to discuss, so drove to his apartment. It surprised me to see Alan there helping him move in, and I realized Victor had told *him* also about our changed plans. *More betrayal! I didn't want to get my hopes set on anything, let alone tell anyone else, until I knew for sure!*

Victor happily accepted my Valentine's invitation but was too busy to talk more right then. I went home and told my house mates the news since so many already knew.

That same night, when I returned from Susan's, there was a phone message from Victor's brother Patrick. In a *very* gruff and *angry-sounding* voice he said, "Judy, I've just been talking to my brother, and he sounds *very* upset! It seems that you have a *great* deal of control over him! I just want to say, I hope you don't abuse that! And that's *all I better say right now! Goodbye!*"

Phoning Victor I asked, "Are you OK?"

"Yes, I'm OK. Why do you ask?" He sounded pleasantly surprised.

"I got a phone message from Patrick, and he sounded quite angry," I informed him.

"I talked to Patrick on the phone and *was* pretty upset; I'm feeling just terrible, *terrible* about Clarice. I'm all broken up. I was very open with Patrick and told him you had a whole change of attitude, but we haven't talked more about it since then."

So that's what the story is! Victor is having second thoughts, obviously!

The next morning, Saturday, I went up to the cabin with Steve Burden, and returned home Sunday night. In the last year or two, he and I had been assigned a few times to work together in the mountains where I do volunteer trail patrol for the Forest Service a couple weekends a month, May through September. I had made arrangements with Steve to help with some heavy work at the cabin *long* before I ever *dreamed* Victor and I might get back together.

On the morning of Valentine's Day Victor called. "I have a big surprise for you! I want you to come to my apartment, and I don't want to tell you what it is until then."

Remembering my schedule, I asked, "When do you expect me to come to your apartment?"

"After we eat lunch today." Victor sounded surprised that I asked that question.

He still doesn't listen, or at least doesn't remember. So I asked, "Do you remember we eat lunch early, because I have an appointment with Lena Talbot?"

"Oh, I forgot about that," he apologized.

"What is the surprise?" I really *wanted* to know.

"Well, I'll tell you now. I talked to Clarice last night and told her you were afraid I might go back to her. She said to tell you—and *this is the good news, this is the surprise*—she said to tell you she will *never* take me back, because she's closed the door! She'll not *ever* let herself be hurt again by me."

He's saying this with a tone of voice and expression as though he has won a million dollars! This is the same Victor—totally covering up his real feelings. He must be hurting! Here's the woman he says was the love of his life, who made him happier than he's ever been with me, but he rejects her. Then he tells both his brother and me he's terribly broken up, yet now sounds marvelously jubilant that she'll never take him back again! He just doesn't make sense to me! **KAREN: All this is manipulation to *not* blame *himself* for his *own* actions! Victor is not expressing any sympathy towards Clarice for her pain and suffering. Just like he didn't with Judy.**

"Thank you for telling me." *Judy, be positive! I tell myself.* And to Victor I assert, *"And* I need you to remember *I won't decide anything* for at least a *year."*

At lunch he told me he had asked to get his chaplain's job back, but the administrator told him she had gone to headquarters to discuss his status quo. "We'll give you a three-month leave of absence until you decide what you want to do." Apparently they recognize his instability.

He asked me to come back to his place that night, after my counseling session and teaching duties, to give me a Valentine's serenade. He played his keyboard and sang several songs, including "All the Things You Are" by Jerome Kern and Oscar Hammerstein II.

"That's so beautiful and romantic!" I genuinely appreciated it. "That's one of the songs I wrote about in the recent letter I gave you."

He looked dismayed. "What letter?"

I was nonplussed at his question, but clarified it with, "The one in which I listed things I would always remember, the one that I put in your car a short time ago."

"Oh, you did say some sweet things in that letter," he recalled.

I'm surprised he doesn't remember my mentioning that particular song that I always have loved hearing him sing. I guess he is too emotionally distraught to remember.

A landscape gardener from Victor's church made him an offer to pay him minimum wage for doing yard work with him every Friday. Victor accepted, and eventually that turned into full time work later.

A Vietnamese lady, who had previously lived with us for a while, asked me, "May I give Victor some money?"

"Currently he doesn't handle his money very well, and I don't know whether he would accept charity. But if you have work for him, and he could *earn* money, I think he would like that and take good care of it."

Later I asked Victor "Are you all right financially?"

"Oh yes, I'm fine. I have $1100 in the bank." About three days later when I offered to pay half of a meal at a restaurant, he said, "Oh no, I'm fine. I have $500 in the bank."

The first of December Victor had moved out of his apartment into a room he rented at Pierce's home, because they charged only half as much as his apartment cost. What he didn't consider—or what he thought didn't matter--was that he had signed a year's lease at the apartment. Victor even took it to small claims court and was told, "A contract is a contract!" So when he returned from Clarice's after Christmas, he paid his lapsed apartment rent. Since he had promised to live with Pierce's until February 11 and didn't want to pay double rent, he gave them his microwave oven in place of the January and February rent. He has no couch because he gave it to his former church pastor's family. He told me earlier he thought he would *not* have to pay income tax, but recently went to a tax expert and discovered he owes $700.

Am I the cause of this apparent absent mindedness in Victor's thinking? While feeling emotionally drained and wrung-out, I'm struggling with guilt— hoping I'm not the instigator of his instability. However there lodges in my soul a strong determination to carefully think through any decisions I make, and get professional help when I'm stymied. **KAREN: You blame yourself for his own poor decision making? Boundaries issue!**

The following Friday I went to the singles retreat and got home about Sunday noon. I called Victor and he wanted me to come over to "take me to a movie." On my arrival, he admitted he had *rented* a couple movies the night before, but hadn't watched them yet. "I want you to watch one of them with me. You choose which one." One was an X--rated playboy type; the other similar one was called "Desire." Although not usually caring to watch this type of movie, I chose one for Victor's sake. He said he was "feeling terribly, horribly depressed," and he guessed he better get back on Prozac. **KAREN: Lack of boundaries. Not ok to go against yourself!**

After the movie ended and we conversed a little, his depression didn't seem much improved, so it was time to head back home and get my own beauty rest.

One day I received in the mail an announcement about an all-day women's convention to take place the following week at Glenkirk Presbyterian Church in Glendora. I decided to attend. Several short seminars there were given by specialists.

At one of these a Dr. Sinimon talked about the Biblical way we can meet another person's needs before our own. He also said to never lose track of what *we* need, and our *own* sense of self. We *choose* to put the other person's needs ahead of ours. At the end of his lecture there was a question and answer period. I raised my hand and asked, "What do you do if you're married to a man whose only need you are able to discover is that he never wants you to ask what his needs are?" **KAREN: Meaning you must just guess. Manipulation. Lack of integrity!**

Everybody laughed, of course, and he said, "Well, there are an enormous number of people like that. You've got to set strong boundaries." **KAREN: Yes!**

Realizing that's what I *haven't* done through the years, I raised my hand again and said, "I was married to this man. Our divorce is final, and he was engaged to marry another woman in June. Three weeks ago he broke up with her and now wants to come back to me."

I heard a big gasp from the audience. Dr. Sinimon asked, "What's the wedding date?" "There's no date yet. I told him he'd have to wait at least a year before I decided." The whole room burst into clapping and cheering.

With a relieved sigh Dr. Sinimon replied, "Oh, good! If you had said there was a wedding date, I would have sent you my card and insisted, 'You get into counseling right away.' Tell your ex-husband: 'Therapy!' He either gets himself into therapy or there's no wedding." **KAREN: Absolutely!**

Several people spoke to me afterward and said, "Hang in there. Don't let him change your mind."

The day after attending, I woke up remembering my determination to record my thoughts and experiences, which I'd been letting slide from consciousness. So today, after listening for the first time to the tape I made January 8 on the way to church, all I can say is WOW! I am amazed! God is really processing that prayer—although I still can't guess the future! The subsequent recording tells more:

> So much has happened since my January 8 recorded prayer that it's unbelievable! I feel confused! I've given up so many times. My love has seemed to be dying often, and there have been so many problems I haven't known how to face. It seems I should be rejoicing that Victor is out of my life. And yet, instead, I'm happy that he's not. No, I don't know if I am happy. I'm sounding mixed up, and I am! But the things that have happened are utterly remarkable. All the hurt and abandonment that I was feeling is gone. It is replaced with anxiety and fear. I'm afraid to go back with Victor--scared that in my weakness I'll take him back and experience the same kind of marriage we had before. So what I'm doing now is just deciding to make no decisions! There is a whole year to work on this. If things gradually fall apart, then I'll know, and perhaps won't feel as abandoned. There are a lot of issues that must be solved.
>
> Some of what I said to Victor to get him to stay wasn't wise. I wasn't truthful, because I was giving Nancy's words instead of my own; but I felt desperate. I believe it was right for me to ask him to stay. And he *did* break up with Clarice. I have confessed my dishonesty to God and to Victor, and believe I am forgiven. I felt like I meant what was said at the time, although immediately afterward the realization hit me that I'd said too much.

Not wanting to forget any part of "my story," my recording continued, describing my feelings and thoughts as well as events and conversations.

This week Victor has worked three days in my yard and accomplished a lot. We played tennis Wednesday night and had a delightful time. He worked Thursday for our Vietnamese friend and Friday at his new job with the landscape gardener. Friday night I went on a "moon walk" with the Singles Club at a hilly park. It felt wonderful to breathe heavy, sweat a lot and work off much body and mind tension.

A couple days later Victor took me to a big-screen theater. On that date he didn't ask me one thing about the seminar I attended or about the moon walk with the singles. I asked him a lot of things about his work and job, but decided to not tell him anything about me unless he asks.

My horrible sense of rejection and heart brokenness is gone. There are moments when I feel tremendously free to be who I am, and am interested in finding out more of who that is.

Merv Jenson suggested he recreate Victor's therapy group—the same three women and him, plus me. I had gone to meet with them one time before at their "marathon," and we worked together for about an hour or more.

Tonight, February 27, the specially re-created therapy group is to meet from five to seven o'clock. We'll see what happens there. I'll find out if Merv Jenson will recommend that Victor have a complete psychiatric evaluation or not, as was recommended by the leader of my Divorce Recovery Group when recent developments were divulged to her. I'm certainly willing to get one too.

I wonder why Victor has never mentioned the thing I wrote that was put on his hi-fi in the garage. When asked, he said he had read it; that was all. But when I read it to the Divorce Recovery Group, they said it *should be published!* In fact the leader said it *must* be published, because it is powerful and might help a lot of people! I wonder if it had any influence on Victor's breaking up with Clarice or not, or on whatever else is going on inside him. He needs time to himself, and I've asked him to build a life of his own, at least *some* apart from me. We'll see what happens tonight and in the future.

My feelings are mixed from one day to the next, sometimes wishing I could still date. But my need isn't as great as before. Spending a lot of time with myself, doing my own things, time at the cabin with friends, time on singles outings, but without the idea of trying to find a "date" suits me beautifully just now.

Last night, in the recreated group, my perspective was validated and enlarged by having the other three women present. They knew Victor well from their previous series of therapy sessions and truly and deeply care for him. It was good to see their reactions and observe their honesty. It made me realize I'm OK. I told the group some of the things that have happened since they met for their "marathon," which was before Thanksgiving.

Then Merv had me stop talking and asked Victor to report. It was obvious, in looking at their faces, they saw him as very confused. Every little while Merv kept giving the women a chance to respond to Victor's statements. In essence, each one of them said, "You are enormously confused, and you are in no possible condition to have a deep relationship with anybody. You must get yourself straightened out. You have to find out who *you* are first."

Mentioning the letters I sent to him, he admitted these helped him get in touch with more of what he felt for me. I expressed appreciation for his thanking me once for one letter, saying it was sweet, but stated disappointment he hadn't talked more about them, wanting to hear both his good and not-so-good feelings.

Merv gave Victor and me the assignment to "sit down together and read these letters and talk about them." I brought up the fact that he hadn't mentioned the piece containing my imagination of what his unspoken contract might have been when we first married. Merv suggested we should go with the letters first, and this would be something to bring up at a later date.

Then Merv introduced a new idea to Victor with, "You asked God to give you a sign as to whether you should go with Clarice or go with Judy, but put the responsibility on Clarice to make the decision until she said, 'Yes.' Then you prayed for God to give you a sign whether you should come back with Judy, and you got that when Clarice said that all marriage plans were off until you had the money in hand. So God told you first to go back to Clarice, and then God told you to go back to Judy. Is God confused?"

There was no response.

Merv continued, "Now if you can't have Clarice, you want Judy; and if you can't have Judy, you want Clarice. What would happen if you couldn't have either one of them?"

Victor looked very uncomfortable as he spoke, "I guess I'd just have to find someone else right away."

"I think you need to look at this 'loving' Clarice," Merv went on. "I'm thinking you *need* Clarice and you *need* Judy. If you can't have Clarice then you *need* Judy, and if you can't have Judy then you *need* Clarice. And if you can't have either one, then you *need* somebody else. I think what you're feeling as 'love' may be much more '*neediness*.'"

Victor didn't like that! His facial expression and body language were obviously speaking blatantly!

Merv pointed out that Victor seemed to be expecting the group to tell him what to do, and they weren't going to! But at the same time, he seemed to resent the fact that they *might try* to tell him what to do! Merv repeated over and over to him many different times and in many different ways, "Victor, we're not here to tell you what to do--whether to go with Clarice or to go with Judy, or go with anything. We are here to tell you we love you and we have very, very deep concern for you."

Victor became so angry that he went into his closed-up, withdrawal mechanism. Merv confronted him, and Victor admitted he was *very* angry with Merv and didn't want to be there, and he'd like to walk out! I thought for a moment he might leave the room and wondered how I was going to get home if he left without me?

Merv rather quickly ended the meeting. Coming home, we briefly sat in the car and Victor admitted he was terribly uptight, but was still committed to me. As I started to get out he said, "Well, if Clarice and I ever get back together again…"

Interrupting, I blurted out, "Victor, you just now said *if* you and Clarice get back together again, and yet you just said you're committed to me and that she won't take you back. You are still unstable. You still don't know what you want!"

Victor is in no condition to have a deep relationship, and I definitely will not consider remarrying him in the near future and don't know whether he will be able to grow past this point. His instability has been there all along, and

I have been his cover-up, his protector. As much as I did not want to mother him, and as much as I did want him as my partner, I was protecting him from growing. I won't do that now! God help me!

Merv Jenson called tonight just as I was going to bed, wanting to know what Victor's reactions were since group last night. My only answer was that he left a message canceling work in my yard today because he "hadn't slept well last night," and promising to call tonight, but didn't.

Merv said he talked to one of the women in group about the session, and they are *all* baffled and think Victor has serious problems. Merv thinks this could be a brain tumor, Alzheimer's, senile dementia or no telling what. All Victor's crying could be a sign of something. But whatever it is, he thinks it all stems from Victor's "unfinished business." He is going to recommend he read a book on mid-life crises, because he's "been in mid-life crises for twenty years."

I retorted, "Thirty or more."

"No. The first twenty years were evidently a delayed teenage rebellion against his mother," Merv explained. "But midlife crisis has to do with mother business also."

Merv will probably get Victor in to see a psychiatrist because he says "Victor should have a total work-up."

I wondered about calling Victor's medical doctor to see if *he* would cooperate in all of this too, because Victor might have a nervous breakdown and end up in a mental hospital. Merv said he was concerned too, and since Victor was "on the edge" last night, that's why he backed off and ended earlier than planned. He doesn't know whether Victor will have the strength to face any of this.

A few days later, during a lunch date, Victor brought up the subject of group therapy. "If we continue therapy, what are you going to work on?"

Delightedly surprised, I responded, "I still have a lot of fear, and am *very* hesitant to discuss anything *with you* unless there are other people present. In the past, when telling you what I felt or needed, it brought the worst kind of behavior from you. Let's not *discuss* anything personal without other people present to give feedback on the transaction. What do *you* want to work on?" Victor chewed several bites of his burrito before answering, and my impatience was nearly burning my ears. "I realize the one thing Merv will insist on is my giving up my relationship with Clarice. I've been talking to her rather often."

"I'm *relieved* you have! Leaving just a phone message was awful." I took a sip of water to wash out uncomfortable emotions.

"I know it. I still love her as much as I ever did. I am *not* willing to give up my relationship with her at this point." He sounded *very* sure of himself!

"It is *your* choice!" I really meant it! "I'll *never* tell you what you ought to do."

There was silence the rest of the meal. As Victor picked up his napkin from his lap and put it on the table, he revealed, "I told Clarice I wished I could be a bigamist and have two wives, because I love both of you, but that's illegal."

My counseling appointment with Lena Talbot is every two weeks. Last week I told her it finally dawned on me that I have been Victor's "patsy" through all of our marriage, understanding that word to mean "enabler"--the person helping the other to *keep* his same problems. Often, instead of keeping *my* identity and informing him of *my* needs, they were dissolved in order to meet *his needs*, protecting his immaturity and stubbornness. I must learn to say, "That's unacceptable. That is intolerable."

The first few years of our marriage I worked hard to *please* him--do everything he wanted me to do. After a while that changed, and I did whatever I believed was the *right* thing to do. Through it all, I've been the stable one who has held the marriage together, doing more confronting and requesting in recent years. I've believed we are equals, but wanted *him* to be the family leader, nearly always communicating to him what I admired in a man and what I needed.

Because I couldn't say he was *perfect all the time*, he seemed to think I was extremely critical, repeating often, "All you can do is criticize and criticize and criticize!" Daily looking for and finding ways to compliment him, I'm beginning to understand that if I express *any* need or want, he interprets it as telling him he is a failure! Or if the slightest suggestion is made, he hears it as an absolute demand! Could that be possible?

This has been a remarkable time! That's one reason I'm recording my thoughts today.

My insides have grown and my emotions have stabilized enormously. I don't feel abandoned or rejected, even though Victor said he was "giving up the love of his life" and was going to "tough it out" with me. He is very needy and distraught, and I'm praying God will keep him from having a nervous breakdown and help him discover what his problems are. I'm finding out who I am, and feel energetic and positive about my future. I will develop my abilities, resources, talents and gifts and move in whatever direction God opens up for me. Not knowing how I'll feel tomorrow or next week, I really thank God for this day!

I have just made the decision to limit my time with Victor, not going to church or church functions with him yet, because neither he nor "the world" must take it for granted that we're back together. More time must pass.

After seeing Lena today, I feel even more validated in what I'm doing. She said Victor is very fortunate; most women would have just given up and walked away. She said he is operating from an infantile position emotionally.

Since the re-created therapy group met, Victor says he doesn't *ever* want to go to Merv Jenson for counseling again. He wants to find a new therapist. Lena thinks he should stay with Merv, because he has uncovered enough to understand the issues. If he went to another therapist, it would waste a lot of time and money for the new person to get to the root of the problem. Merv sees it now. I'm going to encourage Victor to continue with Merv and hope he will make that choice.

It's 5:45 am. During the night a new idea came to me. Still feeling betrayed and invaded by Victor, I need to tell him about it. Each time I'm feeling this way, I've decided to write it on a little card to put it in a special place where it can rest until a counseling or therapy group appointment. It's not good to allow my mind to dwell on so many issues for so long. What is written down can be forgotten until there is a productive time to talk about it.

Victor and I planned to go to the cabin last weekend. I had recently told him that I currently feel awkward, self-conscious and embarrassed to be seen hiking with him. There are several close friends I often see along the trail who know we are divorced and that Victor was engaged to someone else. I need privacy, so left Victor a message last Friday to *not* come to my place Saturday morning to pick me up as originally planned, because I was going by myself *very* early in the morning to have quiet time and write in my journal. He could come up whenever he wanted, and he wouldn't be expected until noon or later.

In this historic canyon all cabin owners are asked to "sign in" in a special book at the pack station. If there were some sort of emergency such as a fire, authorities would know who needed to be evacuated.

I was delighted to greet his arrival the next day until he said, "I signed in under your name."

A wave of anger and embarrassment rushed over me! I reminded him of my embarrassment to be seen hiking with him, and told him *that* was my reason for going alone earlier. "You know I always sign in with the number of people in my party. Didn't you see I already signed in, listing *two* people going to the cabin?"

He looked disgusted as he answered, "Yes, but I signed under your name anyway!"

Trying to be patient, I asked, "Why would you do that?"

"Just force of habit." He almost spit the words out!

Starting already to feel exceedingly embarrassed, I asked, "Did you see anybody there?"

"Yes. Jenny and Don." Now he sounded defensive.

"Victor, one of the main reasons I didn't hike up with you this morning was because of *not* wanting certain people, *Jenny and Don in particular*, and Frank and Cheyanne also, to even *know we were at the cabin together!* If you had just gone up the trail after leaving your truck, no one would have been the wiser for it. But by your going to the pack station and signing in, *everybody* who owns a cabin that comes in that day to sign in will see we're there together. Since I signed in hours earlier stating there were *two* of us, now it looks like I was with someone else and *you're coming in to spy on me!* This horrible fear of being publicly humiliated haunts me, and I'm embarrassed and angry! I feel betrayed!"

I continued, "Some of my fears come from a childish emotional state of being, and certainly not from an adult or mature stance. A lot of it has to do with my relationship with my mother. I fear public humiliation *enormously!* That was the basis for my fear of being seen hiking to the cabin with you, or having people know you were there."

Purposely I left a time gap between sentences so Victor wouldn't feel overwhelmed by my verbosity. Then there was deep quiet.

Wanting so much for Victor to understand what I was feeling, finally more words tumbled out. "It felt like you *deliberately* challenged me by signing under my name, to show me that you were boss and could do as you pleased, regardless of my feelings. I felt unheard, un-listened-to! At times I *panic* like a little girl who needs protection; I haven't learned to put away all my fears. Maybe these emotions are similar to yours when you think I'm arguing with you or criticizing you."

"Hm-m-m-m. I need to think about that," he said very softly.

Perhaps he *did* think more about that, but he didn't mention it.

I'm certain my fear does stem from my childhood and is a juvenile, emotional thing; but I can't help my feelings and don't know how to get over them. As I am recording, I'm still furious, not understanding why he doesn't consider what I request. That one act in itself makes me wonder if I can ever live with Victor again. He is not hearing me! I'd like to be able to get over these fears of public humiliation and people gossiping about me or asking me questions, which I don't even know how to answer because things are so unsettled.

Victor needs to know that Burt, Merv and Lena, without any conferring with each other, say he is operating from the emotional level of a two-year-old, or "extremely infantile." They see this as a result of something that happened between him and his mother. They think he should be able to deal with it in therapy and get beyond it in probably a year or less time, if he's willing to face it! Lena told me I was probably the only one who could confront him on this without hurting him—when the time is ripe.

After lunch at the cabin that day, we slept for about an hour until I got agonizing muscle cramps in my feet and legs, so got up to drink some Gatorade, walked around, moving and stretching, until the painful spasms relaxed. We then decided to do one of our favorite activities—take turns reading to each other. It was pretty cold. We kept the stove going all day, so later on we needed to gather more wood to last for the night. As usual, we found plenty of small, dead branches in the woods around the cabin. We took turns swinging the long pieces against the rock wall to break them small enough to fit in the fuel compartment of the stove. Soon there was a new blaze warming not only us, but our soon-to-be-consumed dinner and also water for dish washing afterward.

Victor wanted to play dominoes, and I agreed to, although not really wanting to. Why was I was so tired? We got through one game, with Victor seeming to be confused how to play, saying one thing, changing it, and going back to still another way. Maybe he had too much on his mind.

Finally I said, "I'm too tired to play anymore and *must* go to bed." It was only 7:15 pm but already dark. We had the Coleman lantern, oil lamps and candles burning for warmth as well as light.

Victor offered, "Let me read to you."

"Sure. I'd like that." But I fell asleep soon after he started reading.

Twelve hours later I awoke, still "bushed" and now achy. It rained a lot, and we did only a few things indoors. Victor put framing around windows and also laid some baseboard. I stapled a new cover on an army cot. It was fun to work with Victor there.

We played Flinch that evening, and again Victor seemed confused how to play. He read the instructions out loud, told me one thing, and then did something different. Finally again I had to go to bed even though it was only 8:30 pm.

Next morning, in spite of my exhaustion, we got up very early to hike out. I hoped we had left early enough to miss seeing anyone we knew, but we met Don again and Victor greeted him. Surviving what was dreaded, I still had more unexpressed anger. Victor traded and carried my backpack up the last long hill to the parking lot, so I carried his smaller and lighter day pack.

After we got back to our cars, Victor tried to give me a hug and kiss in the parking lot, but I refused.

I don't want the public to see us hugging and kissing each other. We are not engaged! There's been no promise to marry him. He is to be courting me only. He must prove he can think about me and my needs and desires, or I'll send him back to Clarice.

Arriving home with bad shivers, I took my temperature, which was almost 101 degrees! A four-mile backpack with a fever! Silently congratulating myself that I made it home, I showered, loaded myself with vitamin C and water, rested a bit, and then taught students from 4:00 until 8:30 pm.

My roller-coaster emotions are lowering my immune system! How can that be changed? Now that I feel better, Victor's presence and help at the cabin is truly appreciated. I am damaging my health; Victor is not doing it! I, myself, do it by worry, feeling hurt, and my own instability. I choose right now to live to age one hundred, productively and healthfully. I choose to take action to accomplish this and stop worrying now! Victor says he doesn't want to live even until he's ninety. He has valid reasons for that because of his work in the convalescent hospital, seeing how older people suffer and hang on. I won't criticize him for that. But I choose LIFE!

Victor and I have enjoyed doing more things together in the last month than we've done in the last ten years of marriage. He's done far more open and honest communicating in the last week than he has during our entire marriage! He admits telling *lots* of people about my affairs. What he *hasn't* told them is that *he really set me up* for some of them, and then *refused*

counseling when I begged for it! I was desperate, suicidal! It still feels like Victor did it--set me up for affairs--so he could despise me without guilt.

Victor is living as though he is counting on our remarrying; I am living as though I won't decide for a year. He is making effort to act as if we are married; I am making effort to show people we're very single. We aren't working "together," but we are both *working!* Never before have I felt he was *trying*, but I believe he is now!

27

TREMBLE

[The remainder of this book is a combination of my story telling and the many actual recorded tapes that I transcribed and edited, with no designation as to which is which. However, the stories are all true!]

Victor called to say he had lunch today with Nancy, and she sent me a gift. When I got home late, he had already left from working in the yard, and I discovered a package on my dresser containing the book, <u>Ten Stupid Things Women Do</u>, by Laura Schlesinger. With it was a letter containing more of Nancy's "truthfulness and honesty." Those quotes are purposeful, because she wrote in a very unhappy and antagonistic way: "If you begged to get Victor back, why are you refusing to show him love? You are still going to therapy, and he's not living with you yet!" **KAREN: Nancy is a good example of exposing yourself to poor counsel.**

She is quite a dramatist! Although she has very strong feelings about what she thinks ought to be done, I am in control of myself and make my own choices. When other people give me counsel, guidelines and even creative ideas, or when they tell me my faults and give suggestions, I listen carefully, ponder what they say, and then make my *own* decisions. I will relate to Nancy with kindness and love and tell her how very much I appreciate all she has to say, but not mention what my plans are. I'm finally learning to think my own thoughts and make my own choices without being overburdened by other people's desires and opinions. Thanks be to God!

Victor and I decided to go on a whale-watch together, since I had a rain check ticket from a trip on which I hadn't seen any whales. We arrived at the coast early and went to a restaurant for a good breakfast. I long for interesting conversation when I eat, so asked, "Would you like to tell me about your lunch with Nancy yesterday?"

He squirmed a bit and finally answered curtly, "Well, I'm *not* going to tell you everything!"

"You don't *have* to tell me anything! I certainly *don't* want you to divulge confidences!" I waited a while before Victor spoke again.

"She said she wanted me to be happy, but . . ."

Does he not want to share with me because he told her he has given up the deepest happiness and the greatest person he has ever known? Has he told her he is going to tough it out with me, like he said in group? Or something else even worse?

After what seemed an interminable silence he exclaimed, "Clarice is such a *wonderful* woman! She wants to please *everybody*! **KAREN: How is that a wonderful person? By what standard?** The first time I met her at a singles outing, she was constantly trying to set me up with her girlfriend. It finally got to me, and I insisted, 'I'm not interested in Angie; I'm interested in you!'"

After another long silence, I remarked, "I'm listening."

Victor sees her wanting to please everyone as an enormous plus; he also wants to please everybody—except me. Often a person who wants to please everybody is somewhat of a chameleon; they will do what they think is necessary to please, rather than forming strong convictions, making good decisions, doing what they believe is right, and setting goals for themselves. I've been quite a chameleon myself in the past. **KAREN: Good insight!**

Hurrah! We got to see three whales, one of them spouting, and I didn't get seasick! The cold wind blowing in our faces, with occasional spray splattering us as the boat bounced along on waves, was great fun.

On our way driving home I pulled out the Schlesinger book Nancy had sent a few days before. Originally opening the package, I had told

Victor that I valued many of Laura's opinions, morals and standards heard during the broadcast on the infrequent times I had listened. So now in the car I asked him if he'd like me to read from her book, and he answered, "Sure."

As I read the first chapter, which discussed how some women identify themselves only in relation to their husbands and don't develop a personal identity for themselves, it struck me that this may be true also for some men, including Victor. It's as though he doesn't know how to have his own identity; he must have a woman in his life. He just can't be alone. I want him to recognize this, but of course I make no comment.

After I finished the chapter, I closed the book with, "That's all I'm going to read for now," hoping he'd make some comment. There were no words.

Recognizing that my old habit would have been to break the silence with, "Shall we put on some music?" or commenting about something outside the car, I decided to not rescue him. *He either will comment or he won't. But I am not going to put anything else into his mind.* **KAREN: Hallelujah!!**

Many minutes passed before Victor spoke again. "After hearing you read this book, I think we might discuss what we are planning to do after we marry, and what some of our goals are for the future."

Amazingly he asked an intelligent question, which proves he was really listening and thinking!

"That sounds like a good idea!" I responded with genuine relief.

"These women's groups, I'm wondering whether you want to handle them by yourself, or if you want my help. And men's groups, whether you would want to assist me or have me do it on my own," he questioned.

Now I feel bewildered confusion! I've never heard Victor even hint about "men's groups," and I haven't the vaguest idea what he's talking about.

"Oh, *men's groups*? Tell me more. I don't recall ever hearing you discuss that before."

"I'm very open for hiking and backpacking," he happily divulged.

Where does that fit? Some *months* previously I had talked to Victor about the possibility of *my* leading a group for women with "empty-nest syndrome." At that time I was considering starting a personal-growth group by hiking or backpacking with them. We could then discuss what we learned from the hiking experience and use that information as challenge and direction for our on-going lives. But Victor has never mentioned *anything* about men's groups before this! I'm stymied! So I continued to probe, and suggested, "Tell me more about this business of men's groups."

"I'm thinking more of a support group," Victor paused. "Some group that would involve more exercise and healthful living, and so forth."

"That's interesting." I stopped and just waited for him. (New behavior for me.) **KAREN: Great!**

"I've always thought I would like to live in the country and have a center for healthful living, and be able to teach about purposeful, good eating, exercise and so forth."

"Oh, has that been a dream of yours? You haven't shared that with me before. How long have you been dreaming about this? It's a wonderful idea," I complimented him.

Oops—I mustn't get into what he sees as interrogation mode again. When I asked that double question I saw the same tensing, withdrawing, irritation and almost anger in his body language again. I regret asking that second question.

"Well, I don't *know* how long I have been thinking of it. I just don't know. . ."

I remained quiet, because he sounded like he was going to say more, but didn't. Silence stretched long. Victor finally replied, "It really crystallized with me and Clarice."

Now I know why he was hesitant.

He went on, "She held cooking schools when she was married to her minister/evangelist husband, and enjoyed doing that. I thought *we* might do something like that!"

He wants to do it now with me? Never have I pictured myself holding cooking schools! No way!

Again I remained silent. Victor said no more after that, and I let quiet fill our car the remainder of the way home.

A few days later Nancy called to ask how things were going. **KAREN: Nancy needed to be dropped off as a confidante!** I filled her in on how we were and some of my concerns. She still pushed the idea that if I really love Victor, we should now be living together, but she finally accepted the reality that I'm not ready for more. She even apologized for urging me.

Nancy also asked about the women's groups. Victor evidently has recently told her about our months ago conversation regarding them, and she wants to help advertise them. But they hadn't even crossed my mind for a *long* time, and I'd forgotten ever mentioning them to her before! When I told Victor a while back that I was considering these, I don't remember his ever responding at all to the idea. I was amazed he even remembered my mentioning it. I now told Nancy my priorities had changed, and it was important for me to develop advertising for music lessons in order to increase my income.

She assured me, "Victor *does* love you. He recognizes that you have a heart of gold, and I know you love him."

I also revealed to her my fear of being publicly humiliated, *especially* when I don't even *know* I'm doing anything questionable, realizing that stems from early childhood experiences.

She responded, "If Victor truly loves you, then he should listen and help protect you from your fears, even though they are childish. Appeal to him from the fact that these are not *his* problems, they're *yours*. In that particular area you are still feeling what you experienced emotionally as a little girl. Tell him that from now on you both need to play a game. When you go out of the house anywhere together you can ask each other, 'Do you feel safe doing this?' If either one feels unsafe, then don't do it. Do something different."

That is a good idea!

I see so much potential in Victor. Or do I really? He has reached great levels of accomplishment—musically, his chaplain's work, certainly his gardening and landscaping—but he has waited for *me* to do whatever needs to be done in our *relationship*.

Because Merv Jenson said Victor had done enormous growing in his group therapy, I was expecting more maturity and better decision-making. He obviously is being more open—sometimes almost cruelly so—and more honest—rudely so. He is a little more communicative on *some* issues. When we do things together, we *do* experience more fun, and I like that part *very much!* He is looking for ways to *spend time with me*, and I like that also! If I could count on his *total commitment* and responsible *initiative* to work at the marriage like he works in the yard and at the cabin, maybe we could begin to hope for much more.

Merv now thinks Victor is healthier emotionally, and his problems are not as serious. He hopes Victor will return to therapy, work hard and accept the confronting. He said it might be possible, in as little as a year, for us to grow to the point where we could do well in marriage.

Recently Victor asked me, "Would it be all right to go visit my brother Patrick?

"Are you asking my permission?" I gently quizzed him. "I have no authority over you. You are your own person and have every right to do what you want." **KAREN: Great!**

Then I covered my mouth and gulped, suddenly realizing that while asserting myself clearly, I still *feared his reaction*. He might perceive me as trying to run things. "If we are going to get along together, it needs to be very clear that I am not your boss! I am your *equal!* It is wonderful for you to tell me your ideas and wishes, and especially your feelings regarding them." Still talking in a firm but gentler manner, I suggested, "We can talk over plans, express our wishes and discuss our disagreements."

Victor appeared somewhat taken aback by my expressing these honest hopes. He took a big breath and blinked hard several times before responding, "I really *want* to go visit him. I *need* to go away!"

"That's good! I understand! However I *do have fear* about your going to your brother's. You've recently felt very confused, and Patrick sounded quite angry when he left his message on my phone. I get the feeling that he and Barb don't want you to come back to me and would work on you to return with a changed attitude."

Hoping Victor would say more, I waited. But when no words came for several minutes,

I said, "I *want* you to go if that's what *you* want. It's wonderful when brothers can confide in each other."

He must have told his brother about his financial situation, because Patrick paid for Victor's flight ticket to visit them for several days. Before he left, I called to say goodbye, and Victor asked to set up a time when we could talk as soon as he returned. Immediately I felt panic and told him so. "Is it going to be bad?"

"No, it will be good."

I'm guessing he wants to talk about the possibility of getting married right away. I'm not ready for that. It worries me some; yet I realize worry doesn't help anybody with anything, so try to think positively.

After his return, Victor told me that one of the first things he said to his brother and sister-in-law when they picked him up at the airport was, "Judy was kind of worried that if I came up here, you might try to change my mind." He says they both laughed and said they just wanted him to be happy.

Victor says he mentioned a few things about his relationship with his mother to Patrick. He (Patrick) said mom gave him lots of wet kisses, too, and neither he nor Barb thought anything was wrong with what mom did to Victor. But I don't think he told anywhere near all! Patrick is eleven years younger than Victor, so probably wasn't aware of his mom's words or actions with Victor, especially at an earlier age. But mom's relationship with Victor concerns me, because both Lena and Merv feel this is serious. I believe it is a strong factor in our marriage problems.

One night we had a real date and went to the play, "American Twistery." When we got home and kissed each other goodbye, I felt very warm towards him, and wanted to be in his arms longer. Feeling horny when going to bed, I told myself, *"Hey, this is fine, but I'll not dwell on it, because this is no time to get sexual!"*

A few days prior, Rudy and Rosemary had invited me to breakfast. While eating with them, I related how Victor thought I was trying to change his personality and/or his character. I told them, "I *like* his personality. I *like* his looks, his manner. The thing I need from him is his respect, his listening ear, and to be valued by him; but also wish he could open up and share his depth."

Rudy asked some pointed questions, including, "What does daddy want for *himself*?"

"He wants to get married next month! But I will no longer give up my identity and my needs and walk on eggshells trying to please him. I *want* to please him, but not if it means giving up who I am."

"I'm sure glad I'm getting counseling now and not waiting so long," Rudy exclaimed. "You can't have a good marriage until you've straightened yourself out. It's obvious daddy needs to get help before he can figure how to live with someone else. I think he needs to go to counseling for *himself,* *besides* group therapy."

"I wish you would tell him that, yourself!" I said, and hoped that Rudy really would do it.

Victor worked two days last week with the landscape gardener and one day for our Vietnamese friend. He spent the other days in my yard. He must be really exhausted; he's put in a vegetable garden and finished planting the plot in front of our house.

Genevieve Chinnock, who is a psychologist friend and a member of the church Victor used to pastor before he took the chaplain's job, was talking to me recently. I mentioned Victor's passivity, and she said she was aware of it. "Judy, I don't want to come across as a smart aleck or know-it-all, but I will say this: Within a short while after you folks arrived at our church, I became *very much* aware that you two *didn't* have a close relationship! You *didn't have a true marriage!* You, Judy, were just a persevering, stick-to-it person. You were making the best of the situation."

I had never, ever talked to her or *anyone else in the church* about our marriage, so this really surprised me! She told me, "A passive-aggressive person is one of the hardest to live with."

Recently I was talking with Merv Jenson about passive-aggressiveness and he said, "A person can be a *passive* type and *not* be passive-aggressive. The *passive-aggressive behavior* stems from deep anger that the person is not able to express in any other way. When they hold that anger in, it eventually comes out in an aggressive way. It's not bad to be passive; but if you have a lot of anger that *isn't released*, it will come out in other behaviors you may not even be aware of. Passive-aggressiveness is *not* a healthy 'state of being.'"

Lena Talbot explained, "There are people who, because of their family situation when growing up, learn at a very young age to completely turn off their thinking and feeling. That's the only way they can cope as a child. But when it becomes an adult life pattern, it makes a relationship very difficult!"

She is currently working with three different men in their twenties and thirties; two are married and one recently became engaged. They are all in therapy, wanting to cooperate and working very hard on this particular problem. She said one of the fellows calls it "trancing-out."

Lena said, "Judy, you need to know that when this happens, it is a *very* difficult habit to overcome. If Victor chooses to work on this, it is something you need to be aware of. When he *does* listen to you and *does* follow through, he needs to have *excellent* feedback and a *lot* of *encouragement!*"

For whatever reason, Victor apparently does "trance-out." And I believe he has also been passive-aggressive. **KAREN: Yes!** Lena said she doesn't know how much hostility he has currently, or whether that is happening. **KAREN: I think the Perfectionism hid it from himself. <u>He may not know he ever acts out that way, which makes it all the more difficult to overcome.</u>**

At another recent counseling session with Lena she said, "Judy, it would be absolutely catastrophic if you went back to Victor now! Within a short while, no matter how much he wants to relate differently, he would be back in the mama's womb. No matter how much you tried *not* to mother him, it would be *impossible* not to do it! He would resent your mothering him, and you would feel you didn't have a real partner. <u>Victor must learn how to take care of Victor!</u>"

One thing I know is that Lena has had far more experience looking at couples and their problems than I have. She has made a study of this. I believe God is using her, so therefore my choice is to accept what she says.

I don't know whether Victor is willing to listen to *anybody* yet. He still says he doesn't want to go back to Merv Jenson. However Merv says he plans to call and invite Victor to return to group. I think maybe he's been waiting, hoping Victor would call him first.

Lena believes if Victor were going to gain benefit from another therapist, the thing for him to do would be to have closure with Merv Jenson. No matter what he does with his future, no matter to whom he goes, he needs to return to Merv and tell him, "I would like to have closure with you. I don't want to come here anymore, and these are my reasons." Then he would be finished.

Lena said, "No therapist is going to want to take him after he's been with Merv as much as he has, without having closure first."

Merv really loves Victor. He thinks Victor is greatly talented and a wonderful person, and he *wants* to see us back together again. He believes it's possible for people to patch up problems in marriages, even when they're as bad as Victor's and my problems are.

"I'm not going to call Clarice anymore," Victor told me, and then later said he probably would be talking to her some, because there were business things to tend to. She's been discussing with him more about her future plans. She wants to buy a house and have a nursing home or retirement home or something like that. She also wants to have her own greeting card business utilizing her artwork. I thanked him for sharing that with me.

Victor says his hostility has melted away now. But I think it could return when we're together. **KAREN: Yes!** Unless he knows the *source* of that hostility, unless he's been able to deal with it, is he going to cover it up when he feels it coming back? Or is he going to be able to be open and say, "I'm feeling angry about such and such?" Is he going to be able to recognize that some of his anger may still be towards his mother or grandmother and not because of me? Is he able to sort things out so as to know which is which? Too many questions are still in my mind!

Some of the things Victor has said and done recently would have devastated me earlier. I don't know whether he has any concept of how cruel, hurtful and cutting these things are. I don't resent his saying them, because I believe he is working at being open and honest, even if things hurt. <u>So rather than choosing hurt and devastation I say, *"Praise you, Lord, that he is getting brave enough to be able to see what his feelings are and verbalize them. This is a real plus; I see it as magnificent!"*</u> **KAREN: Yes!**

I believe Victor now has good motives and prefers *not* to say hurtful things. He's just in the process of changing old habits. I have a choice. I will accept his saying these things now because they are more real and honest than was his cover-up lying.

My life right now is productive. I am enjoying myself and wish so much Victor felt that way too--see himself as having an interesting, fruitful life without our actually being married. If he truly values me, he will see me as worth waiting for. If he really loves me, Judy Wexford Leigh, then he will want to be the very best person he can in relationship with me. He will want our marriage to be *better* than it was before.

I finally braved telling Victor that Lena Talbot urged, "Don't let him go to another counselor," and her reasoning why. "Even if Victor goes with a complete, written-out history and states what he thinks is the problem, it still would take about a year for the new therapist to begin to know how to help. It's obvious Merv Jenson sees the problems clearly and is committed to helping Victor grow. If he wants to accomplish what he needs to achieve in order to remarry, Merv should be his counselor."

Surprisingly Victor said that made sense. He soon decided he would be willing to go back to Merv's group. God is still working!

I went to the Barbara De Angelis seminar on Renewing Relationships last weekend and learned much more that makes good sense. I'm purposely keeping myself very busy these days so there won't be time to worry or do something stupid.

Judy, be patient with yourself and don't push seminar information too fast and too hard on Victor!

Besides going to a well-advertised Divorce Recovery group on Thursday nights at the large Congregational church in Pasadena, I've started going to a Singles Social at the same church on Tuesday nights and want to continue for a while. Victor has hinted numerous times in the past (since our divorce) that I should try to look for a new man, but there are no males in that singles group that attract me—nor anywhere else. **KAREN: You considered it because he said it?** But the interaction and opportunities for intelligent conversation are stimulating. I've made some interesting friends. They help me keep my perspective so I won't get so tied into Victor, in case he changes his mind. There is a good possibility he may; he isn't stable yet and still *frequently* talks long distance to Clarice.

At my next session with Lena Talbot I shared my concerns that Victor might possibly be holding it against me for "making him" break up with Clarice. I didn't *make* him do it, but want him to understand the whole picture. Lena said it was very important that we talk about it. That night I had some lesson cancellations so offered to go to Victor's apartment. He had worked for the landscape gardener all day and was very tired.

Detailing to him how Nancy and I fasted, prayed and collaborated on her getting together with him, I described our conversations and goals since then and her imagination that I was being unfair. Then I read him two of Nancy's letters to me, which shocked him, and he said he realized they must have hurt me. Although there was a *little* pain, mostly what I recognize is that Nancy has *very deep problems of her own*, and she is to be pitied. **KAREN: Yes!**

Victor and I then made a strong verbal contract with each other that *neither one of us* would talk to Nancy again about private things. I have learned my lesson, and will never discuss our personal relationship with other people except professionals. It was unwise to give Nancy *any* details, perceiving her *then* as being much more wise, much more mature and understanding than she really is. **KAREN: Yes!**

I reminded Victor again about my commitment to God, Lena Talbot, Merv Jenson and myself, that there would be no *deep* relationship between the two of us for a *year*. In fact they urged me to keep free from *any* romantic relationship for twelve or more months! They *insisted* I give myself this amount of time to *heal* and *establish my own identity*. That was in January, 1994 when I emphasized my love for him and my desire to remarry him.

If he is having a hard time waiting, he needs to understand *very clearly* that he has *no* obligation to me. He is a free man! We are not engaged! We are still divorced! He is free to call Clarice *any* and *every time* he feels like it, and doesn't need to tell me! He's free to date anyone and go anywhere he wants! If he should decide he doesn't want to get back with me and would like to go back with Clarice, and she questions whether she should do that or not, I would even be willing to call her, if that would help! **Karen: There are two boundary issues here: The offer to fix Victor's relationship** with **"the other woman" which takes away Victor's responsibility in his own personal decision making.** He told me he continues talking with her on the phone and isn't sure what he is feeling. Before I left that evening he said, "<u>I still want to get back with you</u>. <u>Time will tell</u>." **KAREN: Two opposing statements. The second one is "passive-aggressive".**

At another counseling session with Lena I reported feeling stronger these last few days. Any depression is almost gone. She said, "I think you're *stronger than you've ever been in your entire life!*" That compliment really pumped up my joyful energy!

The things Victor still divulges about Clarice don't bother me as much. I'm not so *needy* for him, and know I can live healthfully and happily, even if we don't re-marry. Victor's my first choice. I like his looks, personality, talents, and basic character. If we can learn to build a relationship where there is freedom to say what we feel, think and need and can problem-solve, there is nobody else out there I'd rather be with but him. But I believe this won't happen unless he can deal more deeply with his "mother issues."

One day when Victor was putting tools away after working in our yard, I casually showed him some things stacked near the garage door that I was planning to take to the pack station to be transported to our cabin by the donkey pack train. I mentioned *two* items I was planning to spray paint, and also said I was going to pour the lime from the big bag into the two containers with lids.

A couple days later I returned home from teaching lessons at school and was happy to find Victor working in our yard again. He then informed me he had taken all the stuff *up to the pack station, emphasizing* he had spray painted *three* items and *hadn't* put the lime into the lidded containers. I could hardly believe it! I said I wasn't *ready* to take anything up there yet! And I *definitely* wanted the lime taken from the bag and put into the two containers with tight fitting lids.

Finally I got brave enough to ask, "Were you under the impression that I *asked you to do this?*"

"Yes, of course!" he declared.

"I never *imagined* your doing it! I *didn't want* you to do it! I'm really concerned that you sent the bag of lime as it was rather than putting it into the containers like I mentioned! It was *not* to be sent that way!" I worked hard to not let my tone of voice betray my burgeoning emotional eruption.

"What *difference* does it make?" he asked, disgustedly.

"The paper bag of lime will tear much more easily and perhaps spill when put into the burro bags. Besides it's harder to balance the load on the animals with things so large and heavy. They could put the two containers with lids, one on each side of a burro, to balance the load. And I didn't want the gallon Tupperware container *ever painted*, because it will chip off soon and look ugly."

Somehow Victor had gotten completely confused about what I had said, thinking I was *making requests of him*, but I was only *giving information*! Maybe I talk too fast or need to learn to make clearer statements. Or perhaps he is still so confused emotionally that information gets short-circuited.

Trying to be gentle and not sound blaming, I asked, "What can we do to have a clearer understanding of what we want? It *feels* like you didn't listen to me. It *feels* like you don't care about what is important to me."

"I want you to hear *me too*!" Victor retorted with a flat-handed slap against the wall he was leaning against. "I thought I *told you* that I was going to take the things up Tuesday." He gritted his teeth, showing the white of many enamels.

"I don't recall your *ever* saying anything about *that*. I *do* remember your telling me that Tuesday would be a good day to pack the duplex beds into your truck." (We are leaving tomorrow to take the beds, that mother doesn't need any more, to my sister's place.)

"What's really important," I now emphasized, "is that from now on we are very careful about what we request each other to do. When you're ready to do something here at my place, please *check it out with me before you do anything*, to be sure that's what I want! I also want to *double check* with you to make sure I understand you."

Another insight came to me. "I'm wondering, since sometimes I am verbose, do I use so many words and talk so fast that you get used to turning it off?"

He laughed, "Yes."

"On a scale of one to ten, is it about ten and a half?" I teased.

He nodded and laughed again.

So we got through that conversation with some humor and with some real listening. I don't know whether any problems are solved or not. But I hope he at least sees the point. I hope *I also* see *his* point. I really want to be listened to. I know I talk very fast sometimes. Maybe I *think* faster than Victor and just don't give him time to respond before I jump in again. I must ponder this more!

I have felt increasing excitement regarding Victor the last week or two. He is more fun than he was before, as if he's learned how to *enjoy* himself and how to relax. He hasn't made any commitment for church responsibilities, so isn't obligated for anything. He doesn't yet have a full time job, and maybe that's the reason he feels more freedom to have fun. He is more willing to talk, more willing to listen, and certainly more willing to do things *with* me. He's even asked me to go out to dinner with him a couple times. When I've had to decline because of my own schedule, he hasn't seemed to be too disturbed.

Merv told me Victor would be receiving a letter about when the next therapy group starts. Hopefully he will decide to sign up for it again. I suggested he call his insurance and see if they would reimburse him for therapy expense. Victor thinks he has the money now to pay his income tax, since he's working more hours in landscaping.

I don't know if he's taking better charge of his life financially now, but that's not my problem. I'll just wait and see.

We left Thursday evening to drive up to Clare and Rich's place in the Fresno area. The most wonderful thing about the trip to their place was the fact that we spent so much time alone in the car. On our way there, we played radio music in the dark, and didn't do much conversing. I previously had talked to Victor about the Barbara de Angeles' Seminar called "The Mirror of Relationships," and while riding back home I went through quite a few of my notes and handouts, and we were able to discuss some things. He seemed to listen closely as we went over things, and I was also able to share more about my feelings through the years.

When Victor had gone to visit his brother Patrick and his wife, Barb, they told him I had really blackened the Leigh name. Nancy said the same thing in her letters to him. Victor thinks they were referring to those two long letters from me that he had given them to read. [The Nov. 11 letter in chapter 20, "Exhaust," and the letter and journaling in chapter 22, "Retort."]

As we talked, Victor spoke more openly than ever before and seemed to really *want* to hear what I needed to say. My words became more courageous as I admitted my covering up for years about my feelings and my finally sensing it is time to face reality--just *say* how things were and are! But I told Victor, "I'm determined to continue growing, and don't want to place you in a worse light than myself in anything I say or write." He thanked me for that.

After arriving home, we continued talking for a long time. At *his request*, I again read him that very long letter, mostly my journaling, sent to him January 3 that ends, "Happy Free Anniversary." [Chapter 22.]

When I finished, he said, "Well, you certainly were truthful in portraying what you *felt*, and you were honest in saying what the situation *was*. I don't think you have blackened my name at all." That was kind and very interesting, and it also gave me a lot of relief, especially since Patrick, Barb and Nancy all said it was a horrible, terrible letter.

Then I told him, "The ultimatum was the scariest thing, as well as the most courageous thing, I've ever done! It took many years to get to the place where I was brave enough to do it. I loved you deeply through all those years, admiring your character and basic personality. I've known you were a wonderful, marvelous man in so many ways, but you were severely blocked emotionally. For years you appeared to feel awfully sorry for yourself being married to me. It seemed obvious to me that you didn't want a relationship with me, but *I didn't have the courage to give you freedom to get on with your life.* Your lack of love was destroying me, and it certainly wasn't helping you. It seemed you were just putting on an act for the public's sake. That's the reason for the ultimatum."

He hasn't yet responded to that, negatively or positively. I get the picture that he recognizes truth. I do hope someday he can talk to me more about it.

After more silence, I continued, "When we first married, I was pretty much of a clinging vine and was afraid to be my own person in many ways. Working as a secretary while you were in the seminary, I was afraid much of the time also and expected you to do things *for* me--rescue me. If you had pampered me, I might not have grown. Thank you for not babying me through those years, because you helped *me* grow. It has taken a long time to find my own identity and stand on my own two feet, move on and take charge of my life. I have decided to be happy, even if there is no man in my life until I die."

We talked for hours. What Victor said about his relationship with Clarice and with me was most amazing. "I am still emotionally attached to her and might always be. The realization hit me that I need a purpose. I began to wonder what I'm going to do with the rest of my life. I want to please the Lord, serve and work for Him, and make the most of the remainder of my years. I began to realize that of all the people I have ever known anywhere, you, Judy, are the one who has been my greatest supporter! You are the one who has helped me grow! You are the one who has been the most loyal and stood by me! If I am going to continue to grow and serve the Lord, you are the person who will help me the most! You are constantly growing and reaching out to *be* more and *do* more. I need that sort of a person in my life."

With emotion trembling my body and tears about to bulge from my lids, my lips formed the relieved response, "Thank you *so much* for saying that; I really *needed* to hear it!"

For the first time Victor seemed to look realistically at his situation with Clarice. "If I had married Clarice, I probably wouldn't have grown as much. Clarice gave in to everything all the time. She gave in to most everybody. Her former husband had really dominated her. He 'ruled the roost' and she hadn't learned to stand up to him. It has been ten years since her divorce, and she is *just now* beginning to find some goals. I call these her 'pipe dreams' regarding her art. I don't know if she ever will really accomplish them. I realize probably neither one of us would have grown much. She would have just wanted to please me and back down in everything."

That is excellent insight! -- On second thought, did she "back down" passively when I didn't want to sell the house? That's another totally different kind of insight.

One of the things we both discovered, by taking some of the tests I received at The Mirror of Relationships seminar, is that Victor really *is* changing. His inherent characteristics are different than he saw in himself. He agrees he is much more vibrant, assertive, outgoing and courageous than ever before. We also feel enthused that we perceive each other more realistically, and in many ways are similar. That is exciting!

Before we parted, I repeated again, "Victor, I have no strings on you, nor rules for you; I'm also not telling you yet whether I'll marry you, as much as I want to and love you. If you feel the need to visit Clarice, talk to her on the phone, have her come to visit you, or if you want to date anyone else, you are a free man! You are not tied to me! You are completely free!"

"Thank you. I appreciate that." and he gave me a prolonged hug.

Another day Victor came indoors to wash up from yard work before leaving for his place. I was gazing out the window, luxuriating in the beauty of his mowed grass and blooming flowers, when Victor slid his arm behind my back and gave me a squeeze. As I looked up with appreciation, he tenderly asked, "Would you do 'a special favor' for me tonight?"

Before agreeing, I asked, "What is that?"

"Would you come to my apartment, sit down with me, and let me show you all my collection of notes, letters and mementos I have received from Clarice?"

Mortified, I stalled for a few moments. I needed to establish some sort of control over my rising feelings of disgust, disrespect, shock and revulsion for him wanting to display Clarice's very private material to *anyone*, let alone me! Inside I started trembling again and stiffened my body to try to keep it from showing. After taking several long, deep breaths I asked, "Why would you want to show them *to me*?

"I thought maybe it might 'turn you on.'" he answered hopefully.

"Does looking at it 'turn you on?'" I was trying again to figure this man out.

"Yes." And Victor smiled a rather seductive smile, which had *never* appeared for years.

"Did she write to you about *sexual* things?" *Is this what he means in this context by "turned on?"*

"Just loving things. I thought maybe we could sit down and have it like a bedtime story," he murmured under his breath.

Oh, I'm angry! No, its radical rage I'm feeling! Turn me on? I'm shaking even more! I want to slap him—hard--but will restrain myself. What a pitiful

373

reality that he is so mentally and emotionally screwed up, at this moment, that he wants to flaunt Clarice's heartfelt delicacies by showing them to me! Does he think I don't have any feelings at all? Does he purposely want to crush me and destroy her at the same time? I choose to control myself, and speak very gently and carefully.

"Excuse me. Did I understand you correctly? Are you wanting me to come over to your house and *enjoy* looking at things Clarice sent you?" I questioned.

"Yes." Now Victor looked puzzled at my questioning.

I've got to be gentle but honest—truthful but soft. "That is a terribly rude and unkind request to make of *anyone*, without asking Clarice's permission! **KAREN: You told him so *little* of your truth in that experience! This is a *tiny part of what is* wrong with that request.** That is glaring *betrayal*!" I almost whispered. **Karen: But a betrayal of you also!**

"I never *thought* of that!" was his amazed reply.

I tried to explain. "How could I *enjoy* looking at romantic things my would-be husband has received from 'the other' woman he wanted to marry? I refuse to look at any of them! You need to *return them to her* or destroy them. I don't feel like coming to your place tonight now at all!" **Karen: That sexual boundary was broken early in Victor's life!**

So he left with disappointment, probably feeling criticized.

A few days later, when he came to do some more work in my yard, he brought up the subject again. "I mentioned to Clarice on the phone that I was considering showing these things to you, and she demanded I return them immediately!"

"Absolutely excellent!" I exclaimed, and then asked him, "Did you tell her you already *asked* me to look at them, and I flatly refused?"

He looked surprised again. "No, I just mailed them back."

"I hope *she* doesn't think *I* asked or wanted to look at them! I'm *so* relieved you sent them back! When I thought I was going to marry Jim, I trashed *everything* from *any other man,* except the letters from you that were hidden deeply in a trunk in the basement. I even threw away my book from Marriage Encounter that we did a few years ago. I felt so sad that we had never gone through it, like I requested, so you could show me the places in it that you perceived as my terribly criticizing you. I was stunned you took what I wrote as criticism! I wanted you to explain specifically what hurt you."

"But I refused to go through it with you!" he remembered!

"That's right. But after your complaint, I showed that notebook to both Lena and Merv, wanting to correct any habits of communication that you might interpret as unkind or critical. But they only *commended* me on what was written in that book, so I still don't know what *you* perceived as criticism." *Now I wish it were still in my possession so I could learn how I hurt you!*

"<u>Well, you *have* called me a stuffed shirt</u>!" *He can't let those words rest, can he?* **KAREN: It would have been better to describe his *behavior* rather than name calling. This would have been a good place to ask forgiveness for hurting him.**

"I remember calling you that more than once, and you called it criticism; I agree it was. And when using that term, I truly *meant* that's the way you came across to me regarding the specifics we were talking about at the time. It would have been *unfair and dishonest* to *not* inform you, since you were my husband at the time. I *loved* you, even when you *were* a 'stuffed shirt,' but I despised the pretense, dishonesty and disloyalty you demonstrated to me."

A very long silent period again returned.

Is it wrong for me to want some sort of response from Victor? I'm trying so hard to follow through on what I am learning in therapy, even though it is sometimes <u>so scary to divulge my feelings and thoughts. I still vividly remember the awful thud on my face</u> and being pushed out the door in anger. When no sound or movement comes from Victor, I haven't the slightest idea what my next move should be to avoid that ever happening again. I'll just be quiet for a while. **KAREN: You were never allowed as a child or adult to say, "If you ever hit me again I'm gone!" Has Victor recognized the damage of that hit? Has he asked forgiveness?** [Victor and I dealt with this situation very thoroughly before we discontinued group therapy. He thoroughly apologized and asked my forgiveness, which I gladly gave him. This subject no longer rises as a problem or a fear.]

Finally, after probably at least five minutes and a self-search for courage and a deep breath, I tried to start more conversation. "I remember a time when I was taking the Sierra Club's Basic Mountaineering Training

Course and was beginning to get acquainted with others in the class. Some guy asked if I was married, to which I replied, 'Yes.' And his next question was, 'What do you enjoy doing with your husband?' Totally silent a few moments, I was trying to think of something you actually *liked* doing with me, when another man spoke before I could create a good answer. 'Well, you don't have much of a husband if you don't do things together. What does your husband do for a living?' 'He's a hospital chaplain,' was my answer. Then a woman retorted, 'A chaplain is supposed to know all about relationships and how to be close and friendly!' I felt embarrassed. I wanted *so much* to be able to brag on what a wonderful husband you were and how much fun we had together, but I couldn't think of anything you relished doing with me. That was before we had the cabin."

Again there was no response from Victor.

Another day, when Victor came to take me out to eat, I asked, "May I bring along this folder with information from the Mirror of Relationships seminar? There are still some more things we haven't done yet that we could do at the restaurant."

"Sure," he agreed.

On our way in the car he said, "I've got something here we can read too, if we have time." He reached into his pocket and pulled out a little square book. It looked like perhaps a booklet of love poems. My feelings at that moment were, *I fear being too romantic before we can solve our problems. Reading love poems is like eating frosting without cake, and without eating any dinner before-hand. It's too sickening sweet. I need a meal before dessert. I want to build a fun and interesting relationship that's currently more casual and less romantic, wanting to just enjoy being with Victor and know he likes being with me. No love poems now!*

At the Mirror of Relationships seminar, while reading a list of things one can do to keep romantic relationships alive, I saw one of them *was* to read love poems. Victor loves poetry, and if we can develop a thoughtful and playful relationship, I'll love reading those poems. Just not right now!

After he pulled the book out and handed it to me, eventually he added, "This book was given to me recently by" – pause – "someone."

Immediately I thought it was from Clarice and turned it upside-down on my lap before I had opened it. *He wants to be romantic with me, reading love poems Clarice gave him?*

Victor hesitated a long time, but finally continued, "By someone—not by Clarice, but by someone else." **KAREN: This is manipulation.**

I waited, but he said no more. I put the book back into his pocket. **KAREN: Great!** Having asked permission to bring other material, with his agreement, I was extremely relieved we wouldn't have to read love poems; our time was limited.

As we ate, I showed him a test from the seminar I hoped we could take in the near future. He seemed interested, and I wished we could have chatted longer.

On the way home I asked, "If there was something to talk about that I think might be uncomfortable for you, what would be the best time to do it? There's nothing specific right now. I just want to know the best time to bring up problems. You don't like to talk at mealtime about things that upset you, so I want to avoid that, and don't want to spoil our cabin time either. That is very special."

"Maybe when I come over to work in the yard," he suggested.

"What if we were married? Could we set up a time on a regular basis to discuss anything about our relationship?" was my next question.

"I think that would be okay."

I hope he really means that and remembers we discussed it. **Karen: I have couples write out an agreement and sign it.**

I hiked up to the cabin one Friday and Victor came to join me about 11:00 am the next day. He had brought in his day pack the little book I thought was love poems, but now noticed it was "<u>Secrets for Staying in Love</u>." I then asked if he had been trying to hide something from me when he said "somebody," not Clarice, gave him the book.

"No, it was Pierces" [Victor's church friends and temporary landlords] "who gave it to me. They went on a sightseeing trip and brought it back for me." **KAREN: So why not say that?**

"I thought you were trying to hide something or keep something secret. I don't feel at all sure of you or our relationship, Victor. You have changed in so many wonderful ways, but the very way you hesitated before you said "somebody" gave it to you, made me wonder what's going on.

Your actions, tone of voice and facial expressions, or lack of them, really *throw me* sometimes."

He made no comment.

Later in the day the two of us were relaxing outside in front of our little brown cabin in our freshly repainted-to-match Adirondack chairs, watching the humming birds fighting at the feeder suspended under the eaves. I broke the silence with, "I need to know something. When you found out about that first affair on the island, seven years after we were married, is that what changed your attitude about me from then on?"

"Well, it was a shock. I don't know more than that." He lifted his plastic cup of water sitting on the arm of his chair, gulped down the last swallow or two and set it back down with a whack.

I was determined to continue searching for answers in spite of body language that told me he wanted silence. "My reason for asking is this: When I brought up the idea of divorce, I figured you didn't know anything about my affairs except that one. I am currently going to Divorce Recovery meetings, trying to learn all I can. They talk about owning our own part of the responsibility for divorce. I am willing to own responsibility for my affairs. I made bad decisions. You aren't responsible for that!"

I noticed his shoulders drop slightly. Was that from relaxation or retreat?

"But you seemed to jump at the opportunity to divorce me before you knew about any affair, except that one," I continued. "I honestly don't have a clear picture in my mind what all the problems were, as you perceived them. Why did you want a divorce?"

It took a long time for him to answer again. Sometimes his words were so soft I'd have to ask him to repeat them. "I felt you were *always* trying to be in *control*. Sometimes, after you started getting counseling, you seemed to back off from trying to control. Then I got panicky, and rather than wanting to take over, I really wanted *you* to take over, because it *scared me!*" **KAREN: Having a man's "mom" being in control—he hates it and also fears the loss of it!**

Elated that Victor was actually opening up, but surprised at what he was saying, I spoke as kindly and open-mindedly as possible. "I don't see myself as ever *wanting* to control you, not perceiving myself as that kind of person. But I do know what my wants and needs are and where I want to go. I'm not afraid to talk about them."

After considerable silence, and watching a half dozen hikers move up the trail across the narrow canyon, I went on. "All my life I have pictured marriage as a *partnership*. I never had *any* concept that one person was to rule another, believing the *man* should be head, or leader of the family. But the man and his wife are basically *equal*! There will be times they don't agree, and it may take some real effort to fully understand each other. There will need to be *discussion* and *negotiation*. There will be times when total agreement is impossible. Then I would think that the man would make the final decision."

Breeze caused a flurry of pine needles to light on my lap. I brushed them off to the side, hoping Victor would have something more to say. There was nothing! I soon quietly added more. "I didn't have any *desire* to take over and do what was your responsibility and wasn't even aware of coming across like you describe. I believe that is the way you must have *perceived* me, because you say so; but I can't even *imagine* what areas you felt I was trying to control. I don't know whether it was in sex or child rearing, or the way to run the house or how to spend money."

Suddenly Victor gave a loud and disgusted response, almost shouting, "All of the above!"

Judy, remember to be gentle and concise, I told myself, and then took a long breath. "I'm still not clear. Can you give me an example?"

Victor's voice was loud and articulated, "Well, you wanted to be in control of how to run *worship*! You wanted to control even how I should *smile*!" His body language displayed bitterness and displeasure as his right boot made a deep etching in the hard-packed soil.

Struggling to remember anything about either of these things, I waited awhile for more explanation, but there was none. Eventually, trying to pry out the truth, my words were slow and tentative: "Now, as you imagine a *good* marriage and picture what you *want* ours to be, is there a place for the wife, *once in a while*, to speak up and say something about what she'd like to have in family worship? Or something she might like to change or add to it?"

Victor turned his head toward me, but his eyes didn't look into mine. "Yes, I think so."

"What makes you think our marriage would be any different now than it was before?" I smiled and shrugged my shoulders.

"Well, I think," he shifted his position and almost gave a tiny giggle, "I have matured enough that I won't be acting out as a rebellious kid."

More time passed. I was almost dozing in the warmth and peacefulness of nature. After Victor came back from the outhouse, he actually found some accusing words. "You broke your promise to me that I wouldn't *have* to go to counseling." He sounded almost *elated* that he could remember something negative!

"That is true. I *did* break that promise. I decided it was very wrong to have said what I did, just because Nancy suggested it." There was a pause as I brushed a tiny red spider off my arm. "Do you remember my statement, '*I* must go for more counseling, because I am not handling *my* emotions well?'--actually not asking *you* to go again until much later, after you had already gone for a while, and then stopped?"

Waiting for what seemed like several minutes for Victor's response, but hearing not a word, I finally asked him, "Do you feel I manipulated you and forced you to break up with Clarice?"

"No." He actually looked surprised at my question.

"Your calling her and leaving only a curt message on the phone really shocked me. I thought you had grown more than that. I was amazed that you would be so cruel to someone you said you loved. I actually hurt for *her*!"

There was a very short and almost inaudible "Hmm," as he placed his head on his elbow-propped hand.

Wanting to be sure and get *all* of his attention, I stood up, stretched and turned to face him. "When you felt upset in the meeting that night with Merv Jenson, the three women and I, one of the main things they questioned was your 'love.' How could someone who truly *loved* a woman, break up completely with her, leaving only a message on her machine?"

With his boot he indented another scar on the ground and then crossed his legs. "I realize I was just chicken. I was just thinking of myself." **KAREN: Trauma and broken boundaries created self-absorption. However through good teaching—in the church—we can come to move out of ourselves.**

Now he is being honest! Wonderful! "You were acting mean to me also, when you said you'd call me at 9:30, and didn't until after 10:30, because you were watching TV and 'had forgotten.'"

He quickly uncrossed his knees then folded his arms across his chest. "That was my drug to cut out the pain, because I was feeling so horrible."

Victor's comment about TV being a "drug" gives me great encouragement. He is gaining better insight regarding himself! But his body language shows more resistance to my questions.

"Feeling so horrible about breaking up with Clarice?" I questioned.

"Yes." His tone of voice was raised perhaps in exasperation, and he leaned forward in his chair. **KAREN: Good place for Judy to say, "Then you can call her and ask forgiveness for the hurtful act." Keep it about him, because it *is* about him.**

I hear his pain! I understand his pain! How can I ever get him to recognize I also have had pain?

Softly and carefully I asked, "Has it ever dawned on you that *I, too,* might also be in horrible pain during recent weeks, months or even years?"

A fly lit on Victor's arm and slowly wended its crawly way to his fingers, but he didn't seem to notice it any more than he noticed me, and gave no answer.

After an exceedingly long wait, I again asked another question. "Did you feel rushed by me to break up with Clarice?

"Well, no. I just knew I *had* to do it if we were going to get together." I was relieved his voice sounded more calm.

A fat robin flew past us and landed about ten feet away, cocking his head as if listening intently.

"Had you been thinking about breaking up with her anyway, before coming over the day that I asked you not to move away and instead come back to me?" Now I was feeling braver.

"Well, it crossed my mind." He swatted at another fly this time.

"Before I spoke to you about my 'being wrong,' were you planning to push me harder to sell the house?" *I will not stop questioning until I can see progress in problem solving. But I'm willing to move slowly and carefully.* **Karen: The above issues regarding the break-up with Clarice is one thing to clear up—problem solve—then move on!**

"Yeah! Clarice had been needling me to get that settled, and I *had* to do it if I was going to go up there." His voice had changed to a tone of total honesty and straightforwardness which refreshed almost as much as the cool water I then went to pour for us.

Early the next morning, still curled up under a pile of blankets in our cold cabin, I started "chatting." "I feel bad about the affairs I had. I felt so abandoned for so long. If we had learned to have a good relationship, the affairs would never have happened. It wasn't sex that I needed. It was a *friend*, a *companion*, a *human being who listened to me and spoke his own thoughts to me*."

"I guess you really did have a great need." Victor admitted as he bunched up his red flannel-encased pillow to prop his head. "I felt like you were trying to get me to meet *all* your emotional needs, and I just couldn't do that! I didn't know how, or even have a concept!"

I turned to look at this handsome man with his scruffy, graying beard. "True. A close relationship *was* my need, and I thought marriage would entail *at least* a warm friendship. But when going for counseling to Dr. McGinnis, he said it sounded like I was chasing you too hard—making you too big a priority." **KAREN: I don't hear that! I hear trying to be perfect, to be accepted. You had lots of interests and talents that kept you sustained in many ways.**

I had read a book by Alan Loy McGinnis, The Friendship Factor, while I was on a backpack a couple years previously and was so impressed that I had written him a deeply emotional letter, referring to my dilemmas, and mailed it to the publisher. Surprisingly, Dr. McGinnis *himself* answered it, was located within traveling distance, and offered to counsel me. I went regularly for several months, and then he asked to see Victor. After *considerable* begging, Victor still refusing, Dr. McGinnis offered to see him *one time* without charging! So Victor went, but would never discuss it with me. However, I felt enormously helped and encouraged by this man, and am a better person for having spent the time and money for his counsel.

When we first bought the cabin I had asked Victor for the privilege of lighting the fire on cold mornings, which I enjoy immensely. Victor was delighted, because he prefers to keep warm in bed while the fire is being lit. So this particular day, I climbed out of bed, put on my purple terry cloth robe and started emptying the ashes from the bin in our wood stove into a tall rusty square can. Later these cold ashes would be dumped into a bucket in our outhouse to be used there.

A half hour later at the table, as we drank our hot chocolate and silently consumed our instant oatmeal with hardly even a slurpee sound,

I inwardly complained to myself: *Oh, sometimes I feel so futile in even imagining I will ever be able to have a real conversation with Victor!* Yet I brazenly attempted more.

"Back in those earlier days of our marriage I couldn't read your mind; I had no idea what you wanted. You refused to tell me, or else just couldn't. I did my best for you, putting to use all the counseling and information from newly purchased books. My life priority at that time was to be the *finest wife possible!*" I really emphasized those last three words, longing for him to comprehend my supreme efforts.

It was as though he didn't hear me at all. It felt like he just wanted to blast at me as he scowled his accusing response and flung it my direction. "In the past, you tried to change my *personality* and my *character!*" His head shook with venom. **KAREN: The question is here, "How and when did I try to change you?"**

"I certainly didn't *perceive* myself as trying or even *wanting* to change either of those. I fell in love with you BECAUSE of your personality and character. I wanted a *relationship* with you the way you were! You shut me out! I wanted you to tell me what you needed, what you did and didn't like. I wanted to spend *time* with you and *talk about* problems in order to solve them."

I got up and started clearing the table. "Sure you were imperfect, and so was I! We still are! But I felt like it was YOU wishing *my* personality and character would change! You didn't like me, but you refused to tell me what you wanted and needed. Instead, you *expected* me to conform to your wishes *whether I knew them or not.*"

The teakettle started singing on the wood stove, so I got out two pink plastic dishpans (saved from a hospital confinement) and poured hot water into both of them while continuing to talk. "I *didn't* want control then, and I *don't* want control now! A marriage is *not* one person controlling another. It's giving each other the *freedom* and support to be who they are, as they move through life TOGETHER!"

Silence! We finished the dishes, made the beds and swept the floor. After putting everything in order, we hoisted our backpacks and started down the trail.

I'm feeling such frustration at this point. **KAREN: Because Judy shut down Victor's voice by not asking the how and when question, she**

continues to fail in her attempts to "fix it" all by her own "guess work". This imbalance of responsibility is fairly common in a lot of marriages. *Evidently Victor resented me from fairly early in the marriage. Laura Schlesinger says in one of her books that women can't have all their needs fulfilled by their men. But if the man refuses to have any relationship, leave him. Don't keep hanging on. One of my worst mistakes was trying too hard to push him to have a real relationship.*

In the car on the way home, I realized my vow of reserving time at the cabin for only "pleasant" conversation had been broken. Victor had obviously been uncomfortable much of the time, and I felt bad for that. But now we were riding and had experienced a really pleasant day, so I spoke up again. "In the Mirror of Relationships seminar I did an exercise, telling my partner what kind of things would make me feel most loved. I'm asking you that question now, and I'd like for you to just think about it. What one person feels he needs is usually based on what he *didn't* get when he was a child. What *you* didn't get as a child very likely could be very different from what *I* didn't get. You may feel like a certain kind of behavior is loving, but if you gave that kind of behavior to me, I might not feel like it was loving at all! What *I* need to receive, that feels loving to *me*, might not seem loving to *you* at all. I'd like for you to put some thought on that for us to talk about in the future.

AND, I want to tell you NOW that because of your *willingness to listen and respond honestly* this weekend, I feel more loved than I have for a long time! I really appreciate both you and your willingness! Thank you so much!"

I had planned to make avocado, tomato and lettuce sandwiches, and fix some hot soup when we got home. But on arrival he said, "No, I couldn't digest any avocado because my stomach is too uptight."

"Did it get upset because of our talk?" I asked.

"Of course, yes!" he exclaimed, as though surprised I asked.

"I'm really sorry, but I *needed* you to know what I told you, and I *need* to know the *answers* to the questions I ask. Our relationship doesn't feel at all secure to me yet. You've changed so much in a wonderful way, but it's obvious you haven't made up your mind. We need *more talk* in the future, and I truly value the time we spent at the cabin."

Victor has mentioned more than once that *my* attitude has changed. I have made up my mind to work very hard, search out, find and own the responsibility for mistakes I've made. I must have been critical and domineering at times, since he says I was, but surely didn't realize it at the time, and haven't the vaguest idea when those times were. I need for Victor, or someone else, to tell me, *at the time I am being that way*, so that I can become aware of what I do. But I *don't* see my attitude or motives changing at all! If he *perceives* something, there must be *behavior* he is responding to. I own my *behavior*. But the *motives behind that behavior* are not at all what he thinks—*wanting* to be critical, domineering and controlling.

Since talking to Merv, Lena, my sister Clare and others, I'm starting to realize how terribly fragile Victor has been, recognizing more than ever the importance of soft-pedaling anything I say, and being very gentle and careful how it is said. I'm beginning to comprehend that his refusal to verbalize feelings stems from his childhood, his low self-esteem and his experiences with his mother and grandmother. This inability or refusal to verbalize his needs, wants and feelings was evidently a necessary survival mode of his earlier years.

Sometimes I still wonder why he wants to come back to me. What has really changed? I see him starting to blossom. I've got to figure out how to support him and help him. But he must decide how to support *me* and *help me* too. We both must learn!

Today was a "minimum day" at school, and I got to come home early. Victor, with gloved hands, was carefully rubbing an old rag, dipped in poisoned oil, on the stiff new blades of hard-to-kill nut grass, which keeps invading the front lawn. What patience he has to do such careful, but menial work!

He seemed delighted to see me earlier than usual, and I fixed us cold drinks to sip, as we seated ourselves on a comfortable couch to talk more.

I told Victor I have never, before this past weekend at the cabin, been aware that he saw me as trying to be in control! I'm willing to own whatever I actually *did* that he perceived as purposeful controlling; but so far as my *motives* are concerned, *I don't want to control him! And NEVER have!*

He replied with exasperation, "Well, I certainly didn't perceive you *not* wanting control! I perceived you as *very much* wanting control!"

Oh, a million ouches! How can that possibly be? I want to scream—Damn it!!!! I thought I was very self-observant. It feels like I always wait and wait and wait and wait "forever" for him to take action and make decisions. **KAREN: This is the dilemma of strong people.** *If he refuses, or just doesn't say or do anything, I feel impelled to do the talking or action that needs to be accomplished, because of his refusal to speak or act.*

Again I reiterated, "Owning *everything* I did and said, and *accepting* whatever it was that came across to you like that, I still don't know *what I said*, or *how or when it was said* that caused you to think that. I don't know the words used, the facial expressions, tone of voice, mannerisms or body language. This is a BIG REASON why it is *unthinkable* for us to get married right now! It's only now *barely dawning on me* these last three days that you've perceived me as always trying, pushing, wanting to *be in control*, or thinking I should be in control of the marriage, of us, of you. I *can't imagine* how or when you perceived that, and certainly don't have the *slightest* idea how *not* to do it, since I don't know what, when or how it happened. If anything, *I passionately hate this concept!* You *do* remember, don't you, that I've asked you *many* times what you wished you could change about me?"

He gave a solitary, gruff "Yes."

Getting braver by the minute, I exclaimed, "You lied to me! You were unfair to me! You told me you *didn't want me to change anything!* When I asked, you said I was *perfect!* I knew then that it was a lie, and now I think you said it because *you wanted me to be in control!*"

Silence.

Getting up from the couch, I started pacing the floor. "I was willing to have been told *anything* that needed to change. I was willing to have spent *any amount of money and effort* to learn what was needed. I was willing to have gone through *any kind of emotional pain*, any kind of therapy or counseling in order to achieve a good marriage. *You weren't willing*, or somehow weren't able, to tell me the truth. I don't know how to deal with that!" **KAREN: Good honesty!**

Victor looked like he was almost shriveling into the back of the couch. "I'm truly sorry now."

I walked toward him, sat down and put my arms around him. "I forgive you."

After holding him tenderly for a while, I sat back and waited for a response, which didn't come, so stood up again. "And if we are going to have a relationship in the future, you *must* tell me, *even before I ask*, what I'm doing when you think I'm trying to control! Not being aware of the way I come across or how you are perceiving me"—I flung my arms wide open--"there is no possibility of our getting past the roadblock!"

"Okay," he droned with a submissive tone.

Now he's sounding wimpy and put down. *How can I help him understand?* "I refuse to be a doormat! I will not be a person with no needs, desires, wants or ability to speak for myself," I spoke quietly and clearly. "I also *refuse* to try to run somebody else or say it has to be done my way. There may be certain times I need to do that because of assigned and accepted responsibilities. If I were questioned, I would explain that clearly."

"I think I understand." He sounded a bit more confident.

Victor seeing me as wanting to be in control baffles, frustrates and angers me! And yet I remember, after breaking up with Jim, my brother said he saw me as a person who likes to be in control, and he saw Jim as also liking to be in control. He said that down the road we would really have butted heads had we married. *What on earth do I do that makes people think that? I wish I knew!*

Looking back to the time when my folks had their 50th wedding anniversary celebration, Mother had asked me to be in charge of the musical part of the program. When some of the relatives were here the day before, and I was asking people to go through their parts, I know Diane complained to Clare that I was trying to be in control. Yes, I was *asked* to be in control of a situation where I was responsible for getting people together for practice to perform the next day. I would do it again! If someone has requested that I be responsible for preparing a program that is to be done publicly, and each person has previously agreed to do it, yes, I choose to be in control! I am very much in control of me, and that is a plus. **KAREN: Yes!**

Arriving at home after teaching the next day, I saw Victor hadn't left yet. Wonderful! I must ask him more about this business of his seeing me as wanting to control. I am puzzled and confused. It seems so foreign! I'll make him a good supper and serve him strawberries and ice cream for dessert.

Following the meal, I asked him for more specifics and he obliged with, "You tried to be in control of family worship."

"Please tell me about it so I can understand," I asked, genuinely interested.

He recalled one time he came into the living room for evening worship and said he was going to read an article from a magazine on a certain spiritual topic. He remembers my response: "I'd also like to have something read from the Bible."

We actually hadn't been having *any* family worship for a long time. Part of my reason for saying what I did was because our adult sons were home for a visit. I had imagined he suggested having worship *only for their sake*. To me, family worship *includes* reading the Bible. Victor could have responded, "No, I really want to read this article instead," and I'd have said no more. **KAREN: Why does it have to be either/or? He didn't *have* to be offended. He could have agreed to both!**

Now I told him I did not know *at that time*, or *all the years since then*, that he was offended. There was no word or body language to show it. But shortly before our divorce he *did* tell me I "humiliated him in front of his children" and gave this as an illustration. **KAREN: Wow! That is sad!** Even then I didn't realize, until just now, that he considered this event as *proof that I wanted to be in control!* Victor has a mouth capable of saying "No, I want to do it my way." He needs to use it! **KAREN: Or incorporate others *into* his life. Judy's and Victor's ideas *together* make a richer experience.**

I asked for another example, because the above hardly seemed an answer to my question, and he gave a second illustration. He had come to family worship, a different time, announcing, "I've decided we will talk tonight about how to know whether we're saved or not."

Naively I had asked, "Why did you choose that subject for tonight?" Not knowing whether he was uptight or trying to emphasize the subject, I remember that his tone of voice sounded angry. Steve and Alan were visiting again. Was he going to show them that they were doing or believing something he thought was wrong? And being the mama, I felt an urge to protect them from their dad's wrath. I couldn't *imagine* why he was bringing this up right now! This happened years ago, and now I realize that mothering them was totally unnecessary, because they were adults.

"I wasn't aware of your upset that time either," I honestly admitted. "It was shortly before our divorce you told me this was another example of my humiliating you in front of our sons. Now you say this was my wanting to control you? **KAREN: This would have been a good place to ask him to forgive you. It would have been more interesting to hear his worship talk.**

Silence.

"At the time, I wasn't even remotely aware you were even ruffled. Did you purposely refuse to let me know how you felt? Is that true?" I asked.

Victor sighed and just sat quietly without comment. **KAREN: Silence is power!**

Waiting takes such patience! Why doesn't he answer? Guess I'll just go on. "If I was in charge of worship part of the time, and you asked me why *I* picked a certain subject, or told me you wanted something different, *I would be delighted.* It would give me more of an opportunity to share my thoughts with you and get your input. The golden rule is to do to others as I'd *want* them done to me. Both of those things seem to me like *positive feedback!*"

He only shrugged. **Karen: Power again.**

On still another day I made a request: "I want you to tell me *more* about your perception of me in the years before our divorce. I'm thinking that possibly you felt I came across as scary or frightening."

"Well, you certainly did sometimes!" Victor again spoke emphatically and dramatically!

"You felt afraid of me?" I could scarcely believe what I heard!

"ABSOLUTELY!" He almost yelled, as if I were deaf!

"That seems so foreign to me, but I do *accept it.* Currently I can't even *guess* when those times were or are! What did I do that caused you to feel that?" I asked.

I waited a long time, but he didn't answer. **KAREN: Does Victor even remember? VICTOR: I can remember feeling afraid of Judy, but I don't even have a hint of any events related to that feeling.**

I see myself generally as mild-tempered, calm and cool.

389

In the past he has said I was hysterical. I don't think I have ever gotten hysterical. No, that's wrong. There were times, when I was being tickled as a child that I was hysterical; and there were times, when mother screamed at me, that I cried hysterically. I thought she wasn't hearing me when I asked what I had done wrong. **KAREN: You were "set up" for this kind of relationship!** But she demanded I stop crying instead of answering me. **KAREN: Just like Victor!** Many times I didn't know what I was being punished for and I *couldn't* stop crying! Yes, I *was* hysterical then. **Karen: Created perfectionism.**

I don't remember any time since my marriage when I have been that out of control of myself. No, that's not right either. I was out of control when the evangelist, JA, told me off and I cried all afternoon in the closet.

Realizing Victor was going to leave in a few minutes, but wanting to say more, I excused myself and brought back ice cold lemonade for us to drink. "We're both human and imperfect, sometimes getting emotionally drained or physically exhausted. Sometimes we make unwise decisions. Is that a reason one of us should discard the other? Is that a reason to throw someone out?"

No answer.

"We must learn to tell each other our *perception*! When one of us does something hurtful, the other could say, 'Ouch! That hurt!' Wouldn't this bring us *closer together*, not farther apart?"

Victor still made no comment except, "Well, I'll see you tomorrow afternoon," as he got up and walked to the door.

I feel gigantically afraid to marry this man who now says he divorced me for wanting and trying to be in control. But previously he told me I was perfect and didn't need to change anything. That's a double message if I ever heard one! Who is trying to control whom now? Do I even want to marry this man—ever?

If only Victor had been able to tell me, if not at the moment, but maybe the next day or week or the next month, and say, "Judy, there's something you've done that really hurt me, and I need to tell you. It's bothering me and I'm really aching inside." That would have aided me.

If only he could have helped me see how impotent or emasculated he felt, then I could have been aware. But I didn't even know these things bothered him until all these years later. [I was crying on the tape as I recorded this.]

I must ask Victor not to discard me or throw me out until I have a chance to at least understand what he feels and needs.

There's a wonderful Jacuzzi at Victor's apartment complex, and he invited me to come enjoy it with him. Ah-h-h, how wonderful to have my back massaged by pulsing water and feel the bubbles tickle my skin. It is a delicious and relaxing time. There's no need to talk for a while.

After probably five or ten minutes of sensuous silence and luxury, I turned and looked Victor full in the face and then directly into his eyes. They were a dreamy blue and he started a little smile. *I can't take my eyes off this handsome man.* Suddenly his eyebrows arched way up and his forehead wrinkled as he squirmed and then gave me a rather awkward big wink and turned away.

How disappointing! He broke the romantic spell. Now it suddenly dawns on me what he must have meant when at the cabin he said I even tried to control the way he smiles. I must say something about this again.

"Did you just now feel self-conscious or embarrassed as I looked deeply into your eyes?"

Looking almost shocked, he asked with apparent amazement, "No! Why do you ask?"

"The other day at the cabin you told me I even wanted to control the way you smiled. I haven't been able to even *imagine* what you were referring to. But just now it came to me what I *think* you might have been talking about then."

There was only silence while I just looked down and didn't say a word more for a while.

I wonder if I should ask more so I can understand more. Or should I not say anything unless he asks? Will I make him angry? God, help me in this, my dilemma. I guess I never will know what to expect from him or whether he even heard what I said, or if he cares enough to listen more.

It felt like an eternity passed before Victor finally spoke. "What do you mean?"

Whoosh-sh-sh-sh. A major flood of tension flushed out of my body. Victor actually asked a question!

"It must be difficult for you to look into my eyes," I answered with relief. "You usually squirm when I look into your eyes like I did a few minutes ago." I paused, hoping for more response, but there was nothing.

"When we were first married, I discovered that when I looked deeply into your eyes, longing for you to return my romantic gaze, you usually broke the spell. Sometimes you raised your eyebrows high, like you did just now, often several times, again and again, fast. Other times you gave a big wink, like you did just now, or made a funny face, cracked a joke, or started talking about something totally unrelated to our current situation. Then right after doing these things you quickly looked away really fast, and didn't look back at me for a while. I always felt a big letdown. Did you know that?"

He looked completely puzzled. "Did I know *what*?"

"Did you know when I looked deeply into your eyes, *wanting* you to gaze romantically back at me, and you broke the spell in various ways, or just looked away, I felt *disappointed* then—and still do, even now?"

There was an almost inaudible "Hmmm."

I purposely scooted around a bit in the spa so I could face him directly. "Many years ago I mentioned to you the way you turned your eyes away when I looked deeply into them. For whatever reason, you must feel self-conscious and can't look back for more than a few seconds. I wanted then for you to look back into my eyes in a romantic gaze, without turning away, while we were just talking, or perhaps about to make love. I wanted you to *visually* return my love, but apparently you don't feel able to do that. For many years I was afraid to tell you how I felt when you broke the spell."

Not even a Hmmm. He just looked down. But I continued looking at his face, still hoping for a response.

Trying to cover my disappointment, I went on. "After going for counseling, I learned it was okay for me to express myself—my needs and my desires--and decided to tell you. One time when feeling very romantic and extra close to you I looked deeply into your eyes. It seemed you purposely broke the spell, so I gently explained *how* I had hoped you would respond--how your romantic gaze in return would be very thrilling to me. You must have felt put down or criticized. I'm not sure, but I think that *might* be what you were referring to at the cabin when you told me I even tried to control your smile."

"Hmmm, I didn't know that," he spoke with quiet admission.

What a marvelous relief and joy it is when he makes some sort of acknowledgement that I spoke to him. He actually heard me!

While in the Jacuzzi that day, and ever since then, he hasn't let on that what I said bothered him, or referred to it again. I'm not even sure he really understood what I meant. Since he used to think I was trying to control him by talking about this in the past, maybe he still thinks I am trying to control him. I need to talk in therapy group about all this.

I'm frustrated and bewildered. I had truly hoped that all this communication and explanation would encourage and thrill him. I hoped he could learn how to look deep into my eyes and enjoy it!

Victor: Yes, a long time ago when Judy talked to me about gazing into my eyes and my breaking the "spell" by winking, raising my eyebrows, making a face or cracking a joke, I *thought* she was trying to control my smile. Talking about it *now*, I don't perceive it as trying to control. However I still don't feel *comfortable* looking into *anyone's* eyes for more than a few seconds. I still feel *terribly* awkward and uncomfortable, and usually *do* break the "spell" as soon as I can do so, hopefully without hurting someone's feelings.

Now I understand that I'm barely scratching the surface of his frustrations, his unhappiness and fears.

SOAR

Hooray! Victor called to say he has set up an appointment to start group therapy again Monday night, and expects me to go with him. I have to do some fast shifting of lesson times so I can join him. Tomorrow I leave for a weekend in the mountains to take the Sierra Club's Wilderness First Aid Course.

Last night we went to our new therapy group for the first time, and it went well. Victor gave a history of recent events--our divorce and his engagement, my engagement, which soon ended, and his desire to get back together with me.

I said I owned the responsibility for my affairs, but at the time of my ultimatum, he knew of only one of them, which long ago he refused to discuss or get counseling for. But when the ultimatum mentioned the possibility of divorce, he *figuratively* yelled "Hallelujah," because he had been unhappy for decades. *But I still don't have a clear picture of why he wanted a divorce.* I recently asked him, and his answer was *because I was trying to control him.* So I want to learn how *not* to act controlling. I *don't have,* nor did I *ever* have, any *desire* to control him that I am aware of. And *I still don't know what I do or did that makes him feel that way!*

As I record what took place last night, I have a very heavy throat ache right now from trying to keep from crying. A memory has just hit me with

394

such tremendous force that I'll describe it. I was maybe eight. On a very hot summer day, four or five of us neighbor children were playing in a sprinkler on our front lawn. Mother must have insisted I wear a swim cap to keep my hair dry. It was such fun whooping it up with friends. Suddenly I was being hit hard with a yardstick on my wet, bare legs as my mother painfully grabbed my upper arm and dragged me up onto the front porch, still whipping me all the way with the yardstick.

I cried out, "Why are you spanking me?" I hadn't the remotest idea why.

She yelled at me, "You know why I am!" and hit me all the harder. Over and over I pleaded for her to tell me why, and she said, "You know why," and over and over she whipped me harder each time I asked. She even told me I was lying. As I recall, it seemed like it was maybe several days before I learned why.

Finally either she or grandma told me that mother had called me two or three times to come into the house. I had neither seen her nor heard her—probably from the noise of the water hitting my bathing cap and the noise of our excited voices. I was completely baffled—brokenheartedly stymied—because I wanted so much to always please my mother, and really tried hard to obey.

Here I was being demeaned and punished for some reason, but I had no idea what it was I had done or why the scolding and punishment. And mother continued whipping me because she said I was lying, and I "knew" why she was doing it. That *predicament* felt horrendously more painful than the physical hurt of the whipping. **KAREN: My underlining. Just like the marriage relationship.**

Right now I'm feeling JUST LIKE THAT. I have been "punished" during all these years of marriage, but I've *no idea* what I've done wrong (aside from the affairs). I've tried so *hard* to find out, but haven't been told.

Victor told the group that when he first married me, it was for all the traits I had that were *like his mother*, but that those very traits were the ones that irritated him after he was married for a while. When he was asked in group for examples of how I controlled him, or tried to, he said *he couldn't think of any!* I'm sure there are some in addition to what he's already told me, but I guess they're few and far between and not gigantic. He said he realized the problem was a lot *in his head* from his background and his childhood, but was glad I wanted to learn how *not* to act controlling.

395

On our way home from group we talked, and when we arrived at my house I continued rambling about various things such as the cabin and yard. Finally Victor said, "Would you please stop talking!"

It so surprised me that I said, "Oh, so you're learning to be assertive! Good for you!"

When I finally cut off my flow of words, he explained that he wanted to kiss me and leave. It was getting late.

At my next appointment I told Lena about the examples Victor gave about worship and looking into his eyes. She said, "Judy, you are going to have to come up with an understanding of what you see as control and what Victor sees as control, because *they're totally different!* As long as Victor has one concept of what being in control is, and you have a different concept, you can go on forever and not be able to change anything. Victor will still perceive that you're in control, if your *concepts* are different. He probably needs to think it through carefully, and write out a statement or a paragraph about what he considers 'being in control.' You need to do the same. You need to compare them, so you can come to some mutuality."

That's a great idea! I haven't talked to Victor or the group about it, but I want to do that. **Karen: Yes. This was a wonderful and practical exercise suggested by Lena.**

Lena also said, "Those two examples about worship--if I had fifty women here like I have in my group therapy right now--they'd laugh out loud. They would think it absolutely *funny* that Victor perceived that as control. **Karen: Yes.** And the one about Victor making funny expressions and looking away when you looked deeply into his eyes, they would think it was utterly ridiculous that he would perceive you as trying to be in control." **Karen: Yes.**

She then told me the most amazing thing: "Actually Victor perceived *you* as trying to be in control; however *he* has been the one who has *wanted* to be in control, who *has been in control,* and **who has *gotten you to allow him* to be in control!**" She repeatedly insisted that although he complains that I am controlling, he has been the *very super strong controller of me*!

KAREN: My underlining and Bold type. Wow! Unbelievable! I feel validated by that! Oh, what a thrill to be lifted out of my prison of incomprehension! I want to shout for joy! But I must learn how to keep *him* from controlling *me*! **Karen: Yes!**

Victor called to tell me he had never had an endearing term for me, and he wanted to know if he could call me "Rosebud." Instantly I remembered Nancy telling me that Clarice loved roses and Victor had been planning to get all these different kinds of roses and plant them in her yard. They were going to pick roses and have the whole church decorated with them for their wedding. Clarice was going to carry roses. *I wonder if he called her "Rosebud?" That hits me hard in the gut.*

"Did you call Clarice 'Rosebud'?" I asked, almost holding my breath.

I heard only three words with no change of tone of voice: "No, I didn't."

He surely must know the reason I asked. "I know Clarice loved roses and they were very special to her. I wouldn't want you calling me Rosebud if you had called her that."

Victor chuckled as he said, "No, I called her Spring Flower."

I have decided to let him call me Rosebud. I also have a feeling that part of the time he still is unconsciously role-playing as this magnanimous, wonderful, super-kind man, wanting to be the perfect person. Perhaps this is what Merv called "the mask," and what I referred to as a "stuffed shirt." I know that Victor is basically kind and <u>*wants* to be genuine</u>. Yet I feel like what he often does is a sort of preplanned, non-spontaneous thing--this is what he "<u>ought</u>" to do. **KAREN: My underlining: Perfectionism.**

I have this feeling about his calling me Rosebud. He sounds awkward saying it, but I *choose* to accept that, because he is attempting new behavior. When I grapple with my own efforts at growth, I'm sure I sometimes come across as bungling or ungainly. When he appears that way, I *choose* to accept him! The more we struggle at new behavior, even if we feel inept, the more we'll eventually be able to relax.

Victor told me his cousin Dorothy wants him to go with her next weekend to visit a relative in another state. He asked if it would be all right with me for him to do that. Dorothy hasn't seen this relative for many years, and the cousins all want Victor to come also. He had already committed to go to the cabin with me and was feeling regret that he'd disappoint me; however I strongly promoted his going to be with his relatives. I think that's important.

A few days after Victor talked about his trip, he called and said he made a mistake about the date. "I don't have to go after all. It's going to be the following weekend, so I can go to the cabin with you." He came over and I gave him the things he could carry up in his backpack. He told me what time of day he'd be here ready to go.

That night I found a phone message from him saying his cousin had just called and said she had lost the instructions on how to get to his place, and would he give them to her again. He replied, "That's next Friday." She said, "Oh no, it's tomorrow!" Then he really did apologize to me because it *was* when he originally planned.

I don't know where this confusion comes from. I used to think maybe it was Alzheimer's, but I think it's emotional. Maybe it's either depression or fear. He was exceptionally apologetic.

I returned his phone message with, "Oh that's okay. Anybody can make mistakes. I want you to go and have a good time. Don't feel guilty about it at all. I love you. Just enjoy yourself."

I phoned him the next morning at quarter to six to wake him up as he requested on the message. I went on up to the cabin that day by myself. I got quite a bit more work done. Alan and a friend came up the following day and helped with more outside jobs.

After Victor returned, I told him my fears regarding his going, because in the past Dorothy, Mary Lee and their families had all told him, "Don't, under any condition, go back to Judy." This was because he had told them about my affairs. But this trip he told them he loves me, so they said, "Well, it looks like God is working it out, so do whatever will make you happy."

While I was at the cabin, I mentioned to Alan that I told his dad it was perfectly fine to go with his cousin, and I hoped he'd have a good time.

Alan said, "That was certainly loving."

I appreciated that from Alan, because I know he is still close to Nancy. Nancy said in one of her letters to Victor that she was "going to take every action possible to protect you and Alan from Judy, because she is an evil woman." Naturally I was glad Alan recognized my loving, caring attitude, and was not buying everything Nancy told him. In fact, prior to Thanksgiving, Nancy had talked to Alan about what a *wonderful* person I was. Alan had told her then that he learned his kindness from me. He had hugged me then, and said he appreciated my teaching him kindness.

Now, with Nancy telling Alan I am an evil person, he felt confused. He wondered why Nancy had so totally changed and taken a different way of thinking.

I suggested, "Alan, we can recognize she has emotional problems, and it's futile to *let* ourselves be confused or hurt."

He smiled and said, "I'll try to remember that."

A few days later Victor invited me for dinner at his place and served burritos and pizza. We drank sparkling grape juice and ate ice cream with raspberries for dessert. He played his keyboard and sang to me for quite a while. I sang a little with him. Then we just cuddled and talked. It was great! He acted like he is falling in love with me. I certainly feel that way towards him. I still have some fears, but I enjoyed myself anyway. In the last few weeks I have had more fun, more conversation, more friendship, more companionship and more laughing than I had in the last several decades of marriage. It's super neat!

In a later group therapy session one of the girls talked about her father always ignoring her and not acknowledging that she was even his daughter. She wished she had a different father. I certainly identified with her pain of being ignored, and said the most excruciating pain in my experience was being treated as though I *wasn't there*. I told the group that I'm afraid to talk about it with Victor, for fear it will cause more rejection.

Victor blurted out, "Well, get it out!"

Looking down to avoid people noticing tears in my eyes, I told him, "That sounded like you are angry."

Merv told him to ask a couple other people how he came across, and they agreed he sounded at least disgusted or sarcastic.

When I started to tell *the group* something, Merv said to talk directly *to Victor* and not to the group *about* him. That is good. Because I wanted to *explain* things to others, Merv corrected me many times. Now I must deal *directly* with Victor.

"I have felt abandoned and rejected; sometimes you haven't even acknowledged my *presence in the room*, even though I am trying to talk with you." My body stiffened, trying to block tears from erupting.

Surprisingly Victor nearly interrupted me to ejaculate, "I *won't* run away any more!"

"What a relief that is!" My emotional dam of fear was broken and anxiety flooded down and out—gone!

Merv said that the words "any more" were the most significant words Victor used.

I felt truly heard this time. To the whole group I emphasized, "I *want* us to get together, but I will not ever, *ever* go back to what we had before."

Then turning directly to Victor, I formed my words carefully. "Thank you for listening and *really* hearing me. That is very, *very* important."

Continuing my comments, I said that although Nancy currently didn't want anything more to do with me, and saw me as an evil person, still it was *she* who encouraged me to try to get back with Victor and invite him to at least stay here instead of moving north, so we could work at our relationship. Then turning specifically to him, I requested, "Victor, when we get married, let's send her a thank you gift."

Merv told us that the most significant word I had used was "let's." He asked Victor how he wanted to respond to that. It took a moment, but then he got up and gave me a hug and kiss in front of the group. Wow! That felt good!

Victor told me recently that someone had called him from the hospital, looking for a social worker designee. It got his hopes up, and he was going to see if he might get a job.

Surprised, I couldn't resist saying, "I thought you *hated* social work."

Sounding very positive, Victor asserted, "I certainly don't want to do *gardening* the rest of my life! Social work is beginning to look better and better."

Later he left a message saying he had talked with the hospital folk, but they decided they don't want anyone who doesn't have a *degree* in social work. Consequently there's no hope of a job there.

This must have been a terrible blow for him. He has made so many changes in his life, but he has still not had a breakdown. He never set aside extra money for retirement, and he gets only half of his retirement check because I get the other half. Now he realizes <u>he may never be a chaplain again because his employers have been too cognizant of his emotional instability</u>. <u>That's tough</u>. **Karen: Yes.**

I think we need to discuss more our personal concepts of what constitutes good communication in a marriage. <u>Prior to our divorce Victor demanded we never discuss problems, and he refused to tell his feelings or wants</u>. I guess he expected me to just <u>know</u> them by his actions. And when I tried to express my needs and feelings, he usually either walked out mid-sentence or refused to respond in any way. <u>Now my concept of a healthy marriage certainly includes the freedom of both parties to talk about whatever subject or problem long enough and repeatedly enough, until both are satisfied they understand what is important to the other</u>. **KAREN: There also needs to be a time to let it go, even if the other one doesn't get it. Sometimes one person needs more time to process the conversation and the problems being addressed.** *Yet each person needs to feel safe saying, "I can't talk about that right now. I need time [to calm down, think it through, unwind, and investigate options . . .] and we need to reschedule a better time to discuss this." If the marriage comes to a roadblock where either person seems unable to deal with a problem, the couple should ask a third party to help, whether it be a friend, minister or professional counselor. <u>And some things aren't worth "going on and on" about</u>.* **Karen: Yes, being careful to choose someone that is trust-worthy and wise.**

Recently, when visiting Victor at his apartment, we decided to take a test called the "Mirror of Relationships Control Questionnaire," which was saved from the Barbara de Angelis Seminar. We each answered thirty questions by checking whether they applied never, sometimes, frequently, most of the time or almost always. These had to do with how we had perceived both the other and ourselves during our pre-divorce marriage.

On the part that referred to my behavior, I gave myself an 8 and Victor gave me a 9. The "evaluating your score" section says: "0 to 10 points--Your personality is not dominated by an excessive need to be in control. You are likely to be comfortable with your feelings and tolerant of other people. You realize that you are imperfect; therefore you understand the failings of others. It is easy for you to let events take their own course. Surprises don't throw you off balance. You probably place a high value on spontaneity and the expression of emotions."

On the part that referred to Victor's behavior, I gave him an 18. He gave himself a 15. The "evaluating your score" section says, "10 to 20 points--Being in control is a frequent issue with you. You have more fears and hurt feelings than you let on, but you don't work hard to resolve these feelings. Being in charge isn't necessarily very important to you, but having your own way is. You consider yourself organized and efficient, yet it isn't a major event if things get a little out of control. You have found someone whom you can be honest and open with, but there are limits as to how much you can safely say or do even with that person."

As we talked about this test, he'd often say, "But *that's* the way I *was.* I think I've *matured,* and *this* is the way I see things *now,* and *this* is what I'm thinking, and *this* is what I'm feeling." Currently he puts himself as a 6. I believe he *has* changed from a 15 to a 6. That's remarkable! He didn't seem to be upset that I gave him three more points on controlling than he gave himself for our marriage before our divorce.

It's interesting that I fit in the first category for most of our marriage when he had *perceived* me as a controlling person, and he fit in the second category as the more controlling one.

As Victor was about to leave my place after doing some raking one day, I asked, "Are you any more comfortable with the fact that you are having to wait before we get remarried?"

"Yes, I feel better about it now." His tone of voice was relaxed and he smiled at me when he said it.

Taking a deep breath, I asked a more important question. "If I continue to have no sexual activity with you at all until we get married, how will that affect our relationship?"

"I'll be disappointed, but it's not that important. I still want to be with you!"

What a relief. He is giving me more assurance.

Since then Victor has been talking about how he perceives me *now.* It feels like he is seeing the real Judy more than he ever has. He admits that how he *used to perceive me* was his "own creation"--whatever was going on in his own head. **Karen: Yes.** Some of the negative things he has seen in me are valid. We've agreed wholeheartedly on some things about control.

For instance, I sometimes talk more than I listen, unfortunately, and I frequently interrupt in a conversation, but I'm working to change that. People who live in my house, such as my house mates who rent rooms, need to follow my rental rules, and that's all right. We all understand each other better.

I had invited all our family to gather at my home the evening before Mother's Day for a meal followed by music. Nearly everyone came. We all gathered in the living room after eating. Victor had brought his keyboard and played while Steve sang. Following that, Alan, Steve and Victor played their instruments together as a trio, using music I had previously arranged for them. Then we all sang some songs together while sitting around the glowing coals in the fireplace.

After everyone left, Victor and I sat there for a while longer, relishing the feeling of togetherness and mutuality.

It was so tempting to say, "Okay, let's go ahead and get married and let our family be back together."

But Merv has said, "Don't be in a hurry. You know how unstable Victor has been. Give him a chance to show his stability."

I've *again* decided to wait and *not* set any time goals. But it is *hard*!

On Mother's Day Steve, Lauren, and our grandson, Jensen, met Victor and me at my mother's retirement home for the noon meal and celebration. My sister and her husband also joined us. Mother was thrilled to have all of us with her for a few hours that afternoon. This is the first *public* thing Victor and I have done together since our divorce.

Victor and I had come in separate cars, so as he was leaving, he came across the lobby saying he wanted a goodbye kiss. Fortunately he remembered to ask, "Is it safe?"

I shook my head. "I don't feel like kissing you in public yet. It's going to be a long time before we get married, and Miss Nixon, who has known me since she was my fifth grade teacher, is sitting a few feet away. She told me a few weeks ago, 'Never go back to him.'"

Victor gave an understanding grin and discreetly said a non-physical goodbye.

Before I left mother's place, but after Victor left, Clare, my sister, told me about an incident last week. She went with her doctor husband, Rich, to Oakhurst where he works on Wednesdays at a clinic. A man came in and said, "Oh, I know you." It was Jim, the man to whom I had been engaged. He was there for a pre-marriage blood test, but was surprised to see Rich. He expected to see the nurse practitioner.

Clare, Rich and Jim went to lunch together. Jim told them he had thought many times of calling me, but decided it probably wasn't wise. "Judy is a really fine woman. I have a lot of respect for her. I *did* push her too hard to get married. I *thought* I knew what I wanted, but I was wrong. I just wasn't ready!"

Jim told Clare that when Victor came in and announced his engagement, and I broke down in tears, he realized I still loved Victor. Then when he and Victor went off to play tennis and talked privately for a while, he saw tears in Victor's eyes, and knew he felt bad for hurting me. That truly *surprised* me!

Ouch, these emotions! It's hard to hear all this. It brings back many strong feelings of love for Jim, and my hurt at his decision not to marry me. I did feel pushed, urged and rushed by him; now I feel pangs of sadness.

On arrival home I delightedly discovered a Mother's Day card from Alan and another from Rudy and Rosemary plus a beautiful bouquet of flowers from Steve and Lauren. In spite of these, I had *hoped* to see Victor, but he had already come and gone. I noticed he had planted parsley, carrots and New Zealand spinach in our garden plot.

Since it was still Mother's Day, I looked to see if there was a gift, card or something from Victor, but there was nothing. This is the first year in my memory that he *hasn't* brought me at least a Mother's Day card. I wonder, because of the instability in our relationship right now, does this have a special meaning? I don't feel hurt—just a new kind of 'surprised.' This is a big change for a man that has always seemed to "do the right thing" to impress. Something has changed!

One thing emphasized in therapy is that nobody can read my mind, and I can't read anyone else's mind. If a person wants to know someone's thinking or motives, the best way to find out is to just ask. This took courage, but on a later day I mentioned to Victor that there was no card from him. He looked *surprised*, and said that sometime in the past he had given me a Mother's Day card and I *criticized* him for it, saying I wasn't his mother!

Now *I* was totally *dumbfounded*! Everything anyone has *ever* given me for Mother's Day or any other time has *always* pleased me! It's appropriate and thoughtful for a man to do something special on Mother's Day for the woman who is the mother of his children, whether they're married or not! I can't recall ever even *thinking* critically of any card Victor (or anyone else) has ever given me!

How can I discuss this with Victor and not hurt his feelings?

With some apprehension I began with, "I've always *loved* your cards, and I don't understand how you came to the conclusion that I *didn't!* I must have *really* messed up my words or phrases to cause that."

Suddenly I felt jolted as a new question broke into my consciousness. "You *chose not to* get me a card, but you *thought about it and wanted to?* You *didn't* do it because you thought I wouldn't like it?"

"That's right!" he exclaimed, sounding surprised that I really understood.

Oh good! I didn't hurt him. What a relief. Now I can compliment him.

"Wow! You decided to *refrain* from giving me something for Mother's Day because you didn't want to *insult* me?"

"Yes!" Victor sounded ecstatic.

"Then I see *that* as an especially *loving act!* You *purposely* didn't want to hurt me! Thank you *so much!* That is a *wonderful* gift! But I don't know if I'll *ever* figure out what *I did or said* that caused you to misunderstand. You've *always* done nice things for me on Mother's Day in years past, and I've *always* been delighted. I'm *so sorry* I accidentally gave you mixed messages."

"That's okay," he said half-heartedly.

"Probably sometime in the past I must have said, 'I'm not your mother,' and you connected that to Mother's Day," I reasoned.

Victor gave a nod and shoulder shrug, but there were no words.

Internally I'm nearly flabbergasted—in an especially good way. I see this event as an utterly remarkable change in Victor. For many years—most of our marriage—I haven't noticed effort on his part to think about my feelings. It has always seemed he acted on what he thought he <u>ought</u> to do—what he <u>had</u> to do to appear the perfect gentleman, whether it was genuine or not. Today something about Victor has been TRANSFORMED! He <u>thought ahead of time about my feelings</u> and <u>made a specific decision to change behavior so</u>

he wouldn't upset me. This is RADICALLY NEW! I LIKE THIS NEW VICTOR! Hopefully we will continue to soar to new and satisfying heights in our relationship.

When we were in therapy group again, Merv gave an assignment to draw our "emotional box." We were to describe and explain it in group. I drew my box with the lid completely open. Its padlock of fear was unfastened and lying on the ground outside the box. I printed "procrastination," "verbosity," "not listening" and a few other things inside it. I drew a diving board outside the box, stairs going up to the top edge of the box and continuing inside down to the bottom, and a trampoline inside. I said that sometimes my box of emotions is unlocked. Anxiety is still the latch, but it doesn't hold me inside. Fear is definitely there like the lock lying on the floor, but I have my choice of getting in and out of the box. Sometimes my life is so energetic that I bounce and bounce on the diving board, then maybe dive head first into the box. Generally I hit the trampoline and bounce right back out. Once in a while I'll sit on the trampoline and cry awhile, then drag myself up the stairs and out again.

Some of the people in the group said they were envious of me because I seemed able to move more easily, though clumsily, out of my box than they could.

One of the fellows talked about how *trust* was the key to *his* box. That was interesting. Just the night before, Victor told me he had decided that trust was the key to getting into *his* box where he was usually firmly locked. Now *this* night Victor seemed *different than he ever had before in group!* Merv even remarked that, "More than any other group you've been in, and more than any other night in this group, you, Victor, seem to be *open for growth* and *ready to really work."*

During the intermission I talked to Victor again about Mother's Day, and thanked him for the weeding he had done and all he planted in the garden. Then, referring again to his decision to *not* get me a card, I commented, "You've grown *fantastically!* You're now trying *not* to upset me! You have given me a *marvelous* gift—your *thinking about my feelings* and *not* doing something that might cause my discomfort! I want to bring *that* up during group and tell what I learned about your *growth*, but I'm a little scared."

It was only recently that Victor said he was never coming back to therapy group because Merv made him so angry. It seems miraculous that he finally decided to return. I must be very careful to support Victor in group communication, not doing or saying anything that will cause him to discontinue attending.

After intermission I *did* get brave. I told about how I considered that Victor's *thoughtfulness* in not wanting to offend me *was a gift* he had given me! Then I said, "He *also* did some work in my garden that was needed and planted some more things."

Apparently our therapist perceived that I suddenly shifted to another *position*, like Victor "was *a good little boy* for having done garden work." Merv said words to that effect, and it completely threw me! I felt *terrible*, as if I had done something *awful*. I am totally blank now as to what actually transpired, so I apparently really "fogged." There were tears in my eyes as Merv worked this through with me, and I'm now wearing a rubber band on my arm. If I find myself starting to, or tempted to say something to Victor that I realize is "mothering him," I'm to snap myself with the rubber band and write down what I started to say, and how I changed it. So far, there hasn't been an opportunity, because I haven't talked to Victor since that night. But the rubber band is there, and I'm thinking about it.

The people in group that night noticed the enormous change that took place in my body language. They said they felt sadness and sympathy for the fact that I related to Merv's observations like he had accused me of doing something terrible.

I said, "I *did* feel that way—horrible, awful—like he was condemning me!"

Merv asked me to talk about the first time I ever felt 'horrible, awful, and condemned.' I knew the answer immediately. "When I was about three, mother pulled me out of a church social into the lobby because she saw me sitting on some man's lap. I was probably showing some physical response by cuddling, or something like that, and mother was aghast. She scolded me for what felt like *forever* in front of other people coming and going near us. She said I must never, *never*, NEVER, under *any* condition, sit on *any* man's lap or be acting like "*that*," whatever it was. I hadn't known

I was doing anything wrong. I was just being me. There was absolutely no comprehension of what was wrong in what I did."

After group, Victor said he didn't think I came across as mothering him. I was surprised Merv thought so, because I just wanted them to know Victor *hadn't neglected* me on Mother's Day. His yard work was an appreciated gift, but Victor hadn't called it that. I didn't want *the group* to think he was negligent of me. I want *them* to admire him.

Now today I'm still feeling *terribly ashamed* of my behavior in group. I am *depressed* and fighting a *huge feeling of worthlessness*! Besides that, there is still a deep sadness washing over me regarding Jim. I had thought he really *did* love me and we'd soon marry. While at his farm I planned what to put in each cupboard and what to plant in the garden. At his church I met people who might become close friends. Jim didn't want me to work, so I was considering the possibility of teaching lessons in piano or voice, but not charging for them. Now that hope is gone. Jim needed to deal with his *own* problems. He lied to his mother, telling her he had never asked me to marry him.

My sister Clare said she is thankful we didn't get married, first because it was just too soon; and second because, from her observations, Jim would probably have been a *super controller*. My dear friend Faye also says she's thankful I didn't marry him, and so is my brother. Yet I remember all the good stuff, the tender moments, the loving words and deeds that were lacking in my relationship with Victor that I *did* get from Jim those few months.

My feelings now, *today*, are the same emotions that overwhelmed me as a three-year-old, and also in our last therapy group. I was being natural, doing something spontaneous and loving, feeling so happy, when suddenly there was scolding, public ridicule and inundating humiliation for being so "stupid, wicked and/or evil." [I'm crying on the tape as I record this.] Jim's mother thought it was *terrible* that I wore shorts. Some other "friends" of Jim thought it was *terrible* that I made a trip with him in his motor home before we were married, because they "knew" we were sleeping together.

I believe Jim rejected me because all he had felt for me was sexual attraction. He said, just before he left, "There is *nothing* in our relationship that would make us good friends," even though we had hiked, biked, swam, and played horseshoes together. I had driven his boat while he water-skied. We looked at movies together, read books together, prayed together. We cooked together, did dishes together, and cleaned the motor home together. Yet he said there was *nothing* between us that would make us friends. That hurts! Enormously!

It's that same feeling as when Mother, verbally plunging into me, told me she was ashamed I was her daughter, and that I was shaming my father, the family and the whole town! When she did this, which seemed so often, it would always be about things I hadn't realized anybody thought were "wrong." They were just happy, spontaneous, joyful, energetic living; but apparently I *embarrassed* her! I'm feeling that all over again regarding Jim! And Victor! For what was I being scolded, punished and humiliated? FOR WHAT? Oh, the excruciating, ripping pain as the memories explode into glaring consciousness!

Clare answered a few more questions about Jim and his wife-to-be. I alluded to the fact they probably were going to go on a trip to Canada, because he'd talked to me about wanting to leave around May and go on a year-long trip.

She said, "No, it doesn't sound like he's going to do that."

"How's that?" I asked, feeling very curious.

"Because she wants to continue working." My sister seemed to understand the situation better than I did.

"What does she do?" was my next question.

"She's a psychologist," my sister answered.

I can't *believe* it! He told me he would *never* go for counseling! And now he's going to marry a psychologist? Amazing!

This again stirs up strong emotions. Tears are bulging in my eyes. In a way, there's still love for Jim. But the realization strikes me that my emotions, then and now, are *not* what really constitute love! I'm glad to be back with Victor, even though we aren't positively committed to marry.

When I got home from teaching music lessons today, Victor was working in my yard. He had bought yellow and orange marigolds and planted them along the edge of the driveway. They're lovely! He had done more weeding and put strawberries and corn in the garden. He had planted petunias below the roses. Beautiful! I gave him a good meal before he left.

Merv called one night while Victor was still here, so he talked to both of us. He congratulated us on the way we are working in group therapy, and wanted us to know he really values that. He sees good hopes for us getting back together.

Another assignment he gave us for group therapy was to write about our concept of respect. Victor wrote:

> "Respect and trust are nearly synonymous. If you respect a person, you trust them, and if you trust them, you respect them. The more you know about them, their background, their accomplishments and abilities, the more you can trust them. If you don't know anything about them, you can't trust them."

He read that to me before we left for group.

"That's interesting! Tell me more." I'm struggling to say things that will draw him out.

As we drove along, he surprisingly responded, "The more I'm learning about your background, the more I'm looking at you with new eyes. I realize I really *do* love you, and I really *do* respect you. I want to learn to respect and trust *myself*, because if I don't, then I project that lack of trust and respect on you. That's what I've done. I want to learn to respect and trust myself." **KAREN: Hallelujah!**

I shifted in my seat to look at him more closely and gave him my most gracious smile. "You are growing in such a *marvelous* way!"

He chuckled and said, "I know it."

For my assignment on respect, this is part of what I wrote:

> I want Victor to "re-view" me from a different perspective--to see the real me in a new light. I want him to "look back" and notice what is there that he couldn't see before. He was blinded by his un-dealt-with past. I want him to *spy* on me--to discover the hidden secrets of the real Judy who was always there, but hidden to him because of

410

the historic and negative images he saw superimposed over me. I will feel respected if he can look, then acknowledge what he sees, whether it is good, bad or indifferent. Just notice and *respond!* I need him to be *aware* of me, as a human being, imperfect, but real, who has feelings and wants and needs that are as valid as his. I want him to be courageous enough to look me straight in the eye, and verbalize what he sees, whether I like the content of his statement or not. This, to me, is respect.

For me to give respect to Victor would be the same. Besides that, I would give him honor and hold him in high regard. I have always *wanted* to do that, but it seemed he was blocking me. I want to listen to him without asking for details all the time, and without interrupting him. I want us both to be accurate mirrors of the other, with love as the mirror polish.

Thursday night was my weekly social "outlet," attending the Singles Social at the Congregational Church in Pasadena, next to 210 Freeway. When that was over, I attended a much smaller Divorce Recovery Group in an adjoining room. At both groups a "Healing Workshop" was advertised one night. It was to be a seminar once a week for four weeks at a Methodist church, specifically for those who have experienced loss, whether by divorce, death or some other way. The first night I attended this workshop, it felt to me like huge, empty spaces in my soul were filled, and I looked forward to the next three weeks.

Friday I took Buster with me to the cabin. He is half German shepherd and half Collie and provides both companionship and protection when hiking. As we rounded a bend, there in the trail, sitting a few feet ahead, was a baby bobcat about a foot long. I had never seen one before, and was so thrilled! It looked up at me, and then ran out of sight. Buster made no attempt to chase it.

After arrival at the cabin I put water to boil on the three-burner, old-fashioned kerosene stove, cooked and ate a whole box of macaroni and cheese, made up a container of Crystal Lite, powdered Gatorade and water mixed together, and drank a lot of it. Then I ate a whole package of peanut butter filled pretzels! After resting, I did some more interior painting and cleaned the cabin. Next day I collected a lot more wood, broke it up into smaller, useable pieces, and stacked it in boxes.

In the afternoon I walked down the trail, hoping to meet Victor, and sure enough we met about 4:30. Right away he said he wanted to tell me something as soon as we got back to the cabin. Eagerly I exclaimed, "You can tell me now!"

"No, I want to wait until we get there and sit down and talk." *This is new behavior for him. It's hard to believe he really said, "No," and didn't act like he thought I was trying to control him.*

I felt delighted to wait, and walked in silence through the shady, cool forest, listening to the water singing its lilting song in the nearby creek. We stepped on slightly submerged rocks to cross the stream, climbed the steep slope to the first cabin in our area, passed two more rustic forest dwellings and rounded the bend to where our chocolate-colored, steep-roofed, single-room hide-away came into view.

Victor unbolted the front door, stepped inside and took off his backpack, leaning it against my antique treadle sewing machine. I made up and poured us a cool drink of Gatorade and Tang, mixed together, and we sat on the bed, leaning against the large, bright orange propped cushions.

His first words were, "You've sometimes told me dreams that were so vivid, and I told you I almost never remember dreams. Somehow yesterday I just *knew* God was going to send me a dream, but I felt afraid that I would forget it. So I prayed last night that God would help me *remember* what I dreamed. And I *did* have a *horrible* nightmare! I've been trying to think what it means and what God is trying to tell me." He shifted his relaxed position to sitting up straight. Then after a few moments he squirmed, rearranged his cushions and leaned against the wall. After even more hesitation he spoke again. "Well, I'll just tell it to you. I want to know what *you* think about it."

Shifting my position to get totally comfortable, I responded, "I'm *eagerly* listening!"

There was tremendous hesitancy in his voice as he slowly began to speak. "There was this huge apartment building, extremely tall." He sounded a bit trance-like and sort of far away. "*Somebody* had built a bed attached to the outside of the building. It was up *very high*, many stories from the ground. I was on this bed. I didn't know how I got there or remember *anything* before that. But I began to realize the bed was starting to deteriorate and crack. I looked far below where I saw cars driving on the roads down there, but they looked as little as ants or bugs because they were so far away. I slowly began to realize the bed was going to break off from the building, and I was soon going to crash to my death. I became more and more frantic, trying to look for a way of escape. Finally I noticed a little window about shoulder-height above the bed. I reached up and tried to open it, but it was stuck closed. I got hysterical and started pounding and banging on the wall and yelling for help. As I hollered, I struggled with the window. It was quite small--like a bathroom window. After what seemed a *long* time it opened. It was just barely big enough to squeeze through, but it was so far up, I couldn't get myself into it very far. Someone inside started to help pull me. They struggled, tugged and twisted and eventually were able to pull me through the window until I was standing up inside a room. At last I was safe! Then I looked to see who it was who helped me. It was *you* who had pulled me into the building!"

"Oh, my! What a dream! Is that the end?" I wanted there to be more.

"Yes, that's all. Then I woke up in a cold sweat, shaking and terribly frightened. It made a *tremendous* impression on me! I wonder what God is trying to tell me. I wonder if maybe I'm not doing something right and I'm about to lose eternal life. What do *you* think about this dream?"

"Victor, I'm no dream interpreter. But if you want, I'll tell you what it *seems* to me."

"*Please* do!" His voice sounded almost pleading as he looked straight into my eyes.

I asked, "Have you ever heard people say, 'You've made your bed; now you can lie in it?'"

He tilted his head with a surprised look on his face. "Yes, I have!" he admitted.

"Those were the words that instantly flooded my brain as you described the dream." I watched him closely, feeling some fear about saying what I thought next. "Nobody else built that bed for you. You built it. That was *your* construction, and you've been up there for a long, long time--far, far away from the reality of the contemporary world! That bed was built with your masks, your protective walls, your. . ." I now hesitated, trying to think of a good word.

Victor helped by replying with a question: "My fantasies?"

This man doesn't look angry or even frustrated. He seems eager to hear what I have to say. I'm amazed!

"Yes! Your fantasies! You've lived much of your life on that little narrow bed. But somehow, some way, you came to the realization that your bed was crumbling. Somehow you felt you *had* to *do* something. You were in this process when you divorced me and went searching for somebody else. You found Clarice, and you were going to give up your own home-- our house, our yard, our property, our family. You gave up your job. You were going to move away in order to marry Clarice, and you hardly knew her. You were hysterical as you pounded and yelled for help. Whether your conscious mind told you or not, that ruckus was causing the bed to crumble even more."

After waiting in silence for any response, negative or positive, and there was none, I continued. "You began to get more in touch with your emotions; then I began writing you letters, and finally you realized that you, yourself, were crumbling, and the person who pulled you into the building was me. I believe you are in your *own* building now. You are becoming your *own* person, and not forcing yourself to act like someone you imagined yourself to be. And you are wanting to be in *my* home for the first time also. You've always been 'out there,' way outside of reality, just on the edge." **KAREN: It's also accepting Victor's own feminine side that is strong and can save him from living in the masculine only. Living in only one side will distance us.**

"Thank you for listening and understanding and sharing with me. That makes sense." He sounded both relieved and pleased, which continued to almost astound me!

We talked longer, and then he said, "There's something else I want to tell you. I was thinking about it on the way up here today. When I read to my therapy group the letter you wrote Nov 11 [in the chapter "Exhaust"] they all said they thought you had super-human love. They were amazed you still wanted to try to get back with me. **Karen: Yes.** I felt awful, so I called you, came over, and told you I still loved you. But I felt I *had* to go see Clarice. That was when I prayed to God for a sign."

414

After a long pause and changing position two or three times, he continued, "I realize now I was *forcing* the issue. I *knew* what *I wanted*, and *I* was going to go after it! I was just like Balaam. [The Bible character described in the book of Numbers, chapters 22 to 24.] I *imagined* I knew what God wanted, but for sure *I knew* what *I* wanted! I pressed *hard* for Clarice to give me an answer."

Victor looked at me for some response, but I just nodded for him to continue. Then he repeated with emphasis, "I *knew* what *I wanted!* I not only tried to force *God*, **I forced *Clarice* to make *my* decision for me!"**
KAREN: Wow! Great insight!

This is *miraculous!* This is *amazing!* In the letter I wrote him in December and gave him January 3, I told him he was doing the same thing to Clarice as he had done to me--forcing me to make his decisions for him. For him to say he was like Balaam astonishes me!

I think my letters to him somehow *did* penetrate. Today they have finally reached his *conscious* level. They had previously seemed to bypass his thinking mind as well as his spiritual conscience because of his habit of blocking out things. Somehow there's been enough therapy now. God is reaching down into his subconscious, and pulling things out for him to look at, little by little, as he's able to emotionally absorb new concepts. This is so touching, because I believe that's the work of the Holy Spirit.
Karen: Yes.

This "heart cleansing" is usually more unconscious than conscious. When we allow God to transform us, He reaches down inside and pulls out hidden "junk" for our appraisal. If we give Him permission, He'll clean it up and wash it away. Then He gives us the gift of forgiveness, both for ourselves and for whoever else hurt us. This miracle is taking place in Victor's life, and I'm the lucky and blest observer. I'm also continuing to ask for ongoing cleansing and forgiveness in my life.

Victor talked further about how he had been so *terribly* rebellious. He repeated, "Rebellious against *everything*!" He said, "I was just going to go out there and find out what the world was like, because I *wanted* to! There was *nothing* that was going to stop me! But now I am loving you more and more. I really *want* our marriage to work."

"Victor, this is *heavy stuff* you've been telling me! Are you feeling uptight? Are you feeling upset about it?"

"No, I feel very comfortable." And his words matched his posture, now stretched out flat on the bed with his head on a cushion, looking up towards the white rafters bracing the steeply sloped cabin roof.

It was only a month ago, after asking him some heavy questions, that he couldn't eat supper because he was so upset. I think my confronting him on many of these issues and writing these things in letters has helped to crumble his emotional walls, and crack his dangerously attached "bed." Apparently he didn't think about it at first. But he is finally *talking*, and he says he's *comfortable* and he wants to be *completely open!* Wow again! Thank you God!

As we were returning home the next day, Victor invited me to come over to his apartment. My back and neck were hurting, as they often do, sometimes intensely, from a previous serious neck injury. He suggested I come share his Jacuzzi. Later he gave me a massage and really worked on my back and neck. It helped me feel *so* much better.

While he was massaging me, I told him a bit more about what I was feeling regarding Jim and his rejection. "I realize *you* have broken up with Clarice, but it wasn't *her* rejecting *you*, was it?"

"Well, it *felt* like a rejection when Clarice told me she would never take me back as long as you were alive." He was really pressing hard on my back as he said it, probably not realizing his emotions affected his massaging.

"When she told you again, just recently, apparently it felt even *more* like a rejection?" I questioned, trying really hard to understand.

"Yes," and he stopped so suddenly, I wondered if that was the end of my massage.

This man is getting in touch with his feelings! And the feelings are getting stronger and stronger! He even *looks* like he is feeling more deeply!

"Have you considered the possibility that you might go back to her?" I probed.

"Well, yes! Yes, I could *easily* go back to her! I *love* her!" Now he was doing fast pummeling on my back that usually feels so good. But this time I asked him to ease up a bit.

"I'm not sure whether you understood my question. If I died, or married somebody else or broke up with you now and refused to marry you, would you go back to her?"

"Yes, I certainly would! But I *want* to marry *you*! If I went back to her, I think I'd *insist* on our getting counseling!" Now I felt the long, easy finishing strokes on my back and knew the massage was ending.

As I sat up and wrapped a large towel around my shoulders, I asked another question. "Was *she* against counseling?"

Victor wiped the lotion from his hands on another towel and came to sit close beside me. "Well, I asked her a number of times to go for counseling. She seemed to think we didn't *need* it. She could go to her counselor she had gone to after her divorce."

Here's a man who is growing by megabytes. I don't know what was keeping him from it before. I know these changes come from God. I also give Merv and Lena, our therapists, tremendous credit.

As I was later gathering my things to head back home, Victor said, "Oh, I realize we haven't discussed what the starting date was for the year you insisted must pass before we remarry."

I thought we had already discussed that. February 7 is the date when he decided not to move north and made the break-up call to Clarice. I think so much of what I've said previously hasn't registered. Now Victor's exquisitely refined steel exterior is starting to melt a bit on the surface. That's more crumbling of the bed in his dream. What I've said is finally penetrating his walls, his fantasies, and his masks. I'm genuinely expecting his personality to become more pliable and self-generating.

I told him the year would be over around the first week of February, and he seemed happy. That leaves only about eight months. I'm sure I won't marry him until at least a year has passed, but we can possibly start making plans.

"If Clarice would take you back, no strings attached, even though you were penniless--if she would welcome you with open arms, even though you had no money and no job, would you want to go back to her?" I asked.

"No, I wouldn't. Not unless you died or married somebody else."

"Why?" I was feeling a very strong need to know his answer.

"Because I realize I *love* you. I *want* to be with *you*. I am seeing you in a new light!"

Oh, the joy of observing change, new growth and maturity in Victor. His tender embrace and warm kiss lingered in my whole body as I drove back home.

Months ago, when deciding to write my story, even though there wasn't a vague concept of how it would end, I started toting my mini-cassette tape recorder everywhere I went, even in my backpack to the cabin. Soon after the above communication took place and I arrived back home after dark, I lay back in my recliner with recorder in hand. My housemates were out of town and I relished my concealed solitude. My ballooning emotions and expressive hopes became words and sentences recorded on tape.

I'm ecstatic. I don't even want to stop tape recording right now because I am so thrilled with Victor. He is looking me in the eye now. He calls me Rosebud, and I'm learning to love it. He initiates conversation. He's patient with me. I tell him I'm trying to learn to *not* ask for so many details and *not* interrupt him. He appreciates that. I tell him I don't *want* to come across as mothering him, but that I'm not always aware when I do, so I want him to tell me if he notices it. And I want him to tell me when I get to talking *too* long, asking *too many questions*, and just going on a roll. I want him to speak up and *tell me*, so I'll know! He says he will. I believe he really will! This man amazes me.

One evening after therapy group I was talking to Victor in the car on the way home. "We haven't yet dealt with some things *I* need to deal with. They are *heavy*, and I know it will be hard for *you*. It's about something I wrote that was quite negative. You said you had read it, but haven't commented about it. I need some kind of feedback. I'm referring to the one piece of writing that wasn't a letter, but about my *imagination* regarding your unspoken marriage and divorce contracts."

After about a minute of quizzical expression and cocking his head, he reflected, "I am having a really hard time. I can't remember anything about it." He promised he would try to find and read it.

That is surprising to me because I thought it would have been so powerful it would have made a deep impression.

The next day Victor called me and said he found it. "Is that the one that starts out 'Agony!'?"

"Yes, it is," I assured him.

"I read it over. It is *powerful!* I would be willing to bring it to our therapy group if you would like." He sounded determinedly open and honest.

Feeling really shocked, I answered, "I certainly don't expect you to *do that!* But if you do, Victor, you are a tremendously courageous man! It means *everything* in the world to me that you would even *consider* reading it to them."

29

ATTAIN

One week passed, and I had forgotten Victor's generous offer to present to our therapy group my imagined and written-out diatribe I had given him. Gradually I have learned to mentally submerge any exciting hope about real change in Victor, but habits aren't easily broken. Expectations soon were erased because hopes had been dashed so frequently in the past. This particular night we traveled to group therapy in separate cars, since Victor was coming from an appointment in a different direction.

As I listened to other members reporting their assignments and having their turn "on the hot seat," I was relaxed and totally centered on the various issues others had been detailing. Suddenly Victor spoke up, saying he wanted to present something to the group that I had sent him some time ago. He explained that I had written it more than a year previously, but gave it to him a few months ago. He had forgotten all about it, until I got brave enough to ask him for feedback. He had hunted it up, just for my sake, and studied it; now he wanted to read it to the group.

When Victor had told me a few days before that he was *willing* to bring this to group, I didn't believe him! Now I looked up, *incredulous*, and saw enormous determination in his eyes! His jaw muscles clenched tight for a moment. He took a couple deep breaths as he smoothed the pages he was about to read. Slowly he then got up, stood tall and brave, gave a painful grimace, and haltingly said, "Well, – I'll read it – just as she wrote it."

Agony! The searing, pulsating, jabbing constancy of the rejection is overwhelming. The abandonment, the being discarded, deluges and floods my being. The finality has dawned. There is no hope! There never should have been. I still hear Victor's words as he was packing, getting ready to move out--the loud, forceful, angry words:

"I don't *like* intimacy! I don't *want* intimacy! I *never* have, and I *never* will! When you ask me how I feel, it gives me the *paralysis of analysis.* I don't want anyone to *ever* ask me how I feel, because I don't *know* how I feel, and I *don't want to know!*"

Evidently the following was the base, the foundation, on which our marriage was established, without my (or even Victor) realizing it; at least this is what it seems to me now, years later. In my *imagination,* the following is what Victor *might* have said (could he have comprehended it) when we established our legal contract of marriage:

"I'm entering this relationship with these requirements, these rules, these demands:

> You are to act like you love me. Always.
> You are to pretend I'm perfect. Always.
> You are to tell me I'm wonderful. Always.
> You are to cook my meals, clean my house, bear my children, be available to me sexually whenever and in whatever form I want. Always.
> You must focus on taking care of me!
> The world must never know I am imperfect.
> The world must never know I don't know how to treat you with deep love.
> The world must never know I feel like an inferior person.
> They must never know I hate much of myself.
> I will go through the motions of saying I love you and want you, but I will pull down the shades of my mind. I will put on blinders. I will do it with my most gracious and magnanimous loving voice and demeanor, when I smile and say I love you and everything is perfect.
> Don't ever say you don't understand.
> Don't ever ask for an explanation.

Don't dare ever cry about our unspoken contract.

Don't ever need my deep love.

Don't speak of your needs.

Sweep all problems under the rug. I demand you never speak of them!

If you presume to complain, I will deny even minimal discussion.

I refuse to look at us.

I refuse to see the real you.

I refuse to look at me.

There is nothing you can do to change this status quo because I can't stand being open and real and honest. If I ever did that, my props would fall out; my facade would crumble, my iron walls would melt, and my whole being would collapse into a puddle of nothingness. I would cease to exist.

My armor is a substitute for emotional bones, muscles, and tendons.

Inside it I've hidden a machine that constantly creates and diffuses through the cracks my aura of peace, love and tranquility, along with anesthetic and incense, as a camouflage.

I must never let anyone get close enough to smell the rage and anger that churn constantly in this helpless body and brain."

As he read, there were frequent, surprised, but quietly verbalized exclamations of "ouch" or "oh my," or soft groaning sounds coming from other members of the group. I saw the muscles in Victor's cheeks release their clench and now start trembling as he went on:

"You made waves in my life.

You rocked my boat too many times.

You didn't unconditionally accept my unspoken contract.

You have refused to submit to me.

422

You have refused to be 'one flesh,' which I believe means to think, act and feel whatever I demand.

You are not a wife to me, because my wife should have been a robot, so I am discarding you. I'm dumping you on the rubbish heap in front of God, the church, my relatives and friends, in front of the whole world.

Tearfully he cleared his throat, shuffled his papers, fumbled for his handkerchief to mop his cheeks, and with quavering voice continued reading.

I hope they all see the filth smeared on your face, the tattered rags you are wearing.

I hope they smell the stink of your unwashed body.

I hope they all say, 'Good riddance of bad rubbish,' and clamor around me to sympathize, cajole, pat, hug and support me.

I have washed myself to a spanking clean whitewash.

My armor is gleaming.

The anesthetic-incense mix still wafts about me, and everyone thinks I'm wonderful!

TOUGH LUCK, Judy"

Quiet gasps and astonished silence overwhelmed the room! Victor stood silent for a moment as if trying to decide what to say or do. Then he spoke again. "I acknowledge *all of it!* Yes, that's the way it *was!*" As he was seating himself, he continued passionately, "But it seems so *foreign* to my mind now, because *that* was a *different* person! Today I'm not that person *at all!*"

Cheering and clapping erupted from all of us, and I nodded my tear-dampened face vigorously.

Merv verified what Victor said with, "You were a *roll-playing* Victor then, but now you are the *real* Victor! They are two totally different individuals!"

More clapping and cheering exploded and expanded before Merv held up his hand for us to finally quiet down. He clearly emphasized, "What has just taken place is the most *powerful* thing I have *ever* seen happen in *any* group, at *any* time, to *any* person previously! Something that intense and that deep, and someone willing to bring it and read it! This is just amazing!" **Karen: Yes!**

Everyone praised Victor for his tremendous courage, for being willing to read this, and to acknowledge that our marriage *had been* that way.

As things moved on in group, I internalized: That *is* the story of *much* of our past marriage! However, if I look at it realistically, there were *lots of good times* also, *wonderful times*. Sometimes I *did* feel close! **KAREN: This had to be the case, for you to still love him**. But if there were problems that needed to be discussed, the situation changed abruptly. And as the years went on, things got worse.

During "my time" in group that same evening, I stated that I wasn't trying to "mother" Victor, following Mother's Day, but I definitely was trying to protect him. I didn't want him to get so hurt, discouraged or angry that he might leave therapy; it seems miraculous he was willing to even come again! I didn't want him to change his mind, so I purposely mentioned commendable things about him.

The following week Victor could hardly wait to tell the group about his dream. Again there were audible responses heard as he described it. Merv gave each person an opportunity to comment, telling his or her thoughts and feelings regarding it.

Victor then asked me to tell what I thought about it. As I did, I added more than what I had said at the cabin. "It is significant that the bed was *outside* the apartment building. Living and sleeping out there meant to me that Victor didn't feel like he really *belonged* to *any* family. All the many families in the apartment building--all the people he's been with most of his life--were separate from him. I think he hasn't felt like he really belonged to any of them in an intimate sort of a way. Now that he has found himself *inside* the building, I hope he will be able to form closer bonds with others. The fact that the bed was up on the side of such a *tall* building, I believe, signifies his high ideals and desires to please God; but he has been somewhat out of touch with the real world."

Merv encouraged others at this point to make comments or ask questions. Then he told me to continue with my "interpretation."

"It seems to me Victor began to notice *in real time*, the 'cracking bed frame' in his dream even more, after I began increasing my confrontations with him. His desire to get away from *me* was partially his struggle to get away from the *bed* that he felt was crumbling. He wanted a divorce, thinking I must be the problem. Apparently he had wanted to escape for some time, and in the dream had to pound on the wall and window for quite a long time before it opened. Trying to get through the window by himself was impossible, so he needed another person to help him succeed. At first he thought that would be Clarice."

Merv made some clarification comments and then asked me to continue.

"I feel like I have been by the window, waiting for him to *want* to come in for a long time, believing he would eventually try. I have loved him through it all, and am so thankful I waited. His whole way of looking at me is different than it used to be."

Victor shared how he thought God was trying to show him his way of life had not been good, and he was about to crash and lose eternal life. Then he told the group again that he saw himself as Balaam. He admitted wanting what he wanted, and trying to push both God and Clarice. "I wasn't really looking for God's will in my life at all!" Right then he made a commitment to start spending more time with the Lord and working on his relationship with Him, as well as with me. **Karen: Great!**

I recently told our sons their dad is a walking miracle. He has shown tremendous courage in his growth, and has gotten many new insights. **Karen: Good!**

As Victor and I were hiking again to our cabin one day, I told him how I had bragged on him to his sons about his being a "walking miracle." And I also told them, "Your dad is such a wonderful worker. He can fix or build almost anything. I don't know how I could ever have found anyone who would be so careful in the things he does, both at the cabin and at home. I have a tendency to be sloppier, but he is so meticulous. And now he is becoming much more careful how he treats me, also." They actually seemed excited in their response to hearing that from me.

425

As we finished eating one noon at the cabin, Victor said, "I want to talk with you." He asked if I had a Bible there, and we looked up several verses on reconciliation and discussed them. He has never before seemed to want to dissect ideas with me, but he asked to now! He told me he had already talked to his pastor about developing a study on reconciliation. Pastor Jerold gave him some material on the subject, and also loaned him two books.

Then Victor became very quiet. There was a growing comfort in his silence, and I actually didn't feel impatient for him to talk. At last he quietly spoke, "When I went and picked up these books last night, I talked to Pastor Jerold for probably over an hour. I told him . . . ." [As he paused, I noticed tears in his eyes]. . . . "Well, I don't really know *what* I told him, but he told *me* it appeared I was still suffering terrible guilt from all the mistakes I've made. He suggested I go home and read the story of the Prodigal Son." **KAREN: This is what I love about the confessing church. We have a way of acknowledging sin and being forgiven**.

Putting my arms around him, I just held him close for several minutes. Then after he wiped his tears and blew his nose, he spoke again. "Judy, I see you in a completely different light than I used to. I don't know how anybody could have been more attentive than you've been to me. You've been wonderfully loving to me."

Is he referring to now, just since he broke up with Clarice? Or is he referring to ever since he moved out? Or does he see how loving I was to him our entire marriage? Of course <u>those are things I'd like to know, but maybe it's just as well I don't. I wish I didn't feel this compulsive questioning so often</u>.
KAREN: Good insight!

He added, "When you first told me you wouldn't marry me for a year, I thought it was because you hadn't totally forgiven me, or weren't willing to pardon me. But I realize now it wasn't that reason at all. That's just the way I *felt* at first." Another tear rolled down his cheek, and he just let it drip off.

"The purpose of that decision," I replied, "was for *me*--for *my* growth and *my* settling--so I could live with *myself*. When I realized how upset I was with you right after you broke up with Clarice, and recognized *my* tumultuous feelings, I knew there was no way I could live in a marriage without learning how to manage *my* feelings better."

"I accept that now." Victor took in a very slow breath and I thought would never let it out. Finally there was a long and almost silent sigh. "And I'm willing to wait as long as necessary."

Then he said his pastor wants to invite me to attend his church and join it when I'm ready. Victor wants that very much; he thinks I would like the church. But I told him I am not ready to go there at this point.

Victor also invited me to his high school reunion June 5. I guess I'm ready to go there with him. I will feel awkward and self-conscious, but will do it anyway.

We left the cabin Sunday morning because my big Spring Student Recital was that night. We were hiking out for home when Victor asked what he could do to help set up for the recital. I asked, "Would you like to come?"

Instantly he questioned, "Is it safe?"

That truly pleased me. "I really don't know whether I want you there or not. It feels premature; but I'm thrilled that you asked, 'Is it safe?'"

Before we got home he said, "I'll tell you what. I'll go set up for you and do your grocery shopping for the punch ingredients and carry in all the serving plates and punch bowl. When I finish I won't stay."

He is thinking about *me*--what I *feel* and what *I want*! This is so new--so different! Yeah!

"Victor, you're wonderful." And I again get this big, genuine smile in return that seems to say, "I know it!"

When we arrived at the recital hall, he helped me set up the chairs and even vacuumed the whole room. Apparently it hadn't been cleaned since its last use.

After everything was prepared, Victor went to my place and worked the rest of the afternoon in the yard. I called to thank him when I came home much later, and he seemed happy to hear my voice. He's treating me like I have *longed* to be treated by a man. Now he makes me feel important to him!

The "minithon" for our therapy group was Monday night and lasted six hours. At the beginning, Merv handed out something for us to read and think about:

427

The longer I live, the more I realize the impact of attitude on life. Attitude, to me, is more important than facts. It is more important than the past, than education, than circumstances, than failures, than success, than what other people say or do. It is more important than appearance, giftedness or skill. It will make or break a company, a church, or a home. The remarkable thing is, we have a choice every day regarding the attitude we embrace for that day. We cannot change our past; we cannot change the fact that people will act in a certain way. We cannot change the inevitable. The only thing we can do is play on the one string we have. That is our attitude. I am convinced that life is ten percent what happens to me, and ninety per cent how I react to it. And so it is with you. We are in charge of our attitude.

KAREN: The more we soak up the Lord, the more our attitude is hopeful, joyful, loving, accepting, grateful.

Merv then went around the circle and asked each of us to put in our own percentages. When it finally was Victor's turn, he said he felt that what happens in life is fifty percent and attitude is fifty percent. Towards the end of the evening, after we had a lot of other discussion, Merv asked Victor if he had changed his percentage.

"Perhaps in reality it is ten and ninety. But of course the rebellious child in me would still like to leave it at 50-50." Everybody laughed. Victor said it like he really meant it, and yet he could see the humor. "I don't want to give up that fifty percent of how my life has been affected by what happened, rather than by my attitude."

When Victor did his therapy "work," he showed the picture of a bed he had drawn, which represents our life together. The bed was on the *outside* of the building in his dream, but now he specified, "The bed is on the *inside*. The bedposts are respect, honor, kindness and freedom. The flat part of the bed is love. This bed is the one on which we will build our next marriage."

Tiny blades of hope, which seemed to take forever to sprout, are greening my perspective.

Merv suggested to Victor, "Tell your subconscious to dream on."

When my turn came, I stated, "My purpose in coming to this group was to learn to build a close relationship with Victor. We're making good progress in that direction, but I'm not sure what should come next. In thinking about the first group meeting after Mother's Day, I have come to the realization that although I *wasn't* mothering Victor, I certainly was trying to protect him.

A few days later I had a dream. In it, I was outside a building in a public place leaning over to take something out of a box. Then I heard Merv's voice saying, 'Be careful!' so stood up to see why he said that. Immediately I was horrified to realize I didn't have on underwear, and I had 'mooned' him. Shocked, I wondered, 'how did I get out here like *this*?'

Next in the dream I was going back into a building. People were all around--church people that I knew--and suddenly I realized I had no clothes on at all! Flabbergasted, I was trying to find something to wrap around myself. A little child's play clothes appeared in my hands, which I held in front of me, but they were far too small.

In my dream I recognized my horrible fear of public humiliation. I just *knew* all these people who saw me would now have discovered how awful and shameful I really was, and I would be ridiculed and condemned for life. That terribly sad and horrible feeling was the end of my dream."

Merv said he thought my dream was basically healthy, because the very fact that I told it showed my openness and willingness to share my inner feelings and thoughts. He said, "You're not hiding anything. Nakedness in a dream shows openness and willingness to be vulnerable." **KAREN: Yes. It's often intimidating to others. In some ways that's always been a part of Judy's personality. It got stomped on a lot by mom, husband and others.** He said the dream was a very healthy part of my life—an important part--that I'm becoming open, and I'm becoming free.

As we discussed the dream, I said, "In my growing-up-years, it seemed Mother would verbally cut me down when I was accomplishing the most, was the happiest, and was feeling the most successful. Later, not long before she died, we talked about some of these things and she told me, 'I was so proud of you three children. You were so beautiful and talented. I thought if I didn't keep you humble, *I'd* lose eternal life, and you *three would also*.' She felt a *compulsion* to 'burst the bubble' whenever she thought we might get proud. Yet she pushed us to accomplish, to think, to do and to be perfectionists. **KAREN: With fear not only of being perfect in performance, but also damned by God for lack of being perfect in performance.** We had to 'tow that mark.' When we were successful, happy and contented, she admitted *that's* when she'd feel a compulsion to put us down so we 'wouldn't become proud.'"

Still going on, I admitted: "I fear going over to Mother's retirement home this coming weekend. I'll be leaving from her place in my forest ranger uniform to do my twice-a-month volunteer trail patrol in Gorgonio Wilderness. Mother may get after me for having people see me in my uniform shorts on the Sabbath." **KAREN: What would that mean spiritually?** [Judy: Shorts were "indecent (immoral)" clothing unless at the beach, so they *especially* should not be worn on Sabbath.]

Merv had me role play. I was to play "Mother." So I said rather sarcastically, as Mother would, "Judy, you're going to go out like *that* in those *shorts?* It's the Sabbath! What are people going to *think* of you?"

Merv played me and said, "Mom, I could take them off if you like. Would that be better?"

Everybody burst out laughing. He was making light-hearted suggestions of what could be said to disarm her when she was being critical.

Play-acting again I asked, "Can you *really* worship the Lord up there doing your volunteer *trail patrol?*"

Merv's response was, "Why, there's one thing *for sure!* I'm *not* going to carry any critical remarks with me. I'll just leave them *all here* so I can have a *really* blessed day."

That's good! He's very clever. I can learn from that!

I told the group there was still a tremendous amount of fear under my brave front, even after dealing with much of this heavy stuff. I fear mother's sarcasm, shaming, and put-downs. I fear what Victor may say later. He's not comfortable with my doing this mountain volunteering either, at least on the Sabbath. I fear that this new relationship with him could still evaporate.

Before group ended, Merv gave me the assignment of writing about my fear. I'm to bring it to the next group therapy session.

At mother's tonight I'll get a chance to practice what I learned in group. Tomorrow morning I'll rise early to drive up to the mountains, check in at the ranger station in Mentone with other volunteers, drive to my assigned trail, don my backpack and head up the trail for a couple days.

In my last session with Lena, she said Victor is fortunate to have me. **Karen: Yes!** She helps so much to replace my shredded self-esteem.

I replied, "God is the one who gave me courage and wisdom to do all the confronting in letters. Although some were really tough and critical, I believe they helped Victor see himself and be willing to grow."

Last night I read to Victor what I wrote about fear. He responded, "My, you have always written well, but that is put so beautifully. You really *do* have deep-seated fears from your childhood." He wanted me to know that he loved me, he wouldn't run, and he wouldn't do the things I feared. This is what I wrote:

> FEAR. What's my fear? What has been my fear? A part of me sees myself to be a "bull" in a "china shop"— huge, rambunctious, unmannered, clumsy, careless, destructive, rough, temperamental. **KAREN: You look *anything but* a bull! I always describe you as elegant.** I'm very afraid of that image of me. I get all these 'wild' ideas—or ideas I'm afraid someone will perceive as wild— and I get a visionary glimpse of goals I want to reach, and just plow into ground zero and 'wing it'—risk it—push for it—regardless of what others think.
>
> Then there is a part of me that sees myself as a shy young fawn in a beautiful forest. She is so dainty and careful and light-footed that the grass and flowers beneath her hoofs only bend but do not break, springing up again with no injury from her passing as she gently forages for her sustenance.

[This insert is not part of my essay, but added during my transcription of the recorded tape: When I read the above to Victor, I didn't feel like crying when I spoke about the bull. But when I described the fawn, I fought back the tears. Right now, just reading it as I type, I have tears wetting my cheeks, and it is difficult for me to read the part about the fawn. I'm not really sure where all this emotion is coming from, except that I want *so enormously much* to be the fawn, and I'm so *scared* that I'm always the bull. At least it feels like my mother and my husband have always seen me as the bull. I had forgotten all about writing any of this, or even recording it, until I just was transcribing it. I realize now that often I *am* the fawn. I just wish my mother and Victor could have seen at least *some* fawn in me, at least *once*, and acknowledged it!] **Karen: Yes!**

When I do gutsy things such as going to be with Jim, whom I'd never met in person before I vacationed with him in his motor home, or such as saying some of the confrontational things to Victor, writing all the negative stuff to him and pushing us to a deeper level both in and out of group--I fear being the bull and wreaking havoc on all those around me. **KAREN: I see this as naive on your part. Your "gutsy" is certainly not "giving up" when you confront Victor (and do so much hiking and mountain climbing in your fifties.) Wow!** But I long to be the delicate fawn who doesn't even fracture a blade of grass as she softly moves around.

I don't fear Victor's anger if it is not repressed or hidden. I don't fear his emotional upsets if he is committed to me. The thing that I fear—terribly—is his anger, rage, bitterness, and resentment he is not fully in touch with and tries to bury or deny. I fear his acting nice to cover the reality of un-nice feelings. **Karen: Yes!** Then I don't know what to expect—whether he'll run away, ignore me, or push me aside. I fear that a whole lot.

And yet I fear that whatever I say or do to try to draw us together will come across to him (or to you, Merv, or the group) as my being the bull in the china shop, when I want to be the fawn in the forest.

Knowing myself—if I had to choose between the bull and the fawn, in an issue of relationship with a loved one, and I really believed the 'bull' would accomplish more in the long run for not only myself but also for the people I love, I'd choose the 'bull' no matter how painful. **Karen: Amen!** I'm trying to learn to tame the bull. The 'fawn' scarcely knows how to protect herself in a peaceful forest. **Karen: Yes!** She is so fragile and tender. The 'bull,' in contrast, has such thick skin that bullets and lion's claws are sometimes repelled. But the nerve endings are still there and the pain is often excruciating.

I want to overcome fearing Victor and fearing myself.

When we went to the 50th reunion of Victor's high school graduating class, many of his friends got up in front and told a bit about their life history. Then it was Victor's turn. "I married a wonderful girl," he said as he pointed to me, "but we've been divorced for some time. I just want to say divorce is a terrible, terrible thing, and we're planning to get back together again."

He seemed to be happy he could say that, but I was emotionally divided. I felt so awkward and ashamed that we had ever divorced; and was so unsure, even now, of our stability, I had to concentrate on what was going on around me to figure out how to act appropriately. My feelings were an oxymoronic conglomeration of good, bad, ecstatic and awful!

About a week later we were working hard together, getting things ready to have a garage sale in June, but took a break and went out to eat. While conversing during the meal, I asked Victor several questions. One was, "Where, in our relationship, or in your relationship with Clarice, did you begin to comprehend *my* pain?"

He took a couple bites on his sandwich and chewed them thoroughly before answering. "I didn't understand it *at all* until *very recently,* when your tears really touched me. Only *now* am I *beginning* to realize you had *any* pain. I was shocked that Clarice called you a couple days after I broke up with her and congratulated you on our getting back together," he continued, "like she kind of expected that's what would happen. Some weeks later she told me she didn't even shed a tear or act depressed for three or four weeks after she got my 'breaking up' phone message. *That* felt like a *put-down* to me and hurt a lot." **Karen: 'Yes. Maybe Clarice was the selfish one.**

I recognized immediately that he was still so involved with his own now-starting-to-be-recognized emotions, that it was difficult for him to even *conceive* another person's pain. So I said, "Well, perhaps that's a little of the way I felt after I long ago told you, 'If you can't be a father to our sons, you can get out,' and you answered, 'Okay, I will!' *That* felt like a *huge* put-down to me *then*. More recently you told me you wanted to leave and didn't intend, *at that time*, to even look back or to fight for the marriage. I still feel the enormous pain of *that*, even right now."

Without a comment, Victor just finished his sandwich and pushed his pickle aside as he wiped his mouth and laid his napkin down very neatly.

Oh how I wish he'd say more!

Since there were no more words for a while, I went on. "I'm thankful you had this relationship with Clarice, because apparently you finally began to get in touch with what you really *want* to do and *like* to do with a person you love. You learned so much from her, and now you are treating *me* better. I have *her* to thank for that."

One day when Victor was kissing me he said, "I *like* French-kissing now."

Quite surprised, I asked, "How did *that* happen to change?"

"I don't know," he answered with a shrug.

Teasing him, I kidded, "Oh, did Clarice teach you to like it?"

"No!" he said *emphatically!* "Actually, it's sort of funny. I once started to French-kiss her and it shocked her."

"What do you mean, 'shocked her'?"

"Clarice said she'd never before been French-kissed." **KAREN: Wow! But I'm not surprised somehow. I have known many older women who thought *all* sexual behavior disgusting. They told me that I'd hate being married. They were wrong!—only talking of their sad experiences.**

"Do you mean she'd been married all those years, and yet had never been French-kissed?" I asked, surprised.

"That's right." Then Victor was totally silent again.

After we got into the car to go home, I talked to him about the time he first French kissed me. He doesn't remember it *at all*. [See Chapter 2, "Horizon"] Then I added, "There may be a *big* relationship between what was bothering you way back then and your being turned off by me sexually during much of our marriage."

Later that day he admitted, "We still need a lot of therapy!"

At my bi-monthly counseling with Lena, I told her about the French kissing and Clarice, and she asked, "Well, did that hurt you?"

"No, not at all. If you're going to marry someone you're in love with and sexually attracted to, it seems a normal part. What really hurt heavily was when Victor admitted he hadn't wanted to be married to me for most of the years we were together. I know I didn't *feel* loved for many years."

One evening when Victor seemed in no hurry to leave, I told him there was something I still needed to talk to him about, but that I'd been scared to previously; he said he had time to listen. I recounted the time Steve Haynes, one of my Forest Service Volunteer friends, had gone up to the cabin with me to help with a heavy task, shortly after Victor first broke up with Clarice. Steve has studied psychology and sometimes does counseling; his wife is a Presbyterian minister. I had poured out my heart to Steve, telling him how much I loved my ex-husband, and was trying to understand him, and also told some things that had happened after Victor and I broke up.

In the past, I have been partnered a number of times with Steve on volunteer trail patrol in the Wilderness. The Forest Service sets up who goes with whom. Recently, because of some last-minute changes, I was unexpectedly partnered with him again. During that time I told him the miraculous changes that have been taking place, and how much I still love Victor. I also divulged some of my fears and my temptation to get married right away. He said, "Oh no. Don't you *dare* get married right away! You and Victor haven't dealt with everything you need to yet." **Karen: Yes!**

I asked him to elaborate. He'd never met Victor, but he had a hunch there was "still more stuff regarding his mother. Probably something sexual." Until that was totally dealt with, he thought there would be problems between Victor and me all over again.

He clarified, "I'm not meaning they went so far as sexual intercourse. But from all you've told me, he never admitted feeling his own sexual excitement towards his mother, and feeling guilty because of it. It is as though he denied ever *having* those feelings, and that's *impossible*, judging from what you've told me. I think he needs somehow to be able to go back and *emotionally* re-experience what happened between them, until he *feels* it and *recognizes* it. It will help him understand better what has caused

435

his blocking. I think he needs to remember it *in such vivid detail*, he will actually *have* those same feelings again."

I was afraid Victor would be angry that I talked to Steve about such intimate things. Amazingly he didn't seem to be bothered *at all*! Last night I reminded Victor of his experience with his mother long ago, when she went to his army Basic Training Graduation when he was eighteen. I said something about the fact that he gave her an enema.

Instantly he exclaimed in angry defense, "No, I *didn't* give her an enema! I didn't *ever* do that! What she asked me to do was look at her hemorrhoid. It was her hemorrhoid she wanted me to check!"

Victor's agitation was obvious, and I felt pity for him in his embarrassment and denial. Very gently and quietly I spoke with tenderness, "Victor, I don't know whether you are aware of this or not, but that's the *third* story you've given me about her coming to your Basic Training graduation."

He gave me a bewildered and almost fearful look. "What on *earth* are you talking about, anyway? He looked aghast, amazed and unbelieving!

"I'm going to carefully tell you something, and I want you to hear it *clearly*." I paused, waiting for some kind of 'permission' from him to go on.

"I'm listening," he finally replied.

"It must have been during the first two or three years of our marriage that something came up about your mother. It seems like it was when we were living in Plainfield, New Jersey. At that time you told me about when she rode on the train across several states to come to your army Basic Training Graduation, I think in Missouri. But when you first told me this, I was so *shocked* at what you were saying that I began to really *pepper* you with questions—interrogate you about *details* right then! Apparently she had traveled two or three days on the rails, and something was bothering her stomach or bowels--maybe she was constipated from her travel—and she asked you to give her an enema. Perhaps being in a doctor's family made that seem not so unusual. The first time you ever told me about this, you said you remembered coming into the hotel room to visit her for the first time since she arrived, and you found her *already undressed*, totally *naked*, and *lying on the bed*. She showed you this already prepared enema bag or can filled with warm water, and asked you to give her an enema. Somehow I never thought of this before, but hotels don't furnish enema bags or cans, so she either brought it with her from home, *planning for this ahead of time*, or else *bought one* after arriving. While you were telling me back then, I thought it was really weird! After you gave me these facts, I didn't discuss it more with you at the time because you seemed embarrassed." That was story number one.

"Much more recently--after we decided to divorce, but before you moved out--I urged you to talk to Merv about this business with your mother—meaning about that enema story--but not actually naming which "business" I meant, because I didn't want to embarrass you again, and I thought you would know what I meant. I was relieved you finally set up the appointment and then went to it. When you came home, I asked what had transpired at your session. You reported that you told Merv about when you were a teenager; your mother would kiss you out on the balcony at night when there was a full moon. She would pull your body tight against herself and wet kiss you all over your face, telling you how *romantic* it was to hug and kiss you in the moonlight. Then when your dad couldn't go on a planned date with her because he had to deliver a baby, she'd take *you* with her *instead* and call you her '*date,*' hold hands with you, kiss and hug you, and treat *you* like her *boyfriend*."

Continuing my questioning about what transpired at that session with Merv, I asked, "Did you tell him about what happened when your mother came to your Basic Training Graduation? You answered yes, but you said you really couldn't quite remember exactly what it was that happened. You remembered she either pulled her nightie up or her pajama pants down for you to check something. You said she had a rash or a pimple or something like that.

"Right then, just after you had returned from seeing Merv, I commented, 'That's not the story you told me years ago.' You cocked your head and your mouth dropped open; you looked bewildered and almost scared. This conversation with Merv took place over a year ago. It is story number two."

He blushed, looking sort of bugged-eyed and said, "Huh? Maybe you're right. Huh-h-h!"

"Now you're telling me about a hemorrhoid," I stated.

With emphatic voice he blurted out, "Oh yes! It was the *hemorrhoid* that she wanted me to check when she was back in Missouri! It was *definitely* the hemorrhoid!"

"You never told me the *hemorrhoid* story before today. That's story number three, a totally new story. These are *three different stories.* They probably are *all true.*"

He looked miserably perplexed and just sat there speechless for several minutes.

After this lengthy silence, I went on. "Maybe there are *more* stories. I don't think you're making up any of them."

He squirmed more and sort of rolled his eyes in thought. "Yes, now that I really *try* to remember, I think probably I *did* at *some* point give my mom an enema. I don't think it was back in Missouri."

"It doesn't really matter where or when it was," I offered. "She stripped naked before you came into the room, had everything ready, and you gave her an enema at *her request.* Maybe it happened *more* than once. And you were probably a teenager. I don't know how you could *help* not having *enormous* sexual feelings."

I saw his body stiffen and a look of steel come into his eyes. "I am so-o-o *disgusted* when *you* or *anyone else* talks about my having *sexual* feelings for my mother! I absolutely *never* had *any* sexual feelings around her!" he exploded with venom and his doubled up fist thrashed the air as though wanting to hit something or somebody very hard!

Astonished at his strong emotional response, I decided not to press the subject. Some other conversation went on for a little while, and then he suddenly said, "Well, I *do* remember *one* time when I *did* feel sexual."

"Tell me about it." I listened very carefully, because I knew this memory was important.

"It was when I was living in the Glendale house; maybe I was eleven or twelve years old. I'd been outside playing and don't know what started it--whether it just happened or whether I had been playing with myself or thinking about stimulating things. Anyway, I had an erection, and mother called me into the house for some reason. As I came in, she looked at me intently and said, 'Oh, what do you have in your pocket? Come here. I want to see what you've got there in your pocket.' She took her hand and reached into my pocket and took hold of my penis and held it and said,

'Ah, you've got a marvelous hard-on!' The sexual feelings were *gigantic!* I felt both *enormously* embarrassed and *tremendously* sexual, and also quite *bewildered* and *definitely guilty!*"

"Victor, your mother *knew* what was going on. She wasn't just curious about what you had in your pocket. She knew *exactly* what it was, and wanted to *touch* it. She may have orgasmed just feeling you. She was such a highly-sexed woman. I wonder if there may be a relationship between your mother's wet kisses and your not liking French-kissing during much of our marriage."

"I never thought of that or put those two things together before." He stood there and turned both palms up in front of his body, like he didn't know what to think, or else gave up something he wanted to keep.

Then I asked, "Did your mother kiss you like this?" I hugged and then kissed him, putting my tongue in his mouth.

"No!" He emphatically shook his head.

"Did she kiss you like this?" and I wet my lips so they were very slippery and I slid them all over his face, making little kissing sounds, then moved to his mouth, touching my tongue lightly to his lips and cheeks and even eyelids.

"Oh, yes!" he giggled. "Yes, *that* was the way she kissed me."

"I *know* that was *very* sensual," I emphasized.

Later in the evening, I asked if tonight's conversation upset him.

"Yes, it did upset me some, but the more I get into these things, the less it bothers me. I'm trying *hard* to remember and to get in touch with my feelings."

I asked what disturbed him most, and he said it was when we were talking about his mother. It wasn't the fact I had talked to Steve about these things; it was mentioning about his having sexual *feelings* when being involved with his mother's actions. He said he wasn't angry with *me*.

Karen: Good. When Victor was able to recognize his mother's sensual behavior with him, he could begin to heal.

When I later told Lena about this she said, "You were giving Victor permission to *feel* and to *remember*. Probably all these stories are true. And there may be more."

To my knowledge, Lena has not had any communication with Merv. They've tried to get together several times to set a time to meet, but haven't.

Previously, when I told Merv about the first two stories, he said, "Hmmm, there are probably more that Victor has just blocked out."

The next day I purposely continued the discussion. I knew Victor needed to talk more, although he didn't realize it yet. "It seems Steve was right that you really *need* to get in touch with your feelings. No one is accusing you of doing more than you've told. It's just that you <u>must,</u> being <u>a normal male, have had an extremely strong sexual response to your</u> <u>mother's overtures.</u> **KAREN: My underlining. Cross out "overtures"** **and change it to *sexual abuse!* <u>Any</u>** teenage boy whose mother holds him up tight against her body so he can feel her breasts, and then caresses him and wet kisses him all over his face and lips, would be set up to feel *raging* sexual urges! And it would be *doubly* so if his mother told him how romantic *she feels* in the full moonlight and treats him like her boyfriend. It would be *abnormal* for a boy *not* to feel a powerful sexual response."

Victor's voice again became loud and angry—literally yelling. "*I want you to know I NEVER had ANY sexual feelings around my mom! When she did those things it just felt good, not sexual!* This Steve guy doesn't know my mom or me! I do *not* have, and *never have* had, sexual feelings regarding my mom!"

"I believe you! And that makes me admire you even more!" was my quick but calm response. "That *proves* you were a fine Christian young man and had *very high* moral standards! You wouldn't have considered *allowing* yourself to even *think* of such things, let alone *feel* them."

Victor's tension slowly abated, and he began to relax. I *knew* I had to be cautious in whatever I said now. "Do you remember when your mom walked in on us without knocking when *we* were naked on the bed a year or two after we married?"

"Yes," he answered.

"She acted *so excited*, both in her tone of voice and her movements; she stayed long enough that I think she probably had an orgasm while she was looking at us. She didn't actually *ask* us to have sex and let her watch, but she said she "just *loved* watching my son love his wife. It makes me feel so, so *good*!" I think *she* got sexual satisfaction out of a *lot of her actions with you!* Do you remember a program we went to with your mom, given by Bob Larson many years ago, telling 'why rock music was bad?'"

"Yes," he nodded.

"Bob Larson played some of the 'bad' music to demonstrate. Afterwards, while your mom and I were walking out to the car, separate from you, she said, 'I can see why that music is bad. My fu fu was just a-vibrating.' I figured she must mean she had an orgasm while listening to Larson's demonstration. After we got home, I told you what she said, and you agreed that's what she meant."

Now I wonder <u>how he "knew"</u> that was what she meant. **Karen: Yes! Sexual abuse destroys boundaries and one's ability to create them.**

Apparently when we first married, Victor's concept of privacy was non-existent. I reminded him now that he had told me about his mom *often* taking a bath in the tub in the same open, uncurtained bathroom while he was shaving, or walking in on him while he was using the toilet. He grew up with *no bodily privacy*. He also said he had no special cupboard or drawer to call his own. His grandmother was taking things in and out of his drawers, cupboards and closet daily, since he shared a bedroom with her when he was home from about age ten until we married.

There was another event he had related to me earlier in our marriage regarding a time he was maybe about twenty-two years old and his adopted baby sister, Aimee, was around two. He wanted to speak with his mother, so went up the stairway leading to her bedroom where the door was open. When he got to the doorway, he observed both his mom and baby sister giggling, playing and having a great time. They were both totally naked, and his mom, sitting on the edge of the bed, was holding Aimee up above her lap, facing her, mom's hands around Aimee's waist, while she "taught" Aimee to "bat" mom's breasts around, back and forth with her little hands, like a game, and both were laughing hard about it. Victor's mom saw him at the door and apparently *wanted* him to watch their antics, because she continued the play for some time as Victor watched. When I brought this up to him now, Victor said he didn't at that time think anything was out of place, because he "knew mothers nursed their babies." But when I mentioned that his mom had never nursed Aimee because she was adopted, and I thought that maybe the *play* was all right, but not while a grown son was watching, he said it never *occurred* to him it might not be appropriate.

"But *my* own mother and father never let me see either of them naked until they were very old and ill and needed help in caring for themselves,"

I exclaimed, still hardly comprehending the magnitude of his accepting all of this unquestioningly.

Victor just shrugged, so I continued, "No matter *what* your mother did, that will not make me disrespect her memory. She was a *wonderful* mother-in-law. I think she was a fine Christian. But she was a *human being*, and she probably had needs that weren't always being met. When a person is sexually excited, they can do crazy things and not always think things through. I will *not* criticize or blame your mother. In fact, I--just at this moment--thought of something that never entered my mind before. Do you remember the discussion we had very early in our marriage, after your mother told me she was conceived during the *one and only* time her mother had sexual intercourse with her father?"

"Well, what about it?" he asked rather sarcastically.

"I remember your mother telling me that *her* mother--*your* grandma--said that her *father* --your *grandpa*--believed sexual intercourse was very sinful, except for the explicit purpose of procreation. **KAREN: Yes. Common Christian belief.** He refused to have sex with his wife, your grandma, except for *one time only*, after which he knelt by the bed and pleaded aloud with God to forgive him for his terrible sin. That one-time-only resulted in your mother being born. I believe this man eventually ended up in a mental hospital, didn't he?"

Victor nodded silently.

We both sat and pondered all this in silence for quite a while. Finally I spoke again. "I wonder if your grandmother talked about her husband so critically to your mom, that at some point your mom made a decision to bring up her children to *like* sex--so they wouldn't be like their grandfather. To me, that is an intriguing idea! Your mother may have been so affected by her *mother's* story that she swung the pendulum too far in the *other* direction. **KAREN: Or maybe she was abused also. Sounds like Grandma didn't have good boundaries either. We really don't know.** That would certainly fit in with all this. Your grandma's marriage didn't last long, and you say you have no memory of your grandfather. Could that idea be possible?"

"That makes sense to me," Victor finally admitted. "I'll try to think of it that way."

"And I certainly don't blame *you!* It's *not wrong* for a boy to have a sexual response toward his mother when he is treated that way. It's *normal*. Because you are a Christian, and because you wanted to be *good*, it was *normal* to try to block those feelings and bury them--cover them and determine to *never* remember them again! Apparently that's what you've done. **KAREN: Very kind and gentle response!** "Victor, I don't have *any* bad feelings against you because of this. Right now you have no memory of *any* sexual response to your mom's actions. I believe that's very *normal* for a sincere, honest and respectful boy or man. It also tells me your feelings were <u>**very**</u> blocked! **KAREN: Underlining and boldface are mine.** They probably *had to be* for you to live comfortably in the situation."

So apparently talking about not only what Victor's mother did to him physically and sexually, but especially *his response to it*, is what upset him. At least he had a chance to begin to look at it.

I reminded Victor that Merv suggested he pursue following through regarding his dream about the bed. Merv thought there was some significance that the dream was about Victor's being on a *bed* outside the building, and being rescued through the *bathroom* window. He thought there was enough significance for Victor to pursue that in his recall. I think Merv was telling Victor to pursue his subconscious. Victor said he realized it was okay to go ahead and dream some about that. "But I don't know how to make myself dream, and I haven't dreamed more."

I responded, "It was either Lena or Merv who recently said they wouldn't be a bit surprised if you begin to experience flashbacks, because you're open and willing to remember, and you're talking about it. So you *may* start remembering more."

Lena said Victor was going through what many women go through when they're having flashbacks about sexual abuse from their father. **Karen: Yes!** She says right now it's the "in thing" for *women* to talk about their sexual abuse from their fathers. But it's probably extremely difficult for a man, because it's not the "in thing" to talk about sexual abuse from their mothers. **KAREN: It's difficult for men to be vulnerable to women. Often they tell about it as though it is a sexual escapade, *especially* if it is an older woman.**

I woke up at 4:30 one morning and couldn't sleep any more. I started remembering conversations that had taken place in the last week or two and I am still amazed at Victor. Somewhere along the way I asked him at what point he felt like there was real change that took place in either of us. He said it was mostly *after* he broke up with Clarice, although there were some times before that. One of them was when he came over to discuss about selling the house. He was *amazed* I didn't manipulate him or try to force issues. He felt some real love that night, momentarily.

Another thing I recently asked him was, "At what point did you really want to get *out* of the marriage?"

"I can't put my finger on it, but it's like *years and years—long* before you ever mentioned the possibility of divorce. I was *very unhappy* and wanted to have a fling, and see what it was like to be with other women. *I felt sorry for myself being married.*" **KAREN: Dangerous, eh?**

Another time I asked him, "If you had never known about my affairs, would you still have wanted out?"

"Oh yes! I *would* have! I don't think *that* would have made much difference!" **KAREN: Victor, do you know why? VICTOR: I couldn't seem to do *anything* that pleased Judy.** [Right now, as Victor and I are discussing this, and making small changes or additions that Karen has suggested, I'm feeling *condemned* by Victor. I asked him for examples regarding the above question. I didn't usually even *think* or *imagine* anything to criticize or complain to Victor about except for our *relationship*. But I *did* speak up when I felt angry or hurt when he destroyed something he knew I loved. Just now he gave me the example of the plum tree we used to have at the Bradbury house. I had never especially liked or bought plums at the store prior to living there. But *these* plums were superb! I loved them! I *talked* about how delicious they were! But scads of little shoots kept coming up around the plum tree trunk that annoyed Victor. He often complained about all those "messy" shoots, and periodically clipped them off. One day I looked out in the yard and the plum tree had been sawed off at ground level and was lying on the ground. I gasped and let out a cry. I wept for that tree. Victor hadn't previously mentioned cutting it down, and I was in shock! I believe it's the man's responsibility to take care of the yard, and I loved most all the things he did. We had wonderful gardens, and he kept everything beautifully planted, mowed and trimmed. I tried to make a point frequently of telling him how much I liked what he did in the yard and thanking him. But *just now* he brought up the plum tree—using *that* as an example of how he could *never* do anything right. Yes, I cried then, and again am experiencing tears at the moment. I've never again eaten a plum that tasted like those. Since then I usually don't even look at or buy plums. They remind me of my pain.] **Karen: Victor heard Judy talk about her love of this plum tree, that these were the best plums she had ever eaten, then he cut it down-and didn't even apologize for it. He did not even see Judy, he only saw himself and the plum tree. And then blamed her for not appreciating his handiwork.**

"Would you have fallen for Clarice and wanted to get married?"

"Yes, I think so, even if I hadn't known about your affairs."

So apparently my affairs weren't the problem at all. It seems like he tried to set me up to have them -- over and over.

I continued to question him more, trying hard to understand all of this history. "If I had never gone with Jim and gotten engaged, would that have made any difference?"

Victor's demeanor then changed, and he sat forward in his chair. "There was the matter of *competing* with you to find someone else *right away!* Yes, that probably made me want to get married even sooner!"

All of these things are painful, because I have been constantly searching by self-introspection, prayer, study and reading how to be the best wife possible. I never dreamed of trying to **compete** *with Victor! I wanted to draw him out, help him build self-esteem, and inspire him to be the kind of man I thought he wanted to be. It didn't bring results from him until only recently, but I have grown enormously because of it!* **KAREN: A lot of your marriage was competition. Victor worried he wouldn't look good--holy or masculine. Am I correct? VICTOR: Yes, except being more holy or masculine wasn't my goal. I just needed to know I was good enough to be Judy's husband.** I, Judy, competed only with myself—trying to get better each year at everything—than the year before. Competition never entered my imagination. I always looked to Victor as my superior and thought it was supposed to be that way. That's why I tried so hard to please him. I didn't have even a hint (that I recognized) that Victor might be trying to compete with me. That would have seemed ludicrous.

Victor brought up the fact that he believed for many years of our married life that it was wrong, even *sinful*, to get counseling. There also were *lots* of things about sex that he thought were sinful, and he felt guilty. "Now," he says, "I realize God *created* sex, and it's beautiful!" He's so happy that Merv, our counselor, helped bring him to this understanding. **Karen: Yes, that's wonderful!**

We again reminisced about all those years he thought I was controlling. He had used the words *domineering, overpowering* and *overbearing* many times, like I was trying to run the family. This was so far from my mind, because I believed *strongly* the man should be the leader, and I *encouraged* him to take the leadership role. Yet he had really *believed* I *wanted* to run the family. That was *his perception*.

I asked him, "Did it ever occur to you to say to me anything such as, 'Judy, it seems like when you do or say that, you sound like you are trying to run our family? I believe the *man* should be the leader. I really feel upset about it. We need to talk about it. We need to work some of these things through.' Did you ever *want* to ask me that?"

"No," Victor said. "It would have been so *foreign* to me to even *imagine* asking or telling you anything about how I *felt*. I was brought up believing I should *submit*."

More recently I've asked *who* taught him "to submit," and *how* did they teach him to believe he *must* submit. He said he has no idea! He just always believed it. And he even *today feels* the same way—that he *should* submit to women and to *everyone* in authority. He has to consciously remind himself that is *not* true, and use *will power* to change his automatic response that might be inappropriate. In other words, he has to *work* at not submitting. **KAREN: It was the abuse by Victor's mom and Grandma's domination. Also, Victor's long hospital stay required him to comply with everyone else's instructions while he was so physically helpless as a child.**

VICTOR: Because my dad was a doctor and my mother was a secretary/receptionist in his office and gone much of the time, my Grandma was my "Nanny" and took care of me as long as I can remember. There were pluses and advantages in having both a nanny and a mom, but I saw my Dad really chafe and give in to Grandma

and Mother. From that I learned that submission was the name of the game and that zipping your lip was a wise idea.

Another idea he shared was, "Until I was in therapy group, I *never* had the concept that marriage *could* be a union of two *equals*. I really believed either the woman ran the house, the life, and the marriage, or the man ran it. The idea of people being equal, pulling *together*, talking over plans *mutually* was totally foreign. It never crossed my mind, even though you *tried* to discuss that with me. It was *impossible* for me to *imagine* two people working together."

He said that getting married had actually been a very scary thing for him. He knew that the man *should* be the head of the family, but that absolutely petrified him! He even had highly resented my *telling him* I believed the man was to be the head of the family, and *asking him* to take responsibility. He felt THAT was my domineering him! He didn't *want* to be leader. **KAREN: His was afraid because he would be blamed for anything that went wrong.** He deliberately *refused* to take responsibility and purposely *forced* me into the leadership role. He *wanted* me to be the leader, "Damned if you do, and damned if you don't" and that's the way he thought he liked it, even though I was dragging my feet all the way and trying to change it.

Apparently he got so angry that he decided he would *have* to take over! He *resented* my leadership, so started doing bullish things to my property (my poem book, my grocery cart, and my carefully dug-up bulbs) just to show me who was boss.

He said he remembered, when I wanted to talk to him about our relationship early in our marriage, that he *made a decision then* to absolutely *not* communicate, because that's the way it was *supposed to be!* He told me he had *really believed the man should just suffer through it,* like he saw his father doing. **Victor: My Dad totally submitted to my Grandmother—never raised his voice against her. Very rarely did he raise his voice or stand up to my mother.** Since I was a strong woman, he would just *let* me run his life. **KAREN: Like the women were in Victor's house when he was a kid.** That's why he wanted to leave me and find a "passive" woman. He admits that most of his life he had a habitual "poor me" attitude about nearly everything.

Last night he said again, "I believe most of this stuff was only what was going on *in my head.*"

I talked about all of this to Lena at our last counseling session and she said, "You've got to realize there is *no* person--there is *no* woman--who could have been married to him who could have been any different. It was like you were in the *wrong* place at the *wrong* time. He just wasn't *ready* to love. **KAREN: A woman clear about who she is wouldn't be in this marriage!** There was *no possible way* to change that!" **Karen: God can change that!**

Now, sometime later, I'm thinking, I really *am* a beautiful, tamed female 'bull' that still seems like a young heifer, and at times kicks up her heels and prances through the forest with such agility that the trees and flowers and other animals laugh and dance with her.

When we were at the cabin recently I took the tape recorder and played for Victor the recording of a talk I gave at mother's retirement home last year. I wanted him to hear this devotional, because he has never known my capabilities in public speaking; I had secretly *wanted* to be a co-speaker with him. I also played the tape I made January 8 -- on the way to church [see chapter 23, "Release"], explaining that my purpose in recording it was to rid myself of my horrible, awful feelings of rejection and abandonment.

As we listened to the prayer, tears streamed from my eyes. Even now it was still very touching to me and so poignantly showed my pain. Victor shed tears also and was very warm and loving, and he apologized profusely for the grief he had caused. **Karen: Fabulous!** He wanted to know if he should play it for our group therapy, but I thought it too long and too personal. (On the original tape it was over a half hour long.)

The other day I told Steve that sometimes I am tempted to get married to Victor right away.

He said, "No mother. No! No! Don't! Don't! *Please* be consistent. Follow through on what you've decided. It's going to be good for you and Daddy to wait awhile. Please follow through on what you've planned."

Karen: Very smart son!

I told that to Victor and he seemed shocked that Steve would say that.

Recently I had a conversation with Genevieve Chinnock about my affairs and the fact that Victor told lots of people about them. I now shared with Victor what she told me about this: "Judy, folks have put you on a pedestal--both of you. When they hear about this, you may have more people coming to you for encouragement and counsel, or for someone just to listen to them pour out their stories. Now they'll see you as human, and not being up in the clouds on a pedestal. You may have your work cut out for you in the future."

Regarding this, I said to Victor, "I don't know yet what God's plan is for us. You've talked about wanting to do the Lord's work and wanting to get back into chaplain's work or something like that. Maybe our work is going to be different. Maybe you and I will share, whether one-to-one, in small groups, or publicly. We can tell about our struggles through marriage and what we have learned. I want to be vulnerable and willing to share as much as is appropriate, publicly or privately, whatever will help other people grow. I want to acknowledge what I've done wrong. Both of us need to admit our mistakes. I don't know whether we are ready to do that yet or not."

Victor didn't turn off from this idea. He feels there's something ahead for us. Perhaps we can be of help to other couples. We can testify that God *can* change hearts, can *change us*! His power is so much greater than our comprehension; the unexpected and "unreal" *can* happen! It doesn't always happen the way we *want* it, or the way we *expect* it, but God knows best! We are safe turning our life over to him totally, and putting Him in charge. I want so very much to be able to share that with others.

Last night Victor asked me when we could read another chapter in the book Pastor Jerold loaned us, <u>Restoring a Loving Marriage</u>, by Jake Hessner. We have finished four chapters, and *he's* the one pressing for us to read more. I'm pleased. No, I'm thrilled!

I went to the cabin yesterday morning and hiked back out in the afternoon, a total of eight miles. I had invited some of the singles from both my Thursday night Divorce Recovery Group and the Tuesday night Healing Workshop to hike with me, so I waited at trail head for them, but they didn't show. I went anyway to carry several things in for cabin use. While there I slept, wrote in my journal, and watered some flowers. I slept really well that night after all my exercise.

Victor came over this evening to read more in the excellent book, <u>Restoring a Loving Marriage</u>, by Jake Hessner, that his pastor recommended. Following chapter five we got to talking more and I asked, "Are you aware of how much you have matured in the last few months?"

He seemed a little unsure of what I meant.

I elaborated: "You are relating in so much more of a mature way. You are taking charge of your life. You're being assertive. You are choosing what to read and setting up times to read with me, and you're inviting me on dates and planning things to do. You scarcely ever took charge of things before, and I see wonderful maturity evolving. You are noticing my needs and trying to find out how to meet them. You're more loyal to me. All of these things I see as your growing more stable. Do you have any idea as to how or when that started?"

"I think God is working miracles in my life," he said. "I think God has done it. He's changing me *inside*!" **KAREN: Amen! Like the Prodigal Son, and also like Saint Paul in the New Testament.**

"I think so too. You are a walking miracle, Victor. God has definitely changed you. Do you think the dream you had affected that?"

"I think so," he answered.

"I'm so proud of you! The time has come to tell you something I've wanted to tell you for a long time, but didn't think you were ready for it. I discussed with Lena about telling you this. She said I'm probably the only one who can tell you and get away with it."

"Go ahead and tell me," he encouraged.

"After you had broken up with me and gone back to Clarice, Burt said to me, 'Something must have happened a long time ago in Victor's life. His emotional maturing just stopped. He never grew emotionally past that point. He is stuck emotionally back in his childhood around age two. Something happened in the relationship *with his mother* where he literally was blocked, and stopped growing *emotionally*, but not in other respects. He's had very good success in taking charge of his life in many other ways, but *emotionally* he's been relating to life like a two-year old!' That's what Burt told me, but I don't see you that way now."

Victor took a long, deep breath and just smiled.

"I'm telling you now only because I feel it is in the past. Burt did not discuss this with Lena nor did he discuss it with Merv. But around the same time, probably within the same month, Lena and Merv also, each separately, told me practically the same thing. Lena used the words "infantile" and Merv mentioned the age of his grandson, who was three at that time. They all said something happened to you at age two or three that completely blocked your emotional growth. So until very recently, you have been reacting emotionally from that age."

Victor sat for a long time before saying, "I haven't the remotest idea what that might have been." **KAREN: Victor was eight when his brother died and *his mother was away from home when that happened*. It could be a double whammy of abandonment.**

I responded that I didn't think it was necessary to know, and anyway now he was changing and maturing at a high rate of speed.

30

RAINBOW

Today is my birthday, June 13, 1994—and also the day Victor *had been planning to marry Clarice.* So much trash has been excavated and thrown out from both our lives, and the "dumpsters" are still in the process of hauling it away. My Life Gardener (Jesus Christ) has been raking up the windblown leaves of my traumas and putting things in order. As a birthday treat I'm invited to go over to Victor's apartment complex by 10:00 a.m. and share the Jacuzzi with him again. Following that, he'll favor me with another satisfying massage, which works wonders on the tension and pain in my back and shoulders.

We had lunch together, and he gave me a $50 check and a box of bath soap bars that looked and smelled like roses. He also gave me a massage that was wonderfully relaxing. I came home and slept soundly. My birthday was superb!

Victor came over in the evening because, Rudy and Rosemary, and Alan came with a birthday cake, candles and ice cream and sang "Happy Birthday" to me, since we were in therapy group the night before. It was wonderful to have our family together, and Victor was the epitome of a loving and caring husband and father the entire day of my birthday.

Today is the Fourth of July. In a recent group therapy session we were assigned to read and later report on Paul Tournier's book, <u>To Resist or</u>

<u>Surrender</u>. Victor and I each wrote our reports today at his apartment and the following is what I learned from reading the book:

This book did several things for me. It:

1. Inspired me to want to grow into an ever more deepening personal relationship with God and the other important people in my life.

2. Helped me verbalize more clearly what I was already discovering: that problems and dilemmas don't always necessarily require "solving," but instead may need "altering" by the perspectives, attitudes and insights within us. They may metamorphose so greatly that the perception of the 'problem' changes. That 'alteration' takes place in a seemingly miraculous way as we enter into a relationship with someone (God or significant person) where the telling, sharing, listening, and mutual identification with both empathy and understanding, create a bond between the two. This bonding, or fusion, is the catalyst for transformation--maturing, inner growth--a becoming more in tune with, or in sync with other relationships. It is similar to the concept of my drawing a large enough circle to take "him" in after he drew a small circle around himself that excluded me.

3. Made me realize that my greatest periods of growth have come about many times in connection with my relationships with certain individuals. I was suicidal some years ago. I am not now, and don't believe I ever will be again. My catalyst for change two weeks before the carefully planned suicide was a two-hour conversation with a person, almost a stranger, who said he felt impressed I needed someone to talk to. I went away feeling life was worth living, and I was worth living it! Many relationships since then, with therapists, friends and some near 'strangers,' have stimulated and cultivated who I have become and continue to become.

In the process of writing this report (in Victor's presence, in his apartment, after many previous deep conversations in the mountains), I realize that part of the miracle of Victor's change has come about precisely because of what took place in his relationship with Clarice. Although he thought he loved me when we married, he was so blocked, so stymied in emotional growth, so filled with powerful negative emotions stemming from his early childhood, that it was literally impossible for him to have the kind of deep relationship Tournier discusses and describes in his book, and which I wanted and worked hard to achieve. Victor's only hope was to have that kind of transforming relationship somewhere *outside* of his marriage responsibilities.

Not until he got away from me, experienced his aloneness, recognized his personal need for self-responsibility, went to group therapy, and began to experience intimate sharing and understanding in a new context, was he ready to start to *feel* and to *love*. Even though I perceive his love for Clarice was not a deep, long-lasting, long-term-commitment kind of love, (because it hadn't had enough time and proximity) I believe it was far deeper than he had ever before experienced. It was real, and was felt and recognized as *feeling*. It was believed-in to an intensely greater level than he had experienced with me. He only then began to recognize what it means to love and be loved.

I believe it was that very relationship with Clarice that had the transforming power to change him. It (the relationship) created, along with God's power, the miracle of awakening a self-understanding within Victor that made him see me in a new way. I believe that if it were not for what Clarice and Victor shared and experienced, I would not have the blossoming, thriving, exciting relationship of intimacy I have with him today. I can thank God for Clarice, and I can and will thank Clarice for the gift she gave me.

Victor's report was quite long, so only a small part of it is included here:

> Tournier explores the unconscious influences, the life experiences and memories that determine whether a person resists or capitulates in any given situation. He marshaled some resistance in me because he exposed my favorite weapon--obstinate silence. . . .**KAREN: Your Power! VICTOR:** *Now* **I am convinced that silence** *destroys* **a marriage and superficiality just does not**

"cut it." Honest, forthright communication is what is needed: How you *feel* about things and not just head knowledge. Trying to skirt the *real* problem and talk about peripheral issues doesn't work either, even though I tried that for so many years.

In the last chapters, Tournier gives us the answer to the dilemma of when to resist and when to surrender. "If, then, thought is both so necessary and so difficult and in any case, never sufficient, can we count on divine guidance? Yes, I believe this. But there again we must realize that it is no easy path." He further states that by depending upon God's guidance, we obtain the greatest freedom. That was when he really stepped on my toes and got to "meddling." "What is the will of God? Are we not in danger of ascribing to him our own decisions?" That is *exactly* what I did! Ouch, that smarts! . . .

James 4:7 (KJV) gives us the good advice: "Resist the devil and he will flee from you." I don't think the devil reads lips, because when I tell him to get lost, he is all the more persistent. I wonder if he can tell by my actions that I really don't mean it? . . . **KAREN: Powerful insight. We can see that in others also when they don't mean what they say. That's a lack of integrity!**

Dr. Tournier does not come up with pat answers as to why God is sometimes silent when we plead with him for answers. There is the problem of our limited language. We may be asking the wrong question. We may not be ready for the answer. We may not even understand an answer at the time. **KAREN: If we wait on the Lord, He will give the right question.**

Or God may want us to grow and mature. God may want me to persevere or change my attitude. So, what does He do instead of giving us pat answers? He many times turns around and asks us a different question like He did Job, or like Jesus did with the Scribes and Pharisees! Job did receive an answer, but not one that he expected. He received <u>an *experience* of God instead, a revelation of God that changed his attitude.</u>" **KAREN: My underlining.**

This letter, written by Victor, was done as an assignment for group therapy.

August
Dear Judy,

This is a goodbye letter, a divorce letter, a divorce of *old* relationship—*not* shutting or locking the door to a new relationship.

After we first met, I had a vision of loveliness, a queen, a proper lady for a proper preacher. You are an upbeat person with a positive attitude, a very caring woman, a devoted mother, and an organized, talented, beautiful Christian lady. You put me through the seminary and stuck with me, even when I physically and verbally abused you. I tried to fool you into believing I was a "take-charge" person, a head of the household who knew what he was doing, and you were to be the demure preacher's wife who was to go along with everything I said. Well, that didn't work, so I took the comfortable, well-worn path of the passive, dutiful husband who let *you* make all the decisions (nearly all). For most of our married life you mothered me. You took care of the finances, worked outside the home and did a fine job of raising two boys as well as two foster boys. **KAREN: How much of this was the Christian culture to be perfect, no matter what? And how much came from "woundedness?"**

Do you remember the time the conference president asked me, "Who wears the pants in your family?" **KAREN: Insulting question and wrong question!** I should have told him the truth and said Judy does. [I, Judy, the person writing this book, felt furious when I first read this, because I *detested* the concept of a woman "wearing the pants in the family." **KAREN: This is an insulting question to women!** But now I realize that in Victor's *mind* I *did* make all the decisions because he *refused* to and *forced* me to make them by his passivity and *non*-action. In this letter he was being his *new*, truly *honest* self!] I still had some pride and some concern for your feelings, as I said that you didn't make *all* the decisions. And then I mumbled something about needing to be more assertive in getting decisions for baptisms. This man was questioning my fitness for the ministry because I wasn't baptizing anyone. I suppose it was about that time I began being resentful and hostile toward you. I had been taught, and *really believed*, that marriage counselors and psychologists turned a person or a couple away from God! Certainly a preacher of the "Word" didn't need that kind of counsel! **KAREN: I know another minister who says that. He divorced his wife also.**

The "dance of anger" began in earnest when you asked to *talk about* problems. I said, "Yes, we have problems, but I'm *not* going to a counselor. We will *sweep the problems under the rug* and go on ignoring them."

I'm sure that somewhere, along about that time, I began "putting my Grandmother's face on you," and I became more hostile. The more you wanted intimacy, the more I *purposely* withdrew. The more I withdrew, the more you wanted intimacy. Dr. Lerner, in the book <u>The Dance of Anger</u>, gives her description of this kind of relationship. She says the vast majority of couples she sees have the same problem. Most women are *overfunctioners* in the field of emotions, and most men are *underfunctioners* emotionally. The more the man underfunctions (withdraws), the more the female overfunctions (becomes emotional). **KAREN: Yes. Good book.** I believe this is the basis for most of our marriage problems. I sensed that you were angry with me at times. I'm not blaming you, because it is a natural reaction to my hostility toward you.

I hereby declare that I am divorcing anger! With your consent and agreement, I want to bury the past, with all the blaming game, the hostility and the anger. May it be buried so deep that the "ax handle" can never be found again. Goodbye old relationship. You are divorced, buried, cast into outer darkness. **KAREN: That's burying and denying anger once again. Anger is part of being human.**

Your divorceable husband,
Victor

October: As an assignment for group therapy, Judy wrote this book report on <u>Soul Mates</u>, by Thomas Moore.

I have learned from this book that it is <u>more important to nourish my soul, observe and reflect on Victor's soul, and tend to the care and feeding of the relationship's soul than trying to be a perfect wife or person, or expecting Victor to be a perfect husband or person.</u> **Karen: Amen!**

I am very glad I stayed with Victor through all these years of tensions and lack of intimacy. I would not be with him in our wonderful relationship today if I had not. But even if we *weren't* together now, I believe my growth/metamorphosis is very great, because I learned to survive the tensions, problems and paradoxes. It pays, in the long run, to *not run away* just because of pain or problems. <u>The book helped me realize that my experience with music, both as a listener and as a performer, has also fed my soul! My many hours alone in the mountains have also contributed greatly</u>.

<u>Soul Mates</u> has built a desire in me to increase the breadth and depth of my imagination. It has taught me that wallowing in guilt blunts sensitivity, and self-hatred blocks wisdom and maturity. Accepting and welcoming the <u>shadow side of Victor</u> and myself, creatively, broadens my perspective and infuses me with vitality. It also opens new doors to possibilities, such as trusting and nurturing my intuition, which enhances awareness of my soul speaking. **KAREN: Hopefully Victor can continue to see his**

shadow side. The more we open that shadow side to ourselves and to God, He puts His uncreated light in to replace it, so actual honest change happens.

Pain and suffering *may* be part of the *initiation of new growth*, rather than a sign of problems in a relationship. It can help us reach new levels of intimacy. **Karen: Yes, That's true and good.**

I can be most truly myself when in *relationship with* others. Therefore, developing intimacy and closeness with friends and/or spouse helps me become more of who God planned for me to be, *embracing all of life*.

Victor's growth has become super-fast! Unbelievable! I am ready to marry him! So last night I finally confirmed, "Yes, I will remarry you." He was so excited! He absolutely bubbled with new life! Everybody had told us it needed to be at least a year before we remarried. February 7 was when he and Clarice first broke up. Oh, what a rocky road it was for months after that. Now we are debating if we should wait until *after* Feb. 7. We talked some about having a Valentine wedding.

November: We have continued regularly in therapy and are still learning more about how to be good communicators. We spent several days and dates discussing what sort of a wedding service we would like, where we want to have it, and also the possibility of getting married on the *anniversary* of our first marriage. Yesterday we finally chose to get married on our anniversary, December 22, even though that date is about six weeks short of a year. **Karen: Great!**

I was working on a therapy assignment, listing all the times my mother had criticized me for things which really weren't wrong, but for which she felt embarrassed or ashamed. **Karen: Her narcissism blocked her from seeing you as a separate person!** I had mentioned in group that most of what I could remember were times after I finished elementary school. Merv Jenson suggested I might be repressing <u>some from a younger age</u>, and it might help to write anything more that I remembered with my left hand, which I did. I thought of four or five more after that, and they were from a much younger age.

After spending parts of several days working on the list, I made even more time for trying to remember, because I had learned that *when we* *talk about our trauma memories and <u>work through them, they don't remain</u> <u>"buried" where they can mess up our "today" lives</u>.* **Karen: Amen!**

I awoke one morning during that remembering period, turned up the heat and returned to bed for the specific purpose of spending time trying to think of more things mother had said, or more times she had hurt me with her shaming episodes. While in this frame of reference, I apparently dozed off for a very short while—maybe only seconds. When I awoke, I realized I had dreamed--not about an event, but about a single scene. More important than what I *saw*, were the *three words* that came to me with power and fervency.

The scene: A man lying on a wicker couch on his right side in sort of a curved position. [There was a wicker couch in our living room until I was about six] In front of him, lying and facing the same direction as he faced, was a baby—maybe one or two years old—curled up with her back against the man's belly. The man was sort of curved around the baby, cuddling it. It seems like I saw the scene for only a second or two, but these words blasted into my mind: "GOLDEN PARADOX RETRIEVER." I was instantly wide-awake and baffled and began to reflect on it all.

"Golden" is something of great value. "Paradox" is a pair of opposites in life that help the soul to grow and thrive. "Retriever" brings back something that was lost or maybe never owned previously. This very scene seemed to me to be *the* Golden Paradox Retriever. I decided Victor was the man, and that I—or the little hungry, hurting child in me—was the baby. This child-part of me was now being cuddled, nurtured and protected in a way I don't remember receiving from either my mother or my father, although I always knew they loved me and considered me important. I now had a supportive, encouraging man in my life.

Looking at this dream made me realize that anything and everything of true value that I need to retrieve from the past, *can* be reinstated precisely because of the fact that *now* I am being supported, nurtured, cuddled and *valued*. I will be able to discover many paradoxes in my life that will aid my learning and growth.

As I pondered more on this dream I began to realize how much Clarice had unknowingly fostered my growth. Almost before I realized it, I felt a growing appreciation and affection for her. Soon I felt impelled to write to her. The first letter was written July 4 in Victor's apartment when we were writing book reports, but Merv and our group said not to send it for at least a year.

I waited only five months, because I wanted Clarice to get it before we remarried.

Written July 4 but sent Dec. 7, 1994.

Dear Clarice,

I have just shared with Victor the thoughts I am now going to put down on paper for you. In our therapy group we were assigned to read a small book by Paul Tournier, To Resist or To Surrender. Then we were each to write our impressions of the contents, and discuss them with each other. While doing this, I began to realize you have given me a great gift. I believe Victor was so blocked, so in denial of his emotions and his reality, so filled with intense negative emotions and self-hate--all of this from childhood long before he ever met me--that it was impossible for him to truly love *anyone*. How could someone who hated himself and had a love-hate relationship with the significant women of his early life, be able to reach out to love someone else? Apparently his leaving me and getting therapy were important steps in his growth.

During this process, he apparently learned to explore his depths and share his pain, so that he was able to start growing and maturing. It brought him to the place where he was ready to learn what real love is. Then he met you. At that point he was now beginning to be assertive and self-responsible, to think about other's needs, and to define what he really wanted and how he needed to grow. I believe he began to truly *feel*, both love given and love received, for the first time in his life. Prior to our divorce, he had ordered me to never *ask* him how he felt, because he didn't know what he felt and didn't *want* to know. But now you were there for him, and he was there for you at

461

the right timing. Evidently he no longer *needed* to analyze and guess what real love was supposed to look like. He no longer *needed* to put on an act and force his behavior to fit that supposed mold. He began to be assertively spontaneous. He began to relish fun instead of feeling guilty for having it. He began to look at what he *really* liked, what brought him joy, and no longer was he locked into his people-pleaser mode.

He must have, at that time, started giving love to you from his deepest heart, which he was just discovering, and you must have responded from your deepest heart, which I'm going to guess you had somewhat buried because of your own past. Your relationship flourished because it was *genuine* and not faked to impress someone. I can imagine you both slowly began to recognize the jewels of the other, the fabulous inner beauty God has placed within each of us, but which few comprehend. You both must have begun to see a glimmer of the glory of your real selves being reflected from the mirror of the other. And as you figuratively danced in the shimmering glow of your self-realizations, you actually became more of who God originally intended for you to be.

Victor is a walking miracle. I trust you are too. The transformation in Victor is so far beyond any expectations or hopes I ever had. I loved him the way he was, although he never previously could bring himself to believe that. I would have loved him and welcomed him back with a fraction of the growth he has shown. I am reveling in delight and thankfulness for the freedom he has achieved to become himself--a richly varied and sparkling person with a character of solid granite, which has been polished to reflect the warmth of sunshine.

And you, Clarice, must have been a major human agent (along with his therapist and therapy group members) of his metamorphosis. I shall be forever grateful for this gift you have given me, and I thank you and God from the bottom of my heart.

Sincerely,
Judy

Enclosed with this letter was the following new letter explaining the wait, along with copies of our book reports written July 4 on Tournier's book, <u>To Resist or Surrender</u>, and a music CD.

Dec. 7
Dear Clarice,

The time has come for me to send you the enclosed material. In our therapy group some time ago I read aloud the enclosed letter to you. They all, including the therapist, said not to send it—or at least not for a year or more. They said I was "giving you too much power." Internally I laughed, because I'm not giving away any of my power to anyone. To appreciate and thank someone increases my power.

You really surprised us both by your marriage. We're hoping it is a "match made in heaven." Victor says he wishes I could meet both you and your husband. I would look forward to that—the four of us meeting together some time in the future--if and when you both feel open to it. Not at all, if it would be uncomfortable or painful for anyone.

I have not discouraged Victor from calling you. He values your friendship. I always know when he calls, and sometimes I'm in the same room when he does. He and I are so deeply in love; I couldn't possibly have any envy or jealousy. Our relationship is as opposite from what it used to be as day is from night. We are so happy. [Victor actually called Clarice about once a month for the first seven years after our remarriage. I had no feeling of jealousy or criticism. He decided not to continue when he *finally* realized he was causing her pain to do so.]

I told Victor I signed my other letter "Sincerely," but I truly am learning to feel more for you than that. So I will sign—

Love,
Judy

The more therapy sessions we went to, the more assignments we received. I truly believe we would not have grown as much without having to struggle through the reading of books and writing reports.

The following is part of a report, which Victor wrote about the book, <u>Make Friends with Your Shadow</u>, by William A. Miller:

Miller believes that by *denying* or *repressing* our shadow self [our "bad" self], we tend to project evil onto others, or else this imprisoned aggressor overcomes us when we least expect it. I have recently recognized that the basic problem I have in accepting the thesis of this book is the problem I have with paradox and gray areas. One of the paradoxical statements keeps bothering me. "We are to fight evil, but we are to learn from it." In another place he mentions we are to embrace this "friend" and love it. How can I fight against this evil shadow self and at the same time accept, embrace and love it as a friend? I believe this is partially resolved in the idea that Jesus loves the sinner and hates the sin. If I am to be like Christ, then I can love my shadow self and yet fight against the evil that lurks there. **Karen: Amen!**

We resist it, but we recognize it for good and growth. We are to take that which may appear to be undesirable, unacceptable, and even objectionable and use it positively, constructively, and even creatively, thus bringing ourselves closer towards wholeness and completion. This, in fact, is our task!

There is a danger in the constant preoccupation with the shadow self. This danger is that "by beholding we become changed." I can accept and even love that poor, carnal self; but my *focus*, my gaze, my consuming passion is Jesus Christ, the pure and spotless one. Miller comes nearest to this concept in his statement, "God in His goodness has released us from the power of our own evil. **KAREN: This is a person becoming whole!** But the final release must lie in our decision to *face that evil* and win."

I have faced my shadow self and have realized that I am capable of every evil act under the sun. Now, looking to Jesus, I can, through His grace, gain victory over evil. Praise God.

Sometime later Victor wrote the following during his own personal devotions. I came across it and asked to use it in this book:

Intimacy with God and Spouse

Being intimate involves far more than having sex. It is revealing one's own innermost being, deepest nature, weaknesses, idiosyncrasies, talents, gifts, desires, wants, goals, values and needs.

In my personal devotions the Lord revealed to me how the scriptures can bring intimacy to my relationship with God and with my wife. I read Psalm 19:12 in the Clear Word, an Expanded Paraphrase of the Bible, by Jack J. Blanco: "No man can see his own faults. Lord, deliver me from blind spots about myself."

Who knows me better than God and my spouse? God knows me best, and if Judy has an intimate relationship with God, just look at the potential for growth in both of us!

Early in our marriage I took a dislike to that word intimacy because I thought the more I revealed my inner self, the more criticism I would receive. Without intimacy, a marriage dies. Love dies, whether you divorce or not. Judy said before our divorce, "How can I love a man I do not know?"

Through a miracle of God's grace, I was able to hear what I previously thought was criticism, as loving concern—caring *critique*. I realize now that Judy, before she ever spoke to me about our relationship or the lack of intimacy in it, had been praying for God to give her the right words and tone of voice so as not to offend me. **KAREN: Impossible!** I wasted a lot of years in stubbornness, refusing communication and intimacy. Our love died. Our marriage died.

If I had had an intimate relationship with God, if I had prayed for God to reveal my faults and any blind spots, I might have heard His voice of loving concern in what Judy said. Thank God I finally listened! No marriage is too far gone to save or bring back after divorce, if both parties have an intimate relationship with the Lord and are willing to grow.

EMBRACE

We wanted a very private wedding, so chose our own living room. On our mantel and around it on the floor were white poinsettias and strings of miniature white lights among greenery. The fireplace and mantel would be our "altar." At the other end of the living/dining room was a beautifully decorated Christmas tree, and our coffee table had a lovely seasonal centerpiece of flowers and candles.

We invited only the members of our therapy group and our sons and their families to our afternoon wedding.

I wore an off-white full silk skirt that I had cut and re-made from a formal mother had paid someone to make for me when I gave a concert in Singapore seventeen years previously. My newly designed ankle-length skirt had elaborate, wide, gold embroidery completely circling the bottom. My sleeveless top was gold lamé, and a gold metal stretch belt circled my waist. A very delicate, tasseled, off-white lace stole lay around my shoulders and was gently tied in front. For my head, my dearest friend Faye enhanced a gold headband with peach-colored flowers. I had wanted to carry calla lilies at my first wedding, but they were out of season in December. So this second time around I bought some lovely artificial ones which Faye made into my wedding bouquet.

Rudy's two teenage daughters were the candle lighters. Merv Jenson gave the homily. Adrianne, one of the women in our group, had given us a large, beautiful white candle for our engagement gift. This candle, when created, had been elegantly cut and curled into a gorgeous art piece. We placed it in the center of our mantle with a plain white taper on each side. At the appropriate time, we each lighted the center candle with the side tapers and purposely left the two tapers burning. We don't want to let our individuality die in the marriage, which Pastor Jenson explained in his homily.

After Victor and I read our vows, we sang a duet. I had rearranged the music somewhat and added more words to John W. Peterson's "Of Love I Sing."

> Love is a power far greater than any other power on earth that man has ever known.
> Love is a gem of value beyond the rarest, richest diamond any man could own.
> Love is a crown, when worn by a man, can make that man, though poor, to feel like a king on a throne!
> *Love is a wreath, when worn by a girl, can make that girl, though young, to feel like a queen in her home!*
> [John W. Peterson, italicized words by Judy Leigh]

After the wedding, we all went to Clearwater Café in Pasadena. Since most of us were vegetarians, the restaurant furnished a printed menu at each place setting, listing soup or salad, a choice of three vegetarian entrees and a choice of three desserts. As we feasted on delicious food, we were entertained by a variety of toasts, lighthearted laughter and considerable storytelling.

Victor and I returned home, changed clothes and left for a honeymoon in Carlsbad, about two hour's distance away, which was a wonderful, romantic, funny, sensual and adventurous three-day odyssey.

We had earlier decided Christmas was not a good time for a reception. We sent out announcements of our remarriage, mailed a couple days after our wedding:

Victor and Judy Leigh
are pleased to announce their
REMARRIAGE
which took place on December 22, 1994

We live,
We make choices—for better or worse.
We learn from them.
And we GROW.

We THANK God!
For He has sought us,
Taught us,
And brought us—
To a deeper, fuller LOVE
Than we have ever experienced
Previously

At this same time we also sent out invitations to our friends and loved ones who lived near enough to come to our reception:

We invite you to share our joy
created by God's miracle-working power
in our lives.
We believe God has led us in making a
RECOMMITMENT
to each other and to Him.

Please join us at our special
CELEBRATION
January 22, 1995
3:00 to 5:00 pm.
Please RSVP by January 10

Shortly after we arrived home from our honeymoon, we left for a second honeymoon at our one-room pioneer-style cabin in the San Gabriel Mountains. After parking at Chantry Flats, we hiked in the four miles and spent six days there. Merv had assigned us to read Care of the Soul, by Thomas Moore. We brought it with us and sometimes read for hours at a time. Actually we weren't *reading* the whole time. We would read something, and it would spark a conversation where we bared our inner souls, talking about things in our past and current life. We now recognized, better than before, what we had done or felt previously, and were able to be open about it. This reading and conversation helped to bring about more transformation.

Victor is now determined to share his *feelings* and *thoughts!* There are a lot of situations that he can't *remember* how he felt *then*. There are other times he looks back and recognizes he isn't the same person he used to be. He can't imagine how he ever treated me the way he did, and he doesn't know what was in his mind then. It's very interesting, because now when we talk and reminisce, he's so patient with me when I bring up some long buried things.

It's exciting, because every so often I'll ask him about something I want him to do, and he'll just stand up and say, "No, I'm not going to do that! This is what I'm going to do!" It tickles me because it's so different. I'll smile and say, "Congratulations. I'm so proud of you," even if it might be something I wished he'd do a different way.

It's such a joy to see him take charge of his life and recognize what he wants and needs. Even the way he relates to other people is different. In September I started attending the Church where Victor has his membership. It wasn't long before I asked for my membership to be transferred there.

It is January 22nd, Celebration time! About eighty people have joined us. A friend from the hospital is catering. My sister Clare is our hostess. She and her artistic husband have set up a large display table loaded with memorabilia--my original wedding gown which my mother had made, pictures of our first wedding, pictures and albums of our family and activities through the years, and our original wedding book. Faye has been in charge of decorating the tables. Mother is well enough to attend the celebration.

After the casual buffet meal, a forty-five minute program begins. Victor sings, "All the Things You Are," by Jerome Kern. Our sons, both excellent musicians, each perform instrumental solos. Steve plays on his clarinet, "Cavatina," by Myers (theme song from the movie, "The Deer Hunter"). Then I read, "What Makes a 'New Man.'" This was the entry I had sent in some years previously to <u>New Woman Magazine</u> for their contest, but never received a response. After writing it, I had handed it to Victor for his perusal. After reading it, his response was throwing it back across the table at me saying, "That's impossible!" Now I speak proudly, "This description of a New Man, which I wrote several years ago, is a perfect portrayal of what Victor is today:

WHAT MAKES A "NEW MAN?"

A "New Man" is an "Old Man" who is WILLING TO GROW,
For his honest perspective replaces chronology.

He is REALISTIC IN SELF-EVALUATION,
Acknowledging we all occasionally unearth "oldness" within if truthful.
He shares the pain of his discovery without a deluge.
He is alert and aware
Because he makes time for reflection, re-creation and renewal.

He has INTEGRITY, RESPONSIBILITY, ACCOUNTABILITY.
He is in tune with himself and surroundings
Because his inner self is balanced spiritually, mentally, physically and emotionally.

He is ADAPTABLE and always ready for change,
For he believes that life IS transition.
He is not overly concerned with either criticism or adulation.
He varies his viewpoint by deliberately trading leadership with following.

He is ADVENTUROUS.
His muscle and tan come from either gym or nature--
It matters not which--as long as
He is not afraid to get his hands dirty
Or experience discomfort
As he continually expands his horizons.

He works with ENERGY AND ZEST.
Plays with joy and abandon,

And scarcely recognizes the difference
Because both include concentrated effort and relaxed pleasure.

He is a GOOD COMMUNICATOR,
Spontaneously expressing ideas and feelings as the occasion warrants.
He listens intuitively with ears and eyes,
Verbally reflecting what he hears.

He is EMPATHIC,
Feeling with both heart and brain as he tries to understand.
His power is apparent in gentleness;
His tenderness is revealed even when exuding logical and decisive action

He has A SENSE OF HUMOR,
Leaping to welcome the hilarity of his own foibles
And lagging in laughing at others.
He DRESSES APPROPRIATELY,
Being sufficiently independent to cater to his own style,
Yet conscious enough of fashion so a companion feels comfortable.

He ACCEPTS PEOPLE while motivating them to stretch, discover and
excel.
He works at intimacy,
Alternately drawing back for mutual privacy.

He CHERISHES A NEW WOMAN.

After these last words, the piano introduction starts, and I sing, "I'm in Love with a Wonderful Guy," from "South Pacific," by Richard Rogers, with Victor as my piano accompanist. Following this, Debussy's "Reverie" is played on the French horn by Alan. One of the therapy group members, a beautiful soprano, renders, "I's Yo' Woman Now," from Gershwin's "Porgy and Bess." I play the piano accompaniments for these two soloists.

Merv Jenson, our therapist, gives a joyous celebration talk, highlighting the miracles that happened in our growth as well as our deep commitment and new insights.

We each re-read our individually written vows. Since most of the guests hadn't heard them before, we chose to repeat them now.

Victor's vows:

> I am committed to growth, spiritually and mentally. I am committed to continue being your soul mate. I am committed to the maintenance of the magical in our marriage, and also the adventurous. I am committed to good communication. No more running.
>
> If I am too angry or upset to discuss a problem, I am committed to take responsibility for my feelings, and set another time to discuss the issue.
>
> I am committed to being a true husband to you, Judy, a protection and a support for you, at the same time encouraging your individuality.
>
> I am committed to being your friend, as well as your lover and husband, through good times and bad. I will cherish and respect you through sickness and health, through poverty and wealth, through success and failure.
>
> I will give our marriage relationship priority and not let anyone or anything come between us as long as I live.
>
> I will do these things in the strength of the Holy Spirit and the Lordship of Jesus Christ.

And these are my words spoken to Victor on that special day:

> Today I am committing myself to you, Victor, in a new way. I am releasing any and all pre- conceived ideas of what a marriage is or should be. I am choosing to relax and enjoy the security of *not knowing* what to expect.
>
> Just as mountain climbing and back-packing require careful planning and an attitude of adventure, I have prepared, and will continue to develop myself the best I can, so that I will have joy and exuberance on our high peaks; peace and contentment in our valleys of life's everyday nitty- gritty; strength for the steep and rocky

spots; persistence and endurance for the long up-grades; courage for the frightening events; and awareness, wisdom and discretion to make good decisions together with you.

I vow to honor your solitude, cherish your intimacy, accept your differences, and trust your honesty. I choose to listen when you speak, take time to view the world through your eyes, hear the pulse of life through your ears, feel energy and excitement through your body, realizing I will never *completely* understand your perception, feel your feelings, savor with your taste-buds, smell the fragrance of your pleasures or hear the music of your soul. But I can and will imagine these with you and luxuriate in the fantasies you help me create. In all of these times I will be attentively looking into your soul, observing the nuances of growth, identity and variation, knowing I will never fully discover you, yet delighting in each new facet. I accept you as you are. I love you, Victor,

We then sing again the duet we had done at our wedding, "Of Love I Sing" by John W. Peterson. My sister, Clare, reads First Corinthians thirteen from <u>The Message, The Bible in Contemporary Language</u>, by Steve H. Peterson:

"If I speak with human eloquence and angelic ecstasy but don't love, I'm nothing but the creaking of a rusty gate.

If I speak God's Word with power, revealing all his mysteries and making everything plain as day, and if I have faith that says to a mountain, "Jump," and it jumps, but I don't love, I'm nothing.

If I give everything I own to the poor and even go to the stake to be burned as a martyr, but I don't love, I've gotten nowhere. So, no matter what I say, what I believe, and what I do, I'm bankrupt without love.

Love never gives up.

Love cares more for others than for self.

Love doesn't want what it doesn't have.
Love doesn't strut,
Doesn't have a swelled head,
Doesn't force itself on others,
Isn't always "me first."
Doesn't fly off the handle,
Doesn't keep score of the sins of others,
Doesn't revel when others grovel,
Takes pleasure in the flowering of truth,
Puts up with anything,
Trusts God always,
Always looks for the best,
Never looks back,
But keeps going to the end.

Love never dies. Inspired speech will be over some day; . . . .understanding will reach its limit. We know only a portion of the truth, and what we say about God is always incomplete. But when the Complete arrives, our incompletes will be canceled.

When I was an infant at my mother's breast, I gurgled and cooed like any infant. When I grew up, I left those infant ways for good.

We don't yet see things clearly. We're squinting in a fog, peering through a mist. But it won't be long before the weather clears and the sun shines bright! We'll see it all then, see it all as clearly as God sees us, knowing him directly just as he knows us!

But for right now, until that completeness, we have three things to do to lead us toward that consummation: TRUST steadily in God, HOPE unswervingly, LOVE extravagantly. And the best of the three is LOVE."

"My Tribute," by Andrae Crouch, is next sung as a duet by my niece and her husband. Following that, my new husband completely surprises and elates me by reading something he wrote recently. I have never heard or read anything like this from him before:

My love is like a sleek cat – a black panther –
Mysterious, majestic, beautiful and powerful,
Yet affectionate, sensual, cuddly, nuzzling,
Rubbing up against me begging to have her back scratched.
In ecstasy when caressed, she purrs in the night.

My love is as playful as a dolphin,
As fun-loving as an otter,
As stately, queenly and graceful as a white swan,
As tender as a newborn lamb.
Far-sighted, visionary, insightful is my love.

My love exhibits the quiet courage of the eagle,
Alert and watchful as it soars above the world,
Yet she is a woman with many fears
Who has learned to function, in spite of them,
By the grace of God and the inspiration she gains
From nature, mountains and wildlife she observes
During her volunteer trail patrol in the Wilderness.

My love is as exquisite as a rose.
That is my special name for her—ROSEBUD.
I love you.

The room resounds with cheers, bravos, applause and amens. Excitement reverberates among the guests as well as our family. There is wonderful visiting, hugging, congratulations and reminiscing among all of us around the display tables. Many people crowd around my beaming mother and her caretaker, thankful that she is well enough to attend.

While we were at our cabin a few weeks later, Victor wrote this letter to a minister friend who had been a "classmate" in the Minister's Support Group:

Dear Raymond,

You probably sensed the deep-seated problems in my
marriage from the things that were said in the Ministers'
Support Group. After you moved away, Judy presented
me with what I perceived as "demands." If I didn't get
counseling and make some changes, she'd divorce me. I
thought the changes too great to achieve, so told her to
go ahead with divorce. She said to me later, "I suggested
divorce, but you picked up the ball and ran with it." I am
ashamed to say it, but I had wanted a divorce for years
before, but couldn't bear initiating it. I didn't believe in
divorce and my denomination frowns on it. But I was
determined, acting out of my "rebellious child."

Four main problems surfaced after much counseling
and group therapy. First, I married Judy because she was
a "take charge" person like my mother. When I finally
started growing up, I didn't want to be mothered any
more. I didn't want to be dominated. I wanted to grow
beyond my victim role and head the household, make my
own decisions, such as spend my own money. When we
first married, I insisted Judy handle the money because I
didn't want the responsibility. Now I demanded control
of it, but kept dropping the ball and playing victim again.

Second, I "put mother's and grandmother's face" on
Judy. My grandmother lived with our family all my life,
and I shared a bedroom with her until I was married. My
dad was badgered by both mom and grandmother. So I
learned from him to shut up and walk away.

Third, I couldn't stand criticism. Much of what I
heard from Judy was critique or loving concern about our
relationship, but because of my low self-esteem I didn't
hear it that way.

Fourth, many men see the differences between male
and female as a great problem to be solved by counselor,
psychiatrist or guru. Now I have learned to think of

our differences as a glorious blessing. What a change in relationship can be wrought with this viewpoint. God purposely made woman different from man. Revel in those differences.

Back to the story: I moved out of the house January 1, about two and a half months after the conversation about divorce and started dating very soon after that. Through a singles club I became acquainted with several nice ladies. It was at an outing in a national park that I met Clarice Beagley. She seemed in some ways opposite to Judy. She was "95% submissive," according to a personality test she took, and said our twenty-year age difference meant nothing. I became like a teenager. I dined her, wined her (sparkling grape juice), and romanced her for several months. She lived over five hundred miles from here.

In the meantime Judy met a man, through a relative, who swept her off her feet. Judy's friend wanted to get married in November. I was ecstatic she found someone else and anxious to get married to Clarice the following June.

For some reason Judy's fiancé split up with her a couple months before they were to marry, devastating her. So out of pity and what I wrongly perceived as urging from a counselor, I gave our relationship another try, putting Clarice on hold for about two months while I met with a therapy group. Judy joined us at certain times when the counselor requested, but I felt we were getting nowhere, so before Christmas I went back to Clarice.

According to the "friendly" divorce stipulations, all our possessions were to be divided in half, including the house. Clarice didn't own a home and felt insecure when I told her Judy wouldn't sell the house. Judy also tried, but couldn't get a loan to give me my half of the equity. Judy, her lawyer and I had discussions about this, but made no headway!

Judy invited a mediator to a family counsel. Judy presented her case first. Selling the house now was out of the question—prices were very low, and expensive homes were not selling. Furthermore our sons did not want the house sold. And what would happen to Judy's piano and voice teaching business?

Rudy, our older foster son, reminded the family of the good things that had happened in that house. He, Steve, Alan and I had scraped off wallpaper and repainted the house inside and out. Even Fred, our younger foster son, did his share as Judy worked with him.

Then came the bombshell. Rudy said, "Dad, do you love mom?" The silence was deafening. I heard myself say in a weak whisper, "Yes, I still love Judy."

Rudy continued, "Then why are we in this meeting? You wouldn't put mom out on the street would you?"

Hesitating, I answered, "No, I wouldn't."

I don't remember what happened after that except that Judy and I embraced as we were leaving. She asked me, "Does this mean there is hope for our getting back together?"

I gave a half-hearted, "Yes." But later I had second thoughts and wished I hadn't gotten her hopes up. Clarice kept urging me to force Judy to sell. Time was running out. I was due to move and start my new job. Clarice urged me to settle the business before I moved, so I decided to see a lawyer of my own. That very day Judy asked me to come over and talk. I answered, "Of course. I want to talk to you about something too."

She invited me for lunch. Unbeknown to me, another relative and Judy had been fasting and praying for a week. When I entered the house Judy said, "Before we eat, I have something important to say to you. I have been wrong in the past to make any demands. I love you and I want you back with no conditions, no demands, not even any counseling. I just want you back."

I was shaken to the core. I believe the Holy Spirit was behind those words. They came with such loving power that I could not resist. I had no defense—"I was wrong—no demands—no counseling." It took only a moment to melt into her arms and tell her I loved her and that I would come back to her.

She whispered, "What about Clarice?"

I answered, "I will call her tonight and tell her everything is off.

Judy's mouth dropped open, and she blurted out, "Just like that?"

I lived up to my promise and called Clarice at about 7:00 pm. that Monday evening. There was no answer, so I left a message on her machine (a very insensitive, dastardly thing to do). The Lord led in preparing Clarice's heart. Two days later she called Judy and told her she was glad that I was getting back together with her.

Things got a little scary when I had time to think things through. I went to my brother Patrick's home for a few days in another state. During that time I had a battle going on—my rational mind told me: you've made the right decision, it's where you belong and it will be different this time. But my heart cried out about that young lovely who said she would "fly around the moon three times to marry you, even if you were penniless." A woman who is submissive, accepting of my faults and our age difference--she is willing to do whatever I want? What influenced me to go back to the wife of my youth?

I can't fully explain it. I felt convicted by the Spirit of God—this is the way, this is where you belong; this is the way of peace, reconciliation, a hope of rekindling the flame that is just smoldering now. Another convincing point was what I perceived as a change in Judy's attitude. She tells me now that it was always there--the attitude of acceptance just as I am. But I *now* felt freedom to *choose* to change.

That is what is so wonderful about God. He loves us unconditionally no matter what we do or what nasty attitude we have at the moment. Here was the love of God working through Judy, speaking to the rebellious child in me who wanted to be free to have a fling—"I accept you, I love you just as you are. I want you back." Who can fight against that?

As I sit here at the cabin writing this, tears are streaming down my face because of the miracle of God's grace. I'm sure the greatest changes have occurred in *my* attitude rather than in Judy's. Whereas before, I heard demands to change both my behavior and my attitude, now I hear a loving concern for a change in our *relationship*: more intimacy, doing things together, and becoming soul mates, meditating together, praying together and working together.

We both chose to go to counseling and group therapy together. It was a good choice, a cheerful choice, a wise choice. Our relationship is so different now. We've done more real communicating in the time since we've been reunited than we did in many years previously. Judy feels comfortable now in sharing anything with me. I am more open with her than I ever imagined possible.

Another transformation that has taken place is the death of the power struggle I always *imagined* was there. Instead, now I ask myself, how much can I serve and share and cooperate? The attitude of Christ toward the church was and is loving service. Since we have become soul mates there is appreciation of the other's point of view, respect, even glorying in our different ways of thinking or behavior.

One of my biggest discoveries was that SILENCE destroys a marriage, and SUPERFICIALITY just does not "cut it." Honest, forthright communication is what is needed: How you *feel* about things and not just head knowledge. Trying to skirt the *real* problem and talk about peripheral issues doesn't work either!

I believe the Lord is leading us in a special ministry for troubled couples. Neither Judy nor I feel we are competent counselors, but at least we can be concerned listeners and wise enough to refer folks to a trained counselor when the need arises. Currently we are teaching classes in our home for five couples, once a week for twelve weeks. It's a thrill to see their concepts of marriage relationships change and flourish.

You have been a faithful friend, Bob. I want you to know you had a part in encouraging my own growth. Thanks so much.

Your friend in Christ,
Victor

P. S. The other day Judy told me something that happened just last week: A new member came up to her after church and said, "Oh Judy, you are one of the most beautiful women I have ever seen!"

Judy replied, "Oh my, thank you. You really made my day. That feels good, especially since I just had a birthday last week and I can't say I'm in my fifties any longer." She could hardly believe Judy "was so old." She is a very beautiful, attractive woman herself, around fifty."

So now I am married to the most beautiful "young" woman in the world who is equally wise and wonderful. She still keeps me virile and athletic. No Viagra yet! We love sharing our story with others and give our Lord the credit.

We recently told our story to our church congregation at the end of a sermon our pastor preached regarding marriage. A few days later I received the following letter in the mail from the family who had temporarily rented Victor a room during the time we were divorced. I had sensed a coldness from them ever since, although they were never unkind or impolite. The letter is very validating:

Dear Judy,

I certainly admire you and Victor for sharing your testimony. Your talk unequivocally reinforces the fact that when we are sitting next to a friend in church, we may not know the pain in that person's life. I admire your forthrightness and courage to speak out. In addition, I commend you on the ministry you are embarking upon to work with others.

Although Victor needed encouragement and help some time ago, it may be that we were too quick to take sides. I am very happy that you and he are together again, and that you are both still in the church. We are certainly blessed with the music ministry of your family.

When we went out for breakfast last Sunday, Victor chatted with me about past history and how happy he is now. We are all so human.

Sincerely,
Kenneth Pierce

Just because a person *chooses* to change and grow doesn't guarantee the absence of future problems. We are thrilled with our marriage, and our relationship flourishes. Yet sometimes we regress suddenly, and old behaviors pop up with startling audacity.

Alan's birthday was coming soon, and he was planning to take vacation time and visit us for a long weekend. I asked Victor to think about what he'd like to do special to celebrate his son's birthday. The next day he said he had decided he wanted to take Alan to dinner and a movie.

I loved the idea, but without thinking, blurted out what momentarily popped into my mind: "Maybe you might invite Steve to go out with you and make it a threesome."

There was an instantaneous body language change in Victor and complete silence. We were sitting at the breakfast table, and he sort of slumped and put his elbows on the table with his head in his hands.

I recognized it as "old tapes" playing in his head. After there was no response for several minutes I softly asked, "Was that a 'Yes, mommy?'"

Without changing position or expression he mumbled an almost inaudible affirmative "Uh huh."

Immediately I recognized the challenge, and I chose to respond in a different way from my past. I stood up, slammed my hands on the table and said aggressively, "I am insulted! Very insulted! I am *not* your mother! I am *not* telling you what to do! God gave you a mouth as capable as mine and the ability to say 'No, I don't want to do that!'"

I left the table, grabbed my purse and said, "I'm going shopping. Don't expect me back soon," and drove away.

Three hours later, after doing a lot of praying for wisdom and the gift of forgiveness, I returned. By the time I was entering the house, Victor had come to the door to meet me with an apology, "I'm sorry for what happened this morning."

"I'm sorry too!" and I walked to my desk without any more words. He looked rather surprised and went to his study. We each had a lot of responsibilities to tend to that day, and we soon were otherwise occupied.

Later in the afternoon I said, "We're both busy now, but tonight, before we go to bed, I want to talk about what happened."

"Okay," Victor said with enthusiasm.

That evening, after a good meal, showering and dressing for bed, we lounged in our matching recliners, and I asked Victor to tell me what he perceived happened that morning.

"I reverted to my old 'little boy victim.' I should have realized that before I answered. I really am sorry."

"And I felt anger and refused to be pulled into that game again," I responded.

After considerable discussion, Victor says he now realizes there is *still no* suggestion or request I can make that won't *come across to him* as a 'mother demand,' no matter how gently or kindly I verbalize it. He will *always* feel pressured and obligated to "obey." That is how strongly his childhood habits have been ingrained in him.

I realize that is why he often, in the past, did things I only mentioned "thinking about doing" and didn't really want done, and was baffled as to why he did them. So I questioned him, "If I always preface my suggestions or ideas with, 'This is only an *idea*, and I want *only* your feedback, so please *don't* think it is a request, and PLEASE *don't* do it!' would you recognize it isn't a demand or even a request?"

"Yes, that would be wonderful," he answered. "I would understand."

So now I am putting forth effort to always remember to do that. Isn't it amazing that after this many years of marriage, I can learn something new about my husband that I never realized before?

We walk nearly every day before breakfast, often as much as three miles. There is a restroom, on one of the trails we frequent, where we sometimes stop. I often wait for Victor, sitting on a low wall outside, and find myself feeling irritated when he comes out, because he stops a couple or three feet before reaching me, announcing, "Okay," as though he was ordering me to get up and start walking.

What I would prefer is for him *not* to stop and *not* say anything, and I would just get up before he reached me and walk along with him. Why I felt irritated was a mystery to me, and I inwardly tried to ignore it. After dozens of times, I couldn't stop the feeling, so decided to tell him about it. However I chose to preface it with, "I have an utterly ridiculous feeling that doesn't even make sense to me, and I hope you can laugh at it with me." We discussed it with some giggles (mostly mine), and I discovered he was *consciously being polite* not to move ahead of me. So now I listen for his footsteps and hop up as he reaches me, and he doesn't say "Okay" or slow down, and we both laugh. He loves me enough to stop "being polite."

We have decided to plan to *talk* about our idiosyncrasies, prepare to live in *forgiveness* always, and expect to *bend, stretch* and *laugh* with the daily challenges of loving unconditionally. We *choose* to embrace all of life as we joyfully experience our new life together.

32

GLORIFY

This is December, 1995, one year after our remarriage. Victor and I both have matured considerably. Our life together is wonderful-- our emotional life, spiritual life, sex life and our intellectual life. I have a marvelous, exciting husband. It has definitely been worth all the trouble of "hanging in there" all those years. I thank God for teaching us to reach, stretch and soar to new heights of relationship.

Victor and I are still teaching couples at our home, once a week for a twelve-week course, called "Enhancing Your Marriage and Your Life." We have lots of personal anecdotes to share when appropriate. God is obviously reaching and helping others through our sharing.

The day before yesterday I hiked to our cabin alone, because Victor had obligations at the time. He arrived last night, barely early enough to not need his headlamp. We sat down in our padded Adirondack chairs outside. The gnats were gone by then, and we reminisced awhile before going to bed, reminding ourselves of all the various ways we have grown.

As the last trace of sunlight disappeared from the nearby, thickly forested western slope reaching high in the west, the sky above us commenced its polka dot display of twinkling lights, which peeked through the low hanging branches above our chairs. We held hands, listened to the hooting owl and occasional guttural croak from the creek, reminding ourselves how blessed we are to have embraced *all* of life!

We are so thankful we turned around and faced our ogres. What we perceived as impossibilities in our relationship, we finally chose to deal with as challenges. Running away from problems is far less rewarding. We have experienced both confusion and disconnectedness. There have been logjams and floods of foul and foolish emotion. Our choices and actions have often been crude and disjointed.

But we are a *team*, choosing to forge ahead with curiosity and humor, love and forgiveness, ready to share with others what we have learned as we move toward our life's evening horizon.

I was so inspired by our conversation following Victor's arrival that evening that I wrote the following when we came inside the cabin:

Thankful, Crazy Praises

Praise You, Lord, for a purple pantsuit
and an orange polka-dotted hat
with hair flying in the breeze.

Praise You, Lord, for stately green trees
with dead vines, limply graceful, lolling off their branches,
for paradox, for questions unanswered.

Praise You, Lord, for chewing gum that pops
like the logs in the cabin wood stove,
and for similar crack as full-bellied acorns plop on roof.

Praise You, Lord, for punts and strikes,
for fouls and outs, mysteries and puzzles,
for scented candles and smoke that drifts from chimney.

Praise you for dogs that scratch and cats that purr,
for crows that caw and bats with radar,
for simple words like, "Please" and "Here, dear."

Praise you, Lord, for colors and night's blackness,
for music and cacophony, for utter pure silence,
laughter and groans, hilarity and tears.

Praise You for songs and squeaks and hisses,
for thimbles tapping on wood, for sorrow, for rage,
for sore joints, breeze whispers and smell of sage.

Praise You for wind that shrieks and sun that scorches,
for ponchos and palaces, one-room cabins,
for nine-donkey pack train, tents and horses.

Praise You for running and ripping,
for yearning and yielding, yelling and yellow,
for munching granola bars and filling bird feeders.

Thank you, Lord, for disconnectedness and confusion
and for helping it all to "jell" in the end…
or is it the beginning? – again?

Just let me thank You daily……
praise You moment by moment…
for all the nuances and upheavals of life.

For it is through these ambivalences, quandaries,
daydreams, excitements and boredoms
that I grow, I am challenged.

When mixed up in drastic confusion
You startle me into acknowledging You--
Your exaltedness and glory!

Besides, it is much more of an adventure
than a black pantsuit and colorless hat
with straight hair pulled into a bun.

Amen!

Give thanks in all circumstances, for this is the
will of God in Christ Jesus for you.
I Thessalonians 5:18 RSV

Today, on the *second* anniversary of our *second* marriage, I am making a booklet as a gift for Victor. I'm taking several pages of brightly colored construction paper and tying them at the half-fold with gold metallic ribbon. I have chosen a number of photos of our memorable times together since remarriage, and am placing them on the left-hand pages. The following is what I'll hand print on the right hand pages:

Two years ago today you made a commitment
To love me, support me, respect me, encourage me,
Be faithful to me, be my friend, my companion, my lover, my husband.
I thought it was the happiest moment of my life.
It wasn't!

Each of the 730 days since then have become
More wonderful than the day before.
My heart is more at ease.
My emotions are more stabilized, yet more free.
Each day you have allowed me
To enter your world a bit deeper, a bit farther.
You have shared by increasing degrees your feelings, thoughts and wishes.

You have opened up your mind and allowed me
To start plumbing its depths with my questions.
You may not always welcome my curiosity,
But you have not discouraged it.
You have been generously patient
As I ply the oceans of your thinking,
Endeavoring to know more of you.
You are a very special and magnificent man.
You have even accepted my "bent" for analysis and detail.
You've been willing to expand your view

When you recognize the worth of my ideas,
Yet you can turn my thinking in a different direction
When my logic seems illogical.

I remember our decision about lighting the unity candle at our wedding.
We chose to leave our personal candles burning
To symbolize our individual uniqueness that we want to retain and develop
As we link our lives into ever stronger bonds of love
While becoming everlasting Soul Mates.

Today I realize you have given me
A far richer gift than what you promised.

I am growing, expanding, blossoming, thriving.
I cherish our every moment together:
Holding your hand as we sit in church….
Our "conversational" prayers together….
Watching you tenderly "grandfather" Jenson….
Reading to each other and discussing what we have read….
Cleaning house together….
Creating and outlining future seminars….
Taking "sponge baths" at the cabin in the big washtub….
Looking into each other's eyes and talking
While only candles and oil lamps flicker
And incense drifts sensuously around us….
Helping you build the storage shed….
Caressing your neck and face as we drive in the car…

So many moments—
So many touches—
So many tender looks, caring words,
The sharing of goals and ideals.

This marriage is
A partnership forged with prayerful choices….
A pairing which survived painful intervention….

An ideal relationship I wish all our dear loved ones
Could experience for themselves....
A miracle in the making every single day.
I couldn't hope
For a dearer husband.
I want to make your life
As blessed as you have made mine!

Together we two people create three entities:
Your growing, developing self
My evolving, blossoming self
The woven tapestry of ourselves as a couple...
That intertwining, colorful, undulating union
That will never be boring, dull or regretted...

We are a "building," expanding ever upward and outward...
We, together, are a blurring of individuality
Alternating with distinct separation that makes
Artwork of our togetherness...
A landscape of profound beauty...
A portrait of life far more exciting than could have been
Created by two separate individuals.

Thanks be to God
Who always causes us to triumph!
I love you with all my heart.
We are God's miracle
Always your lover,
Rosebud.

33

EPILOGUE

At this writing, nearly twenty years have passed since our remarriage. What marvelous, wonderful, exploring, adventurous years they have become. We relish every day and are delving deeper into our memory, still learning more about each other, as our joy becomes the impetus for our continuing growth and maturity.

In our discussions regarding the writing of this book we have questioned each other about past events and have discovered more insights. Victor had told me a story many years ago about a time when he tossed a "rock" into the air, but was blinded by the sun and didn't see where it was coming down. It hit him on his head, and he had to be stitched up, leaving an indentation and scar on his scalp.

In our re-reading the chapter "Venture," where he told me in a letter that he would *never* put his child "through tests like I had to take"–his mother taking him for psychological testing to find out his "vocational strengths and IQ"–we have talked at length repeatedly about that rock-throwing event.

When he was probably about five years old there was some kind of work being done with flagstone rock in front of his home or next door. He was evidently outside alone when he picked up a rather large, jagged piece of flagstone and tossed it into the air to see how high he could throw it. When the sharp edge of it came hurtling down, hitting him on the top of his head, it not only made a considerable gash, but knocked him

492

unconscious. He doesn't know who found him lying in his blood some time later, but his doctor father cared for him, stitching him up and bandaging his injury. He doesn't remember more of the incident, but he remembers his father emphasizing that it was *stupid* of him to have thrown the rock into the air.

Somehow, while very young, he early came to the conclusion that the accident *permanently damaged his brain and <u>made him stupid!</u>* This resulted in the profound belief in his deepest heart and mind, that his intelligence had been ruined from that accident and that he would *never* be normal – he was <u>*handicapped for life*</u>. Apparently, somewhere along the way, his mother must have become somewhat aware that he believed himself to be stupid or low IQ. So before he started high school, she insisted on taking him to some sort of a psychological institution for testing. But apparently no one realized that the *decision* to have him tested further *proved to Victor* that he *had* been damaged! He was horribly frightened, nearly to the panic level, that now his carefully hid secret of his stupidity would become public knowledge.

He was in a state of abject fear when his mother dropped him off all alone at the test site. A woman stranger handed him a test and put him in a room all alone. When he finished, she handed him another test. He had not been told how many different tests he would be taking or for how long. He "knew" that no matter how hard he tried, he would fail the tests! He had "*known*" that all his difficulties thus far in school (as he perceived them) were because of the horrible damage he did to himself. And he was certain the tests *would prove it!*

He looks back on that testing as one of the most horrible and traumatic experiences of his entire life. He doesn't know how long the testing lasted, but it felt to him it was the *whole day*, with many tests, each one proving *more clearly* his glaring mental handicap.

Several days later his mom returned to get the test results and told him he was "average." At no time was he "counseled" by anyone or given any special loving encouragement by someone who knew how to instill confidence in him.

From that day on he believed himself to be intellectually backward, poor-functioning in his mental abilities, and stupid. That shaped his self-esteem long years before he ever knew me!

Another subject was conversationally explored as we pursued the completion of this book. Chapter 6, "Peril," relates that Victor said to me, "Long before we met, I *knew* that if a husband and wife were deeply in love, *when they had children* their love would be *spoiled* and the marriage relationship would *never* be the same again. So I didn't want children, because it would *ruin* our love. And it has." **KAREN: I think this is a common belief among men. Carl Whitaker, one of the fathers of family therapy, shared his experience of this one time at breakfast with me. At the birth of his fourth child, he was finally able to be with his wife and the baby.**

During this last week a new insight came to me. Evidently, even as a child, Victor must have sensed *at a subconscious level* that his mother's unhealthy relationship with him interfered with her relationship with his dad. His belief from early childhood was "having children spoils the love between parents." So he "*knew*" early in his life—long before he considered marriage—that he never wanted children. His grandmother told me when she came to visit us, before we had children, that he never wanted any. I was surprised, because Victor had never divulged that information. But apparently, although at least his grandmother *was* aware of this, neither she nor anyone else bothered to search for the *reason why* he didn't *want* children, so no one counseled him regarding that along the way. When I mentioned this to Victor yesterday, he said this new idea had never entered his mind before now, but it made sense.

Oh, how we need to develop compassion for the "child" in us – that "child" may have absorbed distorted "belief-systems" from unhealthy and damaging childhood experiences. This is the major purpose of counseling and therapy: helping us to recognize when and how our belief-systems become twisted and fragmented, and aiding in our reshaping these belief systems until they become balanced, representing who we truly are. **KAREN: I heartily agree!**

This transformation works best when both counselor and client invite the participation of God's Holy Spirit in this gratifying work. God will give us the ability to embrace life, determining to never retreat from problems or fearful realities.

I truly praise God for everything that has happened to me. I wouldn't be who I am without it.

495 WAS CONSCIOUS OF HIS ETERNAL

I EMBRACE MY WHOLE LIFE, AND I EMBRACE MY GLORIOUS GOD WHO AIDED IN AUTHORING MY STORY, EVEN BEFORE I WAS CONSCIOUS OF HIS ETERNAL LOVE AND CREATIVE POWER THROUGHOUT MY EXISTENCE.

A many-hued arch spanned canopied space.
Standing, reaching, stretching,
Faltering, vaulting, soaring…
Until color reflected from face and heart…
Until hands immersed in prismed light…
Until fingers caressed different tints and shades…
Until body and mind absorbed refracted rays…
Faithfully following the curve to the horizon.

The pot is not attained by those who reach for gold,
But by those who fly to EMBRACE each variegated strand.

CPSIA information can be obtained
at www.ICGtesting.com
Printed in the USA
BVHW03*1125050418
512573BV00009B/53/P